The Camden House History of German Literature

Volume 2

German Literature of the Early Middle Ages

The Camden House History of German Literature

Volume 2

The Camden House History of German Literature

Edited by James Hardin

Vol. 1: Early Germanic Literature and Culture
Edited by Brian Murdoch and Malcolm Read,
University of Stirling, UK

Vol. 2: German Literature of the Early Middle Ages
Edited by Brian Murdoch, University of Stirling, UK

Vol. 3: German Literature of the High Middle Ages
Edited by Will Hasty, University of Florida

Vol. 4: Early Modern German Literature
Edited by Max Reinhart, University of Georgia

*Vol. 5: Literature of the German Enlightenment
and Sentimentality*
Edited by Barbara Becker-Cantarino, Ohio State University

Vol. 6: Literature of the Sturm und Drang
Edited by David Hill, University of Birmingham, UK

Vol. 7: The Literature of Weimar Classicism
Edited by Simon Richter, University of Pennsylvania

Vol. 8: The Literature of German Romanticism
Edited by Dennis Mahoney, University of Vermont

Vol. 9: German Literature of the Nineteenth Century, 1830–1899
Edited by Clayton Koelb and Eric Downing,
University of North Carolina

*Vol. 10: German Literature of the Twentieth Century:
From Aestheticism to Postmodernism*
Ingo R. Stoehr, Kilgore College, Texas

German Literature of the Early Middle Ages

Edited by
Brian Murdoch

CAMDEN HOUSE

First published 2004
by Camden House

Camden House is an imprint of Boydell & Brewer Inc.
668 Mt. Hope Ave., Rochester, NY 14620 USA
www.camden-house.com
and of Boydell & Brewer Limited
PO Box 9, Woodbridge, Suffolk IP12 3DF, UK
www.boydell.co.uk

ISBN: 1–57113–240–6

Library of Congress Cataloging-in-Publication Data

German literature of the Early Middle Ages / edited by Brian Murdoch.
    p. cm. — (Camden House history of German literature; v. 2)
    Includes bibliographical references and index.
    ISBN 1–57113–240–6 (alk. paper)
    1. German literature — Old High German, 750–1050 — History and
crticism. 2. German literature — Middle High German, 1050–1500 —
History and criticism. I. Murdoch, Brian, 1944– II. Title. III. Series:
Studies in German literature, linguistics, and culture (Unnumbered)

PT175.G45 2004
830.9'001—dc22
                                                        2003017148

A catalogue record for this title is available from the British Library.

This publication is printed on acid-free paper.
Printed in the United States of America.

Contents

Illustrations

Preface

TO HAVE A VOLUME that is concerned primarily with Old High German as the *second*, rather than the first volume in a literary history of German may at first glance seem surprising. The first volume of this literary history, however, is intended to give an overview of the pre-literary situation and of the movement toward literacy in the context of the Germanic peoples. It also considers Germanic literature on a broader scale, looking at Old English, Old Norse and Gothic, as well as giving a brief sketch of Old High German, a sketch which is developed and given flesh in the present volume. The first volume also contains a detailed discussion of the important early work in Old Low German, the Old Saxon *Heliand,* which might equally well have been included in this volume. Although this volume contains discussions of the literature of Germany (which includes literature in Latin) during what is known generally as the Old High German period, from the beginnings of writing in German in the eighth century down to the middle of the eleventh, of course some of the chapters look forward to the Middle High German period. Breaks determined by language change do not usually coincide neatly with literary developments. The point of the present volume is to give an idea of the first stage of literature in German, and this requires examination also of literature as such written in the dominant language of the period, namely Latin, as the background against which those first beginnings of German emerged; there is so much material there that contributors have had to be especially selective, particularly as it is not always easy to determine which Latin writings "belong" in a German literary history. Alcuin was an Englishman who wrote much of his verse in what is now France, but was a major figure at Charlemagne's court; Gottschalk and Walahfrid Strabo were both German. Sometimes we can only guess that the author of a work was German (the Latin writer of *Waltharius,* whoever he was, uses a pun on a name which only works in German, for example). On the other hand, when we turn to writings in High German, one must consider material not usually considered literary in the modern sense at all, but which does show the emergence of German as a literary language in its earliest stage. With regard to what is considered "high" literature, there is precious little; but there *is* a variety, and all beginnings are important. It is significant and appropriate, of course, that the chapter considering the shorter German verse texts should be the longest. The result of discussing both the extensive amount of Latin and the limited amount of German, too, is inevitably but unavoidably a somewhat fragmented picture.

The broad sweep of modern literary histories, as one of the chapters points out, tends to be fairly dismissive of Otfrid's Gospel poem as unoriginal in subject and wooden in execution. But such criticism, made from a viewpoint of more than a millennium of literary development, has to be viewed in another light: Otfrid is the self-conscious producer of a formal literary work of some substance in the German language at a time and in a context when it was necessary for him to justify the fact. But he did it, and he stands pretty fairly at the beginning of German written literature. He shares the position, perhaps, with a lucky survival, that of the *Hildebrandlied*, from the separate oral tradition, but *written down*, captured in writing in a problematic form in a single manuscript, not nearly as official as Otfrid's work, but in spite of everything a worthy secular parallel at the start of German literature.

Thanks are due, of course, to all the contributors to the present volume, and also to those other colleagues in the field such as Cyril Edwards and Frank Gentry, who have kept the editor in touch with their recent work. At risk of sounding elegiac, ever smaller numbers of universities in the Anglo-Saxon world (and particularly the United Kingdom) now choose to concern themselves with teaching or research in medieval German at all, let alone with Old High German. But the importance of knowing about the origins remains, and coordinating work by members of that endangered species, the Old High German specialist, in various countries has been a pleasure. Thanks are much due, finally, to the indefatigable Jim Hardin for his indispensable and invariably good-humored advice and assistance in the production of this volume and for guiding this project as whole.

Brian Murdoch
Stirling, September 2003

Abbreviations

ABäG   *Amsterdamer Beiträge zur älteren Germanistik*

Braune   Braune, Wilhelm, *Althochdeutsches Lesebuch* (Tübingen: Niemeyer, 16th. ed. Ernst Ebbinghaus, 1979 [cited], 17th ed. 1991)

DVJs   *Deutsche Vierteljahresschrift*

GAG   Göppinger Arbeiten zur Germanistik

PL   *Patrologia . . . Latina,* ed. J. P. Migne (Paris: Migne, 1844–64)

MGH   *Monumenta Germaniae Historica* (Hanover etc., 1826–); see also the website Monumenta Germaniae Historica: http://www.mgh.de

MSD   Karl Victor Müllenhoff and Wilhelm Scherer, *Deutsche Poesie und Prosa aus dem VIII–XII Jahrhundert* (Berlin: Weidmann, 1864, 2nd ed. 1873, 3rd ed. Elias v. Steinmeyer, 1892, rep. 1964)

PBB   [Paul's and Braune's] *Beiträge zur deutschen Sprache und Literatur* (T[übingen] or H[alle])

Schlosser   Horst Dieter Schlosser, *Althochdeutsche Literatur* [Frankfurt am Main: Fischer, 1970] rev. ed. (Berlin: Schmidt, 1998)

St.   Elias von Steinmeyer, *Die kleineren althochdeutschen Sprachdenkmäler* [1916] (Berlin and Zurich: Weidmann, repr. as 2nd ed. 1963 and 1971)

VL   *Verfasserlexikon: Die deutsche Literatur des Mittelalters,* ed. Wolfgang Stammler [Berlin and Leipzig: de Gruyter, 1933–35]; 2nd fully rev. ed. by Kurt Ruh et al. (Berlin and New York: de Gruyter, 1978–2001)
The latter edition is cited unless otherwise stated.

WBG   Wissenschaftliche Buchgesellschaft (Darmstadt)

Wilhelm   Friedrich Wilhelm, *Denkmäler deutscher Prosa des 11. und 12. Jahrhunderts* (Munich: Hueber, 1916, repr. 1960)

Wipf	Karl A. Wipf, *Althochdeutsche poetische Texte* (Stuttgart: Reclam, 1992)
ZfdA	*Zeitschrift für deutsches Altertum*
ZfdPh	*Zeitschrift für deutsche Philologie*

Charlemagne's palace chapel, Aachen Cathedral.

Introduction

Brian Murdoch

THE EARLY MIDDLE AGES are hard to define as a period. As far as the literature and culture of the German-speaking countries are concerned, however, we might try to refine the term in various ways. We might, for example, refer to the Old High German period, which is a philological designation for the earliest stage of the German language, implying a period starting in about A.D. 500, when phonological distinctions between the ancestors of English (representing Low German) and modern German (representing High German) began to assert themselves, and ending around 1050, when a further set of distinctive sound changes within the High German dialects began to make themselves felt. Alternatively, we might choose an historical-dynastic designation and speak of the hegemony of the Franks, or of the Carolingian, Ottonian, and Salian periods. Neither the linguistic nor the dynastic definition is entirely satisfactory. The former would imply a restriction to High German only, ignoring continental Low German, and in any case, Old High German is a shorthand term for a number of different dialects that have, however, some shared features; furthermore, the German language was not written down until around 750. Cultural changes do not, in any case, always coincide with linguistic ones. Most important, though, the focus on the *German* language is itself a distortion, since most of the written literature in the geographical territory and in the period with which we are concerned is in Latin. Taking the second option and using the ruling tribes or houses as a marker is slightly safer, but in the earlier periods in particular we have to remind ourselves constantly of a geographical problem. Germany, too, is a fluid term, and it does not necessarily or invariably refer to the current boundaries of that country. In the earlier stages of the rule of the Germanic tribe known as the Franks, we should have to include much of present-day France.

In pragmatic terms we may define "early medieval" in this volume as the period of time between about 750 and about 1100. The geographical area in question — for which we use the name Germany as a form of shorthand — is that covered, roughly speaking, by present day Germany,

Austria, and Switzerland, plus the Low Countries and some of Italy. Taking the mid-eighth century as a starting date does, however, bring together the earliest occurrences of written German and the establishment of the Carolingian Frankish ruling house in 751 on the assumption of kingship by Pépin the Short,[1] the father of Charlemagne (742–814), who was to succeed him as ruler of the Franks twenty years later. Under Charlemagne's rule there would be a florescence of Latin writing: his presence dominates the historical period in which the first German writings appeared, and possibly influenced them. Of course, the middle of the eighth century is not an absolute beginning, and it is necessary to glance back to the earlier dynasty, the Merovingians, and to look forward to the later ruling houses, to the Saxon Ottonian emperors who ruled for much of the tenth century, and to the Salians in the eleventh and into the twelfth.

Various tribal groups had lived in the lands known to the Romans as Germania, territory that for the most part was never conquered and made part of the Roman Empire, though the Romans exerted an influence on it to some extent. When the Western Roman Empire, the part governed from Rome rather than from Byzantium, finally collapsed, and Italy and Rome itself was captured by the Goths in the fifth century, then former Roman territories like Gaul — modern France — and also Spain, as well as the remote province of Britain, were gradually occupied by Germanic tribes, some of which remained in control of those territories for centuries. Tribal groups in the area now covered by Germany, Switzerland, and Austria included the Saxons in the North (some of whom, with the Angles, crossed the sea to occupy and give their name to England), the Thuringians in the East, and in the South the Alemanni and the Bavarians, with the Langobardi, the Lombards, eventually replacing the East Germanic Goths in what is now northern Italy. The Thuringians, originally a powerful group, were effectively taken over as early as the sixth century by what would ultimately become the most successful of the Germanic tribes, the Franks, from the northern part of the Rhineland. The Alemanni, a confederation of smaller groups — their name, though it gives us the Romance names for Germany like "Allemagne," simply means "all men" — settled in the southwestern part of Germany in the sixth century, but also came under attack by the Franks, and by the middle of the eighth century they, too, were taken over into the Frankish kingdom. The same thing happened to the Baiuari, the Bavarians, in the southeast, another confederation of Germanic tribes, who had formed in the early part of the sixth century. They were subjugated by the Frankish kings and eventually taken over completely when Charlemagne himself deposed their last king, Tassilo, in 788. Charlemagne had already become king of the Lombards fourteen years earlier.[2]

The Franks themselves were a confederation of smaller groups in what is now central Germany, with two branches: Ripuarian, locating them by the riverbanks (of the Rhine), and Salian, originally from the sea, probably the North Sea. Around the middle of the fifth century we hear of a king called Merovech of the Salian Franks — it was claimed (with a certain plausibility) that one of his ancestors was a sea-monster — and under his line, that of the Merovingians, the Franks began to expand into what is now France and the Low Countries. Merovech's grandson, Clovis, set up a kingdom at Tournai (now in Belgium), and gradually established a power base. Converted relatively late to Christianity, Clovis and the Franks became Catholic in 503; other Germanic tribes (most notably the Goths) had adopted the Arian form of Christianity, a variant based on the writings of Arius, which maintained that Christ was created rather than eternal, and which was condemned as heretical at the Council of Nicaea in 325. The conversion of the Franks to the Catholic, rather than to the Arian confession, is important for the history of Christianity in Europe.

Clovis died in 511 and his death provides an illustration of the working of a significant Frankish custom: only male heirs could succeed (which is why Queen Victoria was unable to become ruler of Hanover as late as 1837), but all legitimate male heirs shared their father's lands. Clovis had four sons, which led to what one historian has called a "gangster situation," something that occurred regularly down to the ninth century. The lands controlled by the Franks had developed into distinct areas: Neustria in the West, centered on Tournai; Austrasia, centered on Aachen; and Burgundy. Frequently, one son would emerge as a conqueror of the others, and this happened with Clovis's sons, when Chlothar I of Neustria became king of all the Franks in 558, largely by outliving or outwitting his brothers and murdering a rebellious son; these were the qualities needed to be a successful Frankish king. Chlothar's line continued more or less steadily until the death in 639 of Dagobert I, the last of the effective rulers; although his successors did rule in theory for another century or more, they are known as *les rois fainéants*, the lazy kings, who left the actual running of the kingdom to stewards called Mayors of the Palace. These were the de facto rulers of the kingdom, and they passed the position to their sons. This dynasty produced Charles Martel, "the hammer," who was mayor of Austrasia from 714 and then of the whole of the Frankish kingdom from 719–41, and whose most celebrated deed was the defeat of an Islamic army in 732 at Poitiers, something which was again of considerable importance for the later development of religion in Europe. Charles Martel developed a cavalry, and the Franks became accomplished warriors on horseback, aided by two significant cultural developments: the stirrup for control, and the iron horseshoe.[3]

In 741 Charles Martel was succeeded by Pépin, and ten years later, in 751, Pépin, who had thus far technically still been Mayor of the Palace, deposed the puppet Merovingian king Childeric III and founded his own royal dynasty, that known as the Carolingian. In 768 Pippin's son, Charles, became king, and by 771, on the death of his brother, sole king of the Franks. He would go on to establish his rule over (and convert to Christianity) many of the other Germanic tribes, including even the Saxons, reform Latin learning in Germany and France on a large scale, and acquire the by-name of "the Great" as Carolus Magnus or Charlemagne. He was officially crowned emperor of a newly constituted Roman Empire, a Holy Roman Empire (which, famously, could be argued to have been neither holy, nor Roman, nor an empire), on Christmas Day 800 in Rome by Pope Leo III, whom he had re-established on the pontifical throne the year before.[4] The figure of Charlemagne himself is of the greatest importance to the emergence and development of literature and culture in Germany in the early Middle Ages.[5] The *traditio imperii ad Francos,* the supposed passing of the original Roman Empire to the Franks, was significant, even if it was never based in Rome, was of questionable holiness, and as a unified empire (administered rather differently from the original) was not to last for long. Charlemagne did, however, by war and by treaty, keep the neighboring Slavs, Vikings and (in Spain) Saracens at bay, and established stability in territories that now covered much of modern France, the Low Countries, and the German-speaking countries. His son, another Pépin (who predeceased him) defeated the Avar Huns in 795–796, bringing great wealth into his state, and a taxation system kept his Frankish empire fiscally sound. But this Frankish empire was run more or less along Germanic lines, with the emperor's trusted war companions doing the ruling. The taxation system was also run on rather simplistic lines compared with the earlier Roman one, but Charlemagne arranged for the sending out of *missi dominici,* envoys, to different parts of his lands to ensure that the laws were maintained and the taxes paid. With the papacy he maintained a satisfactory relationship in which he had the upper hand, and from Rome he could look toward Byzantium and the possibility of a complete reunification of the whole Roman Empire. But it was far too late for that, and although each side recognized the other, they were now two foreign states, without much influence on each other.

In spite of the link between the word "Frank" and the idea of freedom, the structure of society under Charlemagne and his successors embraced a range of social possibilities. As far as Old High German literature is concerned, however, to what extent it was associated with the lowest levels, the peasant classes, is debatable. Some of the literature that has survived is clearly aimed at a particular group — Otfrid's Gospel-poem for monastic novices, perhaps, the *Muspilli* or the *Hildebrandlied* for lay aristocracy. In fact, most of the surviving material in Latin as in German is linked with court or monastery. Eileen Power's memorable picture of a Frankish peasant called Bodo links him with popular verses and with the charms for curing certain conditions, however, and other historians have pointed out that travel in the early Middle Ages must have been hazardous: some of the phrases offered in the so-called Paris Conversation-Book hint at downright belligerence, which was clearly necessary sometimes, as was caution, as when one writer, sending a valuable manuscript from one monastery to another, stresses that it has to be hidden in case of robbery.[6]

Charlemagne's establishment of a unified, Christian, Western Empire was to a great extent due to the force of his own personality, and it was broken up under his grandchildren by the Frankish custom of dividing inherited land. The Treaty of Verdun, drawn up between his grandsons in 843, made a basic division into what is effectively modern France and the German-speaking countries, so that we may focus after the death of Charlemagne's son, Lewis the Pious, last emperor of the West *and* the East Frankish territories, on the German(ic) part, known as East Francia, the East Frankish Kingdom or Empire. The imperial title remained in use (although its implication varied) and Otto the Great, the tenth-century ruler of the German lands, assumed the title of German Emperor in 962. The relationship between Charlemagne's successors with the papacy also broke down, and eventually, by the twelfth century, a German emperor would be in open warfare with the pope. Charlemagne, however, became after his death a larger-than-life myth, a holy warrior who lived to the age of two hundred, and was claimed as a hero by the French (whose name for him is the best known) as well as by the Germans (whose language he spoke).

When Charlemagne died in 814 he left his son Lewis the Pious as sole ruler of his empire, and though he was effective at first, the stability he had inherited broke down as his children by his first wife, Irmengard, rebelled against him for favoring his youngest son, born to his second wife, Judith. Civil war ensued, until in 839 Lewis made a settlement giving his oldest son Lothar the Eastern kingdom and Judith's son Charles, who was by then sixteen, the Western part of his lands. Of the other two sons, one had died and the other, Ludwig the German, was given Bavaria. But in 840, Lewis the Pious died, and with his death the empire of Charlemagne effectively disintegrated. Lothar now held the imperial title, but was not strong enough to hold the Eastern part of the old empire. He was defeated by an alliance between his surviving brother and half-brother, as a result of which the much younger Charles became king of the West Franks, of what would become France, while his half-brother, another Lewis/Louis/Ludovicus, whom we may more conveniently refer to as Ludwig (and who was given the by-name "the German") took the German territories. Lothar, still nominally emperor, was left with Italy and the much disputed land between France and Germany — *Lotharii regnum,* Lothar's kingdom, known now as Lorraine, and by the eleventh century that, too, had been taken over into the German empire.

A significant early document containing both Old High German and Old French, the *Strasbourg Oaths* of 842 (recorded by the historian Nithart), is an agreement of mutual non-aggression between Charles and Ludwig and their armies against Lothar, and they make clear the separation of the two territories in more than just political terms: the oaths are sworn both in Old High German and in Old French, so that both groups could understand the situation fully. We have, then, the birth of two nations, speaking different languages, since the Franks, unlike the Romans before them, had not imposed their language on Gaul, where Gallo-Roman developed into French. Our interest is now principally with East Francia, with those areas in which High or Low German was spoken. For all that, links between the two parts of the old empire were maintained; the scholar-abbot Lupus of Ferrières sent monks to Germany to learn the language, and we do encounter works in Old High German written and composed in Western Francia, the most striking example being the *Ludwigslied* at the end of the ninth century, when the separation was well established. This "Lay of Louis" is, in modern terms, a poem in German celebrating a victory by a French king on French soil, and for that reason it is appropriate to refer to the central figure by the French form of his name. The modern name of France, of course, derives from the Franks, as does that of Franken, Franconia, in Germany. Otfrid of Weissenburg (died ca. 870), the first named writer in Old High German, still referred in the 860s to his language as Frankish, and Weissenburg is now Wissembourg, in French Alsace.[7] On the other hand, the word that lies at the root of the modern word *deutsch,* and still much discussed, is applied in its earliest stages to any Germanic language, and certainly both to High and to Low German.

Even if Charlemagne's empire had disintegrated before the middle of the ninth century, in terms of long-term achievement, his unifying of the German part, which included and still includes Saxony, is hardly insignificant. The cultural efforts of Charlemagne are equally important: great men wrote under him and were encouraged by him, and he settled monasteries that became and remained great centers of learning. The fact that the roots of the German written language as a literary language lie in his reign is also important, even if the connection between his educational reforms and the German language may not be particularly direct.

A final general term often applied to the early medieval period is the Dark Ages. The view was once commonly held that with the fall of Rome to the barbarian tribes, all forms of learning, political administration and religion went into abeyance, so that the adjective was a precise one. It is not, however, entirely fair, and it is worth considering again whether under Charlemagne there was indeed any continuity, anything that the Franks had inherited from the Romans, rather than recreated. Of course there were major changes: the Roman military organization had disappeared, many Roman architectural techniques were lost, and in the world of culture in general, some specific areas suffered, at least temporarily, one of these being medicine. Graeco-Roman medicine had made analytical advances that disappeared from view until they were much later reintroduced via the Arab world, which had taken this knowledge from the Eastern side of the original empire. Still, the Germanic tribes and the Franks in particular felt that they had assumed the mantle of the Roman Empire, and their rulers gave themselves Roman names and Roman titles, even if those roles were not quite the same as they had been. A minor, but extremely enduring example of the adoption by the Germanic world of Roman custom and administrative practice is provided by the imitation of Roman coinage. Even recent British coinage, for example, shows the sovereign side-face, like a Roman emperor, with a Latin inscription that up to the 1940s even included the title of *imperator* (referring admittedly to the role as Emperor of India in this case). The Romans had left intact in their former territories not only some of their system of administration, but in many places also their language, which had a written culture, and the Latin language developed into the various modern Romance languages. Of course, this was not the case in the unconquered Germanic territories, but even here Latin would return in a quite specific context.

A coin of Charlemagne with the inscription Karolus and the title
Imp (Imperator), in the style of Roman imperial coinage.

One important aspect of Roman administration had been the codification of laws, gathered for example by the Emperor Justinian in a collection called the *Institutions*. The Germanic tribes and early kingdoms imitated this in codifying their own laws, and they referred back to the Roman legal system as they did so. Their own early law collections are mostly in Latin, although German words appear at a very early stage, often because they expressed concepts that existed only in their own language. Among the earliest German words recorded are the so-called *Malberg Glosses*, the name referring perhaps to a hill of judgment, and the isolated German words are legal terms referring to specifically Germanic customs. Collections of German laws tended to be prefaced with a reference to Rome, however, and the prologue of the early *Lex Baiuwariorum* (Law of the Bavarians) provides by way of authority a brief history of law and law-giving, referring to Moses, the Greeks Solon and Lycurgus, and then in detail to the Romans, with a list of names of the law-compilers. Reference is then made to Pompey, and after him to Julius Caesar, then to Constantine and Theodosius II, followed by an etymology of *lex* and *mos* as "written law" and "custom" (taken from the sixth-century Latin theologian Isidore). To this classical material, however, was added a series of references to Germanic lawgivers: to Theoderic, described as Frankish, but probably the fifth-century king of the Ostrogoths, then to genuinely Frankish kings. The change from pagan to Christian law was noted, as was the fact that the various tribes had their own laws. This basic pattern of ancient, then Roman, and then Germanic rulers recurs (albeit with different names, and with an emphasis on Char-lemagne) in other Germanic law collections. These laws are not Roman law as such; they are collections of tribal customs in some respects, and for much of the early Middle Ages, the Germanic areas of northwestern Europe effectively had two legal systems working side by side, merging only gradually. But some of the laws and the idea of a structured legal code came directly from the Romans.

Far more importantly, however, the Roman Empire had established a state religion, Christianity, which had been adopted gradually by many of the Germanic tribes, including the Franks. By the time of the decline of the Merovingian kings, the status of the church had become very weak indeed against the pantheon of Germanic gods under the leadership of Wodan (Woden, Odin). There was a stronger continuity in what is now France, but the decline was marked in what are now the Low Countries and Germany, and especially in Saxony Christianity was at best far from exclusively accepted. However, these territories were reconverted to Catholic Christianity — the earliest missionaries in southern Germany had been the Arian Goths — by missionaries first from Ireland, who worked largely in the south of Germany, where there was still some kind of ecclesiastical organization, and then from the more recently converted Anglo-Saxon world. Establishing and stabilizing a state religion was a great unifying factor, and the name of the Anglo-Saxon Wynfrith — St. Boniface — is important in this context. This spread of Christianity in Germany, the establishment of bishoprics and monasteries, was based on the Latin language, and in German-speaking areas where there was no tradition in any case of a written language, it was the monks again who began to write things down in the local dialects. This is extremely im-portant in the development of literature in the German language, even though the concepts both of a unified language and of literature in its modern sense were still a long way off. The history of writing in German is, therefore, inextricably linked with the history and development of the Roman Church. German writing — the word literature cannot yet be used — emerges from a culture that is Latin and Christian. If the monks wanted to write things in German, the fact that the alphabet which they were accustomed to use was that designed for Latin presented some problems, but they were not insuperable. If Germanic had sounds that matched none of the available letters, then combinations of existing let-ters had to be made to serve for sounds which Latin did not have, such as the voiced or unvoiced -th- sound familiar in English and still present in many Old High German dialects for much of the period, which was rendered as *dh, th,* or even with the runic letter Þ (thorn), as well as a whole range of vowels and diphthongs.

The runic alphabet, an earlier and angular Germanic writing system designed for carving, provided (occasionally) individual letters that could be used in writing, but these did not survive for long. There are far later examples of runic inscriptions in Norse and Anglo-Saxon, but in continental Germanic there is not much more than a number of inscriptions on brooches found in Frankish graves, for example, and these are rarely more than names and dedications. But from the eighth century on, the first indications of German as a written language used for something more than just small inscriptions appear. Nevertheless, the whole basis of the culture remained Latin and the Church, and it would be many centuries before the trickle of writings in the various early German dialects became an established stream.

Latin was the sole official written language in Germany from the time of Charlemagne on, as it was used for administrative, official, theological, and literary purposes. In the last category, the so-called Dark Ages did not, of course, lose sight of literary and philosophical writing, of theology and history, and even under the Merovingian Frankish and other Germanic rulers, Latin writing continued, indeed flourished. One of the great works of the early Middle Ages, Boethius's *Consolation of Philosophy,* was written when he was imprisoned by an Ostrogoth king in Rome in the early sixth century. Slightly later, Venantius Fortunatus wrote Latin poetry as a Merovingian court poet, while in England Bede, at the end of the seventh century, wrote his history of the English Church and peoples, another major work of the period. The writing of biblical commentaries — detailed analyses of the Bible, verse by verse — also continued as a practice unbroken from the earliest Christian times, reaching a high point in the eighth and ninth centuries in Germany.

Writing was chiefly done in monasteries, and under Charlemagne's stabilization these establishments became important centers of learning. Many of the earlier monasteries in the south of Germany had been Irish foundations, but these were now gradually, under Charlemagne and his immediate successors, regularized under the Benedictine Rule, which was the norm in France and in other parts of Germany. That of St. Gallen, for example, was brought under the See of Constance, and became a royal monastery of some importance under Lewis the Pious and Ludwig the German, and others were founded. The imperial monastery at the Reichenau on Lake Constance was a similar case, as was Murbach in Alsace. All three were in the Alemannic linguistic area. Bavarian monasteries included Freising, Tegernsee, Wessobrunn, Monsee, and both St. Emmeram and Prül at Regensburg. In the various Frankish (Franconian) dialect areas, the most notable were at Weissenburg (South Rhenish Franconian), Lorsch and Fulda (Rhenish Franconian), Würzburg (East Franconian), and Trier, Echternach, Cologne, and Aachen (Mid-Franconian). In the Low German area, Essen, Werden, and Freckenhorst were early and important monasteries.

Most of the monasteries had scriptoria, where manuscripts were copied, and maintained libraries containing the works of the Church Fathers and later theological writers such as Isidore, Boethius, Bede, Alcuin, Hraban, and usually some Christian-Latin and sometimes even some classical poetry.[8] There was a certain amount of interchange between monasteries and libraries as far as scholars and manuscripts were concerned, but in most of the period they were relatively isolated from one another by geographical distance alone. The Rule of St. Benedict was maintained, however, for several centuries, and the Carolingian monasteries (often taking their members largely from the aristocracy) became increasingly important for missionary and then for educational work as the equivalent, almost, of the modern university or college. The monasteries also had a social role as landlords and eventually as centers of local administration. Their secular role was important, and not until the eleventh century was there much sign of any far-reaching change in the nature of monasticism in Germany. This did come about, albeit only gradually, in the wake of the insistence on religious asceticism and the reorganization in Benedictine monasticism which had been centered in the previous century on the monastery of Cluny in France, but it had no real effect in Germany until the middle of the eleventh century, and even then it was limited.[9]

To return to the palace school established in the last decade of the eighth century by Charlemagne at Aachen, there emerged under his rule what has rightly been called a Carolingian (or more properly, since it was associated more firmly with him than with his successors, a Caroline) renaissance. Although the validity of the term "renaissance" in this connection has been debated, there was under Charlemagne certainly a new encouragement of educational and religious policies that affected literature, by which is meant writing in Latin. Charlemagne's cultural policies were expressed in a series of occasional, though full, edicts, rather than set up as a system as such, and the influence and implementation of his ideas often did continue (although emphases were different) into the reigns of his successors. Charlemagne attracted to his court scholars from all quarters, such as the Anglo-Saxon Alcuin of York, whose position was a central one, the Visigoth Theodulf, and the Lombards Paul the Deacon and Paulinus of Aquileia. These men produced textbooks for a system of basic education which was based on the seven liberal arts: the *trivium* (rhetoric, grammar, and dialectic), and the more advanced *quadrivium* (astronomy, arithmetic, music, and geometry), as well as historical and biographical texts, political and philosophical writings, saints' lives, theological tracts, and verse of all kinds, including hymns. Biblical commentaries were perhaps the most numerous and most important writings of the school, but it has to be noted that such commentaries were not original in the modern sense of the word, but drew on the authority of earlier commentators going back to St. Augustine. The forms of classical Latin verse were much imitated, but an accented verse with end-rhymes (which occur naturally in Latin) was used in hymns, and this form was to have later significance in that it may have affected poetry in German. Great efforts were made at the same time toward standardization: of canon (ecclesiastical) law, of the monastic Rule of St. Benedict, of the liturgy, and of the Bible itself, which up to then had still circulated in different versions. The period is not one of major philosophical advances, but of the establishing of a solid base for Western Roman Catholicism in the literate echelons of society, and the establishing (and in some areas re-establishing) of standardized worship in the country at large.

Alcuin, the head of the school, and well aware of the cultural heritage of the classical world, gave biblical or classical names to other members of the court, and even suggested that they might be establishing a new Athens among the Franks. Classical and post-classical works were preserved and edited. Charlemagne's official policy was that Latin should be understood well by clerics at least, and that educational resources be made available in a unified and standard form. It is also important to note the development at this period of a type of writing based on Roman lettering and known as Carolingian minuscule, which provided a clear script.

The various capitularies and letters through which Charlemagne instituted and spread his educational reforms, then, were characterized by an insistence on the standardization of good writing in Latin. He insisted on the education of priests and monks, and in one of the most important edicts, the so-called *Admonitio generalis,* issued on March 23, 789, many of the eighty-two detailed articles on aspects of the behavior of priests and monks mention the need for correctness and standards in learning and teaching. It refers also to the setting up of schools for boys, although this refers to the teaching of Latin, and there is no provision for or indeed any mention of German. As a basis for a Christian society, the *Admonitio* did require that priests should know the Lord's Prayer, but also that they should preach it so that it could be understood by all. A few years later, article 52 of the capitulary that followed the Synod of Frankfurt in 794, determined that God should be worshipped not only in the three sacred languages, but in any tongue. Charlemagne himself seems to have had some interest in the German language, and he collected epic poems (the collection has not survived), although his son, Lewis the Pious, was concerned only with Latin poetry. Charlemagne's biographer, Einhard, tells us that Charlemagne gave the months and the various winds German names; of the names on the months, the only one on Charlemagne's list still likely to be encountered occasionally in older literature is *Hornung,* "February," but occasional attempts have been made to revive others, usually (as under the Nazis) as part of an effort to resuscitate German nationalism. Thus *Brachmonat* for "June" is sometimes found in the 1930s.[10] The educational reforms under Charlemagne were about Latin, although they might have reinforced the missionary work of translating the basic Christian prayers (the Creed, the Paternoster and the professions of faith were translated early into German), and sermons were known to have been read in (that is, translated from Latin into) German. The spread of Latin and the striving for standards within the context of the educational reforms might also have encouraged, tangentially at least, the composition of literary works in and the writing of German as well as Latin, but only to a very limited extent, and writing German was for a long time felt to be unusual.

If by early medieval German literature we mean literature written in the eastern part of Charlemagne's territories, the German part of the empire, that is, then that literature is almost entirely in Latin, and a great deal has survived besides legal texts and schoolbooks that is of considerable importance in the period down to the middle of the eleventh century and beyond. A number of biblical commentaries have been referred to already, and there are, for example, many by Alcuin, who was not born in Germany, and by his pupil Hrabanus Maurus (or Hraban), who was. Hraban was enormously prolific, and we may refer also to his encyclopedic work *De rerum naturis* (also known as *De universo,* Of the natural world), which is based on an earlier encyclopedia by Isidore of Seville, to his complex work of praise for the Cross, the *De laudibus sanctae crucis,* and indeed to his study of languages, or rather, of scripts. Little of his work is original in any modern sense, however. Nor would he have claimed any originality in an age in which learning was based on authority. The Carolingian and post-Carolingian age produced many kinds of prose: theological, philosophical, and political tracts besides the commentaries.

The universality of Latin makes any focus on what we may call German territory artificial to some extent. For example, in the middle of the ninth century, John Scottus, John the Irishman, came to what is now France to head the school at Paris established by Charlemagne's grandson, and wrote major — and original — works of philosophy there. Less well known is the lady Dhuoda (it is not certain that her native language was a Germanic one), whose Latin book of advice to her son William was written in 843. Important historical annals were begun under Charlemagne, and continued under his successors. Walahfrid Strabo (another of Hraban's pupils) wrote prose and verse hagiography; a major figure in the realm of science in the first half of the eleventh century is Hermannus Contractus, Hermann of Reichenau, known as Hermann the Lame, because he appears to have been severely disabled, whose works on mathematics and astronomy are important, though he also wrote historical material and hymns. Writings in Latin on music are plentiful, too. In verse, manuscripts range from the lyrics of members of Charlemagne's circle — Alcuin included — to later high points in the poems of Walahfrid and of another pupil from Fulda, the unfortunate Gottschalk, a writer of some skill who was, however, condemned for heresy. Later on we have, for example, the so-called *Cambridge Songs,* a collection of shorter Latin pieces including both a praise-poem to the Saxon emperors and some comic fables, the religious poems of Notker the Stammerer of St. Gallen, the Latin plays of Hrotswitha of Gandersheim, the folktale of *Ruodlieb* (which has a few German words in it), and the *Ecbasis Cuiusdam Captivi* (Escape of a certain captive), a religious fable in epic form, as well as a complex allegorical poem about the struggle between good and evil by a writer known only as Eupolemius, who was almost certainly German, and the Virgil imitation in the poem *Waltharius,* an heroic work probably by an otherwise unknown monk called Geraldus, involving conflict between early Germanic tribes.

Toward the end of the early medieval period, there are even a few macaronic poems, that is, works written in a mixture of German and Latin. However, the great educator Notker III of St. Gallen (d. 1022), known as Labeo, the Thick-lipped, or more significantly for us as Teutonicus, the German, wrote at the end of the tenth and in the first decades of the eleventh century a number of works in what is known as a *Mischsprache,* a mixture of Latin and German explanations for the use of those learning Latin. He was aware, too, even as late as this, that using German was unusual, and he said so in a letter. Even later comes another important mixed text, the commentary on the Canticles, the Song of Songs, by Williram, abbot of Ebersberg, set out in the major manuscripts in three separate columns, the Latin prose of the Vulgate text flanked by a Latin verse paraphrase in hexameters, with a prose commentary on the right in a mixture of German and Latin.[11]

There are, finally, also some surviving Latin works that were clearly either influenced by, or actually translated from German. The epic of *Waltharius* may be in this category, and a Latin version of a riddle about a bird flying without feathers (a snowflake) looks very much as if there was a German alliterative original. A Latin version of the legend of the Dancers of Kölbigk, men condemned to dance forever by God for trying to abduct a girl, may also derive from a German original. A Latin poem on the life of St. Gall, written originally by a monk called Ratpert in the later years of the ninth century, was actually translated from German, we are told, by Ekkehart IV of St. Gall, who died in the mid-eleventh century, and it is his Latin text which survives, although since Ekkehart mentions the melody, the two forms may have matched quite closely.

The unifying element of Latin as a literary and administrative language within the Carolingian Empire and later has been rightly stressed,[12] not only when that empire consisted of Romance and of Germanic speakers, but later on in the German part alone, in which both Low and High German dialects were spoken. The heterogeneity of these dialects is clear in written German material from the middle of the eighth century down to the twelfth. In the case of the High German dialects the differences are apparent not only in the extent to which a set of sound changes known as the High German Sound Shift has affected the consonants of the earlier common language spoken by the Western Germanic tribes (as opposed to the East Germanic Goths, Vandals, Burgundians, or the Norse group), but also in vocabulary, and in orthography in general. There is no such thing as a pure form of Old High German, and to refer to it as a language as such is at best an oversimplification. The term comprises a group of dialects developing over a period of hundreds of years. The High German Sound Shift, which after about 500 affected the voiced and unvoiced plosives in particular, did so to a decreasing extent as it moved northwest from the Alps (hence "High German," from its origins in the mountainous regions). Thus a Bavarian document might express the word for God (modern *Gott*) as *kot,* where in all the other dialects (with a little fluctuation in Alemannic) one finds *got.* In the region of Aachen, the Franconian dialects sometimes show little effect of the sound shift at all; but a dialect is still classified as High German if any of the relevant changes are visible. Above what is known as the Benrath line, passing roughly through Aachen, Germanic dialects are not at all affected by the sound shift, and these are known as Low German. Old

High German includes: Lombardic, which died out early, leaving only some legal words; the so-called Upper-German dialects of Bavarian and Alemannic; the central dialects of the Franks themselves, with a distinction between East, South Rhenish and Middle Franconian, the latter being sub-divided into Ripuarian and Moselle Franconian and the last of these the High German dialect least affected by the sound shift; we do not have early written material in Thuringian. The continental Old Low German dialects (leaving aside Anglo-Saxon, that is) include principally Old Saxon (the ancestor of modern *Plattdeutsch*), Old Low Franconian (the ancestor of modern Dutch) and the various dialects of Frisian.[13] Apart from Old Saxon, we have very little written material from the earliest period, with the exception of some glosses in a late manuscript. In modern geographical terms, the area in which Old High German was spoken or written covers present-day Germany south of a line through Aachen, say, plus most of what is now Switzerland and Austria, plus some parts of eastern France and northern Italy.

Orthography even within High German is especially variable, as scribes working at monasteries far apart from one another struggled to represent their Germanic language with the Latin alphabet, and in terms of vocabulary, too, the struggle to translate new ideas, usually associated with Christianity and for which there was no ready equivalent, required new words or circumlocutions, and such decisions varied from dialect to dialect. A classic case is the translation of the central Christian concept of *spiritus sanctus* (Holy Spirit) variously as *uuiho atum* or as *heilag gaist*. In the first version, the element *atum* (modern German *Atem*) might well look confusingly secular, while in the second the pre-Christian word *gaist* may have retained, as its modern English equivalent, ghost, still does, the wrong kind of supernatural overtones.

Written down without prescriptive rules in more or less isolated monasteries, then, it is to be expected that Old High (and Old Low) German texts show a bewildering amount of linguistic variation. We may perceive in some documents reflexes of the spoken language, but such glimpses are rare.[14] Given Charlemagne's insistence on a standardized and correct Latin, one might expect some attempts at standardization, at least, in German, and some has indeed been perceived, but it is not systematic, and sometimes the attempt to standardize results simply in what looks like a mixture of dialects in the same text. A separate problem is raised by the question of West Franconian as a German dialect: was there a separate dialect for texts in German still written in monasteries in the French part of the original empire? Nor is it until Notker the German, in the later tenth and early eleventh century, that we see clearly a conscious attempt to rationalize aspects of the orthography of German, in this case in respect of final and initial consonants.[15]

The link between the emergence of German writing of any kind at all and the renaissance and spread of Latin learning under the Carolingians is not a clear one. Rather, the fact that the Church was the instrument of the spread of Latin learning meant that to some extent experimentation with the committing to writing of German might have arisen more or less accidentally, but everything was still firmly within the context of the Church. Not only do we owe every single piece of written German at this period to the Church in physical terms, but the overwhelming majority of what is in any case a very small number of survivals is directly concerned with the Church as well.

Several facts need to be accepted, then, about German-language writings in the early medieval period, and the first of these is that there is, compared with Latin, very little. Even gathering all the fragments, word-glosses (that is, German words written into Latin manuscripts as single explanations, or groups of these gathered together as glossaries) and translations, there is in terms of the modern printed book barely a shelf's worth of material, and as far as texts with self-conscious literary intent are concerned — largely those in verse — we have from before the middle of the eleventh century little more than would fill a single printed volume.[16] German is at this period not so much in the shadow of Latin as completely overwhelmed by it, and where Latin is established and unified, German is to an extent inchoate and confused. Our attitude has necessarily to be one of acceptance of the fact that these are indeed the beginnings, and of a pragmatic acknowledgment of the fact that little surviving Old High or Low German would count as literature in the modern sense, even the poetic texts. Virtually everything that we have may be seen as what in German is called *Gebrauchsliteratur,* functional writing. Glosses — German words written by their Latin equivalents — and glossaries, from the very early translation of a Latin thesaurus known as *Abrogans* down to the careful pedagogical writings of Notker, as well as biblical, liturgical or theological translations are all clearly for a purpose, and that is to aid the understanding of Latin, either as teaching or as reference tools. Even with major poetical texts, the *Evangelienbuch* of Otfrid of Weissenburg is probably a teaching document, an introduction to the proper reading of the Gospels, possibly for novices (while its predecessor in Low German, the Old Saxon *Heliand,* was an aid to proselytizing.) The Old High German charms, though providing occasional flickers of the pagan past, are not only Christianized into what are effectively collects, petitionary prayers, but are in any case clearly designed for largely medical purposes. The charms can be bracketed with prayers, therefore, and are treated that way in the present volume. The devotional intent behind the few small metrical prayers, hymns, and smaller biblical verse-adaptations is straightforward, too, as indeed it is with the descriptions of the beginning of the world in the *Wessobrunner Gebet* and the end of it in *Muspilli,* or in the poetic life of St. George. We are left with two historical pieces in verse — the *Ludwigslied* and *De Heinrico* — the former with a strong religious emphasis and the latter macaronic, and one single, fragmentary and brief heroic poem, the *Hildebrandlied*. Even when we reach the eleventh century, the German verse monuments that survive are in the first instances religious.

All this makes clear that the two terms "literature of the early Middle Ages in Germany," and "Old High and Low German literature," are different. The former designation bespeaks a Latin culture of some richness, plus some early pieces in the vernacular, many patently of philological interest. The second begs the question of what is meant by literature, and may embrace everything written down in the vernacular, including phrasebooks, *Federproben* (pen-testing samples), or fragments which are sometimes almost entirely unintelligible, although we may also find self-conscious efforts at writing in German with an aesthetic intent. The concept of literature in Germany in the early medieval period has to take in not only Latin above all, but all kinds of other writings, from runic inscriptions on brooches from Frankish graves down to stylistically ambitious religious poetry in Old High German.[17] It is no accident that the essay in the present volume concerned with the somewhat amorphous collection of "smaller Old High German poems" is the longest.

Nineteenth-century views of *Nationalliteratur* tended to examine the Latin writings of this period only in so far as they were thought to represent lost German materials. Indeed, many early literary histories went beyond even the simple accumulation of survivals in German, and, sometimes with questionable methodology, focused on the (probably correct) assumption that native works had existed in oral form on the continent in German on Germanic subjects which match texts that we do actually possess in Anglo-Saxon, Old Norse, or Latin, or in later, Middle High German versions. In one of the major collections of Old High German texts there is a work printed in Old High German that really exists (as becomes clear from the notes) only in Latin; it may well have had an Old High German antecedent, but we do not have it. Against the necessary caution of supposing works to have existed, on the other hand, it was suspected in 1875 on linguistic grounds that a 600-line interpolation in a long Anglo-Saxon poem on Genesis had been translated from an Old Saxon original. This was substantiated when a fragment of that Old Saxon poem was discovered just under twenty years later.[18] Finally, in one celebrated case it is not certain even now whether a particular text is even genuine. The so-called "Old High German lullaby" may be a forgery and has indeed been dismissed as such by several critics, such that it is simply not mentioned in most literary histories. The matter is, however, still in doubt.[19]

In spite of their survival in the shadow of a great amount of Latin, it is understandable that emphasis has been placed on the limited number of remaining texts in German dialects from this early period, but they differ from the Latin materials, too, in their transmission. The Latin texts are usually attested with a large-scale and clear manuscript tradition. The vernacular pieces have survived — and "monuments" or "survivals" are both much-used words — in a single manuscript version for the most part (in one case, however, all we have is a later engraving of a now lost monumental inscription),[20] and two further points need to be made. First, that German works (other than translations) have frequently been written on spare or blank manuscript pages, which sometimes makes them difficult to read in physical terms, quite apart from any problems in interpreting the words in a language that has not been written down before. Glosses are written as additions in Latin manuscripts in any case, and these are sometimes in code, abbreviated, or not even inked, but scratched on with a dry stylus. To take some smaller poetic texts as illustrations of the problems, however: the *Muspilli,* a poem about the end of the world, is written in the margins and blank spaces of a Latin text; the *Hildebrandlied,* an heroic poem, was written on the spare front and back leaves of a manuscript; the *Georgslied* may have been written down by someone with a form of dyslexia; and the *Ludwigslied* has features that make one suspect that the scribe was a French speaker. Second, even when the written form is clear, precisely *what* constitutes the text can be a problem. Otfrid's *Evangelienbuch,* his Gospel poem of more than 7000 lines of rhymed verse, is preserved in a well-produced, dedicated manuscript (and corrected by the author), which was also copied in other manuscripts. Thus, we have not only the first named author, but also the first complete, large-scale, self-conscious work in High German, more specifically, in South Rhenish Franconian. It is accompanied by a slightly apologetic Latin letter discussing the fact that it is in German, which anticipates another similar letter written by Notker Teutonicus over a century later. But what constitutes the actual *text* of Otfrid's work? We are in a manuscript culture, and as convenient (and indeed necessary) as it is for us to work from one of the modern printed editions, such editions do not, for example, indicate the different-sized initials found in the Otfrid manuscripts, although these are important to the structuring of the work. Moreover, they frequently omit Otfrid's Latin marginal pointers to biblical verses in the Vulgate. To take a far smaller example, the two charms from a manuscript now at Merseburg are much studied because they contain clear references to pagan gods and to Valkyries; but in the manuscript the two charms are linked with a (never convincingly explained) sign like an H, and they are followed by a prayer on the same page. These features tend to be omitted in print. Furthermore, the Old High German sections of the charms are laid out as prose; however, they fall clearly into alliterative verse, so that a reasonable case exists for printing them out that way, but things are less straightforward with editorial decisions about the placing of capitals (there are none within the text) to indicate proper names. In both cases — Otfrid and the charms — the text is in fact the *manuscript,* and the questions of editorial policy that have to be faced with any ancient text are heightened in the case of Old High German. A more extreme case is that of the so-called *Murbach Hymns,* which are some Latin hymns, every word of which has been glossed in the manuscript. The German words are sometimes printed out without the Latin, as if they were composed as coherent German, which is not the case. More complex still are cases like Williram of Ebersberg's commentary on the Song of Songs, which balances Latin and German deliberately in different columns in the manuscript.

The whole question of what constitutes the text, then, especially with Old High German survivals, is difficult. Even in the examples already adduced there is a difference: Otfrid's manuscript was intended to be the text and was designed as such, even if the modern reader has to encounter it in a different and incomplete form. With the charms, the problem is different. The manuscript version has in pragmatic or philological terms to count as the text, but may also be read as an index of a wider context, so that we may refer back to a pre-written pagan form that is of necessity indefinite. Similar considerations apply, too, with a work like the *Hildebrandlied,* to the interpretation of which further corrective readings might be (and have been) applied.

In spite of all this, some of the German texts can be singled out in literary terms. The *Hildebrandlied* is, in spite of enormous textual difficulties, an impressive work, a happy accident of survival, given that it is a heroic poem whose form and content must have been of antiquarian interest by the time it was written down. As a self-conscious effort in the vernacular, Otfrid's *Gospel Book* is the most significant Old High German work, as is the *Heliand* in Old Saxon, and for this reason merits a full chapter. With Otfrid, while the literary merits may be hard for us to assess, and may appear limited, they are by no means non-existent,[21] and the self-awareness of a writer working in German on a lengthy text for the first time is of considerable importance. So, too, is the presumed stylistic influence of the work, establishing end-rhyme once and for all in High German, for example. At the end of the period, Notker the German is aware of the German language and he uses it with skill, even if his works are of interest mainly for his contribution to the emergence of German as a literary language.

The present volume will necessarily appear somewhat disjointed because the Latin literary culture of Germany and the beginnings of vernacular writings are separate ones, and are thus presented separately, with discussion of the Latin material properly occupying two full chapters. Within the Latin tradition, too, there are understandably some works that seem not to have had much influence outside the immediate monastic culture in which they were produced: the writings of Hrotswitha and the Bible poem (the *Messiad*) of the writer known only as Eupolemius are cases in point. Are there, however, any very precise links between the Carolingian Renaissance and the first signs of writing in German? The influence of Charlemagne's school was not restricted to Aachen, and extended to other monastic centers. Alcuin's favorite pupil was Hraban, to whom he gave the by-name of St. Benedict's own favorite pupil, Maurus, and he was to become a figure of some importance in the further development of writing in Low and High German. Hraban was for many years abbot of the important monastery of Fulda, where an interest in the German language seems to have been encouraged, and the later work of several of his pupils reflect this.[22] It has already been noted that Lupus of Ferrières, one of the latter, was aware of the importance of German, and Hraban seems to have influenced, directly or indirectly, the translation into High German of the prose Gospel harmony ascribed to Tatian (and with it the *Heliand* in Old Saxon), as well as, perhaps less directly, Otfrid's Gospel poem. And yet it remains a problematic question whether other writings in German emerged *because* of the reforms directed toward literacy in Latin, or whether this happened *in spite* of the dominance of that language. Both viewpoints have been argued, and the answer is probably that the work of the monastic centers probably *did* encourage writing in German to some degree, even if a few of the survivals in Old High German seem to go against the spirit of Charlemagne's educational principles. Glosses and translations, of course, were geared to the learning of Latin, and this too is what Notker's works are all about; beyond those we are not left with a great deal of vernacular material.

Even the important work of Otfrid is ambiguous. He studied under Hraban at Fulda and was influenced by his biblical commentaries, which are used extensively in the *Evangelienbuch,* a work designed to aim novices back toward the study of the Latin Bible itself. Nevertheless, to undertake a retelling of the Gospels in complex verse in German was a bold act, even if Otfrid worried in his Latin prefatory letter about using a "barbaric and uncultivated language." In aesthetic terms, the Gospel poem uses Latin devices, including end-rhyme and other rhetorical techniques. Otfrid also added a prefatory verse chapter in German, in which he has a celebrated passage in praise of the German language contrasting with his somewhat disparaging remarks about it in Latin. Both Otfrid and Notker demonstrate, in their awareness of the problems of writing German, the same desire for a linguistic standard that the Carolingian Renaissance had applied to Latin, even if in slightly different ways. The links with the renaissance of writing under Charlemagne are consequential, rather than formal or official, they may be accidental, and they need not be particularly strong.[23]

Where does the early medieval period end as far as literature in Germany is concerned? There is not, of course, an abrupt conclusion, but a series of gradual changes, in society, in the Church, in language. The line of Charlemagne, which had provided rulers of the German part of his original empire, came to an end with the death in 911 of Ludwig the Child. After a brief period of rule by Conrad, Duke of Franconia, a Saxon dynasty was established by Henry the Fowler, and consolidated in the rule of Otto I, known as the Great, from 936 to 973 and then of his son and grandson of the same name. That line died out in its turn with Henry II in 1024, and the Salian house (the name first appears in the twelfth century) ruled from then until the death of Henry V in 1125.

From about 1050, changes in the High German dialects begin to show themselves, the principal among them — this is of course a simplification, and in any case spoken and written changes by no means coincide — being a weakening or loss of unstressed vowels, so that a word like *giburti* would become *geburt,* the first unstressed *i* becoming a neutral sound (referred to as *schwa,* and still represented as *e* in modern German), and the second falling away altogether; and also the spread of umlaut (up to this point manifest only in the modification of short *a* to *e,* as in plurals like *gast/gesti*), until by the end of the twelfth century the High German language had settled in the stage we refer to as Middle High German.

This linguistic change is not matched by social or historical changes of any significance, at least not with any close correlation. Monastic reforms and a greater insistence on asceticism do eventually manifest themselves in Germany, and the split between church and state becomes ever wider. Literature in German moves from being the exclusive province of the monasteries first into the hands of secular canons at cathedral chapters, although it remains largely clerical.[24] But the actual substance of what is written in Germany does not change very much. As far as Latin goes, works like the *Ruodlieb* and the *Ecbasis Captivi,* and writers like Hermann of Reichenau and Hrotswitha, for example, belong in this period, and the process of biblical commentary, of the historical chronicle, of theological writings, continued down to the Reformation. For German, there is no real gap (as is sometimes claimed) in the tenth century and there is no real renewal of literature in the eleventh, certainly not one based on a new piety inspired by the Cluniac reforms. Rather, the trickle of German works (some written down during the tenth century, with Notker the German bridging that and the eleventh) increases a little, again principally in the religious area, although there is a continuous tradition too of healing charms from Old High and Low German again down to the end of the Middle Ages. The process of glossing continues, too. Otfrid's Gospel book (as the Old Saxon *Heliand* before it) mixed biblical narrative with commentary, and the same technique was applied after the Old High German period, in the eleventh and twelfth centuries, to the Old Testament in German in the Southeast, in Carinthia, for example, to Genesis and Exodus, and then to other parts of the Bible. The works are not quite the same and there are different emphases, but the similarities outweigh the differences.

Further historical works appear, and religious poems of various sorts, now in a wider variety, and sermons in the vernacular are also written down, as are prose texts on zoology (the theologically orientated bestiary known as the *Physiologus*) or pharmacy (the so-called *Arzneibücher*). Further *Sammelhandschriften,* collective manuscripts dedicated to German texts — though not many — appear. German continues to develop as a literary vehicle, and one sees the first indications of a more genuinely secular literature in works like the *Kaiserchronik,* a rhymed chronicle of Roman emperors and saints, and in the *Rolandslied* and the *Alexanderlied,* the poems of Roland and of Alexander the Great. These are religious works (and were written by clerics), but are not exclusively so. In the same category fall the earliest versions of a limited number of adventure-stories known (not very helpfully) as the *Spielmannsepen.*

The study of Old High German may be said to go back as far as the sixteenth century, when an early antiquarian interest was shown in the work of Otfrid, and more manuscripts were discovered and printed in the following two centuries. The only text we have, for example, of the *Annolied* is that edited by the Baroque poet Martin Opitz (1597–1639) and published with a commentary in 1639. Since most of the texts we have are preserved in a single manuscript only, some of them have been lost over the centuries, while others have had interesting adventures of their own. A case in point is that of the *Ludwigslied,* first edited in 1696 from a transcript of the original manuscript, which by that time was believed to be lost. In fact it was not lost, and was rediscovered by Heinrich Hoffmann von Fallersleben (1798–1874), the author of the *Deutschlandlied,* and re-edited in 1837. There was some interest in the text in the eighteenth century, and the printed version of 1696, which contains some errors, would have remained the standard version had not Hoffman rediscovered the supposedly lost manuscript. Even so, one of his readings of a single word (but one which was important to the question of the dialect of the piece) in the text was not corrected until the manuscript was examined again with modern techniques in 1968. On the other hand, some manuscripts were lost in the nineteenth century, and others were treated by chemicals to enhance the script, but this caused long-term damage. Luckily, facsimiles and photographs of many of the works exist, and modern computer technology has taken this process further. It is important that this should be so, since the manuscript versions of the works are the real texts.

The nineteenth century saw the birth of Old High German studies proper. Scholars like Jacob Grimm (1785–1863) edited texts in conjunction with the philological and folkloristic work for which they are better known. Scholars began, too, to attempt to integrate Old High German into the literary history of Germany, often with a somewhat nationalistic bias. What survives of Old High German is, of course, fragmented, and it was not until the 1860s that the first critical collection appeared, with soundly edited texts arranged with an eye on chronology. Karl Müllenhoff and Wilhelm Scherer's *Denkmäler* — the use of the word "monument" to embrace all kinds of writings was significant — is still used in the revision by Elias von Steinmeyer, who produced a collection of his own, and others have followed, including one intended for student use, Wilhelm Braune's *Althochdeutsches Lesebuch,* which contains a very good selection, and first appeared in 1875. Since then it has been edited many times, and remains a standard work. A more modern approach is that represented by the recent anthologies of Old High German by Heinz Mettke, Horst Dieter Schlosser, and Karl Wipf, all of whom present selections of the texts with parallel modern German translations. There have also been various major projects concerned with Old High German, spread over many years and in some cases still ongoing. The editing of Notker's works is one example, and the work of compiling all the Old High German glosses is another very long-term project.

The approach to Old High German has varied over the past two centuries. Early studies often placed great emphasis on the Germanic aspects of the works that survive, so that a perhaps disproportionate amount of attention was paid to the pagan gods named in the Second Merseburg Charm, or to the supposed originals of texts that only survive in Latin. Müllenhoff and Scherer even printed what appears to be an Old High German poem, but it is reconstructed from a surviving Latin piece. More recently, the struggle to establish what is meant by "Old High German literature" has led to the full acknowledgement of the fact that much consideration has to be given to what might be thought of as non-literary texts, such as the glosses. The title of a work by Georg Baesecke, one of the leading scholars in the field in the inter-war years, is significant: he entitled his book on what is effectively a thesaurus or dictionary *Der deutsche Abrogans und die Herkunft des deutschen Schrifttums,* thus acknowledging the value of Old High German studies as the beginnings of writing in its broadest sense in German. So, too, the first and last essays in the present work are concerned largely with language. Of course, language and manuscript studies as such are also a continuous process. Beside this has to be set another important fact, stressed most firmly in the years after the Second World War, namely that the bulk of what is most readily accepted as literature in the German-speaking territories during the period is in Latin, and that the Latin language and the Latin church dominate most of our survivals, even if they are in the vernacular. Otfrid's Gospel poem may be derivative in terms of content, but as the author was well aware, for him to produce such a work in German verse at all placed it securely in the literary vanguard. Fascinating though they may be, even works like the early charms or the *Hildebrandlied* were possibly copied down in an antiquarian spirit. Old High German was written down in the various monastic centers in what is now Germany, Austria, and Switzerland, of course, but also in monasteries outside the present German-speaking areas. Some of them remain where they were written, but manuscripts circulated for copying even in the Middle Ages, and sometimes were presumably not returned, ending up a long way from their place of origin. Others were moved in later centuries, and although many are now in the major libraries of the German-speaking countries (such as Munich, Heidelberg, Vienna) there is no center for Old High German material. Indeed, some important manuscripts are in libraries outside Germany. Others have had interesting adventures even in recent times: the two pages of the *Hildebrandlied* were removed from Germany at the end of the Second World War, and although the first leaf was returned fairly soon, the second leaf was not reunited with it for a considerable time. Finally, the search for Old High German (as for other medieval vernacular material) is a continuous one. Glosses are still found and edited, and there is always the possibility — however slight — of a new and exciting discovery at some point. Although it is Middle and not Old High German, the discovery in 2003 of very early manuscript fragments of the *Nibelungenlied* is a case in point.

The concept of German literature in the early Middle Ages still presents us with a series of problems. The definition of Germany is variable, and even to speak of the German language at all is a simplification, when we mean Old Bavarian, Old East Franconian and so on, to say nothing of Old Saxon. In any case, most German literature of the early period is for the most part not actually *in* German, but in Latin. A survey such as the present one will necessarily seem to — and to an extent actually will — be disjointed, a series of disparate views. There are overlaps between Latin and German writings, but they are limited. What has survived in German itself is relatively insignificant, and it is not even always particularly interesting as literature, since for the vernacular material the term has to be stretched to embrace pretty well everything that has been written down. With the exceptions of the *Hildebrandlied* and perhaps the historical works, both of which are dealt with in individual essays, everything in German is *Gebrauchsliteratur* in a Christian context, although, of course, this is true of much of the Latin as well, and it implies by no means an automatic negative in aesthetic terms. Nevertheless, although the early German texts may seem at first glance to be quite unliterary, as in the case of the glosses and the translations which make up so much of the material, and although even with more clearly literary works it is often hard to determine precisely what constitutes the actual text, their importance lies in the fact that they exist at all. These writings show us the birth of a modern literary language.

Latin manuscript with Old High German glosses — a ninth-century interlinear Benedictine Rule *from St. Gallen.*

Notes

[1] It is impossible to be consistent with names, which at this period are in any case almost invariably actually *recorded* in their Latin forms, but are often best-known *now* in a French version, as is the case with Charlemagne (Carolus [Magnus], Karl, Charles). Here the most acceptable modern forms are used (Pépin rather than Pippin), although distinctions are made where useful, so that Ludovicus, for example, is rendered as Lewis in general terms, but Ludwig in the case of East Frankish (German) kings, Louis when we are specifically talking about the (eventually) French-speaking Western part of Charlemagne's old empire, even though this means that the hero of the Old High German poem known as the *Ludwigslied* has to be referred to as Louis III. Merovingian forms are probably best kept separate (as Chlothar, Clovis, and so on, rather than their later equivalents) to avoid having *too* many with the same name.

[2] There is a very full and useful survey of early Germanic history by D. H. Green, *Language and History in the Early Germanic World* (Cambridge: CUP, 1998).

[3] See on the Franks Peter Lasko, *The Kingdom of the Franks: North-West Europe Before Charlemagne* (London: Thames and Hudson, 1971) for the early period, and the standard work by Rosamond McKitterick, *The Frankish Kingdoms under the Carolingians 751–987* (London and New York: Longman, 1983). For background, see J. M. Wallace-Hadrill, *The Barbarian West, 400–1000,* 3rd ed (London: Hutchinson., 1967), 64–114, and there is a good, brief introduction in R. Allen Brown, *The Origins of Modern Europe* (London: Constable, 1972), 34–73. A recent study (with a significant title) of the build-up of the whole *regnum Francorum,* the kingdom of the Franks, is that by Bernard S. Bachrach, *Early Carolingian Warfare: Prelude to Empire* (Philadelphia: U Pennsylvania P, 2001).

[4] On the significance of the coronation and a discussion of Charlemagne's apparent reluctance to seem to hold office from the Pope (a point which would be important again some centuries later), see F. L. Ganshof, *The Imperial Coronation of Charlemagne* (Glasgow: U Glasgow P, 1971).

[5] See *Karl der Große: Lebenswerk und Nachleben,* ed. Werner Braunfels (Düsseldorf: Schwann, 1965), especially the second volume, *Das geistige Leben,* ed. Bernard Bischoff.

[6] Eileen Power, *Medieval People* ([1924] Harmondsworth: Penguin, 1951), 11–33. On social divisions in Frankish society, see the useful introduction by Heinrich Fichtenau, *The Carolingian Empire,* trans. Peter Munz (Oxford: Blackwell, 1968), especially the chapter on the poor.

[7] There is a brief but useful survey of recent views on the birth of the post-Carolingian countries by Stuart Airlie, "After Empire — Recent Work on the Emergence of Post-Carolingian Kingdoms," *Early Medieval Europe* 2 (1993): 153–61.

[8] The standard study is that by Rosamond McKitterick, *The Carolingians and the Written Word* (Cambridge: CUP, 1989), on the organization and economics of the monastic production. See also M. M. Hildebrandt, *The External School in Carolingian Society* (Leiden: Brill, 1992).

[9] See Friedrich Prinz, "Monastische Zentren im Frankenreich," *Studi Medievali*, Ser. 3/19 (1978), 571–90, and K. C. King, "The Earliest German Monasteries" [1961], in his *Selected Essays on Medieval German Literature*, ed. John L. Flood and A. T. Hatto (London: Institute of Germanic Studies, 1975), 98–124, and, on the reforms in Benedictine monasticism, Norman Cantor, "The Crisis of Western Monasticism," *American Historical Review* 66 (1960): 47–67, and Timothy Reuter, *Germany in the Early Middle Ages. 800–1056* (London: Longman, 1991), 243–46.

[10] The text of the *Admonitio* is in A. Boretius, *Capitularia regum Francorum* I (Hanover: Hahn/MGH, 1883), no. 22, the Frankfurt capitulary is no. 28; see P. D. King, *Charlemagne: Translated Sources* (Kendal: King, 1987), 209–20 and 224–56 for translations. On the *Admonitio* and its importance, see Wallace-Hadrill, *Barbarian West*, 98–99. The *De litteris colendis*, Boretius, no. 29, King, 232–32 is also important on Charlemagne's education policy. See *Einhard's Life of Charlemagne*, ed. H. W. Garrod and R. B. Mowat (Oxford: Clarendon, 1915), 30–31 (chapter 29) on Charlemagne's interest in German and the months; translation by Paul Dutton, *Charlemagne's Courtier* (Peterborough, ON: Broadview, 1998), 34–35. In general see Michael Seidlmayer, *Currents of Medieval Thought,* trans. D. Barker (Oxford: Blackwell, 1960), 34–49 for a succinct survey of the Carolingian Renaissance. See also Rosamond McKitterick, *The Frankish Church and the Carolingian Reforms* (Cambridge: CUP, 1977) and John J. Contreini, "The Pursuit of Knowledge in Carolingian Europe," in *The Gentle Voices of Teachers,* ed. Richard E. Sullivan (Columbus, OH: Ohio State UP, 1995), 106–41. The following papers are also useful: Peter von Polenz, "Karlische Renaissance, karlische Bildungsreformen und die Anfänge der deutschen Literatur," *Mitteilungen des Marburger Universitätsbunds* 1959, 27–39; Franz Brunhölzl, "Der Bildungsauftrag der Hofschule," in *Karl der Große,* II, ed. Bischoff, 28–41; Werner Betz, "Karl der Große und die *lingua theodisca,*" *ibid.,* 300–306; Klaus Matzel, "Karl der Große und die deutsche Sprache," *Rheinische Vierteljahrsblätter* 34 (1970): 172–89.

[11] Major surveys are those by M. L. W. Laistner, *Thought and Letters in Western Europe, AD 500–900,* 2nd ed. (London: Methuen, 1957), the huge handbooks by Max Manitius, *Geschichte der lateinischen Literatur des Mittelalters* (Munich: Beck, 1911–31, repr. 1964–65), and on poetry the two works by Frederic J. Raby, *A History of Christian-Latin Poetry from the Beginnings to the Close of the Middle Ages,* 2nd ed. (Oxford: Clarendon, 1953) and *A History of Secular Latin Poetry in the Middle Ages,* 2nd ed. (Oxford: Clarendon, 1957). For discussions of many of the major German-Latin writers, see, *German Writers and Works of the Early Middle Ages: 800–1170,* ed. Will Hasty and James Hardin (New York: Gale, 1995). There are also readable biographical introductions by Eleanor Shipley Duckett, *Carolingian Portraits* (Ann Arbor, MI: U Michigan P, 1962) and Karl Langosch, *Profile des lateinischen Mittelalters* (Darmstadt: WBG, 1965); see also Celia Chazelle, *The Crucified God in the Carolingian Era* (Cambridge: CUP, 2001) and finally, on the poets, Peter Godman, *Poets and Emperors: Frankish Politics and Carolingian Poetry* (Oxford: Clarendon, 1987). Texts are to be found in the great collections such as J. P. Migne's *Patrologia Latina* (Paris: Migne, 1844–64) and the *Monumenta Germaniae Historica* (Hanover etc., 1826ff.), here abbreviated as *PL* and MGH. For a selection of verse, see Karl Langosch, *Lyrische Anthologie des lateinischen Mittelalters* (Darmstadt: WBG, 1968) and Peter Godman, *Poetry of the Carolingian Renaissance* (London:

Duckworth, 1985). Individual editions are noted when texts are discussed elsewhere in this volume.

[12] McKitterick, *Written Word*, 20–22.

[13] There is a brief but useful survey of the dialects by Werner Wegstein, "Die sprachgeographische Gliederung des Deutschen in historischer Sicht," in *Sprachgeschichte* I/ii, ed. Werner Besch, Oskar Reichmann and Stefan Sonderegger (Berlin and New York: de Gruyter, 1985), 1751–66. See also such surveys as Stefan Sonderegger, *Althochdeutsche Sprache und Literatur* (Berlin: de Gruyter, 1974). The outline here is a necessary simplification, especially with regard to the division into East, West and North (Norse) groupings, and there are some shared features between some western and eastern dialects.

[14] Stefan Sonderegger, "Reflexe gesprochener Sprache in der althochdeutschen Literatur," *Frühmittelalterliche Studien* 5 (1971): 176–92.

[15] See Werner Henzen, *Schriftsprache und Mundarten*, 2nd ed. (Bern: Francke, 1954), esp. 44–51; Brigitta Schreyer-Mühlpfordt, "Sprachliche Einigungstendenzen im deutschen Schrifttum des Frühmittelalters," *Wissen-schaftliche Annalen* 5 (1956): 295–304, and Kurt Wagner, "Hochsprache und Mundart in althochdeutscher Zeit," *Der Deutschunterricht* 8/ii (1956): 14–23.

[16] The major collections of Old High German literature are those by Karl Müllenhoff and Wilhelm Scherer, *Deutsche Poesie und Prosa aus dem VIII–XII Jahrhundert* (Berlin: Weidmann, 3rd ed. by Elias v. Steinmeyer, 1892, repr. 1964, abbreviated here as MSD); Elias v. Steinmeyer, *Die kleineren althochdeutschen Sprachdenkmäler* [1916] (Berlin and Zurich: Weidmann, repr. as 2nd ed. 1963, abbreviated here as St.) and Wilhelm Braune, *Althochdeutsches Lesebuch* (Tübingen: Niemeyer, 16th ed. Ernst Ebbinghaus, 1979, 17th ed. 1994, abbreviated here as Braune). Citations from shorter texts are from Steinmeyer or Braune. For selections with translations in modern German, see Horst Dieter Schlosser, *Althochdeutsche Literatur* (Berlin: Schmidt, 1998 = Schlosser) and Karl A. Wipf, *Althochdeutsche poetische Texte* (Stuttgart: Reclam, 1992 = Wipf). The glosses, the *Heliand,* Otfrid and the Tatian-translation, for example, are in separate editions, and are noted in subsequent chapters when cited. For Old Low German apart from the *Heliand,* see Moritz Heyne, *Kleinere altniederdeutsche Denkmäler* (Paderborn: Schöningh, 2nd ed. 1877, repr. Amsterdam: Rodopi, 1970). For material at the end of the period, two major collections are those by Friedrich Wilhelm, *Denkmäler deutscher Prosa des 11. und 12. Jahrhunderts* (Munich: Hueber, 1916, repr. 1960, abbreviated here as Wilhelm) and Friedrich Maurer, *Die religiösen Dichtungen des 11. und 12. Jahrhunderts* (Tübingen: Niemeyer, 1964–70). For a (now somewhat outdated) bibliography, see J. Sidney Groseclose and Brian Murdoch, *Die althochdeutschen poetischen Denkmäler* (Stuttgart: Metzler, 1976).

[17] For considerations of the problem of what constitutes literature in the period, see Heinz Rupp, *Forschung zur althochdeutschen Literatur 1945–1962* (Stuttgart: Metzler, 1965); Horst Dieter Schlosser, *Die literarischen Anfänge der deutschen Sprache* (Berlin: Schmidt, 1977); Werner Schröder, *Grenzen und Möglichkeiten einer althochdeutschen Literaturgeschichte* (Leipzig: Sächsische Akademie, 1959 = Berichte 105/ii); Werner Betz, "Das gegenwärtige Bild des Althochdeutschen," *Der Deutschunterricht* 5/vi (1953), 94–108; Rudolf Schützeichel, "Grenzen des Althoch-

deutschen," *PBB/T* 95 (1973 = Sonderheft/ *Festschrift fur Ingeborg Schröbler*), 23–38. For general surveys see Cyril Edwards, "German Vernacular Literature: a Survey," in *Carolingian Culture: Emulation and Innovation,* ed. Rosamond McKitterick (Cambridge: CUP, 1993), 141–70, as well as my chapter: "The Carolingian Period and the Early Middle Ages," in *Cambridge History of German Literature,* ed. Helen Watanabe-O'Kelly (Cambridge: CUP 1997), 1–39. See also my introductory chapter on Old High and Low German in the first volume of the present history of German literature. Of the various book-length studies of Old High German, the most useful of the earlier compilations remains Gustav Ehrismann, *Geschichte der deutschen Literatur bis zum Ausgang des Mittelalters I: Die althochdeutsche Literatur* (Munich: Beck, 1932, repr. as 2nd ed. 1954), and the best recent volumes are those by Karl Bertau, *Deutsche Literatur im europäischen Mittelalter* (Munich: Beck, 1972f.) and the first two volumes of the *Geschichte der deutschen Literatur von den Anfängen bis zum Beginn der Neuzeit,* ed. Joachim Heinzle: I/i: Wolfgang Haubrichs, *Die Anfänge* (Frankfurt am Main: Athenäum, 1988) and I/ii: Gisela Vollmann-Profe, *Von den Anfängen bis zum hohen Mittelalter* (Frankfurt am Main: Athenäum, 1986); Dieter Kartschoke, *Geschichte der deutschen Literatur im frühen Mittelalter* [1990] (Munich: DTV, 3rd ed. 2000). In English see J. Knight Bostock, *A Handbook on Old High German Literature,* 2nd ed. K. C. King and D. R. McLintock (Oxford: Clarendon, 1976); my *Old High German Literature* (Boston: Twayne, 1983); D. H. Green, *Medieval Listening and Reading* (Cambridge: CUP, 1994), 20–54. See now *Theodisca: Beiträge zur althochdeutschen und altniederdeutschen Sprache und Literatur,* ed. Wolfgang Haubrichs et al. (Berlin and New York: de Gruyter, 2000); *A Companion to Middle High German Literature to the 14th Century,* ed. Francis C. Gentry (Leiden: Brill, 2002), esp. 53–116. Finally, Cyril Edwards, *The Beginnings of German Literature: Comparative and Interdisciplinary Approaches to Old High German* (Rochester, NY: Camden House, 2002) raises some interesting general points about some of the smaller fragments of Old High German.

[18] The reconstructed Old High German poem is MSD VIII (*Spielmannsreim*); on the discovery of the Old Saxon poem, see A. N. Doane, *The Saxon Genesis* (Madison, WI: U Wisconsin P, 1991).

[19] See Edwards, *Beginnings,* 142–65 for an illustration of the manuscript in the Austrian National Library and a detailed discussion of the work and its discoverer. Edwards focuses very clearly on the problems of the manuscript survival of Old High German, as well as providing useful illustrations.

[20] Rolf Bergmann, "Zu der althochdeutschen Inschrift aus Köln," *Rheinische Vierteljahresblätter* 30 (1965): 66–69. The inscription, a picture of which illustrates a sixteenth-century map, was carved on a stone that was probably over a library door.

[21] Cambridge students of German have long enjoyed a handsomely bound volume called *The Beauties of Otfrid* in the Beit Library, a book containing a short introduction, followed by a large number of blank pages and claiming the last line to be the most beautiful. And of course, if Otfrid's work were entirely lacking in merit, the joke would not be funny. See Leonard Forster and Henry Button, "The Story of *The Beauties of Otfrid*," in *Feste Freundschrift: Essays and Short Pieces in Honour of Peter Johnson,* ed. Hugh Ridley and Karin McPherson (Dublin: University College, 1997), 27–31.

[22] Ingeborg Schröbler, "Fulda und die althochdeutsche Literatur," *Literaturwissenschaftliches Jahrbuch der Görres-Gesellschaft* 1 (1960): 1–26; on Hraban, Raymund Kottje and Harald Zimmermann, *Hrabanus Maurus: Lehrer, Abt und Bischof* (Wiesbaden: Steiner, 1982).

[23] Important discussions include Georg Baesecke, *Der deutsche Abrogans und die Herkunft des deutschen Schrifttums* (Halle: Niemeyer, 1930) and his "Die karlische Renaissance und das deutsche Schrifttum," *Deutsche Vierteljahresschrift* 23 (1949): 143–216; Heinz Rupp, "Über das Verhältnis von deutscher und lateinischer Literatur im 9–12. Jahrhundert," *Germanisch-Romanische Monatsschrift* 39 (1958): 9–34; Stefan Sonderegger, "Frühe Erscheinungsformen dichterischer Sprache im Althochdeutschen," in *Festschrift Max Wehrli*, ed. S. Sonderegger et al. (Zurich and Freiburg i. Br.: Atlantis, 1969), 53–81; Joerg O. Fichte, "Der Einfluß der Kirche auf die Mittelalterliche Literaturästhetik," *Studia Neophilologica* 48 (1976): 3–20; Hartmut Günther, "Probleme beim Verschriften der Muttersprache. Otfrid von Weißenburg und die *lingua theotisca*," *Zeitschrift für Literaturwissenschaft und Linguistik* 59 (1985): 36–54. General surveys include Donald A. Bullough, *Carolingian Renewal: Sources and Heritage* (Manchester: Manchester UP, 1991), and the standard works by Ernst Robert Curtius, *Europäische Literatur und lateinisches Mittelalter* (Bern: Francke, 1948, 11th. ed., Tübingen and Basle, 1993); translated by Willard R. Trask as *European Literature and the Latin Middle Ages* (London: RKP, 1953), and those by R. R. Bolgar, *The Classical Heritage and its Beneficiaries* (Cambridge: CUP, 1963) and *Classical Influences on European Culture AD 500–1500* (Cambridge: CUP, 1971).

[24] See on the latter part of the period Friedrich Maurer, "Salische Geistlichendichtung," *Der Deutschunterricht* 5/ii (1953): 5–10, and the two important books by Heinz Rupp, *Deutsche religiöse Dichtungen des 11. und 12. Jahrhunderts,* 2nd ed. (Bern and Munich: Francke, 1971) and Gerhard Meissburger, *Grundlagen zum Verständnis der deutschen Mönchsdichtung im 11. und 12. Jahrhundert* (Munich: Fink, 1970). There are useful essays on this period in *Deutsche Literatur und Sprache von 1050–1200: Festschrift für Ursula Hennig,* ed. Annegret Fiebig and Hans-Jochen Schiewer (Akademie Verlag, Berlin, 1995). Bibliographies by C. Soetman, *Deutsche geistliche Dichtung des 11. und 12. Jahrhunderts,* 2nd ed. (Stuttgart: Metzler, 1971) and by Francis C. Gentry, *Bibliographie zur frühmittelhochdeutschen geistlichen Dichtung* (Berlin: Schmidt, 1992). On the producers of literature in the period (monks, secular clergy, canons) see Ralph Andratschek-Holzer, "Überlegungen zu einer Neucharakterisierung der 'frühmittelhochdeutschen' Literatur," *ABäG* 33 (1991): 81–88. The intimate connection with the Cluny reforms sometimes shown in earlier secondary studies is no longer accepted.

The abbey church at Corvey in Westphalia, the oldest Benedictine abbey in Northern Germany (founded in 822); the western aspect (late tenth-early eleventh century, with some later additions).

Into German: The Language of the Earliest German Literature

Jonathan West

THE ORIGINS OF GERMAN LITERATURE lie in the oral tradition of the pre-literary period but the origins of German *literacy* are to be found in the Latin literary culture of the post-Roman world.[1] Indeed, a division between primarily oral German and primarily written Latin, and essentially regional German contrasting with supra-regional Latin, is a defining feature of German literary and linguistic history from the beginnings of writing in German in the middle of the eighth century to the dawn of the early modern period in the middle of the fourteenth. Yet another three hundred years would elapse before German finally supplanted Latin as the dominant written language in Germany in the 1680s.[2]

At the beginning of the Old High German period (ca. 750–ca. 1050), the Latin context is so pervasive that no text can be fully understood, or even read aloud with any pretence to authenticity, without reference to it. Despite the fact that Old High German and Latin are both Indo-European languages with a large body of cognate vocabulary (for example family terms such as father, brother and mother — Old High German *fater, bruoder, muoter* are cognate with Latin *pater, frater, mater,* and so on.),[3] as well as some striking grammatical parallels,[4] Old High German and Latin developed very different phonological systems, so that, although the Latin alphabet was used to write Old High German, some ingenuity is required on the part of modern scholars to reconstruct how the language might have been pronounced. Moreover, Latin and Old High German were also developing syntactically in different directions, so that word-for-word translation was impossible, and the native vocabulary of Old High German, essentially that of a rural, tribal people, was inadequate to express the new concepts that a Christian education demanded. The great achievement of the monks of what Rudolf Keller calls "The Carolingian Beginning"[5] is that they tackled this linguistic disjuncture, albeit primarily in the cause of Latin literacy, and therefore began, as a by-product of their educational activity and despite the regional and often idiosyncratic nature of their writing systems, the emancipation of German from its subordinated position as the hand-maiden of Latin.

As far as the vowel system was concerned, Old High German still maintained a distinction between long and short vowels, not only in stressed syllables, such as we find in modern German *Bienen* "bees" as against *binnen* "inside," but also in unstressed syllables, at least in the early part of the Old High German period. Thus the nominative singular of *geba* "a gift" and the nominative plural *gebâ* "gifts" are distinguished by the length of the final vowel only. By contrast, Latin had certainly lost distinctions of vowel quantity by the time of the Latinization of Gaul.[6] In addition, a new series of vowels had developed through the phenomenon of umlaut during the late Germanic period, so that the Old High German vowel system had, in addition to short *i, u, o* and *a*, three distinct short *e*-vowels and two distinct long *e*-vowels, as well as four front rounded vowels and ten diphthongs. This meant that the inventory of vowels in Old High German ran to some twenty-seven items, compared with five in late Latin, so that the distinctions of Old High German could not properly be expressed with the Latin vowel symbols. This was naturally of little consequence to German scribes, as they knew how their own language was pronounced. But to characterize Old High German writing systems as inadequate on this basis, as some scholars have done, is to fall into the trap of looking at the evidence from a modern perspective. What is certainly true is that we can only deduce how the language might have sounded from the evidence of the writing, and our knowledge of the history of both Latin and German. A tendency among modern scholars is therefore to regard with suspicion attempts to equate Old High German letters with the sounds of Classical Latin, and to assume that German scribes wrote Old High German as they wrote Latin, even though the Latin they spoke might have undergone the same sound changes as Old High German. Such an idea should not seem strange in an Anglo-Saxon context where Latin words were and are regularly pronounced as if they were English: thus *regina* in the English legal formula *regina versus* . . . (The Queen against . . .) is pronounced with a soft, rather than a hard *g*, and a diphthong (/ai/) rather than a short *i*; the first vowel is also different. This position also explains the use of *c* to indicate the two quite separate sounds [ts] and [k].[7]

One striking feature of Old High German is the absence of any indication of umlaut except with short *e* (to indicate the umlaut form of the presumed Germanic short *a* and using the same symbol as for the short *e* deriving directly from Germanic, which the Latin vowel inventory provided anyway.) It is frequently forgotten that umlaut was not indicated regularly in any case in German orthography until the late sixteenth century,[8] as even a cursory examination of early Luther will testify. Even in Old High German *e* alternated with *a* as a spelling for the umlaut form[9] and this was for many years taken as evidence that umlaut was "in progress" during the Old High German period. However, scholars nowadays tend to see this as a purely orthographical phenomenon, visible in writing only, that is, since umlaut is a sound feature of all the North and West Germanic languages and must have been a feature already of late Germanic. There seems therefore little linguistic justification for the traditional distinction between what are referred to as primary and secondary umlaut. The sound change affected all the vowels in the same period and the spellings are explained by the fact that it took almost a thousand years for orthographical practices to become regularized. Similarly, there was no regular indication of vowel length until the Early Modern period.[10] In particular, early Old High German texts such as the Benedictine Rule, the Isidore translation, and early St. Gallen documents mark long vowels by doubling the symbol (such as *daz loon,* "the reward"), but this practice is anything but consistent and may reflect a period of experimentation encouraged by the confused state of Merovingian Latin before the Carolingian reforms mark a return to a more regular Latin orthography.[11]

It is not surprising that the earliest attested writing in German — apart from the runic inscriptions of the sixth and seventh centuries, and those Latin law tracts of the sixth to eighth centuries that contain some early German legal vocabulary — had a didactic purpose. Acquiring reading and writing skills meant primarily learning Latin. This pedagogical aspect of medieval monastic life in what were mainly Benedictine foundations explains why over 1200 extant Latin manuscripts[12] from the eighth century on were provided with what are known as glosses, that is, German definitions in the form of single words or phrases to aid the inexperienced reader. Sometimes these early definitions or glosses are in a crude sort of code[13] (thus *anus* is glossed as *brslph,* using the next consonant instead of a vowel and meaning therefore *arsloh,* "asshole"[14]), as if the intention was to spare the reader's sensibilities. One should always bear in mind that their purpose[15] was always to elucidate Latin texts, giving translations, paraphrases, grammatical information, etymologies, cultural notes, and semantic and syntactic alternatives.[16]

As glossed texts were used in teaching, the extent of this activity gives some idea of the richness and rigor of monastic education at the time. Nor was it confined to German monasteries. The Venerable Bede (ca. 673–735), in his *De metrica ratione*[17] (On meter) cites examples from various Christian authors including Sedulius,[18] Juvencus,[19] Arator,[20] Prosper of Aquitaine,[21] Prudentius, and Paulinus of Nola.[22] Alcuin's[23] list in York Minster, relevant because it was Alcuin (ca. 735–804) who was called to spearhead Charlemagne's educational reforms, mentions not only these but also Venantius Fortunatus[24] and Alcimus.[25] Other texts on the curriculum included the so-called *Disticha Catonis* (Distichs of Cato, late third century) and Avian's *Fables* (toward the end of the fourth century). John Scot(t)us (ca. 810–877), Martin of Laon (mid-ninth century) and Dunchad of Reims (early ninth century) awakened an interest in Martianus Capella (early fifth century) through their commentaries and *Accessus ad auctores*[26] (introductions using a standard technique of logical investigation).[27] There are other indications of the extent of the curriculum as well. The *Libellus de studio poete, qui et scolasticus* (Introduction to poetry) by Walther of Speyer (963–1027),[28] for example, describes his progress from the age of seven at the cathedral school in his home city in 271 lines of verse. Two years of elementary education with psalmody and hymnody were followed by two sets of two years on grammar and literature, where the scholars read, although a modern classical scholar would find the following list partial at best: Virgil (70 B.C.–19 A.D.), Homer (the *Iliad* in the *Ilias latina* version),[29] Martianus Capella,[30] Horace (65 B.C.–A.D. 8), Ovid (43 B.C.–ca. A.D. 17),[31] Persius (34–62),[32] Juvenal (ca. 60–ca. 130), Boethius (ca. 480–ca. 524), Statius (ca. 45–ca. 95), Terence (ca. 190–159 B.C.),[33] and Lucan (39–65), followed by two years of dialectics and rhetoric. This seems to imply four years for the so-called *trivium*, the first stage of post-elementary education, which comprised grammar, dialectics and rhetoric; the second stage, or *quadrivium*, comprised music, arithmetic, geometry and astronomy.[34] John Edwin Sandys has noted a Latin mnemonic to summarize this educational program: *Gram[matica] loquitur; dia[lectica] vera docet; rhet[orica] verba colorat; Mus[ica] canit; ar[ithmetica] numerat; ge[ometria] ponderat; ast[ronomia] colit astra*[35] (Grammar speaks, dialectics teaches true things, rhetoric colors the words we speak; music sings, arithmetic counts, geometry measures, and astronomy studies the stars). This picture of the literary canon is confirmed by Hrabanus Maurus's *De institutione clericorum*[36] (On the education of clerics) and Notker Balbulus's *Notatio de viris illustribus* (On famous men).[37] In view of the tight focus on Latin, it is not surprising that few of these texts have come down to us in Old High German, but parts of them at least have reached us indirectly in the form of Old High German glosses.

As one might expect, biblical manuscripts[38] were the most frequently glossed texts, as the Bible formed the cornerstone, foundation, and superstructure of medieval education in the West.[39] The St. Paul Glosses[40] on a sixth or seventh century uncial manuscript of the Vulgate (Luke 1:64–2:51), so called because they are now housed in the library of the Benedictine monastery of St. Paul in Carinthia, constitute a good example of early glossing, and there is also an interlinear version of parts of John's Gospel (that is, with every individual word glossed),[41] as well as of Romans and Corinthians.[42] Biblical glosses are also to be found in the thesaurus-like work known as *Abrogans,* in its re-working, the *Samanunga,* and in the alphabetically organized glossaries from Reichenau (referred to as Rd, etc.), all of which will be discussed later. Compilations of canon law[43] and monastic rules[44] were also objects of avid study. We also find glosses on the works of the patristic writers, the major theologians such as Gregory the Great,[45] Ambrose, John Chrysostom, Augustine, Eucherius, Bede, Boniface, and especially Jerome.[46]

Latin codices of Germanic common law were, as has been noted, also the subject of glossarial activity.[47] Particularly well known are the so-called *Malberg Glosses,* German glosses on words in the laws of the Salian Franks. These words are preceded by the term *Malloberg* or an equivalent abbreviation, which has been taken to mean "council hill" and therefore "Germanic legal term."[48] Nor was the world of classical learning omitted from glossing activity: poets[49] in the curriculum such as Terence, Virgil,[50] Horace.[51] Ovid, Juvenal, Persius,[52] Statius, and Avian[53] were all glossed, as were historians such as Sallust (86–34 B.C.), Lucan,[54] and the early fifth-century Christian Paulus Orosius. This classical diet was supplemented by works of early Christian authors such as Avitus of Vienne; Prosper of Aquitaine; the fifth-century writer Sedulius, well-known in the Middle Ages, latterly for his hymns, one of which, *A solis ortus cardine* (From the beginning of the sunrise),[55] was included in Luther's *Gesangbuch* of 1524[56]; the poet Aurelius Prudentius Clemens (348–after 405), usually known simply as Prudentius,[57] whose works, after the Bible, are the most intensively glossed texts of the period;[58] Arator, a sixth-century poet[59] whose 2326 hexameters retelling the Acts of the Apostles and the martyrdom of St. Paul and St. Peter was greatly valued;[60] the *Evangeliorum libri quattuor,* a much-read Gospel poem by (Gaius Vettius Aquilinus) Juvencus[61]; and Boethius's *Consolation of Philosophy.*[62] Of greatest interest, perhaps, was the foundation text used throughout the whole Middle Ages, the encyclopedic *Etymologiae* (also known as *Origines*) of Isidore, Archbishop of Seville in the early seventh century.[63] Early medieval authors such as Aldhelm of Malmesbury (ca. 639–709)[64] and

Walahfrid Strabo (809–ca. 849)[65] also received attention. Sometimes, as the Old High German translation of a tract by Isidore shows, the study of these texts gave rise to sophisticated translations proper. However, it cannot be stressed too much that the intention was probably never to produce material in German, but simply to provide a German bridge to the Latin original. This raises the important question of whether the Old High German words in such glosses are genuine or merely learned calques, interpretative translations of the elements of words. In fact, Werner Betz[66] has shown that the scribes used four different approaches in descending order of relative frequency: semantic loan or loan meaning (*Lehnbedeutung*, such as *bijiht*, glossing *confessio*, the modern word *Beichte* "confession"), where an existing word was employed with a new meaning derived from the Latin; loan translation (*Lehnübersetzung*, such as *lustidôn*, glossing *delectare*), where the Latin word was translated element by element; loan rendition (*Lehnübertragung*, such as *hôrsam*, glossing *obediens*), where an approximate translation of the Latin original was made; and loan creation (*Lehnschöpfung*, such as *findunga*, glossing *experimentum*), where the foreign word is rendered relatively independently of the original.[67]

It should also be pointed out that glossing was not unique to German, and that the practice went back to classical times. Glosses in other Western European languages are, however, usually the product of the same era: the Old Irish glosses, for example, were produced mainly on the continent in manuscripts clustering around the ninth century.[68] In the Irish and Anglo-Saxon missions to the continent, culminating in what has been called the Carolingian revival,[69] dark-age Europe was re-civilized from its western fringes. A consistent migration of Irish monks to continental monasteries and European respect for their exegetical expertise ensured that they played an important role in the Carolingian educational reforms of the ninth century.[70] These Irish glosses, and their Old English and Old High German equivalents provide in Rosamond McKitterick's words "eloquent witness to the common culture created by Christianity in Western Europe."[71]

It is probably a mistake to see the Old High German *glossaries* — collected glosses, rather than those added into a given original text — simply as collections of textual glosses, since glossing was carried on throughout the period.[72] The relevant Old High German texts also derive in part from classical glossaries such as the *Hermeneumata* (school exercises), a third-century Greek-Latin glossary freely adapted in the Middle Ages.[73] The earliest substantial manuscript containing German, the *Abrogans*, for example, is a good illustration of the many manuscripts (or portions of them) that contain nothing *but* glosses — that is, glossaries, though we may think of modern concepts such as "dictionary" or "thesaurus" as well — in which Latin *lemmata* or headwords (in modern terms the "target language") usually precede their German (or German and Latin) *interpretamenta* or explanations. Indeed, there is probably no better illustration of the dependence of Old High German on the Latin original, as subsequent re-workings, translations, and apparently independent texts disguise their Latinate origins.

Like their counterparts in other western vernaculars, Old High German glosses were not only written in the margins of Latin manuscripts (marginal glosses), but above or below the glossed word (interlinear glosses), in the line of text immediately after the word they translate[74] (context glosses, usually as a result of an original manuscript with glosses having been copied and "edited") or simply impressed with a dry stylus on the vellum (scratch glosses).[75] From a literary or linguistic point of view, this topographical classification is probably of little significance. The glosses as a group, however, can be shown even in the early period to have aided more clearly literary productions — the writer of the *Heliand* may well have used a version of the *Hermeneumata*, for example.[76] For modern scholars, the 250,000 German word forms, representing over 25,000 lexical items, provide a repository of vocabulary often otherwise unattested in the language, some of them admittedly *hapax legomena,* unique occurrences. New glosses are being discovered all the time, especially scratch glosses, which often escape the notice of Latin scholars, and have resulted in a spate of new and revised editions over the last twenty years.[77]

The designations for the so-called *Reichenau Glosses,* Ra, Rb, etc., were devised by E. G. Graff, the author of the first comprehensive dictionary of Old High German.[78] The first letter stands for Reichenau and the second for the order in which he edited the Reichenau manuscripts. Rb, for example, is a Latin-German dictionary of the Old Testament, arranged in text order, but may be derived from another text glossary.[79] However, the *Glossae Salomonis* (attributed to Salomo III, Bishop of Constance [890–922] and a nephew of the Salomo I, to whom Otfrid dedicated his *Evangelienbuch*) are largely derived from the works of the patristic writers.[80] Old High German glossaries are organized in two ways, alphabetically and thematically, two traditions that survive almost unchanged up to the eighteenth century in German lexicographical tradition.[81] The best-known thematic glossary is the *Vocabularius Sancti Galli,* but the *Kassel Glosses,* glosses on parts of the body attributed to Walahfrid Strabo, the Viennese Codex ÖNB 1761[82] all belong to this genre. By and large, it could be said that alphabetical glossaries which contain words originally requiring commentary consist of "hard words," that is, essentially peripheral or learned vocabulary, whereas those organized according to subject matter contain core concepts. The prime example of alphabetical organization is the *Abrogans,* but other texts include the Reichenau glossary Rd.

In the alphabetical category, the *Abrogans*[83] (so-called because of the practice of designating medieval and early modern works by the first word, which in this case happens to be Latin *abrogans,* "humility") is attested in three manuscripts, usually designated a, b, c after their editor Georg Baesecke.[84] There is also a re-working of the *Abrogans,* the so-called *Samanunga uuorto* (Collection of words, designated R), which contains biblical glosses.[85] In this family, the Latin headword for "humble" *Abrogans, humiles/humilis* is glossed in a as *aotmuot,* in b as *Dheo-modi* and *samftmoati,* in c as *Theomoti* and *samftmoti,* and in R as *sanftmoti,* the single example giving an illustration of the type of vocabulary involved, the glossing technique and the way Latin orthography was adapted for German words.

The *Vocabularius Sancti Galli*[86] is found in one manuscript (Cod. Sti Galli 913, an eighth-century manuscript from St. Gallen).[87] The glosses are arranged thematically, and selections deal with words for household articles, geographical and natural features and human attributes, useful typical examples of which are *domus* glossing *huus* "house" (*Haus*), *parietas* glossing *uuanti* "walls" (*Wände*), *tegitur* glossing *dachit* "is roofed / roofs" (*dacht*), *cellarius* glossing *puur* "steward" (*Bauer*), *lectus* glossing *petti* "bed" (*Bett*), *ostium* glossing *turi* "door" (*Tür*), *poste* glossing *turisuli* "doorpost" (an equivalent would be "*Türsäule*"). These examples are once again given first to show the general nature of the vocabulary involved and secondly to provide data to show once more the way in which Old High German scribes adapted Latin orthography for their needs.

The *Kasseler Glossen* (Kassel glosses) are another Latin-German glossary arranged according to subject area and probably derived from the same source as the *Vocabularius Sancti Galli,* since their choice of Latin lemmata, headwords, and German translations (in Bavarian dialect) is strikingly similar, especially in those sections which list parts of the body and animals. The Kassel glosses follow a literal translation into Old High German of what looks like a brief sermon on the duties of godparents, the *Exhortatio ad plebem Christianam* (Exhortation to the Christian people) on two leaves of the Kassel manuscript. Apart from the words grouped according to subject, there are sentences the systematicity of which clearly indicates their didactic purpose, for example, *skir min fahs, skir minan hals, skir minan part* (Cut my hair, shave my neck, shave my beard), and a passage which betrays the origin of the scribe and his anti-Italian prejudice, not unknown in medieval German:[88] *sapiens homo spa-her man / stultus to ler / stulti sunt tolesint / Romani uualha / sapienti sunt spahesint / Paioari peigira / modica est luzic ist / sapienti[a] spahe / in romana inuualhum / plus habent merahapent / stultitia tolaheiti / quam spaientia dennespahi* (Wise man, stupid [man]; the Romans are stupid, the Bavarians are wise; there is little wisdom in Italy, they have more stupidity than wisdom).

Eckhard Meinecke and Judith Schwerdt,[89] in a discussion of part of a further thematic glossary from the Augustinian foundation of St. Florian, have shown how a glossary develops from continuous text. They were able to reconstruct the process because the names for herbs in the part under discussion are taken from Book IV of the *Summarium Heinrici* (see below), retaining their original ordering, but with mistakes (for example *sicwurz* for *figwurz*, the translation of Latin *tormentilla* "the plant cinquefoil"), showing that relatively mechanical copying had taken place by a scribe without the required level of knowledge or access to the original manuscript. This is also suggested by the alternative translations given in that text (their example is *huntswurz* against *hundiszunga,* which glosses *cinoglossa* "the plant pyramidal orchis").

A final thematic glossary, the so-called *Pariser Gespräche* (Paris conversation book)[90] is found in a Vatican manuscript and also in a manuscript in the National Library in Paris, from which comes the modern designation.[91] These "conversations" appear to be the Carolingian equivalent of a language school phrasebook for francophone speakers and, with their sprinkling of earthy phrases, they have become a firm favorite with beginners in Old High German. They contain a list of parts of the body — for example, *obethe* "caput" (i.e., *Haupt,* showing the Romance speaker's inability to pronounce initial /h-/ or the consonant cluster /pt/), *bart* "barba" (i.e., *Bart*), *an* "manus" (*Hand,* again dropping the initial /h/), *guanbe* "venter" (*Wampe*) — and useful phrases.[92] The phrases are such as would be used on fleeting acquaintance and can be surprising and just occasionally alarming: *Gueliche lande cumen ger?* glossing *de qua patria?* (From which country do you come?), *Quesasti min erre ze metina?* glossing *uidisti seniorem meum ad matutinas?* (Did you see my lord at breakfast?), *Guanna sarden ger? quot vices fotisti?* (How many times did you fuck?). There is even the odd curse, *Vndes ars in tine naso* glossing *canis culum in tuo naso* (A dog's asshole in your nose!), the last to be used, perhaps, when an invitation such as *Erro, guillis trenchen guali got guin?* glossing *si uis bibere bonum uinum?* (Lord, do you want to drink some good wine?) does not meet with the expected response.

The glossaries could be termed quasi-dictionaries and form one of the bases of the dictionaries, glossaries and encyclopedic works of the later Middle Ages.[93] The *Summarium Heinrici*[94] is a schoolbook which translates the *Etymologiae* of Isidore of Seville, a work intended to encapsulate the sum of human knowledge at the beginning of the Middle Ages in the same way as works like the great grammar and dictionary of 1286, the *Catholicon* of Johannes Balbi of Genoa[95] aimed to do at the end of the medieval period, and it also uses other sources, mainly Priscian (died ca. 530). It was copied frequently and was found in most monastic libraries from Carolingian times on.[96] The first version of the *Summarium Heinrici* has ten books dealing with the following: 1. grammar, 2. rhetoric, 3. animate beings, 4. flora, 5. things which move but are not alive, 6. things which are found under or on the ground, 7. settlements, 8. human offices, 9. clothes, food and drink, 10. war and tools. The second version has six books; the eleventh is an alphabetical glossary with a long and a short version, mostly in Latin but with occasional German glosses. The *Summarium Heinrici* therefore combines the features of thematic and alphabetical glossary in one book, beginning a tradition that lived on at least until the sixteenth century in Renaissance dictionaries.[97] Walahfrid Strabo,[98] who became abbot of Reichenau in 842, is credited not only with the glosses which list parts of the body, but also with those to the Old Testament books from Genesis to the Second Book of Kings. Indeed, it has been suggested that Walahfrid might have been the author of one of the sections of the *Tatian* manuscript, on the basis of the similarities between the language of this second group and that section of the manuscript.[99] The Latin hymnody of the period[100] was also a source for later vernacular hymns. Certainly it produced within German-speaking territories some lasting Latin contributions by the great figures of the era such as Hrabanus Maurus,[101] Walahfrid Strabo,[102] and Gottschalk the Saxon (ca. 803–869).[103] But there are also contemporary German translations, probably also intended for instruction. For example, the *Murbach Hymns*[104] are interlinear (literal word-for-word) versions of twenty-six Latin hymns attributed to Ambrose (few, however, with any degree of certainty). One example is no. 25: *Aeterne rerum conditor / noctem diemque qui regis / et temporum dans tempora, ut adleves fastidium,* which is translated *euuigo rachono felahanto / nacht tac ioh ther rihis / inti ziteo kepanti ziti / thaz erpurres urgauuida* (Eternal creator of [all] things, who rulest night and day, giving time of very time, to take away our pride). That the intention of these versions was to provide a bridge to the Latin text is shown by the imperfect scansion of the German, which simply provides word-for-word glosses of the original. This is particularly noticeable in the passage just cited in the case of *ioh* (and), when we look at its Latin equivalent, which here is the enclitic -*que* attached to the word *diem*. The Latin might be rendered literally in modern English as "night day-and," and the position of the German words are made to do the same thing. Sometimes, too, more than one German word is provided.

Wilhelm Scherer took the designation *Carmen ad Deum* for another similar text from a Cambridge manuscript, one of six extant copies of a Latin prayer, although the German version is only found in the Munich manuscript Cod. Lat. Monac. 19410, brought there from the monastery at Tegernsee, not far from Munich, but probably originally from the monastery at Reichenau. Once again, the German makes little sense without the Latin text, which the glossator appears to have misunderstood in places, but he does add German articles, pronouns, and the occasional understood verb in an attempt to make the German text read more naturally. Interestingly, there is a gloss on the *German* word *porge* (*frido vel spare*) which itself translates Latin *parce* "preserve [us]."

Moving (gradually) to translations in the sense that we might recognize them, the Gospel harmony known in Old High German studies simply as *Tatian,*[105] and which along with the works of Notker and Otfrid's *Evangelienbuch* the largest source text in Old High German, is, like the *Murbach Hymns,* closely dependent on a Latin original.[106] The *Tatian* manuscript has been in St. Gallen since the thirteenth century and contains a Latin version of the Gospel harmony, often known as the *Diatesseron* ("from [the] four [Gospels]") and a German translation in parallel columns made by six separate scribes, of which the last probably corrected the whole manuscript (both the Latin and German were written in Fulda with reference to the *Codex Fuldensis*). The Old Saxon *Heliand* is another example of a Gospel harmony, this time in verse. We know that Tatian, the author from whom the name comes, was a late second-century Syrian, or perhaps an Assyrian, as he described himself, who was converted to Christianity by Justin in Rome,[107] and he compiled his Gospel harmony around A.D.170.[108] He is likely to have written his (now lost) original text in Syriac, the most important dialect of East Aramaic. Later, however, Arabic and, most important for the Old High German text, Latin translations of his work were made early, probably predating the Vulgate, the standard Bible text used since the seventh century in the Western Church, and ascribed to St. Jerome (ca. 432–420).[109] The Old High German text is noteworthy in several respects.

First, apart from being one of the largest sources we have, its dialectal form is often reckoned to precede modern German most directly, and it is therefore often used as the basis for general glossaries and dictionaries.[110] Second, if we reckon Old High German vocabulary to number around 10,000 items, then the roughly 508 items which occur in *Tatian* and nowhere else (apart from the glosses) represent five per cent. These early examples include *balg* "skin, bag" (*Balg*), *balco* "beam" (*Balken*), *thistil* "thistle" (*Distel*), *gasthûs* "inn" (*Gasthaus*), *hantslag* "box on the ears" (clearly not the antecedent of modern German *Handschlag* "handshake"), *quirnstein* "quernstone," *wînreba* "vine" (*Weinrebe*), and many others including a large number of compounds. Old High German is not well enough documented to enable us to ascertain whether the *Tatian* scribe(s) coined some of these items, but idiosyncratic vocabulary is particularly noteworthy when the *Tatian* text stands alone against other sources of the same period, such as Notker or Otfrid, or where a family of related words occurs. A formal relationship exists, for example, between *berahtnessi* (neuter noun), *berahtnessî* (feminine noun), both meaning "glory, honor," as well as *berahto* (adverb) "gloriously," and *giberehtôn* "to glorify," representing an old etymon (there is a Gothic word *bairhts,* meaning "glorious") which does not occur frequently elsewhere, although it survives in Middle High German *bërhttag* "Epiphany," etc.[111] The nouns *asner* or *asneri* "servant" (cf. Gothic *asneis*), and *bruogo* "terror" also reflect an older stratum of vocabulary.[112]

One early German translation that stands apart from all others is the anonymous Old High German version of Isidore of Seville's[113] *De fide catholica ex veteri et novo testamento contra Iudaeos* (Concerning the Catholic faith from the Old and New Testaments against the Jews), normally just known by the German version of the name *Isidor.*[114] The manuscript usually termed P is now in Paris (Bibliothèque Nationale 2326) and is dated shortly after 800.[115] Parts of the translation also occur in a manuscript originally from the monastery of Mondsee near Salzburg (Hanover, Niedersächsische Landesbibliothek, Ms. I. 20) dated around 810 and also in Codex 3093* of the Austrian National Library in Vienna, hence the term Monsee-Vienna Fragments (*Monsee-Wiener Fragmente*), using the old spelling of Mondsee. Apart from the beginning of the *Isidor,* these fragments also contain part of a translation of Matthew's gospel, a treatise entitled *De vocatione gentium* (The calling of the people) by the first editors,[116] and the end of a homiletic text, Augustine's sermon no. 76. Words and sentences from the Monsee Fragments are also preserved in the Junius 25 manuscript in the Bodleian Library, Oxford, which was compiled in the monastery of Murbach around 820 using material from Reichenau.[117] Neither manuscript P nor the Monsee Fragments are original, but are copied from a lost original. P retains the original dialect and the ingenious and surprisingly regular spelling system of the exemplar, whereas the fragments preserve its wording, thus making this group the earliest witnesses to theological literature in Old High German. A possible connection to the court of Charlemagne is indicated also by a book catalog that contains a probable reference to the translation of Matthew in the Monsee Fragments in the Northern French monastery of St. Riquier, founded by Angilbert, who was its abbot from 789 to 814.[118] The language of the original was probably Rhenish Franconian, and appears on the basis of linguistic evidence to be an early work. The Paris manuscript also has a clearly worked out orthographic system.[119] The text is most notable, however, because of the way the translator conveys the sense of the Latin using German word order rather than merely providing word-for-word glosses. For example, the translator may interposes an adjective between the determiner and the noun: *exemplis sanctarum scriptarum adhibitis*[120] becomes *mit gareuuem bilidum dhes heiligin chiscribes* (with ready examples of holy writ), or may go against the word-order of the Latin, so that *portas aereas et vectes ferreos* (III, 2) becomes *erino portun* [. . .] *iisine grindila* (brass gates . . . iron bars). Perhaps the strategy is not always successful. For *Quis est igitur iste deus unctus a deo* (Who is then this god anointed by god? III, 2), we are offered *Huuer ist dhanne dhese chisalbodo got fona gote,* where the phrase *fona gote* (by god) is dependent on *chisalbodo* (anointed), but has in this case become separated from it. There are no examples of extended attributes before the Early Modern period,[121] and the Old High German is difficult to understand. However, the translator shows some skill in using Old High German word formation to overcome the limitations of vernacular vocabulary, so that *Faciamus hominem ad imaginem et similitudinem nostram* (III, 4) becomes *duomes mannan uns anachiliihhan endi in unseru chiliihnissu* (Let us make man like us and in our likeness), avoiding the need for two different roots. Articles, particles, and explanatory phrases are added, omitted or moved where appropriate. For example, *In persona enim Cyri Christus est prophetatus* (III, 3) is translated as *In dhemu nemin Cyres ist Christ chiuuisso chiforabodot* (In the person of Cyrus, Christ is certainly prophesied), which inserts an article and renders *enim,* "for" with the intensifying "certainly" in a different position. Similarly, participial constructions in Latin are often replaced with subordinate clauses, so that the opening sentence of chapter III, *Post declaratum Christi divinae nativitatis mysterium* (III, 1) is rendered *Aefter dhiu dhazs almahtiga gotes chiruni dhera gotliihhun Christes chiburdi ward* (After almighty God's mystery of the birth of the divine Christ was revealed). The resultant text is one of the few in Old High German that can stand on its own, but this should not trick us into imagining that it was actually *intended* to do so, for the translation was once again more likely used as a bridge to a difficult Latin text.[122] After all, if, as many suppose, the text was written by someone at Charlemagne's court, then that writer, too, would have been involved in the educational program.

What is undeniable is that without the foundations laid by glossing, the *Isidor* translation would have been impossible. Literary historians are often tempted to neglect apparently non-literary material like the glosses, but the object of this chapter has been to show that they provide the building blocks and the machinery for the literary constructions of future centuries, certainly as far as the end of the Old High German period, and probably long after that.[123]

Notes

[1] Rosamond McKitterick, *The Carolingians and the Written Word* (Cambridge: CUP, 1989).

[2] Peter von Polenz, *Deutsche Sprachgeschichte vom Spätmittelalter bis zur Gegenwart.* II. *17. und 18. Jahrhundert* (Berlin: de Gruyter, 1994), 57.

[3] See R. E. Keller, *The German Language* (London: Faber, 1978); Carl Darling Buck, *A Dictionary of Selected Synonyms in the Principal Indo-European Languages* (Chicago and London: U of Chicago P, 1949), 79–134.

[4] Hans Krahe and Wolfgang Meid, *Germanische Sprachwissenschaft I: Einleitung und Lautlehre,* 7th ed. (Berlin: de Gruyter, 1969), 16–17.

[5] Keller, *German Language,* 134–235.

[6] Mildred K. Pope, *From Latin to Modern French* (Manchester: Manchester UP, rev. ed. 1952), 9–16; R. A. Lodge, *French: from Dialect to Standard* (London: Routledge, 1993), 37.

[7] See on the vowels Keller, *German Language,* 164.

[8] Peter von Polenz, *Deutsche Sprachgeschichte vom Spätmittelalter bis zur Gegenwart.* I. *14. bis 16. Jahrhundert,* 2nd ed. (Berlin: de Gruyter, 2000), 151. Karl Lachmann's nineteenth-century normalized spelling system for Middle High German masked the linguistic reality.

[9] Wilhelm Braune, *Althochdeutsche Grammatik,* 13th ed. by Hans Eggers (Tübingen: Niemeyer, 1975), section 26–27.

[10] von Polenz, *Deutsche Sprachgeschichte* I, 149–50.

[11] Keller, *German Language,* 152. The consonant system was based on an old contrast of simple versus geminate (i.e., short/ long, single/double) consonants, and an emerging contrast between strong and weak articulation (technically *fortis* and *lenis*).

The Old High German geminates had arisen most especially from the West Germanic consonant gemination, and the Second or High German sound shift, which produced geminate fricatives after vowels (as in verbs like *offan* "open," *mahhôn* "to make"). See on this Keller, *German Language*, 164.

[12] Rolf Bergmann, *Verzeichnis der althochdeutschen und altsächsischen Glossenhandschriften: Mit Bibliographie der Glosseneditionen, der Handschriftenbeschreibungen und der Dialektbestimmungen* (Berlin: de Gruyter, 1973). Note also the ongoing Deutsche Forschungsgemeinschaft project in Bamberg (http://www.uni-bamberg.de/~ba4g11/forschung/forschungsproj.html#Glosse). There is, of course, a considerably greater number of manuscripts in which the language of the glosses is purely Latin, that is, an explanatory *Latin* word is put in to clarify a more difficult Latin word in the text.

[13] Bernhard Bischoff, "Übersicht über die nichtdiplomatischen Geheimschriften des Mittelalters," in *Mittelalterliche Studien: Ausgewählte Aufsätze zur Schriftkunde und zur Literaturgeschichte* (Stuttgart: Hiersemann, 1981), III, 120–48.

[14] Brian Murdoch, *Old High German Literature* (Boston: Twayne, 1983), 26.

[15] Jochen Splett, "Glossen und Glossare" in *Reallexikon der germanischen Altertumskunde*, 2nd ed. by H. Beck et al. (Berlin and New York: de Gruyter, 1973–), XII, 218–26; Nikolaus Henkel, "Glosse 1," in *Reallexikon der deutschen Literaturwissenschaft*, ed. Klaus Weimar (Berlin, New York: de Gruyter, 1997–2000), I, 727; this now replaces Herbert Thoma, "Glossen, ahd." in *Reallexikon der deutschen Literaturgeschichte*, ed. Werner Kohlschmidt and Wolfgang Mohr (Berlin: de Gruyter, 1958), I, 579–89.

[16] Eckhard Meineke and Judith Schwerdt, *Einführung in das Althochdeutsche* (Paderborn: Schöningh, 2001), 167.

[17] Bede's works are most conveniently accessible in the *Patrologia Latina* (*PL* 90–95).

[18] See *Lexikon des Mittelalters* (Zurich: Artemis, 1976–99), VII, 1666–67: an early fifth-century author of prose and verse versions of the Gospels, he was regarded from Carolingian times on as one of the foremost epic poets beside Arator and Prudentius and was widely read; apart from his *Opus paschale* ("On Easter," known in six manuscripts), there are more than 350 manuscripts of his work extant.

[19] Juvencus was the author in the fourth century of *Evangeliorum libri IV*, a Gospel harmony in 3211 hexameters: *Lexikon des Mittelalters* V, 832; *Reallexikon für Antike und Christentum*, ed. Ernst Dassmann (Stuttgart: Hiersemann, 1988–93), XIX, 881–906.

[20] Born in the 480s, Arator wrote *De actibus apostolorum* in two books of 1076 and 1250 hexameters, which were so celebrated that the work was read in public in the church of St. Peter ad Vincula in Rome (*Lexikon des Mittelalters*, I, 868).

[21] Prosper Tiro of Aquitaine (ca. 390–463) was a supporter of Augustine. His *Chronica* (written after 440) begins with Adam and ends with the death of Valentinian III in 455; he also wrote an *Expositio psalmorum* (on Psalms 110–50), a *Liber sententiarum* (which doubtless provided ready material for teaching), epigrams and poems. See *Lexikon des Mittelalters* VII, 266, and *Biographisch-bibliographisches Kirchenlexikon*, ed. Friedrich Wilhelm Bautz (Herzberg: Bautz, 1970–98), VII, 1002–4.

[22] Meropius Pontius Paulinus (ca. 355–431) was, with his Spanish wife Therasia, a driving force behind the new monastic movement. He wrote some fifty letters, corresponding with early Christian luminaries such as Jerome and Augustine, and around thirty poems: *Lexikon des Mittelalters* VI, 1816.

[23] *Biographisch-bibliographisches Kirchenlexikon* I, 118–19.

[24] Born around 540 in Treviso in Germanic Lombardy, and Bishop of Poitiers until his death ca. 600, he was a poet and biographer of numerous Frankish bishops, and especially Radegund, the widow of Chlothar III *Lexikon des Mittelalters* VIII, 1453–54.

[25] Alcimus Ecdicius Avitus (ca. 460–518) was Bishop of Vienne, the most important foothold of the Catholic Church in the Arian kingdom of the Burgundians. He tried in vain to persuade the Burgundian king Gundobad to acknowledge Arianism as a heresy, but succeeded with his son Sigismund, who became a Catholic. Avitus left over thirty homilies, of which three have survived in full, a poem on chastity and an important biblical epic *De spiritalis historiae gentis: Lexikon des Mittelalters* I, 1307, and *Biographisch-bibliographisches Kirchenlexikon* I, 311.

[26] *Lexikon des Mittelalters* I, 71.

[27] *Lexikon des Mittelalters* VII, 1589–91.

[28] *Biographisch-bibliographisches Kirchenlexikon* XIII, 236–39.

[29] See now George A. Kennedy, ed., *Publius Baebius Italicus, The Latin Iliad: Introduction, Text, Translation and Notes* (Fort Collins, CO: G. A. Kennedy, 1998).

[30] James Willis, ed., Martianus Capella: *De nuptiis Philologiae et Mercurii* (Leipzig: Teubner, 1983).

[31] http://www.fh-augsburg.de/~harsch/ovi_intr.html.

[32] http://www.fh-augsburg.de/~harsch/Chronologia/Lspost01/Persius/ per_f.html.

[33] http://www.fh-augsburg.de/~harsch/Chronologia/Lsante02/Terentius/ter_intr.html.

[34] *Lexikon des Mittelalters,* VIII, 2003.

[35] John Edwin Sandys, *History of Classical Scholarship* (New York and London: Hafner, 1967), 670.

[36] http://www.fh-augsburg.de/~harsch/hra_intr.html.

[37] *Biographisch-bibliographisches Kirchenlexikon* VI, 1032–35. The project "Codices Electronici Ecclesiae Coloniensis," which reproduces the catalogue of the library at Cologne Cathedral with excellent digital photographs of the manuscripts, also gives a good idea of what an ecclesiastical library would have been like: the manuscripts are mostly Latin and the few vernacular examples are late. See http://www.ceec.uni-koeln.de.

[38] Klaus Matzel, "Die Bibelglossen des Clm. 22201" (Diss. FU Berlin, 1956); Eckhard Meineke, *Saint-Mihiel Bibliothèque Municipale Ms. 25. Studien zu den althochdeutschen Glossen* (Göttingen: Vandenhoeck and Ruprecht, 1983).

[39] Bernhard Bischoff, "Wendepunkte in der Geschichte der lateinischen Exegese im Frühmittelalter," *Sacris Erudiri* 6 (1954): 189–279.

[40] J. Knight Bostock, *A Handbook on Old High German Literature*, 2nd. ed. by K. C. King and D. R. McLintock (Oxford: Clarendon, 1976), 99. See Lothar Voetz, *Die*

St. Pauler Lukasglossen: Untersuchungen: Edition: Faksimile: Studien zu den Anfängen althochdeutscher Textglossierung (Göttingen: Vandenhoeck and Ruprecht, 1985) and Braune IV.

[41] Lothar Voetz, "Die althochdeutschen 'Glossen' zu Joh. 19.38 (St. Gallen, Katonsbibliothek (Vadiana), Vadianische Sammlung, Ms 70a) — eine Interlinearversion," in *Grammatica ianua atrium: Festschrift für Rolf Bergmann zum 60. Geburtstag,* ed. Elvira Glaser and Michael Schläfer (Heidelberg: Winter, 1997), 195.

[42] Lothar Voetz, "Neuedition der althochdeutschen Glossen des Codex Sangallensis 70," in *Althochdeutsch,* ed. Rolf Bergmann, Heinrich Tiefenbach, and Lothar Voetz (Heidelberg: Winter, 1987), I, 467–99.

[43] Irmgard Frank, *Die althochdeutschen Glossen der Handschrift Leipzig Rep. II. 6* (Berlin and New York: de Gruyter, 1974); Sybille Blum, *Wortschatz und Übersetzungsleistung in den althochdeutschen Canonesglossen: Untersuchungen zur Hs. Frankfurt am Main Ms. Barth. 64* (Berlin: Akademie-Verlag, 1986).

[44] Klaus Siewert, "Althochdeutsche Glossen zur Regula canonicorum des Chrodegang von Metz," *Sprachwissenschaft* 18 (1993): 417–24.

[45] Wolfgang Schulte, *Die althochdeutsche Glossierung der Dialoge Gregors des Großen* (Göttingen: Vandenhoeck and Ruprecht., 1993).

[46] Maria Mitscherling, *Die althochdeutschen Hieronymusglossen* (Diss., Jena, [1975]).

[47] Rolf Bergmann, "Die althochdeutschen Glossen zur Lex Alamannorum im clm 4460," in *Sprache und Recht: Beiträge zur Kulturgeschichte des Mittelalters: Festschrift für Ruth Schmidt-Wiegand zum 60. Geburtstag,* ed. Karl Hauck et al. (Berlin, New York: de Gruyter, 1986), I, 56–66.

[48] The redoubtable Old High German scholar Georg Baesecke provided a survey of their vocabulary in "Die deutschen Worte der germanischen Gesetze," *PBB* 59 (1935), 1–101. There are also a number of translations of legal documents (Braune II) as well as the later *Strasbourg Oaths* (Braune XXI) where we have a formula expressing mutual non-aggression by two of Charlemagne's grandsons, recorded in Latin, Old French and Old High German.

[49] Klaus Siewert, *Glossenfunde: Volkssprachliches zu lateinischen Autoren der Antike und des Mittelalters* (Göttingen: Vandenhoeck and Ruprecht, 1989).

[50] Ernst Hellgardt, "Die lateinischen und althochdeutschen Vergilglossen des clm 18059. Plädoyer für eine neue Art der Glossenlektüre," in *Stand und Aufgaben der deutschen Dialektlexikographie II: Brüder-Grimm-Symposion zur Historischen Wortforschung: Beiträge zu der Marburger Tagung vom Oktober 1992,* ed. Ernst Bremer and Reiner Hildebrandt (Berlin, New York: de Gruyter, 1996), 73–88.

[51] Klaus Siewert, *Die althochdeutsche Horazglossierung* (Göttingen: Vandenhoeck and Ruprecht, 1986).

[52] Klaus Siewert, "Die althochdeutsche Persiusglossierung im Lichte neuer Quellen," in Bergmann, Tiefenbach, and Voetz, *Althochdeutsch,* I, 608–24.

[53] *Aviani fabulae,* ed. R. Ellis (Oxford: Clarendon) 1887; *Aviani fabulae,* ed. A. Guaglianone (Turin: Paravia, 1958).

[54] For both see: http://www.fh-augsburg.de/~harsch/luc_intr.html.

[55] See Joseph Kehrein, *Kirchen- und religiöse Lieder aus dem zwölften bis fünfzehnten Jahrhundert* (Paderborn: Schoeningh, 1853), 34.

[56] *Biographisch-bibliographisches Kirchenlexikon* IX, 1289–90.

[57] *Biographisch-bibliographisches Kirchenlexikon* VII, 1010–13.

[58] Birgit Kölling, *Kiel UB. Cod. MS. K.B. 145: Studien zu den althochdeutschen Glossen* (Göttingen: Vandenhoeck and Ruprecht, 1983); Thomas Stührenberg, *Die althochdeutschen Prudentiusglossen der Handschrift Düsseldorf F1* (Bonn: Röhrscheid, 1974); Meineke and Schwerdt, *Einführung*, 172–73.

[59] *Biographisch-bibliographisches Kirchenlexikon* I, 204.

[60] Henning von Gadow, *Die deutschen Aratorglossen der Handschrift Trier 1464* (Munich: Fink, 1974); Ingrid Kelling, "Die althochdeutschen Aratorglossen" (Diss., Jena, 1964); Armin Schlechter, *Die althochdeutschen Aratorglossen der Handschrift Rom Bibliotheca Apostolica Vaticana Pal. Lat. 1716 und verwandte Glossierungen* (Göttingen: Vandenhoeck and Ruprecht, 1983); Heinrich Tiefenbach, *Althochdeutsche Aratorglossen. Paris lat. 8318. Gotha Membr. II, 115* (Göttingen: Vandenhoeck and Ruprecht, 1977).

[61] *Biographisch-bibliographisches Kirchenlexikon* III, 904–6; Dorothee Ertmer, *Studien zur althochdeutschen und altsächsischen Juvencusglossierung* (Göttingen: Vandenhoeck and Ruprecht, 1994).

[62] Werner Bach, *Die althochdeutschen Boethiusglossen und Notkers Übersetzung der Consolatio* (Diss., Halle-Wittenberg, 1934).

[63] *Biographisch-bibliographisches Kirchenlexikon* II, 1374–79; Erika Ulrich, *Die althochdeutschen Glossen zu Isidors Büchern über die Pflichten* (Diss., Halle-Wittenberg, 1937).

[64] *Biographisch-bibliographisches Kirchenlexikon* I, 97–98.

[65] Eckhard Meineke, "Unedierte Glossen zu Bibelkommentaren des Walahfrid Strabo in Handschriften französischer Bibliotheken" in *Addenda und Corrigenda (II) zur althochdeutschen Glossensammlung*, ed. Rudolf Schützeichel (Göttingen: Vandenhoeck and Ruprecht, 1985), 57–64.

[66] Werner Betz, *Lateinisch und Deutsch: Die Lehnbildungen der althochdeutschen Benediktinerregel*, 2nd ed. (Bonn: Bouvier, 1965).

[67] See S. Sonderegger, *Althochdeutsche Sprache und Literatur* (Berlin: de Gruyter, 1974), 260–61, and Keller, *German Language*, 211–33, for the wider context.

[68] Whitley Stokes and John Strachan, *Thesaurus Palaeohibernicus* (repr. Dublin: Institute for Advanced Studies, 1975). James F. Kenney, *The Sources for the Early History of Ireland, Ecclesiastical*, 2nd ed. (Dublin: Pádraic Ó Tálliúir, 1979), 660–68.

[69] L. D. Reynolds and N. G. Wilson, *Scribes and Scholars: A Guide to the Transmission of Greek and Latin Literature*, 2nd ed. (Oxford: OUP, 1991).

[70] John J. Contreni, "The Irish Contribution to the European Classroom," in *Proceedings of the Seventh International Congress of Celtic Studies*, ed. D. Ellis Evans, John G. Griffith and E. M. Pope (Oxford: D. Ellis Evans, 1986), 79–90.

[71] McKitterick, *Carolingians and the Written Word,* and see also Donald Bullough, *The Age of Charlemagne* (London: Ferndale, 1980) esp. chapter 4 ("A Court of Scholars and the Revival of Learning").

[72] Irmgard Frank, *Aus Glossenhandschriften des 8. bis 14. Jahrhunderts: Quellen zur Geschichte einer Überlieferungsart* (Heidelberg: Winter, 1984).

[73] See Murdoch, *Old High German Literature,* 27 and 30.

[74] Sometimes introduced by *.i.* = *id est* (that is), *.t.* = *theodisce* (in German), *.f.* = *frencisce* (in Frankish) and so on; see Eckhard Meineke, "Unedierte Glossen zu Bibelkommentaren des Walahfrid Strabo in Handschriften französischer Bibliotheken" in Schützeichel, *Addenda und Corrigenda (II),* 57–64.

[75] Elvira Glaser, "Edition und Dokumentation ahd. Griffelglossen" in *Probleme der Edition althochdeutscher Texte,* ed. Rolf Bergmann (Göttingen: Vandenhoeck and Ruprecht, 1993), 9–17; Hartwig Mayer, *Die althochdeutschen Griffelglossen der Hs. Salzburg, St. Peter a VII 2* (Göttingen: Vandenhoeck and Ruprecht, 1994).

[76] Bostock, *Handbook,* 179.

[77] The most important reference text is still the collection published by Elias von Steinmeyer and Eduard Sievers, *Die althochdeutschen Glossen* (Berlin: Weidmann, 1879–1922); this is the standard collection, usually abbreviated Gl. in secondary studies. It has been supplemented by the new dictionary by Taylor Starck and J. C Wells, *Althochdeutsches Glossenwörterbuch* (Heidelberg: Winter, 1990). Steinmeyer's material also formed the basis of the standard Old High German dictionary, which was taken over by Elisabeth Karg-Gasterstädt and Theodor Frings in 1935, and by the Sächsische Akademie der Wissenschaften (Leipzig) from 1948. Schützeichel's Old High German dictionary and works derived from it reflect an entirely separate project funded by the Akademie der Wissenschaften in Göttingen: E. Karg-Gasterstädt, T. Frings, and others, *Althochdeutsches Wörterbuch auf Grund der von Elias von Steinmeyer hinterlassenen Sammlungen* (Berlin: Akademie-Verlag, 1952–); R. Schützeichel, *Althochdeutsches Wörterbuch* (Tübingen: Niemeyer, 1969, 5th ed. 1995);. R. Bergmann, *Rückläufiges Morphologisches Wörterbuch des Althochdeutschen* (Tübingen: Niemeyer, 1991).

[78] Eberhard Gottlieb Graff, *Altdeutscher Sprachschatz oder Wörterbuch der althochdeutschen Sprache* (Berlin: Nikolai, 1834–1842). Words are arranged by roots and the dictionary can be hard to use; an alphabetical index was added as a seventh volume by H. F. Massmann (1846).

[79] Meineke and Schwerdt, *Einführung,* 168–69 (with a reproduction of fol. 56r).

[80] Bostock, *Handbook,* 99.

[81] Jonathan West, *Lexical Innovation in Dasypodius' Dictionary* (Berlin: de Gruyter, 1989); William Jervis Jones, *German Lexicography in the European Context* (Berlin: de Gruyter, 2000); von Polenz, *Deutsche Sprachgeschichte* II, 181–99.

[82] Steinmeyer and Sievers, *Glossen* III, 632f.

[83] Bostock, Handbook, 92–97.

[84] Georg Baesecke, *Der deutsche Abrogans und die Herkunft des deutschen Schrifttums* (Halle: Niemeyer, 1930). Baesecke also supplied facsimiles of a and b: a = Pa, Codex Parisianus 7640, Paris, probably from Murbach, ca. 810; b = K, also called the

Keronisches Glossar (Kero's glossary) = Cod. Sti Galli, 911, St. Gallen, possibly originally from Murbach, ca. 800; c = Ra, Codex Carolsruh. Aug. CXI, now in Karlsruhe, originally from Reichenau, between 802 and 817. The text can be found in Steinmeyer and Sievers, *Glossen*, I, 1–270, and there are extracts in most readers. See also Jochen Splett, *Abrogans-Studien* (Wiesbaden: Steiner, 1976).

[85] Jochen Splett, *Samanunga-Studien: Erläuterung und lexikalische Erschließung eines althochdeutschen Wörterbuchs* (Göppingen: Kümmerle, 1979) and "*Samanunga uuorto,*" *VL* VIII, 570–72. Heinz Mettke, ed., *Altdeutsche Texte* (Leipzig: VEB Bibliographisches Institut, 1970), 23–24 gives in a useful summary of the data the reference in Steinmeyer and Sievers's collection (Gl.) and then the individual glosses from a, b, c and R (the *Samanunga*).

[86] Georg Baesecke, *Der Vocabularius Sti Galli in der angelsächsischen Mission* (Halle: Niemeyer, 1933); Bostock, *Handbook,* 100.

[87] Reproduced in Steinmeyer and Sievers, *Glossen,* III, 1–8; short extracts are found in Braune, I, 2–3, and in Charles Clyde Barber, *An Old High German Reader* (Oxford: Blackwell, 1964) and Mettke, *Altdeutsche Texte,* 24.

[88] Bostock, *Handbook,* 101.

[89] *Einführung,* 175, 177.

[90] The manuscript is Cod. Reg. lat 566 f. 50v. See Bostock, *Handbook,* 101; Murdoch, *Old High German Literature,* 32–33; Wolfgang Haubrichs and Max Pfister, *In Francia fui* (Stuttgart: Steiner, 1989).

[91] Ms. lat. 7461, text reproduced in Steinmeyer and Sievers, *Glossen,* V.

[92] The words for body parts already exemplify beside the lack of initial /h/, the reflex of West Gmc */w/ as /gw/ (which later becomes /g/) characteristic of Frankish loan words in French (e.g., French *guerre* from Frankish **werra* "war") See now Nicola Quatermaine, *The Language of the Franks in Gaul* (Diss., Manchester, 2002).

[93] See Frank, *Aus Glossenhandschriften des 8. bis 14. Jahrhunderts.*

[94] Reiner Hildebrandt, ed., *Summarium Heinrici* (Berlin: de Gruyter, 1982).

[95] *Biographisch-bibliographisches Kirchenlexikon* III, 365–66. The full title of the work is *Summa grammaticalis quae vocatur Catholicon.*

[96] *Biographisch-bibliographisches Kirchenlexikon* VII, 957–65.

[97] West, *Lexical Innovation,* and see also his *A Developmental Edition of Dasypodius' Dictionary* (Newcastle: University of Newcastle upon Tyne, 2001).

[98] *Biographisch-bibliographisches Kirchenlexikon* XIII, 169–76.

[99] E. Schröter, *Walahfrids deutsche Glossierung zu den biblischen Büchern Genesis bis Regum II und der althochdeutsche Tatian* (Halle: Niemeyer, 1926).

[100] See in general J. Szövérffy, *Die Annalen der lateinischen Hymnendichtung* (Berlin: Schmidt, 1964/65).

[101] Brian Murdoch, "Hrabanus Maurus," in *German Writers and Works of the Early Middle Ages,* ed. Will Hasty and James Hardin (New York: Gale, 1995), 74–78.

[102] Brian Murdoch, "Walahfrid Strabo," in Hasty and Hardin, eds., *German Writers,* 143–45.

[103] *Biographisch-bibliographisches Kirchenlexikon* II, 275–76.

[104] Eduard Sievers, ed., *Die Murbacher Hymnen* (Berlin: Waisenhaus, 1874; repr. with an introduction by Evelyn Scherabon Firchow, New York: Johnson, 1972); S. Sonderegger, "Murbacher Hymnen," *VL* VI, 804–10; Dieter Kartschoke, *Geschichte der deutschen Literatur im frühen Mittelalter* (Munich: dtv, 1990).

[105] Smaller early translations include, of course, various versions of the Lord's Prayer and of the *Credo* (see Braune VI, XII).

[106] Meineke and Schwerdt, *Einführung*, 144–48; Murdoch, *Old High German Literature*, 35–36; Bostock, *Handbook*, 157–68. The old edition by Eduard Sievers, *Tatian: Lateinisch und altdeutsch mit ausführlichem Glossar* (Paderborn: Schöningh, 1884, repr. 1966), has now been replaced by Achim Masser, *Die lateinisch-althochdeutsche Tatianbilingue des Cod. Sang. 56* (Göttingen: Vandenhoeck and Ruprecht, 1991).

[107] Walter Henss, "Zur Quellenfrage im Heliand und althochdeutschen Tatian," in *Der Heliand*, ed. Jürgen Eichhoff and Irmengard Rauch (Darmstadt: WBG, 1973), 191–99.

[108] K. Th. Schäfer, "Diatessaron," *Lexikon für Theologie und Kirche*, ed. Josef Höfer and Karl Rahnen, 2nd ed. (Freiburg: Herder, 1967–68), III, 384. Knowledge of Tatian is derived mainly from his other extant work, written around A.D.150, the *Oratio ad Graecos*, see E. Schwartz, *Tatiani Oratio ad Graecos: Texte und Untersuchungen* (Leipzig: Hinrichs, 1888). See also *Biographisch-bibliographisches Kirchenlexikon* XI, 552–71.

[109] The history of the Vulgate text is not as simple as the traditional attribution to St. Jerome would make it appear, see the preface to Roger Gryson, ed., *Biblia Sacra Iuxta Vulgatem Versionem* (Stuttgart: Deutsche Bibelgesellschaft, 1994), xxix.

[110] This is a simplification derived from an old view of the emergence of Modern German. Fréderic Hartweg and Klaus-Peter Wegera, *Frühneuhochdeutsch* (Tübingen: Niemeyer, 1989), 36–48, present a more reliable picture.

[111] See G. F. Benecke, W. Müller and F. Zarncke, *Mittelhochdeutsches Handwörterbuch* (Leipzig: Hirzel, 1854–61), I, 106.

[112] Bostock, *Handbook*, 167. On the other hand *ougazoroht*, "well known," *ougazorhto* "publicly," *giougzorohten* and *giougzorohtôn* "reveal" seem to occur only in Tatian; also *sihwanne* "sometime," *sihwaz* "something," *sihwelîh* "a certain," *sihwer* "someone," *sihwuo* "somehow," as opposed to *sohwer*, etc.; *sûbiri* (Notker has *sûber*); see E. Gutmacher, "Der Wortschatz des althochdeutschen Tatian," *PBB* 39 (1914): 1–83, 229–89, 571–77.

[113] *Biographisch-bibliographisches Kirchenlexikon* II, 1374–79.

[114] Klaus Matzel, "Ahd. Isidor und Monsee-Wiener Fragmente" in *VL* I, 296–303; Alfred R. Wedel "The Old High German Isidor" in Hasty and Hardin, *German Writers*, 248–51; Kartschoke, *Geschichte der deutschen Literatur im frühen Mittelalter*, 106–11; Gustav Ehrismann, *Geschichte der deutschen Literatur bis zum Ausgang des Mittelalters, 1: Die althochdeutsche Literatur* (Munich: Beck, 1932, repr. as 2nd ed. 1954), 273–86.

[115] Hanns Fischer, *Schrifttafeln zum althochdeutschen Lesebuch* (Tübingen: Niemeyer, 1966), 4.

[116] Stephanus (Istvan) Endlicher and H. Hoffmann von Fallersleben, *Fragmenta Theotisca* (1841; 2nd ed., Vienna: Beck, 1934).

[117] Eckhard Meineke, *Abstraktbildungen im Althochdeutschen: Wege zu ihrer Erschließung* (Göttingen: Vandenhoeck and Ruprecht, 1994), 361–73.

[118] Meineke and Schwerdt, *Einführung*, 136.

[119] Bostock, *Handbook*, 118–23.

[120] Full texts are found in *Der althochdeutsche Isidor*, ed. Hans Eggers (Tübingen: Niemeyer, 1964) and *The Monsee Fragments*, ed. George A. Hench (Strassburg: Trübner, 1890). Examples are from chapter III, 1, and this and the following extracts can be found in Braune, VIII. See also Kurt Ostberg, *The Old High German Isidor in its Relationship to the Manuscripts (Eighth to Twelfth Century) of Isidorus, De fide Catholica* (Göppingen: Kümmerle, 1979).

[121] Keller, *German Language*, 440–41.

[122] Murdoch, *Old High German Literature*, 41–43.

[123] My thanks for this and the final chapter in this volume go especially to Dr. Máire West, without whose editing the chapters would have been far less readable; and to Professor Brian Murdoch, for his wise and far-reaching suggestions.

Charms, Recipes, and Prayers

Brian Murdoch

IT CANNOT BE EMPHASIZED SUFFICIENTLY that all the material that we
have in Old High German was written down in the context of the
Christian Church. Nevertheless, some German texts, even though committed to writing by monks, contain at least some clues to pre-Christian,
pagan writings and religious thought. Of particular interest in this respect are the few glimpses of Germanic religion that have survived in the
early German charms. It is understandable, too, that even though all the
pieces we have are Christianized, a disproportionate amount of attention
has been paid to that aspect of these small texts. By charms (the word
derives from the Latin *carmen,* with the sense here of a solemn or
chanted incantation) are meant short texts, the earliest of them oral in
origin, in verse or prose, designed in their original form to effect — to
conjure, in fact — some sort of cure or change by the power of the word
alone, often assisted by the invocation of deities. Thus, one classical Latin
charm from Pliny, for removing a fishbone from the throat, requires the
charm-worker to lay hands on the sufferer and say *Lafana piscator, exi et
fac quae te iussit Iuppiter!* (Fisherman Lafana, come out and do as Jupiter
commands you).[1] Actions can be called for as well, and sometimes otherwise arcane "magic words" (*abracadabra* is probably the most familiar)
are used. Charms often contain the instruction that things are to be said
aloud, but magic words (and, later, Christian formulas or names) may
also be written down to be used as periapts, as portable charms or amulets, in the sense of the modern good-luck charm.

Charms are known to most cultures, including ancient India (there
are a great many in the *Atharva-Veda*) and the classical world, and there
are likewise large numbers of charms extant in medieval Christian Latin,
as well as in most European vernaculars. General comments on these
texts apply, then, not only to German but also to ancient and even relatively modern texts in a wide range of languages. Charms whose form
and content is very close to examples in Old High German, for example,
were collected in the nineteenth century in the Western Isles of Scotland,
and further parallels have been found at considerable geographical dis-

tances as well.[2] The charms that survive in early German, however, while they may preserve elements of what we may think of as their original forms, have all been assimilated into Christianity with the inclusion or addition of prayers, or a change in their context to something recognizably Christian. Thus, for the texts we possess, the designation of prayer would be more apposite, even if the notion of magic never quite disappears. It must not be overemphasized, however.

There are, then, some unusual features in a presentation of the early German charms as part of a literary history. Not only do they represent a cultural phenomenon not restricted to German or even Germanic culture in any case (and even in German it continues unchanged into the High Middle Ages and beyond), but they interlock with other forms of writing that seem at first glance to be different. Categorization is a particularly difficult problem, even when it is accepted that all early German charms are, in the form we have them, Christian. Many of what are termed charms are designed to heal, or at least to make a situation better, and thus they overlap to some extent with the medical-pharmaceutical approach to healing, represented by the recipe, the prescription. The word *recipe* simply means "take (ingredients)," and medical recipes in their turn may be linked with the cookery recipe. In another, rather different direction, the Christianization of the German charms makes for an equally firm link with liturgical prayers, specifically with the collects, the petitionary prayers offered when faced with a given situation, such as prayers for the sick, or to ensure that a negative situation might not arise. The factor which brings together these apparently different types of writing — recipes, charms, and prayers — is the concept of amelioration, of making something better. Charms, indeed, may be found in liturgical contexts, in theological manuscripts, or in medical collections.

This need for amelioration may apply when something has already come about, a disease or a misfortune. A pharmaceutical recipe prescribes ingredients and also actions designed to heal that suffering physically (just as a cookery recipe is based on ingredients to remove hunger), and a charm is intended to do the same thing, while a prayer, finally, might ask for God's help to the same end. A different categorization may be made in the distinction between actual and potential misfortunes. Whereas for the former the word "charm," with its magical overtones, has been used, for the latter the alternative term, "blessing," might indicate, albeit imprecisely, a precautionary request that something negative might not in fact happen at all, that a journey be undertaken safely, for example. In simple terms, a recipe can effect, a charm demand, and a prayer request a cure, so that all are potentially thaumaturgic; while blessings (which are also prayers) request protection, and are prophylactic. The overlap, though, has already been indicated: medical recipes are preserved for future use, and charms, though they often imply orality as well, are also written documents, intended presumably for potential use, and they can also be written out deliberately for use as protective amulets. The magic words written for this purpose may come from pre-Christian times, but liturgical phrases or individual words, such as the names given to the Magi, serve the same purpose and themselves become magic words later. Convenient as it might be to divide even the surviving early German charms according to whether they contain a command that the magic should take effect, or a request that God permit healing or prevent misfortunes, this is not useful, since in fact most charms contain both elements, so that the German distinction between *Zauberspruch* and *Segen* is at best blurred. With Old High German, there is even a case for abandoning the term *charm* altogether,

Although we have in Old English, for example, several collections of medical recipes (known as Leech Books, which also contain charms), examples of medical recipes are rare in early German. Indeed, in the Old High German period proper we have only the two so-called *Basler Rezepte,* the Basel Prescriptions, which seem to describe medicines for a fever and for a tumor. The name comes, as usual, from the present location of the manuscript, a work by a theological writer on the natural world in which they are an addition, but it is not clear where or by whom they were copied, though it was possibly in Fulda. The first has no heading, so that the nature of the recipe has to be deduced (a different Latin version of the German text precedes it in the manuscript, and is sometimes referred to as the first Basel recipe), but the second German recipe (which seems to have Anglo-Saxon elements in it) is headed *widar cancur,* against a cancerous growth. The varied ingredients of the first are largely roughage, which would not hurt the patient and might do a small amount of good. In the second, the ingredients would have had a caustic effect; applied to an external tumor (rubbed until it bleeds), and then dressed as prescribed with egg white and honey (which is a healing agent), there is a possibility that the cure might even be effective. Similar remedies appear in the Anglo-Saxon collections. There is no indication whether either was actually used, although some details of a prescribed regimen are present in the fever prescription; we do not have anything to match the observational classical writings on the actual practice of medicine.[3] Only at the end of the early period — in the eleventh and twelfth centuries — come the larger-scale medical collections, the German *Arzneibücher,* specifically the Zurich pharmacopoeia (with some parallel fragments in a Bamberg manuscript), and the slightly later Innsbruck pharmacopoeia. Once again, these contain charms as well as recipes, but even to refer to these texts as German is not strictly accurate, given that the titles in the former and much of the text in the latter are in Latin. They do offer a series of recipes for various (petty and everyday) ailments such as headaches, sore eyes, toothache, sprains and stomach-ache, as well as for "worms" — by which is meant almost any disease — and also for epilepsy. For epilepsy, the Innsbruck collection provides a far-fetched recipe involving swallow's blood, to be administered to the patient during a waxing or a waning moon, and so presumably (and luckily) not specific to an epileptic seizure, even though medically it would have had no effect whatsoever.

The Innsbruck text also demonstrates how charms are regularly found in medical contexts. Under the heading *Contra Fluxum sanguinis. de naribus* (against nosebleeds), we have first a Latin injunction to say a brief Christian charm in rhymed Latin, and then, with the heading *iterum* (alternatively), we have an instruction to powder burnt egg-shell and inhale it through a reed.[4] The prescription begins in German and continues in Latin, with a note that it is very efficacious, and that it might have a styptic effect. Various smaller prose pieces belong also to this later period, including an eye remedy from the eleventh century, which prescribes bathing the eyes in running water, but calls also for the pronouncement of a blessing on the eyes, so that it is a mixture once again. The Zurich recipe collection calls only for new cheese to be applied to the sore eyes, and there is a later blessing or charm without any practical alternative found in a Cambridge manuscript. There are also, in different manuscripts, descriptions of what to do in cases of paralysis (*contra paralysin theutonice*), which seems to include any sort of cramp, gout or lameness; there are also late individual recipes for postnatal problems or for stones.[5]

Early German writing has preserved no cookery recipes, but it is worth noting as a brief digression, since the term recipe now usually has culinary implications, that later cookery books in other cultures do sometimes contain medical recipes and charms as well. An English manuscript as late as the end of the fifteenth century, for example, contains, side-by-side with recipes of the order of *Samon rostyd in sause*, not only remedies like *A gode medecyn for the colyck* and what we may call folk remedies (such as using a piece of burnt blue cloth to staunch a wound), but also *A charme for the blody flux* requiring five Paternosters. The manuscript, though late, does illustrate the complexity of categorizing the various types of text with which we are concerned, and it highlights once again the interesting question of the contexts in which charms in particular are preserved.[6]

Some of the Old High German charms consist of a simple command — which may have been accompanied by some action — to the effect that a disease should leave a person. More commonly, the structure of a charm is frequently bi-partite, consisting of a narrative of an event that has happened in the past, followed by a command that the existing situation be made better, that blood should stop flowing, for example. However, the early German pieces are almost invariably followed by a prayer, usually the Paternoster, which contains the notion of "Thy will be done," or the Amen, meaning "let it be," so that they are effectively *tri*partite. Whatever they may have been in their pre-Christian stage — and we have very few in which this stage is clearly discernible — they have come close to the formally structured collect, in which an introductory invocation is followed by a specific request, and then by a liturgical-formulaic conclusion, such as *Amen,* or *per Jesus Christum Dominum nostrum,* "through Jesus Christ our Lord." Like recipes, too, charms can also acquire titles indicating their purpose. One feature that is not always stressed about the charms, and especially those where there are pre-Christian elements, is that they are frequently difficult to understand, prompting much scholarly speculation on the individual words and the content of the narrative on frequent occasions, and indeed leading us off into mythological or cultural-anthropological by-ways. In many cases, one might well suspect that a comfortingly mysterious obscurity is a relevant feature of the charm as such.[7]

The simplest of the charms in formal terms are those against disease as such, known often as worm-charms, since they see disease as spread by invisible worms (if we substitute the concept of bacteria or germs, the medical aspect becomes clear), and call on the worms to leave the patient. Again, parallels to the German examples we have are known from ancient times, and they may be accompanied by an action. One such charm, headed *Contra vermes* (against worms), in a Low German form, and of which there is an equivalent in High German (both in theological manuscripts), seems to conjure the disease from the marrow to the bone, then to the flesh, and eventually out into an arrow, which may have been fired away. This looks like pure magic, but the Low German form ends with the prayer *Drohtin uuerthe so,* "Lord, let it be," "Amen," while the High German version calls for three — a ritualistic number — *Our Fathers.* The precise malady involved is unclear, however.

In Old High German, only two or three charms contain references to the pre-Christian Germanic gods and goddesses known from Norse and other literatures, or from Christian formulas which demand that they be forsworn.[8] But the fact that there are some that name Wodan and possibly Donar (Thor), or refer to *idisi* — Valkyries — indicates that oral invocatory magic of this sort had once been known, even if by the time it was written down it had been assimilated by the Christian church. The best-known examples in Old High German are the so-called *Merseburger Zaubersprüche,* two pieces in a central German dialect written in the tenth century on a blank page of a manuscript that contains liturgical material and a fragmentary prayer in German. Although they look like prose, the pieces are in Germanic alliterative verse, long lines linked by their initial sounds (the form is discussed in more detail in chapters 5 and 7), and they are more complex in structure than the worm-charms. Each contains a narrative section and then a command, and attached to them in the manuscript is a Latin prayer. The first four-line piece describes how valkyries released some prisoners, and in the last line comes the command: "escape from the bonds." The second piece describes how Phol (a figure identified as widely as being either Apollo or St. Paul, and probably not clear even to the scribe, who inserted the *h* later) and Wodan were riding in a forest when Wodan's horse sprained a foot. Now, however, we are told that a number of goddesses (either four, or two with appositional alternative names) try a cure, but then Wodan himself effects the cure. Not only is the work written out continuously as if it were prose, but there are no indicators of names, and some of what *are* assumed to be names are obscure. Between the first and the second piece, too, is a sign looking rather like a capital H, which may just be an abbreviation for "another," but to what extent it links or separates the two charms is also unclear. The last part of the second charm, however, is a command:

> ben zi bena, bluot zi bluoda,
> lid zi giliden, sose gilimida sin!
>
> [bone to bone, blood to blood,
> limb to limb as if glued].

The literary power of this alliterative conjuration lives on: there is an English version ("bone to bone and vein to vein") recorded in the nineteenth century. The prayer just below this on the manuscript page in Latin prose now asks for God's help for an individual (whose name can be added), and the addition of this prayer presumably made the rest of it acceptable to the church. By the time it was written, the pagan names may have become little more than magic words. At all events, it is difficult to determine what precisely we mean by the text of the Merseburg charms. Strictly speaking, in spite of the efforts made to isolate the pagan "original," the text can only be the written form from the Merseburg manuscript. Laying it out as verse, adding capitals to indicate distinct names (not all of which are at all clear), ignoring the joining symbol, and omitting the Latin prayer — all of which different editors have done — take us an increasingly long way from what has actually survived. So, too, does an excessive interest in conjectural reconstructions of a presumed original.[9]

The first of these two pieces is, moreover, usually designated in modern editions as a spell for the release of prisoners, and the second is seen as intended to cure a lame horse, but both interpretations are questionable, and the first extremely unlikely. The two pieces are clearly designed to have a curative effect, and although in other cultures we do find love-spells and also curses, all other surviving Old High German charms are for potentially curable conditions. It is far more plausible that *both* charms refer to temporary traumas like sprains, paralysis, or cramp (from which the prisoner had to be freed). The second charm might apply to any sprain, even though a descriptive passage talks about a horse, and we do sometimes find clear distinctions between human and animal charms.[10] Likewise, there are in German (as elsewhere) several charms aimed at specific conditions in horses, and they are indicated as such in their titles, even though the many ailments of the horse are not always easy to identify now; there is no such specific indication in this case.

The Merseburg pieces are unusual in naming pagan figures, however, and this seems to happen elsewhere only in one other piece, a complicated epilepsy charm known in two versions which may (or may not) name Donar, Thor, in the opening words *Donerdutigo. dietewigo;* those words are so corrupt, however, that they are even more likely to represent, in this written form, merely abracadabra words. More importantly, the situation narrated in the second Merseburg charm, that of Wodan's injured horse, appears later in German (and in many other cultures) with a Christianized content, in which Christ or St. Peter take over the central role. In many other charms for different ailments, too, the narrative portion involves not pagan, but biblical figures, albeit not always in what we would understand as their biblical roles. Legends, or apocryphal stories of the infancy of Christ, for example, may be found, and sometimes, too, the content is Christian, but the details are unclear. There is a reference in the Old High German epilepsy charms to Adam's bridge, and a conflict between Adam's son and the devil's son, but in spite of confident assertions as to what this might mean, in fact it again remains obscure.

Charms for sprains (of humans or horses) are common, but charms exist for a number of conditions. The epilepsy charms are more complicated, and presumably are intended to be used, probably by a priest, when someone is actually having an epileptic fit. One version calls for three Our Fathers, the other involves touching the affected person on either side and pronouncing the charm three times. By the time this was done, of course, the seizure would probably have passed.[11] Probably the most common type, however, is the hemostatic charm. These charms to stop bleeding (some of which are even headed as being specifically against nosebleeds), are very frequent, as might be expected, and those that we have in German are clearly Christian. They most frequently take the form of Longinus charms or Jordan charms. The former links the piercing of Christ's side by the soldier in John 19: 34 with the centurion who bears witness at the Crucifixion in the synoptic Gospels. Known traditionally as Longinus, legends become attached to him in the Middle Ages — he is sometimes blind, sometimes a saint, sometimes a Jew. The ideas merge with an infancy legend in which Christ is wounded by a lance, but stops the bleeding. The Jordan charms are based on an incident found in very early apocryphal writing in which the Jordan stands still at Christ's birth or, more usually, baptism.[12] The static Jordan is known in various apocryphal texts in different contexts, and both the piercing of the side and the static river are alluded to in many charms, frequently in combination, as in two late Old High German Bamberg blood charms. There is a striking reduction, however, in a Low German charm from a Trier manuscript that merely reports that Christ was wounded, the blood stopped, and that the present blood should also stop flowing, before calling for three Amens and three Our Fathers. By the time all this had been said, one hopes that the blood would indeed successfully have been stanched. The numerous charms involving the blood of Christ in their narrative section look very much like Christian creations, of course. Although the Jordan and Longinus texts are very common, other hemostatic charms are known even within Old High German, including a complex blood charm (or series of charms) in a manuscript from Strasbourg which invokes at one point a saint called Tumbo, dumb, possibly deriving from the verb *stupeo* (*stupidus*), connected with the modern English word *styptic,* causing blood to stop.[13]

It is impossible to give illustrations of all the charms, but one of the blood charms may serve to show what the majority (the Merseburg charms are exceptional) look like, and what the special textual difficulties can be. This is a tenth-century prose Longinus/Jordan charm from

Rheinau, in a Zurich manuscript. Most of it is Latin, but there are some German words:

> Longinus miles. lango zile. cristes thegan ast astes.
> Adiuro sanguis per patre*m* et filiu*m*. et sp*iritu*m *sanct*u*m*
> vt no*n* fluas. plus qua*m* iordanis aha [qua]ndo *christus* In
> ea baptizatus est [a] s*p*[iritu s]a[n]cto.
> .III. uicib*us* pat*er* no*ster*. cu*m* glo*ria*.

Even before we examine a translation, various features are clear: the mixture of Latin (italics indicate an abbreviation in the original) and German, for example, and the demand for three *Paternosters* and a *Gloria* at the end. In fact, it is not easy to interpret fully, and the slightly garbled text is typical for charms, elements of which may well not have been comprehensible to the scribes concerned, who, equally, may not have expected to understand all the words. Here, the German portions are italicized:

> The soldier Longinus, *may he long bear witness, [?] Christ's warrior at the cross [?]*
> I conjure you, blood, in the name of the Father, the Son and the Holy Ghost that you flow no more than the Jordan *river* when Christ was baptized in it by the Holy Ghost.
> Three Our Fathers and the Gloria.[14]

That text is found in a manuscript containing sermons in Latin, though it also has two Latin fever charms and the Latin biblical passage on the woman with an issue of blood in Matthew 9:20–9:22. The manuscript that contains the Bamberg blood charms noted above, however, is a medical one, and in it there is a significant suggestion that these be used for the poor, rather than the more costly medical recipes.[15]

Medical recipes are clearly designed to cure ailments of some kind, and those written down are at least likely to have been tried; blessings designed to ward off evil will be felt after the event to have worked if nothing does happen. However, it is worth raising the important question of whether or not the charms, too, would (have been felt to) work. The question is not a naive one: why else should they be preserved in such relatively large numbers, and why indeed are they included not only side-by-side with liturgical writings, but also in specifically medical manuscripts? Indeed, medical textbooks in most languages throughout the Middle Ages contain charms as well: the English *Liber de diversis medicinis* (Book of various medicines), a large medical text from as late as the first half of the fifteenth century, contains, as the Latin title implies, mostly medical recipes, but there are also descriptions of amulets (inscribed host wafers to protect against fever) and a Latin charm for easing childbirth which calls on Christ (the verb *adiuro,* "to conjure" is used) for help, but also recalls in narrative terms that when Christ was born, all pain was eased.[16]

As a simple answer to the question of whether the charms worked, most of the early German charms seem to be aimed at transient traumatic situations such as sprains, cramps, nosebleeds or cuts, problems that pass or improve of their own accord relatively quickly. This includes the epileptic fit, which, while alarming, does not last long, and pronouncing the words of a charm, and more importantly saying a familiar prayer several times would at least calm the patient. It is likely to have been a considerable improvement on some medical recipes deigned to cure epilepsy, acquiring the ingredients of which often scarcely bears thinking about, let alone the possible effect on the patient.

The question of who used these charms is a separate problem. In their original forms the magic charms might have been used by folk healers or herbalists — we have very little idea. Quasi-magic material of this sort can be used by local practitioners or those who acquire a reputation for such skills, but their range would probably also have embraced love spells, or curses. Texts of such things exist, but we do not have early German examples. The charms are all concerned with healing, and there is no reason to suppose that the Church, which condemned the use of magic as such, was antagonistic to the use of these charms once they had effectively become prayers. Liturgical prayers were the province of the clergy in any case, and given that a great number of charms were recorded with liturgical prayers attached in monastic documents means that the priests might well have used them. The ecclesiastical proscriptions (of which there are many, as in Charlemagne's *Admonitio generalis* as early as 789, for example) against the use of magic clearly would not, then, apply to these Christianized pieces. The early Middle Ages had lost sight of classical advances in medicine, and what we might see as a herbalist culture was all that was on offer. Monastic herb gardens existed, but medicine as such was also practiced by lay healers known as leeches in medieval England, for example, and there may well have been interchange between herbalists and the secular clergy. A talisman is carried by an individual, and it is possible that charms could have been said by the individual too. The social history of the whole area is unclear and the overlap with superstition and folklore remains.[17] However, with the only barely possible exception of the first Merseburg charm, virtually all the recorded early German pieces are medical, and we do not even have examples of any of the perhaps clerically acceptable, useful, but occasionally more dangerous possibilities offered in medieval Latin, such as charms to capture snakes or banish mice and rats.[18] It is of interest that German charms, in the early period at least, seems to be restricted to those which are at least potentially usable, and even here the range is fairly limited compared to Anglo-Saxon; there are no extant early German charms for assisting childbirth, for example.

Most of the familiar liturgical prose prayers, such as the Our Father or the Creed, were of course translated into Old High German, but there is an early Rhenish Franconian rhymed prayer, the *Augsburger Gebet,* probably of the late ninth century, rendering into four lines of German verse the Latin prose prayer *Deus qui proprium* . . . (O God, whose nature it is . . .) from the Litany of the Saints. There are also several smaller prayers in the language, usually brief rhymed pieces that postdate Otfrid's Gospel poem. Indeed, in the Freising manuscript of the *Evangelienbuch* copied by the ninth-century scribe Sigihard, someone has added two German couplets, known (probably wrongly) as *Sigihard's Prayer,* which ask in general terms for God's mercy. Further prayers seek deliverance from the devil, also in general terms. The prose *Franconian Prayer* also requests God's help, right belief, and health and prosperity in general terms, and in this case the manuscript unusually has a Latin translation which has been made of the German prayer, rather than the other way around. Among the various Old High German prayers against the devil, finally, comes what seems almost equivalent to an amulet, but is an inscription to be placed (so the Latin title tells us) over a house to keep away the devil. The rhymed *Zurich House-Blessing* appears to challenge the devil to pronounce what is probably a magic word, *chnospinci.* In this case the aim is entirely prophylactic.[19]

Charms and recipes deal with existing situations. Except where charms have been written out to use as amulets, they are not designed specifically for warding off future or potential evil, as is the case with the Zurich blessing. Other pieces in Old High German do, however, fall into this essentially prophylactic category, and may be viewed as specific petitionary prayers or collects. Individual saints may be called on within the church for assistance with particular problems, and in the transitional period between Old and Middle High German we find as an example of this a way of dealing with a sore throat. The brief prose piece, largely in Latin with some German, is effectively a prayer to St. Blasius or St. Blaise, one of the fourteen auxiliary saints (*Vierzehn Nothelfer,* the Holy Helpers), who, according to legend, saved a child from choking, and who was a cult saint in Germany. It asks that St. Blaise should come soon and help. This is not exactly a charm; there is a request, but not a command, and the narrative dimension, though present in the legends of St. Blaise, is only implicit, and three Our Fathers are again called for at the conclusion. A general blessing against throat problems seems to have been issued in the medieval period as part of the feast of St. Blaise on February 3, at which time of the year it might well (then as now) have had considerable application.[20]

Preventative prayers can anticipate any eventuality. Early German examples in rhyme ask, for example, that bees might not swarm elsewhere, or that valuable dogs might not run away or be stolen. The Lorsch bee blessing calls for bees to return and not to swarm in the woods, where they cannot be reached, and invokes Christ and the Virgin. The dog blessing asks for the safe return of the dogs in Christ's and St. Martin's name, and there is a Latin parallel to the latter text. A slightly later prose piece from Graz asks God to prevent hailstorms. All three blessings are understandable in their historical context: bees and working dogs were valuable and useful commodities, and hail could ruin crops. Although these are all prophylactic, rather than requesting amelioration of something that has happened, all three have elements of the charm about them, a hint, as it were, of magic, indicating yet again the difficulty of categorizing these pieces. That the first two are rhymed and hence incantatory is itself close to ritual magic; it is interesting that an Anglo-Saxon equivalent of the bee blessing tells the bees to sit still, addressing them as *sigewif,* warrior women, possibly with a suggestion of the valkyrie idea about it. The German bee blessing is commanding in tone, forbidding the bees to swarm elsewhere, while the dog blessing refers to Christ and St. Martin in a non-biblical context. The Graz hail blessing opens with a triple *Ivie riffe* and a double *hin vil michel,* almost an equivalent to "rain, rain, go away." Other requests can be for almost anything, and there is a Zurich prayer, for example, which is, according to the Latin superscript, for the preservation of virginity. The example of the Virgin Mary is invoked in German with this request for chastity, but once again there are echoes both of the charms and of medical prescriptions in the addition that *Diz gebet ist uilgot tagilich gelesin* (this prayer is very effective if read daily).[21]

A final type of specific blessing is represented by rhymed prayers asking for protection on a journey, known also as lorical prayers, from the Latin word for a breastplate, although that can also mean a general prayer for divine protection, as in the Cologne *Morgensegen,* a well-known benediction on rising, with a parallel in the Muri prayers. Most examples of the *Reisesegen* proper are later and in Middle High German. There are several illustrations of the so-called *Tobiassegen,* for example, referring to the deutero-canonical book of Tobit, in which Tobit (Tobias) sends his son into the land of the Medes, where he is protected by an angel. At the end of the Old High German period, though, is the Weingarten *Reisesegen*,[22] which opens (after a Latin blessing with the signs of the cross) with a description of gestures, as the speaker sends with each of his five fingers five-and-fifty guardian angels. The central part is impressive:

> offin si di diz sigidor, sami si dir diz +segildor
> Bislozin si dir diz wagidor, sami si dir diz wafindor

[May the door of victory be open to you and (*the sign of the cross is to be made here*) the door of blessing. May the door of danger and the door of weapons be closed to you.]

Once again there is a ritual tone in the verse, and the piece concludes with a prose prayer to Christ and the saints, but this is very clearly a blessing.

Gathering all these different types of writing — and again, we are unable to assess how many similar pieces were simply not written down — into a coherent section of a literary history is difficult, the more so as we have had to take account of recipes, which are not literary in any modern sense. There are genuine literary high points, such as the German incantation of the second Merseburg Charm, which is impressive (although not unique) in its own right. But not only are the Merseburg Charms difficult in that we are not completely certain of the content (how many gods are involved, for example), but without the Latin prayer attached, they are functionally incomplete. The Weingarten travel blessing is a more coherently impressive piece within a more coherent religious context. Nevertheless, above all else, all the material described in this chapter is functional, *Gebrauchsliteratur* in the strictest sense. Recipes, charms, and prayers are designed to have a specific effect within a human situation, whether that effect is to be brought about by the application of prescribed ingredients, or by the will of God.

Notes

[1] Alf Önnerfors, *Antike Zaubersprüche* (Stuttgart: Reclam, 1991), 30–31.

[2] A perceptive introduction is provided by Lea Olsan, "Latin Charms of Medieval England: Verbal Healing in a Christian Oral Tradition," *Oral Tradition* 7 (1992), 116–42. On the range of parallels to one of the Old High German charms, see Rolf Ködderitzsch, "Der 2. Merseburger Spruch und seine Parallele," *Zeitschrift für celtische Philologie* 33 (1974): 45–57. Also of general use is Felix Grendon, "The

Anglo-Saxon Charms," *Journal of American Folklore* 22 (1909), 105–237, and Peter Assion, "Literatur zwischen Glaube und Aberglaube," in *Glaube im Abseits* (Darmstadt: WBG, 1992), 169–96.

[3] MSD LXII; St. VII; Eis, *Handschriften*, 26–27. See R-M. S. Heffner, "The Third Basel Recipe" *Journal of English and Germanic Philology* 46 (1947): 248–53, Peter Assion, *Altdeutsche Fachliteratur* (Berlin: Schmidt, 1973), 136, and my *Old High German* (Boston: Twayne, 1983), 48–49 on the putative efficacy of the recipes. Earlier opinions varies on the nature of the fever referred to in the first two recipes, and it has even been seen as a remedy for epilepsy; see also Irmengard Rauch, "Basler Rezept I" in *Festschrift für Herbert Kolb*, ed. Klaus Matzel and Hans-Gert Roloff (Bern: Lang, 1989), 523–27.

[4] Wilhelm, XI and XXV. See my paper "But Did They Work? Interpreting the Old High German Merseburg Charms in their Medieval Context," in *Neuphilologische Mitteilungen* 89 (1988): 358–69.

[5] The eleventh-century Munich *Augensegen* is in St. LXXIII. The Cambridge prose text is in Wilhelm XXIII. The *contra paralysin* prescriptions are in St. LXXII under the heading "Gegen Gicht," the word "Gicht" not having the force only of the modern word for "gout" (the word *Gicht* is itself associated philologically with diseases that can be conjured) in spite of the gloss *vergiht* for *paralisin* in one case: St. LXXII and Wilhelm VI. For the *Frauengeheimnisse* and the recipe against stones, see Wilhelm XIII and XXIV.

[6] The manuscript belonged to Samuel Pepys and is in the library of Magdalene College, Cambridge as Pepys 1047. See G. A. J. Hodgett, *Stere hit well: Medieval Recipes and Remedies from Samuel Pepys's Library* (Cornmarket: London, 1972). The collection even has a rather optimistic preventative remedy for what seems to be the Black Death.

[7] Verena Holzmann, *"Ich beswer dich wurm vnd wyrmin": Formen und Typen altdeutscher Zaubersprüche und Segen* (Bern: Lang, 2001) is a recent attempt at categorization. The book contains well over 300 texts in Old and Middle High German, but takes, unfortunately, virtually no account of secondary literature on the charms, of which there has been a great amount in recent years; she omits even such studies as Isaac Bacon, "Versuch einer Klassifizierung altdeutscher Zaubersprüche und Segen," *MLN* 67 (1952): 224–32; Irmgard Hampp, "Vom Wesen des Zaubers im Zauberspruch," *Der Deutschunterricht* 13/1 (1961): 58–76; Manfred Geier, "Die magische Kraft der Poesie," *DVjs* 56 (1982): 359–85. She includes Arno Schirokauer, "Form und Formel einiger altdeutschen Zaubersprüche," *ZfdPh* 73 (1954): 353–64, and Irmgard Hampp, *Beschwörung, Segen, Gebet* (Stuttgart: Silberburg, 1961). See finally Gerhard Eis, *Altdeutsche Zaubersprüche* (Berlin: de Gruyter, 1964). Bibliography to 1975 in J. Sidney Groseclose and Brian Murdoch, *Die althochdeutschen poetischen Denkmäler* (Stuttgart: Metzler, 1976), 48–57. On the comparison with the collects, see my paper: *"Drohtin, uuerthe so!* Funktionsweisen der altdeutschen Zaubersprüche," *Literaturwissenschaftliches Jahrbuch der Görres-Gesellschaft* 32 (1991): 11–37. Relevant editions of charms are in MSD (nos. IV, XVI); St. LXII–LXXVIII and LXXX; Braune XXXI; Wilhelm XVI–XXIII; Schlosser, 108–13; Wipf, 64–97. Steinmeyer and Wilhelm are the most useful, and all the charms referred to here are in these texts. See also Holzmann for texts, as well as the

dissertation by Carol Lynn Miller, "The Old High German and Old Saxon Charms" (Diss., Washington University, St. Louis, 1963) with diplomatic versions.

[8] See in general Wilhelm Boudriot, *Die altgermanische Religion in der amtlichen kirchlichen Literatur des Abendlandes vom 5. bis 11. Jahrhundert* (1928; rpt. Darmstadt: WBG, 1964). The early Saxon baptismal vow (MSD LI, St. III) calls for the forswearing of various of the Germanic deities by name, including UUoden and Thunaer. See on the pagan elements J. A. Huisman, "Odin auf dem Holzweg, oder die Irrfahrt eines altgermanischen Zauberspruchs," in *Altgermanische Beiträge, Jan van Dam zum 80. Geburtstag gewidmet,* ed. Friedrich Maurer and Cola Minis (Amsterdam: Rodopi, 1977), 1–9.

[9] The manuscript facsimile is in Hanns Fischer, *Schrifttafeln zum althochdeutschen Lesebuch* (Tübingen: Niemeyer, 1966), 16a. Compare this with Steinmeyer's text, no. LXII. Translation into Modern German or another language takes it even further away, of course.

[10] There is a huge amount of secondary material interpreting the Merseburg charms. Beside Ködderitzsch, and with a range of different historical, philological, literary and medical interpretations largely of the second charm, see as examples: Felix Genzmer, "Die Götter des zweiten Merseburger Zauberspruchs," *Arkiv för Nordisk Filologi* 93 (1948): 55–72; Kenneth Northcott, "An Interpretation of the Second Merseburg Charm," *MLR* 54 (1959): 46–50; Achim Masser, "Zum zweiten Merseburger Zauberspruch," *PBB/T* (1972), 19–25; Hellmut Rosenfeld, "Phol ende Wuodan Vuorun zi holza," *PBB/T* 95 (1973), 1–12; Lynn L. Remly, "Murder at a Gallop: the Second Merseburg Charm," *Midwestern Journal of Language and Folklore* 2 (1976): 31–39; Susan D. Fuller, "Pagan Charms in Tenth-Century Saxony? The Function of the Merseburg Charms," *Monatshefte* 72 (1980): 162–70 (with a rejoinder by Heather Stuart and F. Walla in *Germanic Notes* 14 (1983): 35–37); Murdoch, "But Did They Work?"; Meinolf Schumacher, "Geschichten-erzählzauber," in *Erzählte Welt — Welt des Erzählens: Festschrift für Dietrich Weber,* ed. Rüdiger Zymner (Cologne: Chora, 2000), 201–15; Cyril Edwards, *The Beginnings of German Literature: Comparative and Interdisciplinary Approaches to Old High German* (Rochester, NY: Camden House, 2002), 78–114 (two papers, the second of which is expressly concerned with conjectures). See also on the question of equine medicine and the charms Ute Schwab, "In sluthere bebunden," in *Studien zum Altgermanischen: Festschrift für Heinrich Beck,* ed. Heiko Uecker (Berlin and New York: De Gruyter, 1994), 554–83.

[11] See my paper "*Peri hieres nousou.* Approaches to the Old High German Medical Charms," in *Mit regulu bithuungan,* ed. J. Flood (Göppingen: Kümmerle, 1988), 142–60. The title refers to the designation of epilepsy as the sacred disease; even now, of course, it can only be controlled rather than cured, since it is strictly a condition, rather than a disease.

[12] On the idea of the static river, see F. Ohrt, *Die ältesten Segen über Christi Taufe und Christi Tod in religionsgeschichtlichem Lichte* (Copenhagen: Levin and Minksgaard, 1938); on the motif in general, see my "The River that Stopped Flowing. Folklore and Biblical Typology in the Apocryphal Lives of Adam and Eve," *Southern Folklore Quarterly* 37 (1973), 37–51. See Adolf Jacoby, *Ein bisher unbeachteter apokryphen Bericht über die Taufe Jesu* (Strasbourg: Trübner, 1902) on the antiquity of the legend.

[13] For a full range of blood charms, see Miller, *Charms*, 96–130. The Strasbourg *Tumbo* charm is on 98–103, with a discussion of the various conjectures about this complex piece, part of which seems to be a variation of the infancy story or of the Longinus legend. In general, see the typology of hemostatic charms O. Ebermann, *Blut und Wundsegen* (Berlin: Mayer and Müller, 1903) [misprinted as Erdmann in my book *Old High German*].

[14] Wipf, 80–81, prints the text from the Zurich manuscript, amends it, and comments in detail on its difficulties, 284. It is in St., 379, who includes it because it contains some Old High German words; however, mixed language is the case in virtually all the charms that are extant. See also Miller, *Charms*, 115. Here the residual reference to Longinus and to the Jordan legend suffice.

[15] Gerhard Eis, *Altdeutsche Handschriften* (Munich: Beck, 1949), 52.

[16] *The Liber de diversis medicinis in the Thornton Manuscript (MS Lincoln Cathedral A.5.2.),* ed. Margaret Sinclair Ogden (London: OUP, 1938), 56 and 63. The text, of course, is in English for the most part.

[17] See E. A. Wallis Budge, *Herb-Doctors and Physicians in the Ancient World* [1928] (Chicago: Ares, 1978); Richard Kieckhefer, *Magic in the Middle Ages* (Cambridge: CUP, 1989); Assion, *Fachliteratur,* 133–36.

[18] See Lea T. Olsan, "Latin Charms in British Library, MS Royal 12.B.XXV," *Manuscripta* 33 (1989), 119–28. Önnerfors, *Zaubersprüche* has several classical love and curse spells, and see John H. Gage, *Curse Tablets and Binding Spells from the Ancient World* (London: OUP, 1992).

[19] *Augsburger Gebet,* St. XVIII; *Sigihards Gebet,* St. XX); prayers against devils, St. LXXX and LXXXI; *Fränkisches Gebet,* St. XI; *Zürcher Hausbesegnung,* St. LXXV. Some of these smaller texts will be examined again elsewhere in this volume.

[20] St. LXXIV, Wilhelm XIX. There are many later prayers in various languages invoking the help of St. Blaise.

[21] St. LXXVIf. has the bee and dog blessings; the hail prayer is in Wilhelm XX, and the chastity prayer from Zurich is in Wilhelm XXVI. On a parallel to the bee blessing see Henk Jongeboer, "Der Lorscher Bienensegen und der ags. Charm *wiþ ymbe,*" *ABäG* 21 (1984), 63–70, with reference to bee magic, and also Edwards, *Beginnings,* 108–10. The text does not really imply that the Virgin has already commanded a swarm of bees in the past, however.

[22] St. LXXVIII; this and a number of the later *Tobiassegen* are given in Holzmann, *Ich beswer dich,* 282–99. Wipf, 94–97 prints it in its Latin context. The paper by Hugo Moser, "Vom Weingartner Reisesegen zu Walthers Ausfahrtssegen. Ge reimte Gebetssegen des frühen und hohen Mittelalters," in the *Festschrift für Elisabeth Karg-Gasterstädt, PBB/H* 82 (1961) *Sonderheft,* 69–89 is important, and for a survey taking the charms and this into account see Jean-Paul Allard (with a "Note additionelle" by Jean Haudry), "Du second charme de Mersebourg au viatique de Weingarten," *Etudes Européenes* 14 (1985): 33–59. There are some interesting comments on the petitionary prayer as such by D. Z. Phillips, *The Concept of Prayer* (London: RKP, 1965), 112–30. The *Morgensegen* is in Wilhelm XXX and XXXI.

Latin Prose: Latin Writing in the Frankish World, 700–1100

Linda Archibald

THE EARLY DEVELOPMENT of Germanic languages and literature has been much studied, even though the amount of surviving evidence on which to base such studies is quite limited. It must not be forgotten that the language of formal, official and academic communication was still predominantly Latin, and the volume of surviving Latin texts from this period exceeds that of the vernacular pieces many times over. The decline of the Roman Empire and the rise in power of the so-called barbarian tribes of northern and western Europe had resulted in a corresponding decline in the classical purity of the Latin language. In the western part of the Frankish empire it was becoming difficult to distinguish where Latin ended and the new local dialects began. The beginnings of modern Romance languages such as French, Italian, and Spanish can be traced back to this period.[1] In the spoken language particularly the structures of classical Latin were being stretched to the limits. People on the western fringes of the Carolingian empire spoke a very different language from Latin used for writing, but at least they could see connections with their daily usage and follow the gist of texts read aloud. In the central and eastern areas, where Germanic dialects and languages prevailed, there was far less similarity between the languages of daily life and the classically inspired language of written records. Educated people in these realms needed to be bilingual if they were to operate equally well in spoken and written contexts. It is around this time, therefore, that we begin to see large numbers of glosses, translations, and multilingual editions of key documents. For some reason, perhaps because the focus of scholarship has largely been on the figure of Charlemagne and his empire, much other Latin material not directly connected with him has not yet been edited, translated and analyzed for modern readers. Some of what are still the standard editions of the Latin texts are more than a century old. Perhaps the best examples are the Bible commentaries by German writers such as Hrabanus Maurus, still accessible largely in the

Patrologia Latina collection edited by J. P. Migne in the mid nineteenth century — and in addition, authorship can be disputed in many cases. The secondary literature is fragmented among different disciplines including history, theology, and philosophy as well as literary studies, all of which makes this field rather inaccessible compared to the more compact and popular vernacular literatures.

One unifying force in all this linguistic variety was the Christian church and another was the influence of the great Germanic leader Charlemagne (742–814, ruler of the Franks from 768, sole ruler from 772 and emperor from 800). The need to hold different parts of the Christian world together was a major factor in the retention of Latin as the principal means of communication for official documents. Charlemagne's empire eventually covered many territories, broadly speaking, what is now France, the Low Countries, Germany, Austria, Switzerland, and northern Italy, and his subjects spoke many different languages and dialects. Indeed the scholars whom Charlemagne gathered around him were drawn from distant corners of his empire and from the countries bordering on his territories. Beside Franks like Angilbert (ca. 740–814) there were scholars like Theodulf (ca. 750–821), a Visigoth from Spain, and Paulus Diaconus (ca. 720–800) and Paulinus of Aquileia (ca. 726–802), both Lombards, as well as various Irish monks and scholars such as the ninth-century geographer Dicuil. The best-known teacher in the group around Charlemagne was the Englishman Alcuin of York (ca. 735–804). These diverse scholars formed the core of the so-called Carolingian Renaissance and their eagerness for classical models in their poetic experiments did much to revive the older forms of Latin and promote a consistent approach to grammar and spelling across the Frankish territories. Their Latin poetry is to some extent an interesting amusement for court events, or a footnote toward the end of the history of Latin literature, but the vast collection of prose writings is their most lasting legacy.[2]

Since the mass production of manuscripts was largely centered around monasteries, most of the written texts produced display a pronounced clerical influence. Dominant themes and genres are therefore those of Biblical commentary and elementary education. Works of pure theology are less common but there is a lot of material on daily custom and practice in the religious life. There are also large numbers of biographical and historical writings that mix religious and secular content. Topics in the legal and political domains include a number of works on the legal position and responsibility of the ruler in particular, while scientific writings included a number of works on astronomy in particular. Perhaps most informative of all are the many letters written to and from the different centers of learning and power by leading figures of the day. Altogether the Latin prose writings of this period give us a full picture of the lives of educated people, their beliefs and their attitudes toward the major issues of the time.

The most famous preoccupation of the Carolingian scholars was their thirst for knowledge and their desire to capture and catalogue known facts about the world. Most of the territories ruled by Charlemagne had been exposed to the Christian gospel, but the spread of finer points of Christian doctrine in any detail was patchy. The skills of proselytizers and priests were likewise variable, and for this reason many of the early Latin prose works in the Frankish speaking region are collections of short excerpts of the Bible such as lectionaries intended for use in church services, or little set pieces like the catechism, the beatitudes, individual prayers, and psalms. Such works were useful in areas where new Christian churches and communities were being planted since they formed the basis for simple sermons that could be delivered to unsophisticated audiences. After about 800 there was a period of consolidation in which monasteries began to focus less on basic texts and more on increasingly detailed interpretations. Political stability and wealth fostered a hunger for study among a new literate elite, and of course the medium for most of this scholarly activity development was Latin prose.

To promote deeper understanding of the Bible, many monasteries set up a vast network of borrowing and copying from other monasteries. One of the favorite genres was that of the Biblical commentary. At first older, established works were collected, such as the commentaries of Jerome (around 347–419), who translated the Bible into Latin, or of Gregory the Great (around 540–604) who wrote many commentaries including one massive and much-used commentary on the problematic book of Job. These scholarly works explained the deeper meanings of the scriptures, showing how literal and spiritual levels are present in apparently simple narratives, treating the biblical text on a verse-by-verse, indeed a word-by-word basis. Another favorite in Carolingian libraries was the famous *Etymologiae* written by Isidore of Seville (around 560–636).[3] Isidore retained links with the North African Christian tradition, and thus with the older Greek and Latin past, at a time when the rest of Europe was more concerned with evangelization and political consolidation of the Christian religion in the different regions. The *Etymologiae*, which was incomplete when Isidore died, is an encyclopedic work covering the arts and the sciences in twenty books (there are sections devoted to medicine, to men and monsters, to food and drink and to war, for example), the headings introduced with often far-fetched etymological explanations. One section is devoted to languages and races, another to a kind of etymological dictionary. This preoccupation with words and their origins or meanings in Isidore's work represents the start of a new generation of commentaries — those which catalogue the natural world in such a way that everything reflects and reveals the will of the Creator. It is, in a way, a Gospel without the Bible narrative, since it is based on the premise that God speaks through everything in the world if one can only learn to interpret that message. It is difficult to overestimate the influence of these works: the notion of allegory is fundamental to Christian writings of all kinds, and it is these early Christian authors, and many more like them, who set down the theory and practice of Christian exegesis.

The greatest Carolingian commentator of all is Hraban, that is, Hrabanus Maurus (around 776–856), also known as "Blessed Maurus Magnentius Rabanus" or *Praceptor Germaniae*. Hraban studied under the English-born scholar Alcuin (around 732–804) at his school in Tours, and spent most of his life at the monastery of Fulda where he was a teacher and author of many books. He became abbot of Fulda and later archbishop of Mainz where he is remembered for his commitment to education. Following the tradition — and often the text; biblical commentaries were rarely original— of Alcuin, Bede and the earlier Church Fathers, Hraban wrote commentaries on most sections of the Bible, and his most popular works include those explaining the first five books of the Old Testament and his commentary on the Gospel of Matthew.[4] He also spent five years between 842 and 847 collecting everything he knew into an encyclopedic work called *De rerum naturis* or *De universo*.[5]

There is little in these works that could be called original. Hraban borrowed liberally from the early Church Fathers, or from more recent authors such as Bede of Northumbria, who wrote a similar work entitled *De natura rerum*.[6] He also drew on his former teacher Alcuin for his commentaries, and on the works of Isidore of Seville for his encyclopedia. He saw his task as collecting and collating information, breaking it into smaller pieces and laying it out for learners to reflect on. This tireless pursuit of meaning in everything, these lists of allegories explaining one image in terms of another, drawing parallels with people and events in the Bible, provide a storehouse of images and concepts with which to build a specifically Christian literature. They show the working behind creation, revealing connections between words and things, and finding etymological derivations to fill some of the gaps in human understanding. To modern readers the logic of Isidore, Alcuin, and Hraban may seem suspect, and their beliefs may appear fanciful on occasion, but in their time they provided valuable reference works and study texts that taught many generations of readers to question the world about them and enjoy the fascination of learning.

One of Hraban's early pieces, *De institutione clericorum* (On the education of clerics),[7] written around 810, contains some individual ideas of his own, notably his support of classical, and therefore pre-Christian Latin authors and texts in the field of education. This was a contentious issue in the ninth century, since there was widespread ambivalence toward the Latin literary heritage that Western Christians had inherited. On the one hand, the language was respected, even revered, since together with Hebrew and Greek it was deemed to be one of the holy bearers of God's written word. On the other, there was deep suspicion of the old tales of pagan gods and goddesses and the bawdy myths and drinking songs of the secular Latin tradition. Monks from Ireland had brought with them a love of storytelling, and reverence for the written word that is seen in their extraordinary calligraphic skills. The Anglo-Saxons had a more critical attitude, being wary of the corrupting influences of some classical authors, but they contributed a talent for grammatical accuracy. Alcuin in particular labored to correct the errors in the Latin texts housed in Charlemagne's libraries (and also to establish a sound Bible text) and return them to an earlier standard of grammatical accuracy.[8] Others such as the Italian grammarians Paul the Deacon and Paulinus of Aquileia retained a more acute appreciation of the pre-Christian golden age of Latin and even Greek writings, and were reluctant to dismiss centuries of their forefathers' achievement simply because of conflict with the Christian worldview. Christian authors borrowed freely from the classical language and its literary genres and patterns, but they constantly reminded themselves and each other of the moral dangers contained in the old texts.

In his role as a teacher Hraban very likely concentrated first on the Gospels and the Psalms, followed by all the other books of the Bible. He was responsible for teaching monks to read and write good Latin, and to master such tasks as preaching and teaching Christian doctrine. This is why so many of his works have an expressly pedagogical function. The old Roman system of the seven liberal arts was revived and imitated by Frankish authors, supported by the patronage of the royal families.[9] These seven subjects consisted of the *trivium* — grammar, logic and rhetoric — and of the *quadrivium* — geometry, arithmetic, astronomy and music. It is no coincidence that the first three language-based subjects were considered the essential starting point and the key skills necessary for children of noble birth and boys destined for the priesthood. Mastery of the spoken and written word opened a gateway to the world of learning and a career in the church or in the service of the nation. Regarding the teaching of languages, grammar, and rhetoric, the recognized authorities were the classical Roman texts such as Cicero's *De oratore* from the first century B.C., which recommended a severe and straightforward style, and Quintilian's *Institutio oratoria* (ca. A.D. 95) which provided guidance for speakers who needed to persuade people in a legal context. In the late Latin period (ca. A.D. 430) Martianus Capella wrote another influential text in alternating verse and prose called *De nuptiis Philologiae et Mercurii* (On the marriage of Philology and Mercury) which used a device of extended personification showing a female Philology with Mercury, the god of eloquence, as her suitor and husband. This text made much use of classical references throughout and was therefore not well suited for purely Christian applications. Many of its lessons were later borrowed and clad in a more Christian guise by Cassiodorus (around 485–570) in his much used *De institutione divinarum litterarum* (On the teaching of divine letters). Another Christian link to the classical education system is Boethius (around 470–524), whose *In librum de interpretatione* (On the interpretation of books) laments the loss of classical learning, with particular reference to Greek authors such as Aristotle and points out how useful these works are to a Christian audience. All these older texts were read in the Carolingian period, in excerpts if not in toto, and new works on the topic were also written. Bede's *De orthographia* was influential on the British tradition, and in the ninth century Alcuin wrote a book entitled *Ars grammatica*[10] and Hraban followed suit with his own book *De arte grammatica*. Besides these works on the theory of what should be taught to young learners there were many books (in manuscript form) of the type called *liber manualis,* handbooks that contained many quotations and little homilies for the edification of the reader. These were produced in great numbers and it is often hard to identify a clear authorship and source for them, especially since the content was so rarely original. One exception in this genre is, however the handbook[11] written by Dhuoda for her son William around 843. This long work written in fluent Latin prose, with some set pieces of Latin verse, is one of the few early examples of a major work written by a woman. Frequent modesty formulas betray the author's own lack of confidence in her ability and entitlement to debate deep points of theology. Where difficult concepts occur, such as the Holy Trinity, the author pleads ignorance and refers the reader to more learned authorities. The evidence of the book shows beyond doubt, however, that Dhuoda was well read and astute both intellectually and in the ways of the world. A noblewoman located in the southwest of the Carolingian empire, near what is now the Spanish border with

France, she was separated from her fourteen-year-old son William thanks to the bargaining and double-dealing of her wayward husband Bernard of Septimania. Her book instructs her teenage son to follow the teachings of the Church and be obedient to his father. Although she hints at some of the dubious temptations that William's father was renowned for, she never once criticizes Bernard or suggests that he is worthy of anything but the greatest respect. She advises William to be wary of bad influences, urging him with frequent quotations from the Bible to follow this or that example of model behavior. When a man, even a religious man, displays human frailty, she urges William not to judge too harshly, but to choose instead role models who are honest and admirable. The importance of the family's noble lineage is underlined, but there is equal emphasis on acting in an honorable way so that the good name of both maternal and paternal ancestors should not be harmed. In its mixture of maternal love, religious devotion, and practical advice this book provides a rare view of the family from the perspective of women and children and is in itself evidence of the benefits of education in the higher levels of society. As it turned out, Dhuoda's exhortations to feudal loyalty and the avoiding conspiracies and intrigue appear to have been much needed since William was executed for treason while still a young man.

Once young scholars had learned to read and understand the Christian scriptures with the help of commentaries and to compose their own sermons using various textbooks, they were ready for the third great preoccupation of the clerics: theology. Most Christian authors wrote position papers and treatises on points of doctrine, and in the first six centuries of the Church these texts laid down the shape and extent of Christian belief. In the Frankish world, however, in a context of church planting and the consolidation of a relatively new religion in a vast realm, there was an understandable reluctance to formulate original thoughts and a tendency to repeat the mainstream ideas of others or try to eliminate unorthodox beliefs or practices. Titles of works beginning with *adversus . . .* or *contra . . .* are a sure indicator that the author is an establishment figure taking issue with some controversial aspect of Christian thought. One such heresy, that of Adoptionism, was refuted by Alcuin in his *Adversus Felicus haeresin libellus* (Against the heresy of Felix).[12] The argument centered on the relationship between the divinity and the humanity of Christ, and it drew in a large number of clerics and other figures including even Charlemagne himself. In the end the matter was settled at a council held in 799 at Aachen; Alcuin's arguments formed the basis of the final resolution of the problem. These debates, and the texts which were composed in their name, show how the unity of the

Christian message was continually under pressure and how different players used the old skills of rhetoric to argue their views.

One distinctive voice in this period dared to explore new theological ground: John Scot(t)us Eriugena (ca. 800–ca. 880). As his name suggests, he was an Irishman by birth (*Eriu-gena,* Ireland-born) and he is one of the many foreign scholars who traveled from other lands to join the Franks in building up their territories as an established Christian empire. He spent most of his adult life in the Western Frankish cities of Paris and Laon. His treatise entitled *De divina praedestinatione,*[13] written around 850, added fuel to the contemporary debate on these matters, but he is remembered more for his *Periphyseon,* or *De divisione naturae,*[14] which he wrote between 862 and 866. This work reveals his familiarity with pre-Christian Greek writings; its approach is speculative and philosophical, using reason and argument to lead to faith, rather than simply listing articles of dogma culled from accepted authorities. The structure of the work is four long books in dialogue form and the source is an older Greek text called the Pseudo-Dionysus, though there is evidence too of a wider reading of early patristic authors in both Greek and Latin traditions. Technical terms from the Greek abound, but these are carefully explained, since few readers could be expected to have any knowledge of that language. These definitions synthesize classical and Christian concepts in a way that makes Eriugena one of the most innovative thinkers of his time. He takes the Carolingian fascination with the workings of the natural world one step further, leading to accusations that his transcendental interpretations stray into a distinctly unchristian form of pantheism. His book is, however, deeply Christian, and it was much read in its own time and in later centuries, providing inspiration for the mystical tradition that was popular in German branches of the Church, even though succeeding generations eventually condemned it as a form of heresy.

Points of theology were, however, not often the prime focus of attention. An inordinate amount of time and energy was spent writing down rules of conduct and formulating guidelines for the religious life. The Rule of St. Benedict, written around 530 and much studied well into the Carolingian period, formed the basis for monastic life in the West. It could, however, be interpreted in different ways by different local communities and in the struggles between branches of the royal family, the monasteries were often a target for displays of secular authority. Kings, abbots and bishops were frequently called on to make rulings on the customs to be followed by those under their care.

A fourth type of Latin prose writings can be loosely called biographical, although works in this group range from largely mythical saints' lives retold from earlier authorities, to tales of key clerical or political figures who were known personally to the author. Perhaps the most famous biography in this period is that of Charlemagne, the *Vita Karoli Magni*[15] by Einhard (around 770–840, also known as Eginhard). Another graduate of the school at Fulda and later of the palace school at Aachen, Einhard completed his most famous work in around 830, proud of the fact that he was an eyewitness to the greatness of the emperor and as such qualified to compose a record of his life. He followed the style of the Latin author Suetonius (around 69–122) whose *De Vita Caesarum* provided a suitably respected classical model. As one would expect of a work written in court circles with relatives of the great man still in positions of power, the account of the hero is extremely positive. In clear, correct, almost classical Latin, Einhard recounts the major deeds of the emperor, not forgetting his charitable works. His depiction of Charlemagne has many human touches, for example a description of the imposing figure of Charlemagne with fair hair and a happy disposition, but he does not forget to mention also his thick neck and protruding stomach. Similarly Einhard tells how Charlemagne loved hunting and swimming but in later years hated the royal physicians who advised him against the rich diet of roast meats that he loved. In thirty-three chapters Einhard covers Charlemagne's immediate ancestors, his rise to power, military campaigns, his daily life including an enthusiasm for learning and kindness to the poor, and then finally his duties as emperor and his death in 814.

A second author, Notker Balbulus (around 840–912), or Notker the Stammerer, also wrote a life of Charlemagne called *Gesta Karoli Magni imperatoris*[16] around 883. This text has survived in fragmentary form. He composed a longer *Martyrologium*[17] which updates the stories of various martyrs told by earlier authors including Hraban. The boundary between hagiography and biography is blurred in this period, since authors frequently included legends and miracles as well as what modern readers would regard as facts, and often adherence to source material derived from an older text interferes with the main story.

A large body of surviving material deals with the preservation and daily operation of the laws of the land. In Frankish territories this was a particularly complex matter, since no single set of laws was recognized universally. The older, pre-Roman laws co-existed alongside the Roman tradition, the newer Church laws, and the rulings of contemporary monarchs and senior clerics. Valuable records of land transfers, marriages, genealogical origins, and inheritances depended on these older legal frameworks, and any claims in the ninth century and beyond were argued on the basis of these old records and customs. This is why the Carolingian libraries contain so many copies of the *Lex Salica* (Laws of the Salian Franks), *Lex Ribuaria* (Laws of the Ripuarian Franks), *Lex Alamannorum* (Laws of the Alemanni), and *Lex Burgundionum* (Laws of the Burgundians),[18] even though it is unlikely that the letter of these old laws continued to be used in contemporary transactions. These documents appear to hark back to the sixth century, even though the first manuscripts are later and the majority of surviving examples are from the ninth century. They consist largely of long lists of crimes ranging from the giving of herbs leading to the death of the patient, to non-appearance to answer a charge, to more serious offenses such as theft, rape, and murder. The punishments usually consist of fines, which are specified exactly in the appropriate currency, to be paid by the guilty person, or in some cases, by his or her family. High importance was given to land and property matters because these were the basis for tithes and taxes, and for mustering armies, and they formed the foundations of worldly power and influence.

Studies by Rosamond McKitterick[19] in particular have done much to illuminate this vast field, and thanks to her we can appreciate just how much Frankish society depended on the Latin written word while conducting its daily business. This is not to say that there was a high level of literacy or a widespread enthusiasm for legal studies. In this period, as in all others, the surviving records chart the lives of the ruling elite, not the concerns of the vast numbers of ordinary people. It is not even certain that the landowners and nobility were competent readers and writers, since most of these activities were carried out by notaries and scribes. The standard method of dissemination of information was by proclamation or reading aloud.

This complex mingling of different legal traditions, often mediated by visiting scholars from a completely different geographical and social background, led to much debate about competing standards. It is a story of claims and counterclaims, exploited by those who had the knowledge to play one set of rules against another. There is evidence, too, of a large number of Carolingian forgeries, suggesting that some people at least knew how to exploit those whose faith in the written word was not underpinned by a deep knowledge of its production and history.

Among the practical writings found in this period are some that could be called scientific, including lists and tables used for calculating dates and times. A certain amount of knowledge had been inherited from

Greek and Middle Eastern scholars but many of the underlying theories had been lost, leaving chroniclers unable to work out the contradictions in the disparate sources they worked on. Confusion over the dates of Easter or different feast days, or the different calendars used by different authors, or inability to calculate the likely recurrence of natural events led some to reflect more deeply on the nature of the physical world. The most famous of these early scientific writers was Hermann the Lame (1013–1054) also known by his Latin name Hermannus Contractus. One of the most brilliant thinkers of the time, he developed an interest in music and the planetary spheres and obtained information on some ancient theories, most probably through secondhand Latin sources received via Spain rather from original Greek or Arabic authors. He admits to collecting such works avidly, and wrote two important pieces on the astrolabe,[20] a mathematical instrument used for navigation and for measuring heights and distances. He constructed astrolabes himself and his two papers give details on how to make them and use them, with suitable adjustments for his own location in Frankish territories. These texts were widely copied and used until well into the fourteenth century. Large monasteries such as Reichenau and St. Gallen, and famous centers of learning such as Aachen and Fulda were also repositories for numerous small manuscripts containing snippets of factual information on the life and work of these communities. Lists of names and dates, tariffs and shopping lists, measurements and plans for new buildings and designs for all the trappings of the religious life are also an important resource for historians of this period.

The final category of Latin prose which completes our characterization of this period is that of letters. The long Roman tradition of epistle writing and the New Testament letters of St. Paul provided suitable models for the Carolingians. Topics range from letters sent by clerics to their flock, or to contacts in distant parts of the Christian community, to doctrinal or political polemics, designed to be circulated and read by supporters and opponents alike.[21] Since separation from home and loved ones is often the greatest motivation for letter writing, it is not surprising that British scholar Alcuin was one of the most prolific letter writers, with more than two hundred on record, although some of the pieces which have been ascribed to him may not in fact be genuinely his work.[22] Sometimes current events or issues prompt the writing of strongly worded public letters, such as that by Archbishop Hincmar of Reims (806–82), for example, who was moved to write a piece entitled *De divortio Lotharii* (On the divorce of Lothar)[23] which was openly critical of that king's decision to leave his wife Theutberg and marry Waltrade instead. Although the argument may have been based on the standards of behavior expected of a Christian king, the motivation of this piece almost certainly had to do with the power struggles between Lothar and Charles the Bald, whom Hincmar supported. Never one to be afraid of conflict, Hincmar appears to have written letters about every prominent issue of his day, though much of this material has probably been lost. Some letter writers, such as the prolific Einhard, for example, reveal much personal detail which adds interest and depth to the sometimes dry material of sermons and speeches.[24]

This large and varied body of Latin prose writing provides the context within which the new Germanic literature emerges, and the recent re-awakening of interest in these authors is to be welcomed: it is important that they should not be neglected within the context of the beginnings of German vernacular literature, even if the connections are not always close or immediately apparent. Although the future — and a longterm one at that — was to bring a fragmented literary landscape across Western Europe, following the trend toward nationalism and linguistic diversity, both form and content of these new literatures were to be much influenced by the Latin prose of this period.

Notes

[1] For more detail see Roger Wright, *Late Latin and Early Romance in Spain and Carolingian France* (Liverpool: Francis Cairns, 1982) and also his later volume *Latin and the Romance Languages in The Early Middle Ages* (University Park, PA: Pennsylvania State UP, 1996).

[2] M. L. W. Laistner, *Thought and Letters in Western Europe AD 500–900*, 2nd ed. (London: Methuen, 1957).

[3] *PL* 82, 73–728, and ed. W. M. Lindsay (Oxford: Clarendon, 1911).

[4] The largest collection of Hraban's works is in *PL* 107–12.

[5] *PL* 111, 9–614.

[6] Bede's works can be found in *PL* 90–94.

[7] *PL* 107, 295–420.

[8] See Vivien Law, "Linguistics in the Earlier Middle Ages: the Insular and Carolingian Grammarians," *Transactions of the Philological Society* (1985), 171–93.

[9] For further information on the classical tradition see D. L. Wagner, ed., *The Seven Liberal Arts in the Middle Ages* (Bloomington, IN: Indiana UP, 1983) and Ursula Schaefer, ed., *Artes im Mittelalter* (Berlin: Akademie, 1999).

[10] *PL* 101, 849–902.

[11] *Dhuoda, Handbook for her Warrior Son, Liber Manualis,* edited and translated into English by Marcelle Thiébaux (Cambridge and New York: CUP, 1998).

[12] For a full study of the ideas and writings connected with the Adoptionist heresy see John C. Cavadini, *The Last Christology of the West: Adoptionism in Spain and Gaul 785–850* (Philadelphia, PA: U Pennsylvania P, 1993).

[13] For more detail on the thinking of this important author see Deirdre Carabine, *John Scotus Eriugena* (Oxford and New York: OUP, 2000). The text is edited by Goulven Madec (Turnhout: Brepols, 1978).

[14] *Periphyseon (De divisione naturae)*, ed. J. P. Sheldon Williams and Ludwig Bieler (Dublin: Institute for Advanced Studies, 1968–81).

[15] *Einhardi Vita Karoli Magni*, ed. G. H. Pertz and G. Waitz, 6th ed. by Oswald Holder-Egger (Hanover, Hahn/MGH, 1911, repr. 1947).

[16] Ed. Hans F. Haefele (Hanover: Hahn /MGH, 1959).

[17] *PL* 131, 1029–1164.

[18] See Rosamond McKitterick, *The Carolingians and the Written Word* (Cambridge and New York: CUP, 1989), especially Chapter 2, "Law and the Written Word," 23–75, for a description of the different laws and a good summary of key issues. The Laws themselves are edited in the many volumes of the Monumenta Germaniae Historica subsection *Leges,* especially the folio volumes and the quarto series *Leges nationum Germanicarum.*

[19] See for example, Rosamond McKitterick, ed., *The Uses of Literacy in Early Medieval Europe* (Cambridge: CUP, 1992); also Rosamond McKitterick, ed., *Carolingian Culture: Emulation and Innovation* (Cambridge: CUP, 1993).

[20] *De astrolabio* (On the astrolabe), *PL* 143, 389–408, and *De mensura astrolabii* (On the measurements of the astrolabe), *PL* 143, 481–90.

[21] There is a large collection of these letters (*Epistolae Karolini aevi*) in the six later volumes of the Monumenta Germaniae Historica subsection *Epistolae* (vols. 3–8). It might be noted that the letters of Lupus of Ferrières (vol. 6) merit attention for the interest that he shows in the German language; see Brian Murdoch, "Lupus of Ferrières," in *German Writers of the Early Middle Ages: 800–1170,* ed. Will Hasty and James Hardin (New York: Gale, 1995), 88–91.

[22] An excellent introduction in English to Alcuin's thought through his letters can be found in Stephen Allott, *Alcuin of York — His Life and Letters* (York: William Sessions, 1974).

[23] *PL* 125, 659–80.

[24] For translations and analyses of Einhard's work, including his letters, see Paul Dutton, *Charlemagne's Courtier: The Complete Einhard* (Peterborough, ON: Broadview, 1998).

Latin Verse

Stephen Penn

L ITERARY ACTIVITY in early medieval Germany, as throughout most of medieval Europe, was dominated by the production of Latin texts rather than those in the vernacular, and these texts form an important part of the history of German literature in the early period. From the beginning of the reign of Pépin the Short, the first Carolingian ruler, largely as a result of reforms instituted by Charlemagne, the Latin language had acquired an unprecedented authority among educators, courtiers, and ecclesiastics. Its privileged status was maintained, as recent research has suggested, by the curricular centrality of *grammatica,* the first of the seven liberal arts, within the most powerful educational institutions of the Carolingian empire (both within and outside the Germanic kingdoms).[1] As a written literary language, by comparison, Old High German remained comparatively neglected, lacking both the authority of Latin and the weight of an established literary tradition. Therefore, relatively few vernacular texts were copied and circulated, and many survive, sometimes fragmentarily, in unique manuscripts. That these had been read within the context of a predominantly Latin culture is often clear from their authors' words, but a more subtle dialogue between Latin and the vernacular is also apparent from the texts themselves. Typically, the vernacular manifested itself in glosses and translations, whose derivative status is clear. Translation of German verse into Latin was unusual, but the preservation of a complete Latin text from the eleventh century (the *Galluslied*) suggests that even in such cases, the Latin rendering was generally prized above the vernacular original (which was either lost or destroyed). It was not invariably the case, nevertheless, that German literary culture resisted vernacular innovation. This is nowhere more apparent than in the small number of texts that combine Latin and German within a single line of verse.

The Germanic kingdoms fell under Carolingian Frankish control throughout the early history of this period. The production of Latin texts (broadly construed so as to include the composition of prose tracts, commentaries and marginalia, as well as educational documents) was inextricably linked with the activities and educational policies of Charlemagne and his Carolingian successors. This should not frustrate our attempts, nevertheless, to speak of "German" poetic traditions, authors, or texts. Nor should we assume that the educational infrastructure that Charlemagne had established through the activities of his advisors and educators, and through his wide-ranging educational reforms, simply dissolved with the accession of Otto I in 936. Indeed, the labels "Carolingian," "Ottonian" and "Salian" do much to obscure the cultural and political continuities that run through the period extending from the mid-eighth to the mid-tenth centuries.

Carolingian Poetry

The court functioned as the political and administrative core of the Frankish empire, but under Charlemagne, it also became the focus of a broader process of cultural reform. The writing of verse and prose was the central literary activity, but it was not an isolated pursuit, nor were any of the Carolingian poets confined to poetic composition as a vocation. Many were actively involved in political life, either as advisors to the king, as diplomats, or as missionaries, and those who were devoted to scholarship alone were engaged in research of various kinds besides poetic composition. This should not be taken to imply, of course, that poets were employed by Charlemagne in a casual or unsystematic manner. Charlemagne sought to attract the best scholars in Europe into his service, as the principal means by which to bring about the revival of learning to which he was so passionately committed. Charlemagne, like the majority of Frankish kings, did not remain in a fixed location throughout the period of his rule, and we should avoid considering the "court" as a single place in which a king and his attendants and advisors assembled. Nevertheless, there were locations from which the court operated for sustained periods. The most significant of these for Charlemagne and his successor, Lewis the Pious, was Aachen (Aix-la-Chapelle), which is often regarded as the capital, or at least the northern capital of the Carolingian empire. This was the location of Charlemagne's "Palace School" (completed in 794), in which king, courtiers, and poets could live and work together. Though Aachen itself, as a German city, might legitimately be regarded as a center of German literary activity, Charlemagne's court was not populated exclusively — or even principally — by German scholars and advisors. Alcuin (Albinus), the most renowned and influential of his advisors, was born and lived for most of his life in York before moving to Aachen at Charlemagne's request in the last decades of the eighth century. Alcuin was an accomplished scholar and a prolific poet, whose educational policies, together with his own poetic achievements, exerted a profound influence on the poets of Aachen, whether German by birth or not. It was he, above any other scholar, who encouraged the self-conscious classicism so often associated with Carolingian verse generally, and with the work of the Aachen poets in particular. In a brief elegy almost certainly composed by Alcuin, *O Mea Cella* (O my cell), the poet speaks wistfully of the rich scholarly life of Aachen, lost with Alcuin's own relocation to Tours (where he became abbot) in 796. Here, he refers to himself as "Flaccus" (Horace) and to his fellow teacher and former student, Angilbert, as "Homerus," reflecting both his commitment to literary scholarship, and to the authors and texts of ancient Greece and Rome. He addresses his remarks to Aachen itself (whose scholarly environment is the "cella" of his title):[2]

> In te personuit quondam vox alma magistri,
> Quae sacro sophiae tradidit ore libros.
> In te temporibus certis laus sancta tonantis
> Pacificis sonuit vocibus atque animis.
> Te, mea cella, modo lacrimosis plango camaenis
> Atque gemens casus pectore plango tuos;
> Tu subito quoniam fugisti carmina vatum
> Atque ignota manus te modo tota tenet.
> Te modo nec Flaccus nec vatis Homerus habebit,
> Nec pueri musas per tua tecta canunt. (vv. 13–22)

> [In you the gentle voices of the teachers could once be heard
> expounding with their hallowed lips the books of Wisdom.
> In you at set times the holy praise of God
> resounded from peaceful minds in peaceful words.
> For you, my cell, I now lament with tearful poetry;
> groaning, I bewail at heart your decline,
> for you suddenly fled from the songs of the poets
> and a stranger's hand now has you in its grasp.
> You shall belong neither to Flaccus nor to Homer the poet,
> and no boys sing songs under your roof.]

It was ironically at Tours, rather than Aachen, that these lines, and the majority of Alcuin's many poetic works were composed. Nevertheless, his vision of scholarly life at Aachen, albeit an idyllic rather than a literal one, clearly reflects its perceived importance as a literary and intellectual center in eighth-century Europe.

The classical models and conventions Alcuin felt to be so important to the practicing poet are conspicuous in the works of all of the most celebrated Aachen writers, and were emulated extensively by their Ottonian and Salian successors. The heroic devices of Virgil's *Aeneid* became familiar to the Carolingian audience as celebratory conventions in political poetry, while the *Eclogues* acted as a model for the flourishing pastoral. The dactylic hexameter (known chiefly to the Carolingians from Virgil's *Aeneid*), and the metrically identical Leonine hexameter (but distinguished by having medial and final rhyming syllables), established themselves as popular forms both within and outside the context of heroic verse. Among the most skilled of Charlemagne's courtiers in his employment of metrical conventions was the Spanish Visigoth Theodulf of Orléans (ca.760–821). In a laudatory verse epistle to Charlemagne, Theodulf chooses the dactylic hexameter (together with other Virgilian conventions) to convey his admiration to the king (divisions between feet are marked with an oblique slash):

> Tē tōt/ūs lāūd/ēsquĕ tŭ/ās, rēx/, pērsŏnăt/ ōrbĭs; (v. 1)

> [The entire world resounds in your praise, my king;]

It would be impossible, Theodulf suggests, to do justice to Charlemagne's magnificence in a poem of this kind, but he clearly felt that the formal and descriptive conventions of classical poetry would bring him closer. The emperor's appearance is described in intricate detail, with extensive use of Virgilian heroic imagery. There is no aspect of this man, we are told, which cannot be praised: *est non laudabile cui nil* (v. 19). Theodulf's scholarship and poetic skill must owe something to the wealth of textual resources available to him as a student, though no firm evidence exists to associate him with any single center of learning.

Poets of the Carolingian and Ottonian courts were eager to lavish praise on their rulers (and patrons) through the dignified medium of Latin, and to magnify this praise through the use of elevated stylistic forms and classical allusion. One of the most elaborate Carolingian panegyrics occurs at the beginning of the *Karolus Magnus et Leo Papa*, a text attributed at an early stage to the Frankish historian Einhard (ca. 770–840), author of the celebrated prose *Vita Karoli Magni*. The poem is thought to have formed the concluding part of a longer work, whose preceding sections have been lost. The poem tells of the meeting between Charlemagne and Pope Leo I at Paderborn, but also gives an impressive description of the building of city walls around Aachen, here described as *Roma seconda* and *ventura Roma* (the future Rome).[3] The poem's hexameters, like those of Theodulf, portray the emperor in flamboyant detail, highlighting his classical-heroic qualities. So extensive are the Virgilian echoes in the poem that it has been described as a "refashioning of the *Aeneid*," in which Charlemagne is the new Aeneas.[4] The poet depicts the king as an outstanding leader, a just legislator, and a peerless warrior:

> Armipotens Karolus, victor pius atque triumphans
> Rex, cunctos superat reges bonitate per orbem:
> Iustior est cunctis cunctisque potentior exstat. (vv. 27–29)

> [Charlemagne, a powerful warlord, a compassionate victor
> and triumphant king, excels in goodness all kings in the world,
> standing out as more just and powerful than them all.]

Latin Panegyric writing was to flourish in the Ottonian period, but the work of Theodulf and his contemporaries also finds an isolated, roughly contemporary parallel in the German vernacular. The German *Ludwigslied*, which is discussed in more detail in other chapters of this volume, tells of the victory of Louis III of France over the Vikings in 881, and was probably composed relatively soon after this date. The manuscript in which it is found originated outside Germany in St. Amand sur l'Elnon,[5] and although it is not a poem about a German king, nor one that can be connected with German territories in any obvious way, it is otherwise similar in thematic, if not in stylistic or rhetorical terms, to contemporary Latin panegyrics composed in Germany. Its author's use of a Franconian dialect of Old High German may not have brought it the prestige of Theodulf's Latin poetry, but it can leave us in no doubt of its Germanic provenance:

> Einan kuning uueiz ih,   Heizsit her Hluduig,
> Ther gerno gode thionot: Ih uueiz her imos lonot.
> Kind uuarth her faterlos,   Thes uuarth imo sar buoz:
> Holoda inan truhtin,   Magaczogo uuarth her sin. (vv. 1–4)

> [I know of a king,   who is called Louis,
> who readily served God: I know he was rewarded.
> As a child, he was fatherless,   but he was compensated for this:
> The Lord God was his guide,   and his teacher.]

Theodulf had regarded Charlemagne as a divine agent, fulfilling God's commands and bringing his word to the heathen. Louis is here seen in a similar light, but the poet gives greater emphasis to the association between king and God. Though the relationship between the poet and the French Carolingian king must remain uncertain, it seems clear that, as with the Latin tradition, he hoped that his poem would survive as a monument to this distinguished historical figure.

The Carolingian court was not the only environment in which poetic culture flourished. The monastic school of Fulda is associated, in different ways, with three distinguished German poets in Latin: Hrabanus Maurus (ca. 784–856), Walahfrid Strabo (ca. 808–849), and Gottschalk of Orbais (ca. 805–869). Hraban, who himself studied under Alcuin, was a teacher who became abbot of Fulda between 822 and 841, after which he was forced into political exile. In 847, after settling his differences with Ludwig the German, he became archbishop of Mainz. One of the few things that can be said with any certainty about Hraban is that he was a prolific writer, even if the real extent of his writings is likely to remain open to question. The majority of his works were biblical commentaries, but he also produced some notable educational tracts, including *De rerum naturis*,[6] which followed closely the expository paradigm established by the popular encyclopedia known as the *Etymologiae* of Isidore of Seville, and an innovative commentary on Priscian's *Institutiones grammaticae*.[7] With few exceptions, these prose commentaries and educational texts have attracted far greater attention than Hraban's poetry. Part of the reason for this may lie with the ongoing, problematic debates surrounding authorial ascription and poetic merit.

It is unfortunate that the celebrated Pentecostal hymn, *Veni, Creator Spiritus* (Come, creator spirit), cannot be ascribed to Hraban with any certainty.[8] Addressed, as its title suggests, to the Holy Spirit, the poem presents an appeal for spiritual guidance and for protection from "the enemy." The hymn's significance in church history is marked by its habitual use throughout medieval Europe at the coronation of kings, the ordination of priests and at the celebration of papal inauguration. Its opening also appears in the nineteenth passus of Langland's *Piers Plowman,* nearly five centuries after it was first recorded, when Will is urged by Conscience, at Pentecost, to pray.[9] Over twenty hymns have been ascribed to Hraban in total (with varying degrees of certainty), including one celebrating the birthday of Christ (*Hymnus de natale Christi*), one on the purification of the Virgin (*Hymnus in purificatione Sanctae Mariae*), one on the Ascension (*In ascensione Domini ad vesperum*) and two martyrological hymns on St. Marcellinus and Peter the Martyr. Among his longest and most complex writings is *De laudibus Sanctae Crucis* (In praise of the Holy Cross), two books of poems that take a variety of elaborate visual shapes (*figurae*) and are each followed by a prose *declaratio* (an expository passage relating to the substance of the poem). Poems of this kind, sometimes referred to as "figure poems" or *carmina figurata,* enjoyed a degree of popularity during the Carolingian period.[10] Hraban carried them to new heights of creativity and ingenuity.

The poems within *De laudibus* raise a sequence of carefully defined theological questions connected with the cross. The sixth of these, *De quattuor virtutibus principalibus quomodo ad crucem pertineant, et quod omnium virtutum fructus per ipsam nobis collati sunt* (On the four cardinal virtues, how they may relate to the cross, and how the fruit of all virtues, through it, are bestowed upon us), considers the function of the four cardinal virtues (prudence, justice, temperance, and fortitude), and concludes with an extended metaphorical description of their "fruits."

The second of the Fulda poets, Wala(h)frid Strabo (Walahfrid the squinter), studied first in the monastery of the Reichenau, on Lake Constance, and probably traveled to Fulda to complete his studies, under the guidance of Hraban, in 827. He returned to the Reichenau later, becoming abbot there in 838. Like Hraban, he was a gifted scholar and wrote commentaries on a number of biblical texts. He was long thought, indeed, to have produced the *Glossa ordinaria* which, during the later medieval period, became the standard academic commentary on the Bible, although this sequence of marginal and interlinear biblical explanations is now known to have been the work of more than one scholar and to have originated probably in the commentaries of the twelfth-century theologian, Anselm of Laon. The removal of the *Glossa* should not detract significantly from Walahfrid's achievement as a scholar, however. Among those texts which certainly were produced by him are several lengthy hagiographical prose tracts, including a life of St. Gall. His first poetic work, written while Walahfrid was still a very young man, describes a vision experienced by Wetti on his sickbed, which, as its preface (addressed to Grimald) reveals, was first recorded in prose (*prosaicis verbis*) by Haito.[11] The text of the *Visio Wettini* (Wetti's vision) was written for Grimald, by whom, he suggests, he was urged secretly to make a copy in hexametric verse (*versibus hexametris furtim exemplare coactus sum*).[12] The longest of its sequence of narrative verses, entitled *De Wettino et eius aetate* (On Wetti and his time), tells of a nightmarish vision of demons, who are eventually driven away from Wetti by an angel. The account is a detailed one, written in memory of a man whom Walahfrid clearly respected highly, as the opening lines of this section of the poem reveal:

> Spiritus alme veni, nostraeque adjungere Musae
> Unius ut vitam praestanti fine capessam.
> Perge Camoena, virum quem supra, tolle, reliqui,
> Nam Wettinus erat celebri rumore magister,

Artibus instructus septem de more priorum,
Cui fortuna dedit scholis adnectier illis
Quis gaudere solet nitida et lasciva iuventus. (vv. 173–79)

[Kindly Spirit, come and join my Muse, that I may treat of one man's life that came to a distinguished close. Come, Muse, extol the man whose praises I left off above. Wetti was a teacher of great renown, instructed in the seven arts in the manner of our ancestors. Fortune granted that he be charged with those scholarly pursuits which it is usual for sleek, light-hearted youth to enjoy.][13]

As Walahfrid suggests in his preface, the poem is written in dactylic hexameter lines, in keeping with its elevated, if not strictly "heroic," subject matter. The vision it describes is related as historical fact, having taken place, Walahfrid suggests, on Sunday 30 October, 824, in the eleventh year of Lewis the Pious's reign. Nevertheless, it adheres to recognizable dream-vision conventions (those, in particular, of the so-called otherworld vision[14]), and, as a critique of contemporary ecclesiastical corruption, contains a number of satirical commonplaces. It arose, we are told, as a result of Wetti's reaction to a health potion, which causes him first to vomit, and then to refuse food. When he finally retires to bed, he is met by the vision of a devil, who, dressed in priest's clothing (*clericus in specie*), tells him *Cras torqueris, meritumque rependitur omne* (Tomorrow you will be tortured; you will receive your every desert, v. 213). After the devil has been driven away, Wetti awakens, and is approached by his brothers. Soon, the angel who expelled the devil returns, dressed in white, and is now described as having been sent from highest heaven. The angel praises Wetti for his devotion to God, and recommends to him the 118th Psalm. After this, a series of other visions follow. The angel leads the monk down a *via amoena* (pleasant path), where he is met with a remarkable sight:

Dum vadunt, montana vident, quae sidera tangunt
Marmoris in specie pulchro commixta colore,
Quaeque in circuitu praecingens igneus amnis
Ambit inexhaustos tribuens intrantibus ignes.
In quo multa nimis monstrata est turba reorum,
Inque locis aliis diversas facta sequentes
Agnovit poenas, multosque recumbere dudum
Quos habuit notos; ibi maior et alter in undis
Ordo sacerdotum praefixo stipite vinctus
Terga dedit vinclis, quae curis carne superbis. (vv. 312–21)

[As they went along the way they saw mountains that touched the stars; they were tinged with a beautiful hue and looked like marble. Circling around the mountains ran a river of fire which poured its unquenchable fires on those who stepped into its waters. In it could be seen a vast throng of damned souls; and in other places Wetti observed different punishments being meted out for sins, noticing that many whom he had known were lying there. There in the stream stood priests of higher and lower rank, tied to upright stakes, their backs turned towards the bonds which shackle those which are proud in the flesh.[15]]

This vision of Hell draws conspicuously on both pagan and Christian literary conventions, most notably, as David Traill has pointed out, on the image of the classical Phlegethon (a river of fire in the underworld).[16] The presence within the river of fire of figures whom Wetti recognizes, including the different *ordines sacerdotum* (orders of priests), serves as a reminder of Walahfrid's (and Haito's) desire to expose the corruption of the contemporary clergy. A devotion to worldly pleasures and desires, Wetti learns, has led many priests astray, and has turned monks away from the teaching of the fathers of the Church. The angel warns him, later in the poem, that after his virtuous childhood, he has renounced the apostolic lifestyle, and succumbed to the worldly temptations of many of those he sees around him. However, the fact that he is now repentant *toto corde* (with the whole heart], and looks on these past errors with tearful regret, gives the angel faith in his ability to deliver to his audience a warning about the dangers of physical indulgence.

For Walahfrid, the process of composition was clearly a self-conscious one, as his loyalty to his teachers and patrons, as well as to the muse, reveals. At the beginning of *De Imagine Tetrici* (On the statue of Tetricus), a long poem about a statue of Theodoric the Great (identified as "Tetricus" in the text), he conducts an extended imaginary conversation with his muse, Scintilla (spark).[17] The statue the poem describes stood in front of the palace in Aachen, brought there by Charlemagne in 801. It is a highly crafted poem, which draws conspicuously on Virgilian language, themes and poetic conventions. Walahfrid asks Scintilla why she fails to respond to him during the months of spring, which are presented in idyllic pastoral detail:

Iam spatiis crevere dies, dulcescit et umbra,
In flores partusque novos, et gaudia fructus
Herba recens arbos datur, et genus omne animantum (vv. 4–6)

[Now the days have grown longer, and the shade grows sweet
With young and new flowers, and the delights of fruit
A new tree grows on the grass, together with every kind of
    living thing.]

The response is a nostalgic one, which looks to the days of peace and leisure that the older poets (*veteres poetae*) enjoyed. Today, though, *pro siluis, hederis, echone, coturno* (instead of groves, ivy, echoes, and fine phrases), we have *immanes tumultus* (horrid commotions) all around. After this wistful opening, the poet, with Scintilla's guidance, examines the statue itself, before concluding with laudatory words on rulers and teachers known to him, including his respected mentor, Grimald.

Gottschalk of Orbais, who became friends with Walahfrid during his time as an oblate at Fulda, enjoyed a less comfortable relationship with Hrabanus Maurus than his companion. Having been sent to Fulda by his parents, Gottschalk soon discovered that he had no desire for a religious career, and asked Hraban's permission to leave. Predictably, the abbot declined, and Gottschalk, after attempting to escape from Fulda and to renounce his vows, was sent, on Hraban's recommendation, to the monastery at Orbais. It was here that he developed his controversial theory of predestination, which was condemned by Hraban in a lengthy prose treatise. Gottschalk's faith in his theory is witnessed by some of his surviving prose writings, but the criticism it attracted from his contemporaries, which culminated in a formal condemnation at the Council of Mainz, left him politically and intellectually isolated. His sense of isolation is conveyed most famously in his evocative poem *Ut quid iubes, pusiole?* (Why are you asking, little boy?)[18] in which he imagines his response to a young boy who asks him to sing. The first six strophes are offered as an explanation of Gottschalk's reluctance to sing, and are linked by the refrain *O cur iubes canere?* (O why are you telling me to sing?). This is not the occasion, he argues, in six-line, rhymed strophes, for the performance of poetry:

> 3. Mallem scias, pusillule,
> ut velles tu, fratercule,
> pio corde condolere
> mihi atque prona mente
> conlugere.
> O cur iubes canere?[19]
>
> [You should know, little one,
> That I would sooner, little brother,

That you sympathized with pious heart
And, with humble spirit,
Grieved for me
O why are you telling me to sing?]

From strophe seven Gottschalk's attitude — and his refrain — changes. Because the child has asked him, he now has cause to sing, and does so willingly. Only one word of the refrain, *hoc* (this), is now repeated, except in strophes eleven and thirteen. The emphasis of the poem now becomes religious, as Gottschalk declares, *canam patri filioque* (I shall sing to the Father and to the Son). It becomes the song he has been asked to sing:

8.   "Benedictus es, domine,
pater, nate, paraclite
deus trine, deus une,
deus summe, deus pie,
deus iuste."
Hoc cano spontanee.[20]

["Blessed art Thou, Lord,
Father, Son, Holy Ghost,
God in Three, God in One,
Almighty God, kindly God,
Just God." This I sing voluntarily.]

The poem was probably composed during Gottschalk's period of exile at the Reichenau. It has been regarded as "among the most outstanding works of ninth-century rhythmical poetry," and as a "masterpiece, both in form and content."[21] It was transcribed with an accompanying melody, which has been reconstructed, using modern musical notation, by contemporary scholars.[22] We should not, of course, allow Gottschalk's genuine exile to blind us to the popular topos underlying the song; Dronke identifies exile as "one of the most frequent and moving themes of Germanic poetry."[23]

Another center of literary activity from the Carolingian period on was the monastery at St. Gallen, in what is now Switzerland. Among the most prolific and original of the St. Gallen writers is Notker Balbulus (Notker the Stammerer), who resided there during the ninth and early tenth centuries. Notker was not the only literary figure of St. Gallen to bear that name, though he was the only one to write consistently in verse. The third monk of the same name, Notker Labeo (thick-lipped Notker), who later attracted the alternative epithet "Teutonicus" (the

German) and who died in 1022, is at least as significant as a literary figure, but wrote almost exclusively in prose. He made innovative use of the German language in works such as his Old High German translation and commentary of Martianus Capella's educational poem, *De nuptiis Philologiae et Mercurii* (On the marriage of Mercury and Philology).

Notker Balbulus, however, is chiefly associated with sequences of verses composed according to strict syllabic rules. These survive in a number of liturgical cycles, which begin with a sequence for Christmas day. Among his other Latin writings are a life of St. Gall and a prose life of Charlemagne (*De Karolo Magno*). The latter cannot be ascribed to Notker with complete certainty, though it is now generally accepted that he is most likely to have been the author. Notker produced some of the most finely crafted poetic sequences, but, as F. J. E. Raby has rightly pointed out, he made no claim to have invented the form of the sequence himself, despite having often been credited with this.[24] In the proem to his *Liber Hymnorum,* he speaks of having composed long songs in his youth, which have now begun to slip from his memory.[25] While considering the problem of how they might be collected together and recorded, he is visited by a priest from Gimedia. The priest shows him a book of antiphons, some of which are arranged into sequences. With the guidance of his two masters at the monastery, Iso and Moengall (Marcellus), Notker sought to imitate these. Delighted with his efforts, we are told, Moengall collected these verses together into cycles (*rotulae*).[26] In each of Notker's sequences, the lines of adjacent strophes correspond syllabically. This can be illustrated with two strophes from the first sequence from the *Liber Hymnorum,* entitled *In Natale Domini Nostri Jesu Christi* (On the birthday of our Lord Jesus Christ):

Gaude, dei genitrix,	Christe patris unice,
quam circumstant obstetricum vice	qui humanam nostri causa formam
concinentes angeli	assumsisti, refove
gloriam deo.	supplices tuos[27]
[Rejoice, mother of God,	[Christ, one with the father
around whom, as midwives,	who, for our sake,
the angels stand,	assumed human form,
singing glory to God.]	revive your worshippers!]

From the Latin text of the above (strophes nine and ten, respectively, in the sequence), it is not difficult to perceive the pattern of exact syllabic correspondences. Lines one, two, three and four contain seven, ten, seven and five syllables, respectively. Notker employed a variety of syllabic patterns in his book of hymns (and elsewhere), many of which are unique to the sequences in which they occur. Though not all of his poems took the form of sequences, these were undoubtedly his preferred mode of expression, and that with which his name is invariably associated.

Ottonian and Salian Literature

Otto I ("the Great") succeeded his father, Henry, as king of Germany in 936. Though the Ottonian court did not function as a center of literary activity comparable to that of the Carolingians, the tenth century nevertheless witnessed a flourishing tradition of Latin poetry in Germany. The most significant collection of lyric poetry of the period survives in an eleventh-century manuscript produced in Canterbury, whose constituent texts originated in Europe (a large proportion in Germany). Until recently, the manuscript was thought to contain forty-nine poems, but a newly discovered leaf brings the total to eighty-three.[28] The origin and relevance of these poems is obscured by the fact that they are most commonly identified collectively as the *Carmina Cantabrigiensia* (*Cambridge Songs*, abbreviated here as *CC*), after the university library in England in which the manuscript is housed. Though the manuscript is English, it is certain that the poems were of continental origin. We need not assume that every one was of German provenance, but there is sufficient evidence, as Ziolkowski and earlier editors have suggested, to indicate a German exemplar.

It hardly seems necessary to point out that a collection of *carmina* were written to be sung, rather than read. Nevertheless, these diverse songs were composed not merely with a view to being performed, but also with the expectation that their audience might reflect on both the theory and the practice of musical production. A large proportion of the songs make explicit reference to one or other of these. The two were carefully distinguished throughout the Middle Ages[29] and are kept separate by the authors of the songs. Musical practice is examined in the proem to *Lantfrid and Cobbo* (*CC* 6), a narrative about two inseparable brothers. Here, the poet considers the three different ways in which musical sound can be produced. In the first place, we are told, it might arise *fidium concentu* (out of the harmony of strings, 1a.2), and *pulsu plectro manuque* (by strumming with the plectrum and hand, 1a.3). Alternatively, we might choose to use wind instruments (1b):

> Aut tibarum canorus redditur flatus,
> fistularum ut sunt discrimina queque

folle uentris orisque
tumidi flatu perstrepentia pulchre
mente musiconant;

[or the blowing of wind instruments is rendered tuneful,
inasmuch as there are differences in the pipes,
and, making beautiful sounds as the bellows of the
    stomach work
and as the mouth is puffed out and blows,
they sound soothing to the soul;]

Last, music might be produced by singing: *plurimarum faucium homi-
num uolucrum animantiumque* (with the melodious voice of many a
throat by people, birds and animals, 2a.2). It is in these ways, we are
told, that the deeds of Lantfrid and Cobbo were to be remembered by
the singers and musical performers of medieval Germany. The musical
concerns of the opening strophes of this poem are typical of those expressed at the beginning of many of the *Cambridge Songs*, and of those
which form the substance of what are likely to be poetic fragments (such
as *CC* 2 and 30).

Musical theory is the theme of two poems about Pythagorean philosophy. The first, and longest, contains an anecdotal account of Pythagoras's discovery of musical harmony, which resulted, we are told,
from his observations about the sounds of a blacksmith's hammers.
When he realized that different weights of hammer resulted in different
sounds, he knew that "some formless power/of tones lay hidden," and
thus "for the first time made known / a beautiful art by adding form"
(*forma addita/artem pulchram/primus edidit*). It is not until the following strophe (3a), however, that he arrives at his understanding of harmony:

Ad hanc simphonias tres
subplendam istas fecit:
diatesseron, diapente,
diapason,
infra quaternarium
que pleniter armoniam sonant (3a.1–6)

[To complete this art he made
these three concords:
the fourth, fifth,
and octave,

> which sound out a harmony fully
> within a quadruple proportion]

In the remaining lines of the stanza, and in the stanzas which follow, the poet considers some of the other discoveries which Pythagoras is credited with having made, including, crucially, that of the Greek letter upsilon, *Y*. The letter is interpreted symbolically as a representation of the choice between the wide pathway (*semita lata*) and narrow pathway (*semita angusta*) which confronts the Christian traveler (*viator*) in his journey through life.

The second poem to examine music from a Pythagorean perspective is *CC* 45, one of a number of texts identified as *modi* in the Cambridge manuscript. The term is often used as a label for verse sequences, but this poem comprises only a single ten-line strophe. The poem makes reference to musical performance in its opening line, and the words of the *modus* are accompanied by musical notation in a later manuscript.[30] This might potentially reveal something about the contexts of reception of the other *modi* in the collection, but it sadly cannot offer any firm clues as to whether this is a German text.

There can be no doubt, however, of the German provenance of two distinctive poems, *CC* 19 and 28. These are macaronic texts, each consisting of Latin and Old High German halflines. *CC* 28, *Suavissima Nunna* (Sweetest Nun), was almost completely destroyed by a disapproving medieval reader, and was further damaged when chemicals were later applied in an unsuccessful attempt to recover the missing portions. A number of other songs in the collection suffered a similar fate, including another love song, quite possibly not of German provenance, of which only a single complete line survives (*CC* 39): *Nosti flores <carpere>, serta pulchra texere* (You can pluck flowers, plait beautiful garlands). Peter Dronke is the only scholar to have attempted a complete reconstruction of the *Suavissima Nunna* text, which, though inevitably highly conjectural, has acted as the departure point for most contemporary critical discussion.[31] The poem takes the form of a dialogue between a man and a woman, often assumed to be a cleric and a nun (hence its more familiar title, *The Cleric and the Nun*). Positive clues to the identity of the man are scarce (though the woman is certainly addressed as *nunna*), and there is nothing within the poem to suggest that he need necessarily have been a cleric. The speakers take turns, beginning in Latin and switching to German at the caesura. Dronke's reconstructed text begins as follows:

Suavissima nunna, ach fertrue mir mit wunna!
Tempus adest floridum, gruonot gras in erthun.

[[Sweetest] nun, [ah] trust [me joyfully]!
[Blossom]-time has come, the grass is green on [the earth]]

Whether or not we are willing to work with a heavily reconstructed text of this kind, we can be in no doubt as to the innovative nature of the poem itself. The syllabic correspondences of the two half lines suggest a writer who had equal mastery of Latin and the vernacular, and who was willing to combine them in a rhythmically striking way. The second macaronic poem, traditionally referred to as *De Heinrico* (On Henry), uses a comparable half-line split between Latin and German (except in the opening line, which mixes the two languages in both half lines). It is possible in this case, however, as Ziolkowski has pointed out, that the Latin text may have been composed before the German half-lines were added. Though textually coherent, the poem is not without its problems. The poet will tell *de quodam duce* (of a certain duke), *themo heron Heinriche* (Lord Henry, v. 3). Leaving aside the sense of grammatical disorientation that results from the mixing of Latin and Old High German inflections in this line, we are immediately confronted by the problem of identity. The poet provides no easy clues as to the identity of the noble Henry, nor of the emperor, Otto, into whose court he is welcomed. The dating of the poem in the last half of the tenth century, as recent scholars have recognized, does not leave us with either a single Otto or a single Henry to whom the poet could be seen to be referring unambiguously.

Properties which might enable us either to establish or to affirm the German provenance of any poem or sequence from the *Cambridge Songs,* alongside linguistic ones, are principally generic or thematic. Notable here are *CC* 14 and 15 (two sequences in what is usually held to be a German series of *modi* extending from *CC* 11 to 16),[32] normally referred to as *Modus Liebinc* and *Modus Florum,*[33] respectively. These *modi* both relate tales of trickery and deception, each involving Swabian tricksters. The *Modus Liebinc* tells the story of the Snow Child, a child born illegitimately to a *coniugis lascivia* (wanton wife) while her Swabian husband, a tradesman, was abroad. When the husband returns, after having been washed to distant lands by a storm, the wife tells him that the child was conceived as a consequence of her having eaten snow:

At illa
maritum timens

dolos uersat
in omnia.
mi tandem
mi coniunx, ait
una uice
in Alpibus
niue sitiens
extinxi sitim.
inde ego grauida
istum puerum
damnoso foetu
heu gignebam. (3b)

[But she,
fearing her husband,
applies deceit
to everything.
At last she says, My . . .
my husband,
once
stricken with thirst
in the Alps,
I quenched my thirst with snow.
So, pregnant from that,
alas, I gave birth
to this son
in a ruinous childbirth.]

This Latin text is the earliest version of this story, which enjoyed popularity in Germany and throughout Europe in the Middle Ages. A later version of it is found in the Old French fabliau, *L'Enfant qui fu remis au soleil*[34] (The child who was returned to the sun), in which the target of the initial act of deceit is once again a trader, and it is also thought to have exerted an influence over the portrayal of Joseph in the English Coventry and N-Town play cycles.[35] The wife's act of trickery is repaid when the husband, after a period of several years, repairs his damaged ship, and returns to sea. On this occasion, however, he takes the child with him, and sells him to another trader for one hundred pounds. When he returns home, he tells his wife that, as a consequence of a storm, he was blown into shallow waters. The sun, he suggests to her, scorched all of them (*nos omnes grauiter/ torret sol*, 5b, 5–6), and the result, predictably, was that her Snow Child melted away (*il/le tuus natus/liquescebat,* 5b, 6–8). The *Modus Florum,* like the *Modus Liebinc,* is an early version of a tale which later became very popular throughout the Middle Ages (particularly among German poets). It is introduced as a *mendosa canti-lena* (lying ballad), a description that characterizes both the *modus* itself (it is a work of imaginative fiction, which could not have been classed as a *historia* [history]), and the fictional act of lying that the poet describes. This act is performed in response to a challenge presented by a king to the eligible bachelors of his kingdom:

> "Si quis mentiendi gnarus
> usque adeo instet fallendo
> dum caesaris ore fallax
> predicitur, si ducat filiam." (2b)

> ["If anyone experienced in lying
> should apply himself to deception
> so well that he is called a deceiver
> by the emperor's own mouth, that man may
> marry [his] daughter."]

The value of the *Cambridge Songs* rests partly on their generic and thematic diversity, but this should not be allowed to obscure the significance of more uniform literary collections and series. Among these are the poems of the nun Hrotswitha of Gandersheim, who lived from around 930 and probably died before the end of the tenth century. Hrotswitha is chiefly remembered for her contribution to medieval drama, but her verse compositions, if generally held to be unaccomplished metrically (largely on account of their irregularity), also occupy a significant position in the history of Ottonian literature. Eight of these take the form of lives of biblical and celebrated religious figures (among the latter, some are historical, others legendary). The longest is dedicated to the life and works of the Virgin, which is accompanied by a much shorter piece on Christ's ascension (*De Ascensione Domini*). The remaining six relate to the deeds of non-biblical saints and martyrs. Hrotswitha produced two further poems, one devoted to the life and deeds of Otto I (*Gesta Ottonis*), and the other to the establishment of her monastery at Gandersheim. Her life of Otto, like the majority of her other poems, is written in leonine hexameters, Latin lines with a central break, rhyming there and at the end. It occupies over 1500 lines, and begins with a conventional celebration of the king's magnificence, in which he is described as *pollens imperii regnator caesariani* (powerful ruler of Caesar's empire).[36]

Alongside lyric poetry, poetic sequences, and longer verse forms such as those produced by Hrotswitha, the Ottonian period also saw significant developments in the trope genre, particularly the famous *Quem Quaeritis* (Whom do you seek?) trope. Raby's definition of the trope remains a convenient characterization of this literary genre: "[a] trope is a text which is employed (with the accompaniment of music) as introduction, intercalation, or addition to a portion of the liturgy."[37] It was traditionally thought that the trope, as a dramatic genre, originated in St. Gallen, but it has since been argued that France would be a more likely location.[38] Tropes were performed by singers, and were not dramatically enacted, but the relationship between tropes and later medieval forms of drama is clearly a genetic one. The *Quem Quaeritis* formed part of the Easter Mass, and takes the form of a dialogue between the Marys who seek the body of Christ, and the angels who surround the empty sepulcher:

1. Quem quaeritis in sepulchro, o Christicolae?
2. Jesum Nazarenum Crucifixum, o caelicolae.
3. Non est hic; surrexit, sicut praedixerat. Ite, nuntiate quia surrexit de sepulchro.

[1. Whom do you seek in the sepulcher, O followers of Christ?
2. Jesus of Nazareth, who was crucified, O divine ones.
3. He is not here: he is risen, just as he foretold. Go, announce that he is risen from the sepulcher.[39]]

This version of the text was preserved in a St. Gallen manuscript dating from the tenth century (and in other German manuscripts[40]), and it seems clear that it was used there. A different (roughly contemporary) manuscript, however, preserves a more elaborate form, with an additional strophe. With good reason, editors and critics have generally assumed that this form must have preceded that which was found in St. Gallen.

The eleventh century witnessed further literary innovation, and St. Gallen again features prominently in this phase of Latin literary history. This century is often regarded as the beginning of a new political period, that under the rule of the Salians. Whether such a label is appropriate must remain open to question, and it seems that political processes (chief among them being the accession of Conrad II in 1024), no less than literary ones, were marked by continuities with Ottonian culture as much as by departures from it. The *Galluslied* (Song of St. Gall) is a Latin translation of a German vernacular hagiographical poem written by Ratpert, who studied at St. Gallen in the ninth century. Its translator was Ekkehart IV, a later St. Gallen scholar (usually held to have lived between the late tenth and early eleventh centuries) who also completed Ratpert's metrical account of life in the monastery (the *Casus Sancti Galli*). St. Gall himself had been one of twelve Irish monks who traveled to Europe with St. Columbanus in the sixth century, and who was known to the students of St. Gallen as the saint after whom its great abbey was named. Ratpert's decision to compose the poem in the vernacular, and Ekkehart's perception of the need to dignify it by translating it into Latin, are testimony to popularity and perceived importance of the theme of Irish saints in early medieval German literature.[41] In the opening strophe, St. Gall is described magnificently as the son of Ireland and a father to Swabia:

> Nunc incipiendum est mihi magnum gaudium.
> Sanctiorum nullum quam sanctum misit Gallum
> Filium Hibernia, recepit patrem Sueuia.
> Exultemus omnes, laudemus Christum pariles
> Sanctos aduocantem et glorificantem. (1, 1–5)

> [Now the greatest joy is about to rise up in me.
> Ireland has sent no holier son than Gallus
> [and] Swabia has received no holier father.
> Let us all celebrate, let us praise Christ together,
> Who engages and glorifies the saints.]

The narrative traces the missionaries' journey from Ireland across Frankish Europe to St. Gall's resting place in St. Gallen. Though only extending to seventeen five-line strophes, it is an account that contains a wealth of historical and geographical details. The poet mentions many of the travelers' stopping-places, including Luxeuil, Swabia, Zurich, Tuggen, and Arbon, from where they finally travel, as a single group, to Bregenz. St. Gall becomes ill and weak as he travels, and has to rest (on Columbanus's recommendation) at Bregenz. Eventually, he turns back to Arbon, where the priest Willimar, a friend, provides him with a bed. He then walks on with his companion, the deacon Hildebald, until the two find a suitable place to stay. This place, St. Gall decides, will be the place where he will remain and devote himself to God. He tells Hildebald

"Requies haec est mea per saeculorum saecula:
Semper hic habitabo, deum meum inuocabo.
Hiltibalt percare, iam noli me uetare:
Libet sic iacere, noli sustinere." (8, 2–5)

["This is my resting place forever:
I will live here always, and pray to my God.
Hildebald, dear friend, do not oppose me:
It pleases me to lie here thus; do not sustain me."]

It is here that St. Gall establishes a hermitage, and at this point in the
poem that we are presented with details which identify it as a conventional martyr's life. The poet begins with two miracles: St. Gall's taming
of a bear and his expulsion of a demon from a young girl "whom Satan
had made mad" (*quam Satan uexat rabidam*, 11, 2). The demon is described in vivid detail as it leaves the girl's body, "wild and black as a ra-
ven" (*toruus colore tamquam coruus*, 11, 3). When the girl thanks him for
curing her, and offers him gifts, he donates these to the poor. The people of Arbon wish to make him bishop, but he declines, inviting a friend,
John, to assume the role in his place. His death occurs shortly afterward,
and he is buried by John.

Latin Epic in Germany:
From *Waltharius* to the *Messiad* of Eupolemius

Three of the longest and most distinctive of the eleventh-century Latin
poems from Germany are all, to an extent, literary experiments. The *Messiad* (a modern name), whose author identified himself by the pseudonym of Eupolemius, dates from the end of the eleventh century, and
takes the form of an allegorical biblical epic. The *Ruodlieb*, a roughly
contemporary poem by an unknown writer, also draws heavily on epic
convention, as does the *Ecbasis Cuiusdam Captivi per Tropologiam* (Escape of a certain captive, told in a figurative manner), a fable about the
adventures of a young calf. These were not the earliest examples of epic
writing from medieval Germany, however, and it is necessary to place
them within their broader literary context.

"Epic" is a difficult term to use in the context of early medieval
German writing, whether Latin or vernacular. One reason for this has to
do with the relative scarcity of epic poetry surviving from Germany in the
early medieval period; only four examples survive in Latin, and only one,
the fragmentary *Hildebrandlied*, in the vernacular. The remarkable diver-

sity among those few works that might be characterized as "epic" further frustrates any attempt to apply the term in a uniform and unambiguous way to the oldest German literature. It is not easy to define "epic" succinctly, but any definition would have to acknowledge that the term identifies an extended narrative poem which concentrates on the deeds, principally in war, of a central heroic figure. Heroism and war are certainly at the center of the earliest of our Latin epics, *Waltharius* (ninth or early tenth century), and to an extent of one of the latest, the *Ruodlieb* (late eleventh century), which survives as a sequence of fragments. The *Messiad* of Eupolemius also centers on a battle, but this is a battle on a cosmic scale (an early example of what has been referred to as the "combat myth").[42] The last of the four Latin epics, *Ecbasis Cuiusdam Captivi*, is a more problematic poem in many respects. War and heroism do not figure as prominently (nor as literally) in its narrative, and it could not be said that the events of the poem take place on an epic scale.

Unlike its vernacular Germanic counterparts (in both Germany and England), the medieval Latin epic shared many of the themes and formal conventions of the classical epic poetry of Virgil. The poets of Charlemagne's court, of course, had regarded Virgil as the supreme poetic model, and the desire to emulate him did not diminish in the subsequent centuries. All four poets adopted the Virgilian dactylic hexameter as the metrical norm in their poems, which in classical poetry had been one of the formal defining features of heroic verse. Unlike the authors of *Ecbasis* and *Ruodlieb*, however, neither the *Waltharius* poet (except in the much-debated and possibly unconnected preface) nor Eupolemius felt the need to impose on themselves the additional constraint of leonine rhyme. The first line of *Waltharius*, in which the poet, a monk, introduces Europe and its constituent kingdoms to his brothers, scans thus:

Tērtĭă/ pārs ōrb/īs, frātr/ēs, Eūr/ōpă vŏc/ātŭr

[The third part of this earth, brothers, is called Europe]

In spite of its Virgilian meter, and plentiful Virgilian echoes and borrowings, *Waltharius* is, thematically a Germanic poem (in terms, at least, of its distorted reflection of earlier Germanic tribal politics). The eponymous hero of the narrative is a prince of Aquitaine, who is captured by Attila, leader of the Huns, under whose guidance he is raised. His friend and ally, Hagano, is taken as a hostage from the Franks, who is himself taken by Attila. The last of Attila's prisoners is Hildigunda, a princess, and daughter to Heririk, the king of the Burgundians (another Germanic tribe). Waltharius, as is to be expected, is renowned as a warrior, and possesses many of the defining characteristics of the Germanic and the classical hero (many of which, of course, coincide). Fleeing from Attila with Hildigunda, to whom he is now betrothed, Waltharius is forced to fight against his friend Hagano, although the battle is ultimately abandoned. Whatever the outcome of this Christian-Latin version however, the narrative is part of an heroic tradition and one of the major points at which Latin writings seem actually to touch the Germanic world. It is discussed more fully elsewhere in this volume in the heroic context.[43]

The *Ecbasis Cuiusdam Captivi* was written after *Waltharius,* though the question of its more precise date of composition remains unresolved, and there are as many reasons to place it in the early eleventh century as in the early tenth (though Edwin Zeydel's dismissal of many of the claims for the earlier date is difficult to overlook).[44] The author is thought to have been a German Benedictine monk, but his precise identity is unknown. His poem is of epic proportions, running to over 1200 lines, and borrows heavily from classical texts (including, most notably, Virgil's *Aeneid* and a number of Horatian writings). Its theme, however, is unusual for the epic genre, and it has been suggested that it might be appropriate to regard it as the earliest example of a new genre, the beast epic. The author was clearly aware that his text might meet with a perplexed, or even hostile response from some of his readers, as his introductory comments suggest:

Sunt etenim quidam, si me depingere quiddam
Audierint falsi, certabunt legibus aequi
Ac mea transmisso transfigent carmina telo.
Consuescunt multi, quam qui sint carmine docti,
Longos accentus per miros vertere flexus.
Nam pede composito certans insistere metro,
Sillabicos cursus cum sim discernere tardus,
Tempora temporibus eque coniungere cecus,
Rectius hoc faciam, linguam si pressero blesam. (vv. 17–25)

[Certain people, if they hear me depicting something
Fictitious, will oppose with the laws of truth
And transfix my songs with a piercing weapon.
Many, especially those learned in poetry, are accustomed
To carry along melodies through artful variations.
So in striving to adhere to meter composed by foot,
Since I was late in learning to distinguish the course of
    syllables,

And blind in properly linking one tense with another,
I would do this better by restraining my stammering
    tongue.]

The poet's efforts to justify his decision to work with a fabulous narrative, rather than a historically verifiable one, may well have appeared — within the context of medieval hermeneutic procedures — entirely necessary.

The *Ecbasis* is strictly two fables rather than one; the second, or "inner" fable is embedded within the first. The outer fable, in turn, is framed by the author's own remarks about fabulous narratives, his childish reluctance to study, and his frustrated efforts to master the leonine rhyme scheme. Structurally, therefore, this is a complex text. The outer fable, we are told, begins *[p]ost octingentos domini, post ter quater annos* (after eight hundred and thrice four years of our Lord, v. 69), during the month of April at Easter. It is here that we are introduced to the solitary calf, grieving that he has been separated from his mother, and unhappy that he is locked away during the months of spring. After praying to Jesus, he decides to attempt to escape, which he achieves by chewing through his restraints. He flees to the shelter of the forest, where he meets a wolf (identified as *forstrarius*, "the forester"), who leads him to his cave-like dwelling. The wolf asks the calf why he has entered the wood, and tells him: *silve novus incola surgis,/Tu recreare venis tenuatum corpus ab escis* (you appear as a new denizen of the woods,/ You come to restore by food a body weakened [vv. 110–11]). The calf, perceiving the wolf's design, prays (to Jupiter) that his sins may be forgiven, and that he should be allowed to return safely. He then speaks aloud of his escape from captivity, and asks to be pardoned for this minor sin (*noxa*). The wolf agrees to grant him a single day's reprieve, during which time he invites him join him in a rich banquet. At midnight, as "night was rejoicing in passing the center of the sky" (*nox per medium gaudebat currere caelum*, v. 163), the wolf's companions, the hedgehog and the otter, return to the cave with additional supplies. When finally the animals retire to their beds, the wolf's sleep is disturbed by a mysterious dream. The dream occurred, we are told, *post noctem mediam, quando sunt somnia vera* (after the middle of the night, when dreams are true, v. 227).

Though this dream (*visio*) has all the hallmarks of what medieval dream theorists, following the influential system outlined in Macrobius's *In Somnium Scipionis* (Commentary on "The Dream of Scipio"), might have referred to as an *insomnium*, a nightmare, it is clear that it is believed by the otter and the hedgehog to have prophetic significance. This brings a further level of structure to the poem, since the dream now functions potentially as an interpretative meta-narrative (and as a narrative which, like the *Ecbasis* itself, may potentially convey truth through a fictional or fabulous episode). The otter recognizes the significance of the dream, and warns the wolf that he should release the calf, lest the swarm of flies, representing animals of the forest, should devour him. The wolf is unwilling to agree to this request, even though he has eaten no meat for the last seven years. When the other animals learn of his response, they are angered, and make for the cave. The wolf panics, and tells his friends of his fear of the animals, and especially of the fox. When they ask him to explain his worries, he presents them with a story of how the two became enemies. This narrative forms the "inner" fable, which begins on line 392. When the wolf finishes speaking, his friends, fearing the other animals, abandon him. The wolf himself is finally led to his death by the saccharine invocations of the fox, who asks him, *quid agis, dulcissime rerum?*" (how do you fare, sweetest of things?" v. 1143). It is the bull, rather than the fox, who commits the act of killing, while the calf escapes to freedom.

The *Ruodlieb*,[45] unlike the *Ecbasis* or *Waltharius*, survives in a fragmentary form. This time the names and a few actual German words in the text very clearly indicate a German-speaking author. The text exists in eighteen fragments, some of which are incomplete, and it lacks a conclusion (the last fragment does not anticipate closure, and the narrative it contains might conceivably lie some distance from the conclusion). It tells of the experiences of a young, noble hero, Ruodlieb (not named until the fifth fragment), who, unable to win recognition for acts of service to his lords, leaves his mother and his native country to seek "foreign kingdoms" (*extera regna*, v. 18). After traveling for a short time, he enters a new kingdom and is met by one of its king's huntsmen. He befriends the huntsman, and is taken to the king's court, where he is made welcome. When war breaks out between the king's people and a neighboring land, Ruodlieb is made commander-in-chief of the army, which he leads to victory. After the battle, he takes the defeated army back to the king, who treats his enemy mercifully. The king proposes to initiate peace negotiations with the neighboring kingdom, and sends Ruodlieb to its leader with the news. After debating the proposal in private with his counselors, the king agrees, and the two leaders arrange to meet in the same location as they had fought. The meeting takes place and peace is established between the two kingdoms, after which a messenger arrives with news from Ruodlieb's mother. She asks that he return home, as the lords who previously treated him so unfairly have, she suggests, repented. He is asked by the king, before leaving, whether he would prefer to receive a gift of wisdom or money from his host. Choosing the former, he is presented with twelve rules, varying in their nature from general maxims to specific caveats, which are to guide him on his journey home.

The advice Ruodlieb receives from the king informs the structure of the remainder of the narrative (from the end of fragment five to fragment eighteen), a point which has led some to adopt what Grocock describes as a "didactic" interpretation of the text.[46] Such an interpretation is problematic, in that it would render redundant those episodes (none of which is insubstantial) occurring before the parting gift of wisdom is offered. The points of wisdom themselves, moreover, are explored only partially in the text that remains. The episodes which follow as a consequence of meeting a red-headed stranger (the first warning) alter the structure of the narrative significantly, and demand that Ruodlieb draw on more of the king's points of wisdom. As the two approach a village toward the end of the day, they discover that the road ahead is thick with mud. In his second point, the king had warned Ruodlieb not to stray from the muddy road through the village. Following the king's advice, he remains on the road, but the stranger chooses to take an easier path across the bordering fields, incurring the anger of their owners. When the two finally reach the village, Ruodlieb chooses to lodge with a young man and his old wife, as the king had advised in his third point: *quo videas iuvenem quod habet senior mulierem hospicum tribui tibi non poscas interanti* (wherever you see that an old man has a young wife, do not ask for accommodation on your journey). The stranger chooses instead to stay with an old man and his young wife, and he and the wife enter into an adulterous relationship. The episode contains all the elements of the classical fabliau: trickery, adultery, and a strong vein of narrative realism. Though the scene in which the wife and the stranger have intercourse is missing from the manuscript, the behavior of the two at an earlier point in the narrative, when the old man leaves to use the lavatory, makes such an outcome seem virtually inevitable:

> rufus et in solium salit infeliciter ipsum,
> una manus mammas tractabat et altera gambas,
> quod celabat ea super expanendo crusenna.
> (Fragment 7, vv. 117–19)

> [The wretched redhead jumped into the master's chair,
> one hand caressed her breasts and the other her thighs,
> and she hid all this by spreading her fur cloak over her.]

At the beginning of the eighth fragment, the old man lies dying, having been struck by the redhead when he stumbles on the two making love. The redhead, unlike the old man's wife, is unrepentant, and is put on trial by the governor of the village. He calls on Ruodlieb to defend him, but the text breaks off, and the succeeding fragment contains no obvious clues as to the outcome of the trial. It has generally been assumed that the redhead is eventually put to death.

The concluding episodes of the poem describe Ruodlieb's meeting with his nephew as he nears the end of his journey, the romance between the nephew and the daughter of a noblewoman with whom they stay briefly, the wedding of the two lovers, and the prophetic dream of Ruodlieb's mother, which predicts that her son will enjoy glory in the future. The last fragment of the poem, in which Ruodlieb meets and captures a dwarf who guards a treasure, brings him within sight of glory (and of marriage), but ends abruptly while the character is speaking. The dwarf had promised to reward Ruodlieb with the treasure of two kings, Immunch and Hartunch (both of whom, he had suggested, would be easily defeated) if he allowed him to go free, and with the prospect of marrying the beautiful daughter of Immunch. We are left only to anticipate that the hero would have been successful.

Although there has been little agreement about the issues of genre surrounding the *Ruodlieb,* there can no doubt that its author produced an epic of a kind which had not yet been seen in Germany. One of its most distinguishing — and innovative — features is its author's use of the themes and imagery of romance. Latin scholars recognized this early on: Edwin Zeydel, who provided the first English translation of the poem, regarded it as "the earliest courtly novel," and Gordon B. Ford, a later editor and translator, added the subtitle "the first medieval epic of chivalry from eleventh-century Germany" to his translation.[47] Peter Dronke, in his study of poetry from the eleventh century to the beginning of the twelfth, described it as "the first medieval verse romance."[48] Though important, such characterizations should not be allowed to obscure other aspects of the poet's style, and his innovative incorporation of a broad variety of genres (such as fabliau) into his text.

Linguistically, the *Ruodlieb* is an eccentric piece of writing, and more difficult to read than either *Waltharius* or *Ecbasis.* Though it might be argued that the unusual word order which characterizes many of the half-lines may result from the demands placed on the poet by his rigid adherence to the conventions of the leonine hexameter, this is hardly a persuasive explanation, especially given the comparative regularity of the leonine *Ecbasis.* Prepositions that occur *after* the noun phrases they govern (as in *quem super ut saluit equus altius ipse saliuit,* fragment 1, v. 42), and conjunctions that appear midway through the clauses they introduce grammatically (as in *copia dum fit,* fragment 2, v. 26) are by no means unique to this poem, nor are they wholly avoided by others who chose to work with leonine meter (including the *Ecbasis*-poet). Nevertheless, it seems fair to argue that such features appear more frequently than in any comparable poem.

The *Messiad* of Eupolemius, despite its epic trappings, is arguably the least conventional of any of the epic texts of medieval Germany. Eupolemius is a pseudonym, and although not all scholars have accepted the attribution, the author again appears from internal evidence in the poem to have been German. Possibly influenced by the *Psychomachia* (War of the Soul), by the fourth-century Christian writer Prudentius, the work presents an abstract battle between good and evil. The text, which occupies two lengthy books (each of over 600 hexameters), opens with a Virgilian declaration of the poet's theme. It is here that the character of Cacus is introduced, who acts as the personification of evil in the poem:

> Contra Messyam violenti prelia Caci
> Detestanda cano, dudum quem fortibus armis
> In dominum pugnasse suum nimiumque potenter
> Instruxuisse ferunt acies Iebusea per arva,
> Que circa Solimam sita sunt. (vv. 1–5)

> [Of the execrable battles of Cacus against the Messiah
> I sing, who for long, with powerful arms, is said to
> have fought against his Lord, and who
> marshalled his armies through the Jebusite lands,
> which are situated around Jerusalem.]

The poet first presents a series of Old Testament figures as allegories of good against evil, and then, in the second book, shows us the ultimate triumph of Messias — Christ — after being killed with five wounds outside Jerusalem and then restored by God. Eupolemius's *Messiad* is a difficult poem in many respects. Beyond its generic ambiguity, there is the problem of its theology. Jan Ziolkowski, perceiving the poem as "insistently dualist," nevertheless seeks to deter us from interpreting it as a "heterodox" text.[49] Like the other German epics, the *Messiad* drew on the established conventions of the ancients and on ongoing literary and ideological debates. It looked ahead, moreover, to the celebrated European theological poetry of the centuries to come, although it seems to have had no direct influence.

The end of the eleventh century, like the beginning of the eighth, witnessed the production of an extraordinary variety of Latin verse forms in Germany. This remarkable productivity would continue into the twelfth century with important writers such as Hildegard of Bingen. If the volume and diversity shown from the beginning was unparalleled in the vernacular, there was, nevertheless, some relationship between the two languages, as attested by translations from the vernacular (and, far less frequently, *into* the vernacular), and by the composition of macaronic poems. This should not, of course, prevent us from perceiving the Latin texts of early medieval Germany as a largely independent tradition.

Notes

[1] See Martin Irvine, *The Making of Textual Culture* (Cambridge: CUP, 1994), 305–33.

[2] Peter Godman argues that the poem is unlikely to have been addressed to a specific monastic "cella": Peter Godman, ed. and trans., *Poetry of the Carolingian Renaissance* (Norman, OK: U Oklahoma P, 1985), 124 n. This is a sensible suggestion, but compare the translation of Helen Waddell in *Medieval Latin Lyrics*, 4th ed. (London: Constable, 1933), 96–99 (repr. Harmondsworth: Penguin, 1952), 106–9.

[3] See vv. 94 and 98 in Godman, *Poetry of the Carolingian Renaissance*, 202.

[4] Godman, *Poetry of the Carolingian Renaissance*, 24.

[5] For a detailed study of this work see Brian Murdoch, *Old High German Literature* (Boston: Twayne, 1983), 93–105.

[6] This text is sometimes referred to as *De universo* (On the Universe), *PL* 111, 9–614.

[7] On the *Excerptio de arte grammatica Prisciani* see Giulio Lepschy, ed., *Classical and Medieval Linguistics* (London: Longman, 1994), 173.

[8] F. J. E. Raby, the editor of *The Oxford Book of Medieval Latin Verse* (Oxford: Clarendon, 1959), 468, acknowledges that the text is ascribed to Hraban in a tenth-century Fulda manuscript, but prefers to identify this as an anonymous hymn.

[9] *Piers Plowman: A Complete Edition of the B-text*, ed. A. V. C. Schmidt (London: Dent, 1987), passus 19, 210–11.

[10] See Karl Strecker, *Introduction to Medieval Latin*, trans. Robert B. Palmer (Berlin: Weidmann), 75.

[11] *PL* 113, 1063B.

[12] *PL* 113, 1063B.

[13] David A. Traill, *Walafrid Strabo's Visio Wettini: Text, Translation and Commentary* (Frankfurt: Lang, 1974), 45.

[14] On this convention, see the introduction to Traill's *Walafrid Strabo's Visio Wettini*, 12–18.

[15] Traill, *Walafrid Strabo's Visio Wettini*, 50.

[16] See Traill, *Walafrid Strabo's Visio Wettini,* 126 n. 314.

[17] The text for this piece may be found in *PL* 113, 1089B–1092C, the extract concerned being at 1089B. It is also edited and translated by Michael W. Herren, "The *De Imagine Tetrici,*" *Journal of Medieval Latin* 1 (1991): 118–39. The translation here is my own. On the image as such, see Paul Edward Dutton, *Carolingian Civilisation: a Reader* (Peterborough, ON: Broadview, 1993), 49.

[18] This is a free translation of the periphrastic title, which literally means "you command so that what?" (The subjunctive verb of the result clause has been elided.)

[19] See Godman, *Poetry of the Carolingian Renaissance,* 228 (text); 229 (translation).

[20] See Godman, *Poetry of the Carolingian Renaissance,* 230 (text); 231 (translation).

[21] See Godman, *Poetry of the Carolingian Renaissance,* 228 (n.) and Peter Dronke, *The Medieval Lyric* (London: Hutchinson, 1968), 34.

[22] The melody, first edited by E. de Coussemaker, is reproduced in Dronke, *The Medieval Lyric,* 236–37.

[23] *The Medieval Lyric,* 36.

[24] F. J. E. Raby, *A History of Christian-Latin Poetry, from the Beginnings to the Close of the Middle Ages* (Oxford: Clarendon, 1953), 211.

[25] *Notker der Dichter und seine geistige Welt,* ed. and trans. Wolfram von den Steinen (Bern: Franke, 1948), 2, 8.

[26] *Notker der Dichter,* 2, 10.

[27] *Notker der Dichter,* 2, 12–13. (English translations in the text are my own.)

[28] *The Cambridge Songs (Carmina Cantabrigiensia),* ed. and trans. Jan M. Ziolkowski (Tempe, AZ: Medieval and Renaissance Texts and Studies, 1998). All English translations of poems from the *Cambridge Songs* are Ziolkowski's, unless otherwise stated. Also ed. Werner Bulst (Heidelberg: Winter, 1950).

[29] See D. L. Wagner, ed., *The Seven Liberal Arts in the Middle Ages* (Bloomington, IN: Indiana UP, 1983), 177.

[30] "Let us sound melodies loudly upon the harp with musical skill." Ziolkowski, ed. 122–23.

[31] Reconstructed text and translation are taken from Peter Dronke, *Medieval Latin and the Rise of the European Love-Lyric,* second edition (Oxford: Clarendon, 1968), 354–55. The diplomatic text can be found on pp. 353–54. Dronke indicates conjectural insertions in the translation with the use of square brackets. On this text and on the fragmentary *CC* 39 see most recently Cyril Edwards, *The Beginnings of German Literature* (Rochester, NY: Camden House, 2002), 122–25.

[32] For a recent discussion of this and other "German" series see Ziolkowski, ed., xxxiii.

[33] These are the titles given in the Wolfenbüttel manuscript, which were adopted by Bulst and others as convenient titles for the sequences. See Bulst, ed., 33–37; Ziolkowski, ed., 209n. and 217n. *Modus Florum* translates unproblematically as *The Sequence of Flowers,* or, as Ziolkowski renders it, *The Song of the Flowers.* The other title is more difficult. Ziolkowski suggests *Sequence to the Liebo Tune,* a tune which, he

argues, might have accompanied an earlier poem about Liebo. See Ziolkowski, ed., 212.

[34] An edition of this text, the earliest version of the French Snow Child, can be found in Anatole de Montaiglon and Raynaud Gaston, eds., *Recueil général et complet des fabliaux des XIIIe et XIV e siècles imprimés ou inédits* (New York: Burt Franklin, 1964), 3, 215–20. There is a translation of the Latin poem in Brian Murdoch, *The Grin of the Gargoyle* (Sawtrey: Dedalus, 1995), 156–59.

[35] For a discussion of the relationship between the French version of the Snow Child story and later English literature, including the mystery plays, see John Hines, *The Fabliau in English* (London: Longman, 1993), 211–12. See also Ziolkowski, ed., 211 (n.).

[36] Hrotswitha of Gandersheim, *Hrotsvithae Opera,* ed. Karl Strecker (Leipzig: Teubner, 1906): *Gesta Ottonis,* prologue, v. 1.

[37] *History of Christian-Latin Poetry,* 219.

[38] *History of Christian-Latin Poetry,* 221–22. For a detailed history of the trope, with a consideration of the connection with St. Gallen, see O. B. Hardison, *Christian Rite and Christian Drama in the Middle Ages* (Baltimore, MD and London: Johns Hopkins P, 1965), 178–219.

[39] Text and (corrected) translation from John Gassner, ed., *Medieval and Tudor Drama* (New York: Bantam, 1963, and London: Applause, 1987), 35.

[40] See Raby, *History of Christian-Latin Poetry,* 211 n. 3.

[41] Peter Osterwalder, *Das althochdeutsche Galluslied Ratperts und seine lateinischen Übersetzungen durch Ekkehart IV* (Berlin and New York: de Gruyter, 1982) has the text. On the role of Irish saints in the Latin and vernacular literature of early medieval Germany, see John Henning, "Irish Saints in Early German Literature," *Speculum* 22 (1947): 358–74.

[42] On the relationship between the *Messiad* and the combat myth tradition see Jan Ziolkowski, "Eupolemius," *The Journal of Medieval Latin* 1 (1991): 1–45 (3f). The text is edited by Karl Manitius, *Eupolemius, Das Bibelgedicht* (Weimar: Böhlau/MGH, 1973).

[43] Texts in Karl Strecker, *Nachträge zu den Poetae Latini I* (Weimar: Böhlau/MGH, 1951, repr. Munich: MGH, 1978); Gregor Vogt-Spira, *Waltharius: Lateinisch/ Deutsch* (Stuttgart: Reclam, 1994); Dennis M. Kratz, *Waltharius and Ruodlieb* (New York: Garland, 1984), 1–71, and (English only) Brian Murdoch, *Walthari* (Glasgow: Scottish Papers in Germanic Studies, 1989).

[44] See Edwin H. Zeydel, ed. and trans., *Ecbasis Cuiusdam Captivi* (Chapel Hill, NC: U North Carolina P, 1964), 5–9.

[45] Numerous English editions and translations of the *Ruodlieb* now exist. Edwin Zeydel's edition of 1959, *Ruodlieb: The Earliest Courtly Novel (after 1050)* (New York: AMS, 1969), includes an English translation and textual notes. The English translation of Gordon B. Ford, published as *The Ruodlieb: The First Medieval Epic of Chivalry from Eleventh-Century Germany* (Leiden: E. J. Brill, 1965), is the most faithful English translation currently available. Ford has also produced an edition of the Latin text: *The Ruodlieb: Linguistic Introduction, Latin Text and Glossary* (Leiden: E. J. Brill, 1966). The most recent edition and translation (cited) is that of G. W. Gro-

cock: *The Ruodlieb,* ed. with translation and notes by G. W. Grocock (Warminster: Aris and Phillips, 1985).

[46] See Grocock, ed., *The Ruodlieb,* 10–11.

[47] These were by no means the earliest scholars to see the *Ruodlieb* as the earliest medieval romance. See the discussion in Grocock, ed., *The Ruodlieb,* 9f.

[48] *Poetic Individuality in the Middle Ages: New Departures in Poetry 1000–1150* (Oxford: Clarendon, 1970), 34.

[49] Ziolkowski, "Eupolemius," 4.

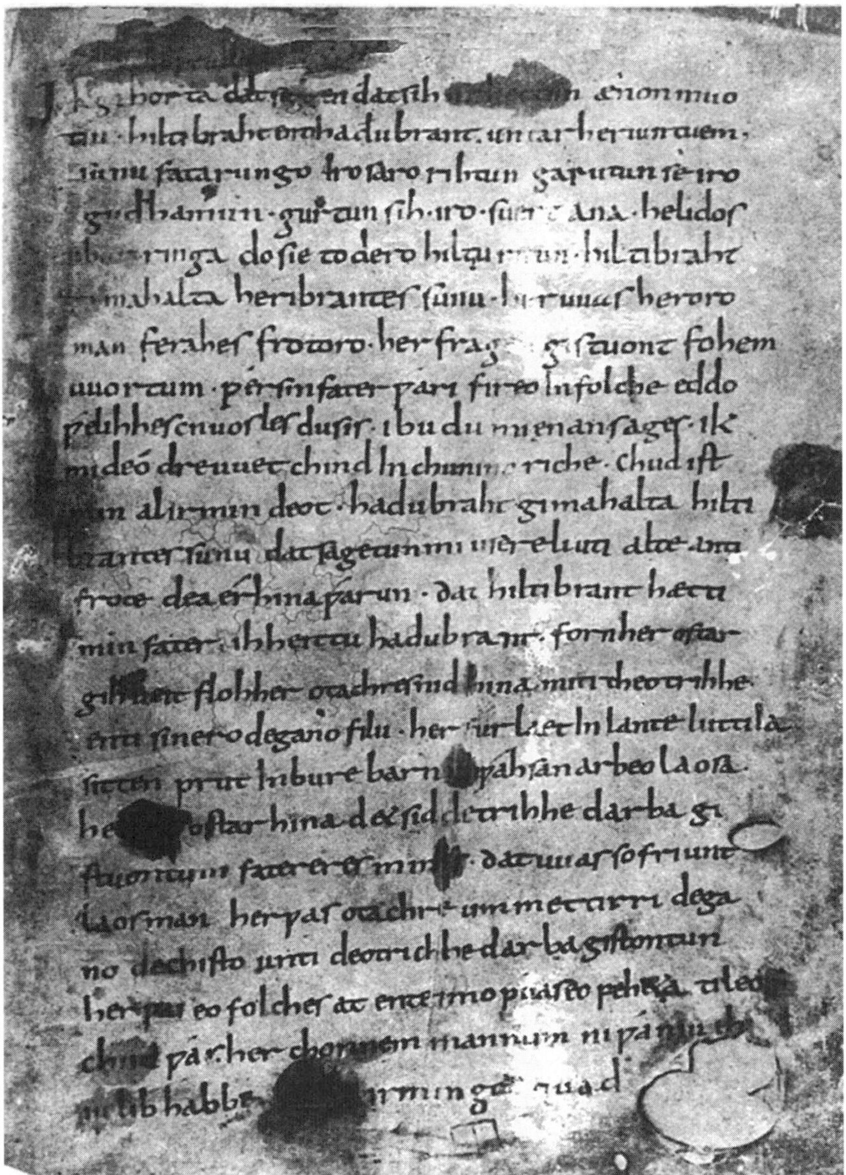

The Hildebrandlied

Heroic Verse

Brian Murdoch

IT IS A VALID ASSUMPTION that there must have been in and before the Old High German period a tradition of orally transmitted heroic poetry associated with the warrior aristocracy and consisting of tales of kings, warriors and heroes, a poetry of action and conflict, set within a particular class of society, and comparable with early poetry in many other cultures. Having oral roots, poetry of this kind — usually known as oral-formulaic poetry — would use the kind of poetic formulas that are found in writings as old as the Homeric epics, set phrases that fit into the established meter, a technique probably most familiar from the English ballad, where a line like "come saddle me my milk-white steed" serves regularly as a metrically convenient, but not otherwise significant indicator that someone is about to set off somewhere. The use of set formulas allows the oral poet to construct the action or dialogue of a work — these are main features — on the skeleton of metrically suitable lines. Poetry of this kind, in the vernacular, on themes of heroic behavior, can be found in virtually every culture, both at epic length and in shorter form, and the fact that examples survive in Old English and especially in Old Norse makes it likely that there was similar material in High German. We know too that Charlemagne was interested in such songs and may have collected them, but his successors and the Church disapproved of secular works and also controlled the means of writing, so that in German they were simply not committed to script.

This makes any assessment of the heroic tradition in Old High German very difficult indeed: we may make comments on the likely form, but the nature of the performance, or of the poet himself, is impossible to pin down. As far as the material itself goes, however, Alcuin of York famously asked in a letter "what has Ingeld to do with Christ?" implying that there must have been poems or songs about the Germanic hero Ingeld (who is known to us from the English heroic epic of *Beowulf*) for him to disapprove of. There may well have been High German songs on themes such Siegfried and the Nibelungen, since such works are attested not only in Norse, but in the later, Middle High German *Nibelun-*

genlied. The *Nibelungenlied* was shaped also by the conflicts in the early Frankish ruling house (told with great vigor by Latin chroniclers like Gregory of Tours), and individual vernacular songs about these struggles may also have existed. The survival of a Latin poem (written in Germany) about the probably Visigothic hero Walther is another pointer, and Middle High German and Norse evidence, plus frequent allusions in Latin writing, means that there may have been songs about the hero Dietrich of Bern (based on the Gothic king Theoderic the Great), or mythical figures such as Wayland the Smith, or other less familiar topics. Early histories of German literature devoted much attention to these presumed heroic poems and cycles; Felix Genzmer's book *Vier altdeutsche Heldenlieder*[1] gives an account first of three different works whose putative existence is based on Latin and later evidence; but his fourth example throws all this into relief, because it actually does survive. In Old High German, only one short heroic poem made the — not well charted — transition from oral composition to writing, and that is the *Hildebrandlied* (also *Hildebrandslied*), the Lay of Hildebrand, a work with which there are, moreover, vast difficulties in establishing what we mean by the text.[2] The problem of early German oral poetry is that we do not really know what it was like, and even studies such as those carried out by Milman Parry and Albert Lord on modern oral composition are not entirely enlightening.[3] So too, the *Hildebrandlied* is not simply a written representation of an oral poem. It was copied from a text already written down, and it is also difficult to place it as a written work into a context within a literary history of early German. Moreover, the context in which it was copied was that of the Church, and although the content of the work may predate Christianity in Germany, this text does not. In the early period surviving texts in German (and even in Latin) dealing with the hero in any form are rare, and the notion of any kind of development, even of the increasingly strong Christian element is tenuous. Latin allusions and the existence of later works make us constantly aware of the lost prehistory of the heroic song in Old High German. But we simply do not have the material.

    In the simplest terms, what constitutes the text of the *Hildebrandlied* is the incomplete work of sixty-eight alliterating long-lines that survives on two outside leaves of a manuscript containing Latin biblical texts, written down, probably at Fulda, perhaps by two scribes, between 830 and 840. The manuscript is now in Kassel, after some vicissitudes during and after the Second World War. Establishing a working text leads us into problems of transmission. Some of these are easily resolved, as when a few words are repeated (indicating that the text we have was copied from a written exemplar of some kind), but other are less straight-forward. Scholars have suggested that something is missing within the text, or that some lines should be rearranged. The work is also incomplete, though whether the scribe or scribes (who used some Anglo-Saxon letters) ever managed or even intended to write down the whole work is unclear. Equally unclear is why they wrote it down at all. Although we owe the survival of this one heroic poem to the Church, both its subject (although there is evidence of an attempt to Christianize the content) and its form were alien to the monastic culture. Metrically, some lines seem impossible too, although we do not have very much in Old High German with which to compare the forms, and have to use Anglo-Saxon or Norse examples to get an idea of the Germanic alliterative long line — a form, that is, in which the two parts of a line broken by a strong caesura are linked by stressed initial, rather than by final sounds. There are, finally, considerable problems with the language as a whole, because the *Hildebrandlied* is not strictly *in* Old High German at all; our surviving text probably represents a Bavarian original, badly adapted into Low German.[4]

The manuscript version is at least the second written form of a text that was, in its oral origin, probably Old High German. However, linguistic evidence, especially names, and the presumed setting of the story in northern Italy, support the supposition that this text had itself succeeded a version in the (only sketchily preserved) High German language of Lombardic. The historical characters mentioned in the work and some linguistic elements have led to the suggestion that there may even have been a Gothic predecessor before that. But the text we have is fixed, and, for all its manifest imperfections, this unique Old High German heroic poem is still a work of considerable literary value.[5]

The early Germanic hero is primarily a warrior, albeit often singled out by some exceptional quality or rank, and heroic poems are frequently concerned with battles, although this does not imply that the hero is what in Latin is called the *miles gloriosus,* the "swaggering soldier," full of his own importance and concerned with how he may establish a reputation for himself. The hero is, it is true, concerned with his reputation insofar as it must not be blemished, but his deeds, however brave, are also determined by the political constraints in which he operates. He may fight with a will, but what is of greater importance is the way in which the hero (and hence his reputation) copes with the blows of fate. Fate, however, can be malicious, so that the only choice the hero has is to accept it.[6]

The context of the *Hildebrandlied* is a distorted history associated with the powerful fifth-century Gothic king Theoderic (Dietrich) the Ostrogoth, who, according to legend, is perceived as having been driven out of his "rightful" kingdom by Odoacer, the man whom, in genuine history, he killed to secure his own kingship of Italy. Theoderic is seen as having taken refuge with the Huns under Attila, which is anachronistic, since Attila died before Theoderic was born, although his father *had* been associated with them. In the legend, Theoderic, accompanied by his faithful retainer Hildebrand, returns to fight for and regain his own country. Theoderic's historical treachery in having had Odoacer killed in 493 was recast in the legend on the strength, presumably, of his later success as king of Ostrogothic Italy, which he ruled until his death in 526.[7]

In the *Hildebrandlied*, the warrior Hildebrand is faced with the necessity of fighting his own son, a theme that is well-known in other literatures, in Greek and Old Irish, for example, so that it is easy to make comparisons.[8] Hildebrand has, in our poem, fled with Theoderic from the anger of Odoacer, presumably to the court of the Huns, whose king, again presumably Attila, is mentioned. He left behind a bride and a baby son and it is this son that he has to face in single combat on his return. Hildebrand is a great warrior, and he tells us that he has fought for thirty years as an exile — presumably a stock phrase for "a long time" — without defeat, but now, by an irony of fate he has to kill or be killed by his son.

A narrator opens the song (which he claims to have heard, an indication of the passing on of the material by oral transmission at some earlier stage), and tells us the names of the two warriors who are to fight each other as champions from opposing armies, armies whose presence as an inner audience must not be forgotten.[9] We are also told at once, although the warriors themselves find out either later (in the case of Hildebrand) or not at all (in the case of his son), that they are a father and son. The warriors arm — the question of armor is important to the work — and before the fight starts Hildebrand, as the older warrior, addresses Hadubrand "with a few words"; the narrator tells us this, underlining that this is a man of deeds, not words. "Child," says the older warrior, with an irony that runs through the work, "I know all men in the kingdom" (presumably Italy is meant). But he cannot know his own son.

Hadubrand's reply is introduced with the patronymic formula "Hildebrand's son," and the reiterated patronymics (Hildebrand's father is also named) again underscores the irony of the situation throughout by reminding us of the relationship set by the composite *sunufatarungo* (son-and-father) used at the start. Hadubrand says that his father was Hildebrand, but adds that old, wise men from *his* people (we may note the possessive), men who are now dead, have told him that Hildebrand fled with Theoderic from the wrath of Odoacer — this is part of the legendary version of Ostrogoth history. Hildebrand, he says, left behind a young wife and a child with no inheritance:

> her furlaet in lante luttila sitten,
> prut in bure barn unwahsan,
> arbeo laosa . . . (vv. 20–23)

[He left behind him in poverty a bride in the bower, with an ungrown child, deprived of inheritance.]

There has been some discussion of the precise meaning of these lines, which may mean simply that the child (the term *unwahsan,* literally "ungrown" is not clear) was left in the women's quarters, and it has been suggested that any reference to Hildebrand's wife is a distraction. But her designation as *prut,* meaning a young, recently married wife, is important and indicates that she presumably had no more children before Hildebrand fled, so that this is the sole legitimate heir, thus increasing the tragedy. The wife is not mentioned again; she is present in a later ballad reworking of the story, but this is not relevant to our poem. The matter of inheritance, either in the technical legal sense, in the moral or in the genetic sense will, however, become a major theme.[10] Hadubrand is proud of his father's reputation as a warrior, but cannot believe that he can still be alive, and concludes that although his father was known to all men — the question of knowledge is also central to the work — he was too fond of fighting, and therefore the son does not *think* that he can still be alive.

Hildebrand has seen the reality of the situation. The rest of the work shows us his gradual and inexorable entrapment in the inevitable fight, balanced by a commensurate hardening in his son's conviction that his father is indeed dead. Hildebrand is Theodoric's champion, and his duty to his overlord and to his own men is clear, even if he has to fight his sole legitimate heir. Hildebrand attempts to avoid this fatal necessity, but in actuality his attempt has the opposite effect. He makes the unambiguous comment that Hadubrand has never fought with such a close relative, and then offers him the gift of a plaited gold arm-ring. The narrator (who usually remains in the background) tells us all this detail directly, and the sudden visual focus on the arm-ring is pivotal to the whole work:

> want her do ar arme wuntane bauga
> cheisuringu gitan, so imo se der chuning gap,
> Huneo truhtin . . . (vv. 33–35)

[He took from his arm a ring made of plaited Roman gold, given to him by the king of the Huns.]

It is offered as a gift, perhaps even implicitly as part of that lost inheritance, and it is a mark of prowess as a warrior; but it is also recognizable as coming from the Huns, and the mistrustful Hadubrand tragically reads it as indicating that Hildebrand is himself a Hun. He refers to him later as an old Hun who has only survived so long by such trickery, someone who will offer a gift and then throw a spear. When Hadubrand speaks again, not only does he cite equally unreachable witnesses, sailors, but claims to have heard from them that Hildebrand is definitely dead, fallen in battle.[11]

There has been much discussion over the next part of the text. There are grounds for suspecting that it might be corrupt, and different arguments for keeping what we have. If we take the text as it stands (the most pragmatic solution), Hildebrand comments that this man before him has never been an exile, but at all events he is aware that his attempt at reconciliation has failed. He would indeed have to be cowardly to refuse battle, he says, using the word *arg*, cowardly, and we know from surviving Lombardic laws that the use of this term demanded satisfaction by combat. Like it or not, Hildebrand has to accept — he now says so — that cruel fate (*wewurt*) must take its course. The text has him add a brief invocation to God at this point, but references to God are rare in the work and look as if they have been added perhaps by the monastic scribes or their predecessors to add superficial respectability. They do not make the work Christian; the whole tone is fatalist, and God has no real role here. All possible escape routes have been blocked and there are no witnesses who might offer proper knowledge. In the face of the armies, Hildebrand is forced now to kill or be killed by his only son. Hildebrand now reminds the younger man that, if victorious, he may legally claim the battle gear and accouterments (including the gold torque), all of which would presumably constitute in any case Hadubrand's inheritance on Hildebrand's death. Hildebrand is forced by duty and his role as a champion to fight, Hadubrand must earn his inheritance in the same way, although he clearly has inherited Hildebrand's battle-prowess since he is a young champion.

The battle description is brief and incomplete, but there is only one logical outcome. Even though in the *Jüngeres Hildebrandlied*[12] (Later *Hildebrandlied*) both men do survive, it is clear that Hildebrand must kill Hadubrand. A late Norse work, the *Ásmundarsaga Kappabana,* in fact, has Hildebrand on his death bed speak of having killed his son; but even without that later parallel, if Hildebrand were to be killed by his son here, or if both were to die, the story could simply never have become known, or at best, Hadubrand would merely have boasted that he had killed a trickster Hun. Hildebrand himself is the only one who could have recounted the true story, and only then, when for him it is too late.

The tragic irony in the work is clear. Hadubrand has inherited his father's capabilities as a warrior, but Hildebrand retains his armor and his reputation, and his status is enhanced, not because he has defeated a younger warrior, but because he has done his duty to his leader, Theoderic, and to his own code of honor, even though he did not wish to do so, trapped by a cruel fate into doing so. Can we condemn either man? Hadubrand has no reason whatsoever to believe that this stranger is what he claims to be. Hildebrand has abandoned his wife and son, but that is the fate of the warrior under authority going to war, and his failed attempt to offer a gift to the son is the act of a man of deeds, a man of few words. Hildebrand's inner imperative is politically determined by the presence of the two opposing armies, Theoderic's army must win, and Theoderic's chief supporter has a feudal duty to ensure that they do. But Hildebrand is also faced with an existential problem. To prove his identity in the face of disbelief from the one person he wishes to convince, he has to demonstrate his prowess, and can only do so by killing precisely that person. The fatal entrapment is complete.

There are various themes in the work: the uncertainty of human knowledge and the problem of inheritance are as significant as the nature of duty. Of greater importance, perhaps, even than the need for the true hero to accept fate even when it is manifestly cruel — Hildebrand is putting an end to a whole line of warriors (his own father, Heribrand is named in the work) — is the isolation of the central figure, unable to prove his own identity except by the successful completion of a specific act (he could not, for example, even fight to lose, or Hadubrand would still have thought that this man was an old trickster). Once again we owe gratitude to the church for the preservation, for whatever reason, and in a far less than perfect form, of a highly important and lastingly powerful text.[13]

Arguments for the existence of lost Old High German material linked with the battles of the warrior hero Walther are based on a work we do have and which has been touched on already in an earlier chapter, a heroic poem in over 1,450 Latin hexameters (with learned quotations from Virgil) that was almost certainly written by a German speaker. The Latin *Waltharius,* like the German *Hildebrandlied,* is based loosely on early Germanic tribal history, and once again it has as its themes bravery in combat, reputation, property, and the conflict between duty and loyalty on the one hand and (this time) friendship on the other.[14] The work used to be ascribed to Ekkehard I, a monk at St. Gallen who died in 973, but this attribution is no longer accepted. A rhymed preface to the poem in some of the manuscripts ascribes it to an otherwise unknown monk called Geraldus, perhaps writing in the ninth century, though here again earlier and later dates have been suggested. The author seems to have been German because, although the poem is in Latin, it contains a wordplay on the name Hagano as hawthorn (compare modern German *Hagedorn*), which only works in German.

The poem is more clearly Christian than the *Hildebrandlied,* and was composed by a monk, but the essence remains heroic.[15] *Waltharius* opens with the Huns threatening in turn the Franks, the people of Aquitaine (originally the Visigoths), and the Burgundians, all of whom elect to treat with the enemy and to pay tribute, with hostages sent as guarantees to Attila's court. The king of the Franks sends Hagano, a noble youth, because his son, Guntharius, is too young. Waltharius, prince of what we may call the Visigoths, and Hiltgunt, a Burgundian princess, are also sent. Some of these characters have historical antecedents of a sort (Waltharius may be linked tenuously with a Visigoth king ruling at Toulouse called Walja), but their tribal affiliations are not historical. The name of the people of Aquitaine is not actually given. Attila treats the hostages well, but when Guntharius's father dies, the new king refuses to pay any more tribute, and so Hagano is forced to escape. Waltharius, now betrothed to Hiltgunt, is a great warrior, and Attila wants to keep him, but Waltharius organizes a feast, and while Attila is drunk, the pair escape with much treasure. None of the Huns is willing to pursue them. When they reach the land of the Franks, Guntharius hears of them and decides, against Hagano's advice, to claim the treasure, and Waltharius is forced to make a stand in a defensive position in the Vosges Mountains. He defeats most of Guntharius's twelve champions and wounds Guntharius severely, but Hagano, who is at first reluctant to fight his old friend and fellow-hostage and who has, moreover, just preached what sounds like a sermon against avarice, eventually has to do so because he is Guntharius's vassal and also because Waltharius has killed a relative of his. In the Latin poem, however, this final fight is abandoned. There may have been a tradition in which Hagano killed his friend, but here, after Waltharius loses a hand and Hagano an eye and teeth, Hiltgunt tends their wounds, and the gold of the Huns (based on Germanic tribute, of course) is shared. Waltharius and Hiltgunt rule Aquitaine for thirty years. There is a surviving fragment in Anglo-Saxon, and a reference to Hagen (Hagano's) reluctance to fight in the later *Nibelungenlied,* so that clearly the tale as such was known, and not just from a Latin poem by a young writer.

The work is really about the relationship between Waltharius and Hagano (one of the manuscripts designates it as such), specifically about the way in which the latter is torn between a reluctance to attack his old friend (who is also, of course, a formidable warrior), and loyalty to his king and people. Only when Waltharius has killed most of the warriors set against him and has wounded Guntharius severely, does Hagano agree to the battle. Whereas in the *Hildebrandlied* the outcome of the battle is determined logically, in this case a reconciliation is far more plausible. The fighting is vivid, because there is more space, and the pitched battles as Waltharius defends his position in the mountains are varied. As far as Hiltgunt is concerned, Waltharius behaves chastely on their flight, and her role at the end as a conciliator is interesting. This time, too, the influence of Christianity goes well beyond the insertion of a few lines, but we can still pick out primitive elements, as when Waltharius beheads his vanquished opponents. Geraldus's preface points out, what is more, that his aim in writing was not the glory of God, but entertainment.

If *Waltharius* is itself rare as an heroic poem in Latin from ninth or tenth century Germany, there is a learned tradition, established already in Merovingian and developed in Carolingian Germany and after, of the panegyric, the Latin praise poem, usually addressed to a ruler, and sometimes containing elements associated also with the heroic poem.[16] Developed in Frankish territories by Venantius Fortunatus, for example, in the seventh century, later exponents included Theodulf of Orléans, a Goth who came to the court of Charlemagne in 780. Such praise poems stress the ethical aspects of the person celebrated, such as their love of justice and peace, for example, but their roles as warriors can also at least be noted. Theodulf's *Ad Carolum regem* (To Charlemagne the King) refers to the various pagan races *quas dextra ad Christus sollicitante vocas* (which your strong right arm has called to Christ.) The panegyric is reflected in Old High German in Otfrid's praise of King Ludwig the German, one of the dedicatory poems to his Gospel book, and in the macaronic poem known as *De Heinrico*. The panegyric is not always closely linked with the heroic tradition, although Otfrid does say, for example, of Ludwig that he was often in danger and was forced to fight, but was always victorious with God's grace. An anonymous Carolingian Latin poem with the title *De Pippini victoria Avarica* (The victory of Pépin over the Avars), is a little closer to the heroic poem in its celebration of a specific conquest, that of the Avar people by Charlemagne's son, Pépin, King of Italy, in 795–96.[17] Pépin is praised as the warrior king who, with the help of God, conquered Unguimer and the Avars without, in fact, the need for a battle (in spite of the use of the word victory), when the Avars, also known as the White Huns, surrendered to superior force. Not only is the power of God stressed in bringing about the victory, which is something quite different from the objective combating of fate in the *Hildebrandlied*, but Pépin is praised and the hope is uttered that he might live long. There is still the notion of the victorious warrior, but the contextualization is entirely Christian and the stress is different.

Closer still to the heroic poem is a later Latin praise poem of about the year 1000, preserved in a collection from the Rhineland, known because of the present location of the manuscript as the *Cambridge Songs,*[18] and whose general importance has again been discussed in an earlier chapter. The *Modus Ottinc* is about the three Saxon rulers of the Holy Roman Empire between 936 and 1002, all called Otto. Written in the service of Otto III (983–1002), most of it is about Otto I, known as the Great (936–73), and it focuses on his victory over the Magyars on the River Lech in 955. This is not a general panegyric, but opens with a vivid picture of the fear of Otto's court when the Magyars raise their standards against him. Otto acts with resolution, and his war-leader Konrad addresses the troops, urging them to bravery and announcing that he will be the *signifer*, the standard bearer. The battle is described and the Lech flows with blood as the Germans are victorious. This takes up the bulk of the poem. Of Otto II we hear that although he has all the right ethical qualities, he was not often able to rejoice in a victory, although Otto the Great was *ante et post/sepe victor* (often victorious before and after). Otto III is also praised. The focus on the Battle of the Lech shows the emperor doing his duty to defend his people, and the battle itself is told in vivid terms, but there is no hint of conflict, as there was in the *Hildebrandlied* or in *Waltharius*.

If the language of the *Hildebrandlied* is problematic, the Old High German *Ludwigslied*, though linguistically far clearer, ought not to be in German at all. It celebrates a victory by what we may call a French king (and may therefore refer to as Louis, in spite of the language of the poem), and it was written at some distance from German-speaking territories. Its theme, however, is that of the warrior-king facing a battle, and it has in it elements both of the heroic poem (in this case completely Christianized, however) and of the panegyric. The *Ludwigslied* survives in a manuscript now in Valenciennes, in northern France, but was written at the nearby monastery of St. Amand sur l'Elnon. Unsurprisingly, most of the manuscript is in Latin, but there are two additions, both in the same hand, which are not. One is our poem in German and the other is a poem about a saint, in Old French.[19] The explanation of this anomaly probably lies in the fact that St. Amand had an international reputation, and its school attracted men — largely aristocratic — from all over the old Frankish empire, so that presumably the *Ludwigslied* was composed by a German speaker, probably a nobleman, living, working, or studying in St. Amand, but originally from the Rhineland, since the dialect is largely Rhenish-Franconian. His class accounts for the expression of closeness to the king himself, and also perhaps for the interest in the battle theme. It is unlikely that the language represents a Frankish official royal language, or that the poem was written in Germany and copied in France; nor (although it has been suggested) is the poem about the East Frankish, German, king who shared the Latin name of Ludovicus (the equivalent, of course, either of Louis or Ludwig). The details given in the work can only apply to the West Frankish kingdom and to Louis. When it was first composed the *Ludwigslied* celebrated a king who was still alive and who had just won a victory that was felt to be very important, by the time the poem came to be written down, probably not long after, the victorious king was dead. Within a year, in fact, a victory poem for a warrior king had become a memorial.

Similar to the *Hildebrandlied* in length, this work is, however, composed in fifty-nine end-rhymed long lines (grouped in strophes of two or three lines), the form that comes to dominate in Old High German after Otfrid. The hero is Louis III of France, great-great-grandson of Charlemagne. Charlemagne's grandsons Ludwig the German and Charles the Bald had, by the middle of the ninth century, become kings of the separate territories of the West and East Franks respectively, and although the territories are not quite the same, they may be referred to as France and Germany. Another grandson of Charlemagne, Lothar I, son of Lewis the Pious, was nominally emperor and ruled in Lothar's kingdom, Lorraine. The French king Charles the Bald was succeeded in 877 by Louis II of France, known as the Stammerer, who died only two years later. His two young sons, Louis III, the hero of the poem, and his brother Carloman, divided the kingdom between them, according to Frankish custom. Louis III was just about old enough to be seen as a viable ruler, although his particular part of the kingdom, the northern part, was under fairly regular attack from an enemy from outside, the Vikings, while internally (and from Germany, too) he faced opposition and the threat of usurpation. However, in July 881 he and his brother defeated one such attempt (by the Duke of Provence), and immediately after this Louis rode north, and with his cavalry defeated a Viking force at Saucourt in Picardy on 3 August 881.[20] The *Ludwigslied* was composed as a song of praise about the king and his victory, possibly for use too as a propaganda piece for a young king on an insecure throne.[21] According to all the chronicles, the Vikings, a great and much-feared threat to Western Europe at this period, were soundly defeated; but Louis died almost exactly a year later, and Karloman soon after that. His far younger half-brother, who ruled as Charles the Simple (meaning "straightforward") eventually gave the Vikings — the Northmen — land for their duchy, Normandy.

The *Ludwigslied* was composed, therefore, sometime between August 881, when the battle took place, and August 882, when the king died, and when it was written down in St. Amand by a French-speaking scribe (we can tell this from some of the linguistic features in the copying), a Latin title was added, describing the work as a memorial. In the written form we have, the text has a potential function different from the presumed original one. Apart from the form, there are three other distinct differences from the *Hildebrandlied:* the work, though concerned with a battle, is based this time on a recent historical event, well attested in contemporary chronicles, rather than having a distant and distorted context; second, the narrator plays a far more dominant role, whereas in the earlier poem the focus is on dialogue between the protagonists, even if the narrator does supply significant points of information; and third, the events of the *Ludwigslied* are interpreted by the narrator in a Christian sense. We still have a work of literature in which an important warrior, this time a king, faces a difficult battle with courage, but the philosophy of heroic behavior has undergone a change.

The poem tells us that there was a king called Louis, who lost his father when young and who shared his kingdom with his brother Karloman. The Vikings attacked when he was away, but he returned and defeated them. Some major historical details are omitted from the poem, notably the date and place of the battle, but this is presumably because at the time of composition these details were well known. However, other things are also omitted: we are told that Louis was away, but not that he was fighting another Christian, presumably because this might conflict with the overall ethos of the work. Beside the facts, the narrator offers a great deal of interpretation, however, all consistent with a theocentric rather than with a fatalist view of human events. Louis is protected by God, whom he serves gladly, was apparently happy to share the kingdom with his brother (although the Frankish kings were never notably fraternal), and he speaks directly to God, who asks him to go and join battle against the pagan Vikings in aid of the Franks as God's own people. The poet also offers a view of why God permitted the Vikings to attack Frankish territory in the first place; their divinely determined function (not an uncommon interpretation) is to serve as God's instrument to punish wickedness in the Frankish people, and at the same time to test the valor of the young king. The situation is therefore established, but the king is away. There is, of course, no question of what has been interpreted as a kind of metaphysical puppetry here; God exists outside time and history, while Louis and the Franks are in it, and have to make their own decisions with their own free will, without knowing the end. Hildebrand has to make the decision to fight against his own son, and this is based on duty; Louis makes a decision in God's name to engage in a dangerous battle, in which there is no perceived divine intervention even at the end, simply a comment on the poet's part thanking God and the saints for Louis's victory. The last lines of the *Ludwigslied* are, like the last lines of the Pépin poem, a straightforward praise of the king, who has behaved as a hero, with a standard conclusion commending him to God's care.

The active role of the warrior king is shown in speech, first with God:

> Hluduuig, kuning min   Hilph minan liutin!
> Heigun sa Northman   Harto biduuungan
> Thanne sprah Hluduig: Herro, so duon ih
> Dot ni rette mir iz,   Al thaz du gibiudist. (vv. 23–26)

["Louis, my king, help my people! The Norsemen have oppressed them greatly." Then Louis said: "Lord, I shall do all you ask, if I am spared."]

Having agreed to act as God requests, Louis addresses his troops, promising them rewards if they survive, or compensation for their relatives if they fall. The battle is presented briefly and vigorously, showing the king fighting especially well, since *thaz uuas imo gekunni* (that was in his blood, v. 51). Hildebrand was aware of the workings of cruel fate and of his duty to his overlord and to his own reputation, but Louis is presented as having a different awareness of human existence: *giskerit ist thiu hieruuist / so lango so uuili Krist* (our life's length is determined according to the will of God, v. 36) he says, and the Franks go into battle with the liturgical words of the *kyrie eleison* (Lord have mercy on us), on their lips. They are not yet as confident of heaven as a reward for death in battle against the pagans as some later crusaders are sometimes shown to be in literature. They are made aware by the king of their Christian duty to fight against the pagans, however, and almost the only description offered of the Vikings is that they are *heidine man*, heathens.

Not every editor has chosen to print the Latin heading added to the poem. That heading, however, is a vital instruction to the reader for the reception of the work as we have it, however it may originally have been conceived. The *Ludwigslied* is a *rithmus teutonicus,* a German rhymed poem, inscribed to the blessed memory of King Louis, son of Louis, who was also a king. Any disputes about his legitimacy as a king are ruled out even after his death, but above all else the church has placed Louis's victory into a coherent spiritual context and has thus fully assimilated the hero. The arguments in criticism of the work about whether the work is Germanic-heroic or Christian in essence are irrelevant, and can be resolved with a compromise as simple as it is obvious: the work is Germanic *and* Christian, and it places the acts of an idealized Germanic warrior-king into a Christian framework, a hero who fights for the state because this is what God wants him to do.[22] The propagandistic aspect of the *Ludwigslied* acquired a different *kind* of political validity with the death of the king himself. It has become a memorial to an instance of appropriate (and hence more generally applicable) behavior on the part of a Christian king, a hero who has followed his duty to his people who are also God's people, just as he is God's king. And yet the poem does not promise him heaven. Just as the older Germanic hero, Hildebrand, lives on in the poem which is *his* memorial and testimony to his reputation as a warrior, so, too, the victory of Louis over the Vikings survives as a memorial to the king's reputation as a Christian hero.

Notes

[1] (Darmstadt: WBG, 1953). See too Gerhard Eis, *Drei deutsche Gedichte des 8. Jahrhunderts aus Legenden erschlossen* (Berlin: Ebering, 1936). Some early literary histories devoted almost entire volumes to supposedly lost heroic material.

[2] The edited text (which is also referred to as the *Hildebrandslied*) is in MSD. II, St. I, Braune. XXVIII, with German translations in Wipf, 150–55, and Schlosser, 60–63, and an English version by James Walter in *German Epic Poetry,* ed. Francis C. Gentry and James K. Walter (New York: Continuum, 1995), 1–8 (the so-called *Younger Lay of Hildebrand* (text and translation) is on 295–302). There are facsimiles in Georg Baesecke, *Das Hildebrandlied* (Halle: Niemeyer, 1945), Hanns Fischer, *Schrifttafeln zum althochdeutschen Lesebuch* (Tübingen: Niemeyer, 1966), plate 12–13, and *Das Hildebrandlied,* ed. Hartmut Broszinski, 2nd ed. (Kassel: Stauda, 1985) as well as in many secondary studies (which often contain a text as well). On its recent history see W. F. Twaddell, "The *Hildebrandlied* Manuscript in the USA," *Journal of English and Germanic Philology* 73 (1974): 157–68.

[3] Albert B. Lord, *The Singer of Tales* (Cambridge, MA: Harvard UP, 1960); Franz H. Bäuml, "Medieval Literacy and Illiteracy," in *Germanic Studies in Honor of Otto*

Springer, ed. Stephen J. Kaplowitt (Pittsburgh: K and S, 1978), 41–54. See Wolfgang Haubrichs, *Die Anfänge* (Frankfurt am Main: Athenaeum, 1988), 104–5. For a clear survey of the problems of *Heldendichtung,* and for a stimulating indication of just how much is unclear about the Germanic oral poet per se, see Roberta Frank's 1992 Toller Memorial Lecture, "The Search for the Anglo-Saxon Oral Poet," *Bulletin of the John Rylands University Library of Manchester* 75 (1993): 1–36.

[4] The fullest study of the language is that by Rosemarie Lühr, *Studien zur Sprache des Hildebrandsliedes* (Frankfurt am Main and Bern: Lang, 1982).

[5] There is an enormous bibliography on the work, and here, only the most useful items can be noted. See H. van der Kolk, *Das Hildebrandslied: Eine forschungsgeschichtliche Darstellung* (Amsterdam: Scheltema and Holkema, 1967), and on more recent criticism the (revised) paper by Maria Vittoria Molinari, "Sul carme di Ildebrando: nuove prospettivi critiche e interpretative," in *Ildebrando: Quattro saggi e i testi* (Alessandria: Edizioni dell'Orso, 2001), 47–79. The volume contains other important pieces in English and German. See also J. Sidney Groseclose and Brian O. Murdoch, *Die althochdeutschen poetischen Denkmäler,* Stuttgart: Metzler, 1976), 31–41. On the prehistory of the text, see Willy Krogmann, *Das Hildebrandslied in der langobardischen Urfassung hergestellt* (Berlin: Schmidt, 1959), Richard Lawson, "The Hildebrandslied originally Gothic?" *NMitt* 74 (1973): 333–39, and Siegfried Gutenbrunner, *Von Hildebrand und Hadubrand: Lied-Sage-Mythos* (Heidelberg: Winter, 1976). Richard d'Alquen and Hans-Georg Trevers, "The Lay of Hildebrand, a Case for a Low German Written Original," *ABäG* 22 (1984): 11–72 make a late (but not convincing) attempt to show that the text that we have began life in Old Low Franconian.

[6] See on the hero in general: C. M. Bowra, *Heroic Poetry* (London: Macmillan, 1952); Jan de Vries, *Heroic Song and Heroic Legend,* trans. B. J. Timmer (London: OUP, 1963); Gwyn Jones, *Kings, Beasts and Heroes* (London: OUP, 1972); W. H. T. Jackson, *The Hero and the King* (New York: Columbia UP, 1982); Brian Murdoch, *The Germanic Hero* (London: Hambledon, 1996).

[7] See Peter Heather, "Theoderic, King of the Goths," *Early Medieval Europe* 4 (1995), 145–73. Two important papers on the question of lost epic material focus on Theoderic: Wolfgang Haubrichs, "Ein Held für viele Zwecke," and Stephan Müller, "Helden in gelehrten Welten," the latter with reference to the eleventh-century *Quedlinburg Annals* in *Theodisca,* ed. Wolfgang Haubrichs et al. (Berlin and New York: De Gruyter, 2000), 330–63 and 364–86. Both papers are relevant to the *Hildebrandlied.*

[8] Wolfgang Harms, *Der Kampf mit dem Freund oder Verwandten in der deutschen Literatur bis um 1300* (Munich: Eidos, 1963); Werner Hoffmann, "Das Hildebrandslied und die indo-germanische Vater-Sohn-Kampf-Dichtung," *PBB/T* 92 (1970): 26–42, and especially A. T. Hatto, "On the Excellence of the *Hildebrandslied,*" *Modern Language Review* 68 (1973): 820–38, and in Schwab and Molinari, *Ildebrando,* 15–45.

[9] See the interesting contextualization of the whole theme by Victor Morris Udwin, *Between Two Armies: The Place of the Duel in Epic Culture* (Leiden: Brill, 1999).

[10] Ute Schwab, *Arbeo laoso* (Bern: Francke, 1972). See also Kenneth J. Northcott, "*Das Hildebrandlied*: a Legal Process?" *Modern Language Review* 56 (1961): 432–

38; Norbert Wagner, "Cheiseringu getan," *ZfdA* 104 (1975): 179–88; Alain Renoir, "The Armor of the *Hildebrandslied,*" *Neuphilologische Mitteilungen* 78 (1977): 389–95, and William C. McDonald, "Too Softly a Gift of Treasure: a Re-Reading of the Old High German *Hildebrandslied,*" *Euphorion* 78 (1984): 1–16. There are interesting illustrations of the armor of a Germanic warrior in Simon MacDowall, *Germanic Warrior, 236–568 AD* (Oxford: Osprey, 1996).

[11] See Ute Schwab, "*Imo was eo fehta ti leop,*" in Schwab and Molinari, *Ildebrando,* 81–146. Other useful interpretations of the work as such include Frederick Norman's *Three Essays on the Hildebrandslied,* ed. A. T. Hatto (London: Institute of German Studies 1973), as well as Werner Schröder, "Hildebrands tragischer Blindheit und der Schluß des *Hildebrandsliedes,*" *DVjs* 37 (1963): 481–97; Roswitha Wisniewski, "Hadubrands Rache," *ABäG* 9 (1975): 1–12; Herbert Kolb, "Hildebrands Sohn," in *Studien zur deutschen Literatur des Mittelalters,* ed. R. Schützeichel and U. Fellmann (Bonn: Bouvier, 1979), 51–75, and H. H. Meier, "Die Schlacht im *Hildebrandslied,*" *ZfdA* 119 (1990): 127–38.

[12] On which see George T. Gillespie, "Heroic Lays: Survival and Transformation in Ballad," *Oxford German Studies* 9 (1978): 1–18.

[13] The Austrian poet Heimrad Bäcker read a poem called "zu spät für hildebrand" as part of a series for Radio Oberösterreich in May 1992: the brief poem juxtaposes Old High German words and their modern meanings, capturing the essence of the poem between *sunufatarungo* and *welaga nu* (father and son; alas). It is published in *Dichterzeit,* a supplementary (extra) volume of the journal *Die Rampe* in 1993, p. 51, and is cited as an indicator of the ongoing force of the work. That it should have returned to the South is also interesting.

[14] Standard edition by Karl Strecker, *Nachträge zu den Poetae Latini I* (Weimar: Böhlau, 1951, repr. Munich: MGH, 1978). There are Latin, Old English, Norse, Middle High German and Polish analogues in Marion Dexter Learned, *The Saga of Walther of Aquitaine* ([1892], repr. Westport, CT: Greenwood, 1970). See also Karl Strecker (German trans. by Peter Vossen), *Waltharius* (Berlin: Weidmann, 1947); B. K. Vollmann's translation and commentary in *Frühe deutsche Literatur und lateinische Literatur in Deutschland 800–1150,* ed. W. Haug and B. K. Vollmann (Frankfurt am Main: Deutscher Klassiker Verlag, 1991), 163–259; Gregor Vogt-Spira, *Waltharius: Lateinisch/Deutsch* (Stuttgart: Reclam, 1994); Dennis M. Kratz, *Waltharius and Ruodlieb* (New York: Garland, 1984), 1–71 (text and English translation); Brian Murdoch, *Walthari* (Glasgow: Scottish Papers in Germanic Studies, 1989) (English translation).

[15] See Emil Ploss, *Waltharius und Walthersage* (Hildesheim: Olms, 1969) and Karl Langosch, *Waltharius: Die Dichtung und die Forschung* (Darmstadt: WBG, 1973). Again, there is much secondary literature; significant papers include W. Stach, "Geralds *Waltharius*" *Historische Zeitschrift* 168 (1943): 57–81; Max Wehrli, "*Waltharius.* Gattungsgeschichtliche Betrachtungen," *Mittelateinisches Jahrbuch* 2 (1965): 63–73; Otto Zwierlein, "Das *Waltharius*-Epos und seine lateinische Vorbilder," *Antike und Abendland* 16 (1970): 153–84, and Ursula Ernst, "Walther — ein christlicher Held?" *Mittellateinisches Jahrbuch* 21 (1986): 79–83. See also Harms, *Kampf mit dem Freund.*

[16] The best survey is that by Annette Georgi, *Das lateinische und deutsche Preisgedicht des Mittelalters* (Berlin: Schmidt, 1969). For examples, see *Venantius Fortunatus: Personal and Political Poems*, ed. Judith George (Liverpool: Liverpool UP, 1995).

[17] Ernst Dümmler, *Poetae Latini aevi Carolini* (Berlin: Hahn/MGH, 1881). The poem by Theodulf is on 438–39, that on the Avars, 116. The latter is translated in Murdoch, *Walthari*, 109–11, and in Paul Edward Dutton, *Carolingian Civilisation* (Peterborough, ON: Broadview, 1993), 43–44.

[18] The text is in the collection of Old High German texts, MSD XXII, as well as in Karl Strecker, *Die Cambridger Lieder (Carmina Cantabrigensia)* (Berlin: MGH, 1926, 2nd ed. 1955), poem 11; text and facsimile in Karl Breul, *The Cambridge Songs* (Cambridge: CUP, 1915). The poem is also in a manuscript in Wolfenbüttel. Text and modern German translation in Horst Kusch, *Einführung in das lateinische Mittelalter* (Berlin: VEB Verlag der Wissenschaften, 1957), I, 210–17. On the work see Georgi, *Preisgedicht*, 131–32, and Markus Diebold, *Das Sagelied* (Bern and Frankfurt am Main: Lang, 1974), 13–17.

[19] Text in MSD XI, St. XI, Braune XXXVI, Schlosser, 100–103, Wipf, 156–61. Translation into English in Bostock, *Handbook*, 239–41. Bibliography in Groseclose/Murdoch, *Denkmäler*, 67–77. Claudia Händl, *Ludwigslied: Canto di Ludovico* (Alessandria: Edizioni dell'Orso, 1990) prints historical parallels, and see on the manuscript Paul Lefranq, *Rithmus teutonicus ou Ludwigslied?* (Paris: Droz, 1945). Erika Urmoneit, *Der Wortschatz des Ludwigsliedes* (Munich: Fink, 1973) analyzes the language in detail.

[20] On history and the poem, see Ruth Harvey, "The Provenance of the Old High German *Ludwigslied*," *Medium Aevum* 14 (1945): 1–20; Elisabeth Berg, "Das *Ludwigslied* und die Schlacht bei Saucourt," *Rheinische Vierteljahresblätter* 29 (1964): 175–99; Brian Murdoch, "Saucourt and the *Ludwigslied*," *Revue belge de philologie et d'histoire* 55 (1977): 841–67; Paul Fouracre, "The Context of the Old High German *Ludwigslied*," *Medium Aevum* 54 (1985): 87–103.

[21] See the important papers by Raimund Kemper, David Yeandle and Paul Fouracre in the collection *mit regulu bithuungan*, ed. John L. Flood and David N. Yeandle (Göppingen: Kümmerle, 1989), 1–93, on the historical-political approach to the work. See further Kemper's papers "Das *Ludwigslied* im Kontext zeitgenössischer Rechtsvorgänge," *DVjs* 56 (1982): 161–73, and "Das *Ludwigslied* — eine politische Lektion," *Leuvense Bijdragen* 72 (1983): 59–77. Also useful are Holger Homann, "Das *Ludwigslied* — Dichtung im Dienste der Politik," in *Traditions and Transitions: Studies in Honor of Harold Jantz*, ed. Lieselotte E. Kurth et al. (Munich: Delp, 1972), 17–28, and Robert Müller, "Das *Ludwigslied* — eine Dichtung im Dienste monarchischer Propaganda für den Kampf gegen die Normannen," in *Sprache-Text-Geschichte*, ed. P. K. Stein et al. (Göppingen: Kümmerle, 1980), 441–77.

[22] See Hans Naumann, *Das Ludwigslied und die verwandten lateinischen Gedichte* (Halle: Klinz, 1932); Werner Schwarz, "The *Ludwigslied* — a Ninth-Century Poem," *Modern Language Review* 42 (1947): 467–73; Max Wehrli, "Gattungsgeschichtliche Betrachtungen zum *Ludwigslied*," in *Philologia Deutsch . . . Festschrift Walther Henzen*, ed. Werner Kohlschmidt et al. (Bern: Francke, 1965), 9–20; Heinrich Beck, "Zur literaturgeschichtlichen Stellung des ahd. Ludwigsliedes," *ZfdA* 103 (1974): 37–51. See also, with interesting comments linking two of our texts,

Friedrich Maurer, "*Hildebrandslied* und *Ludwigslied*," *Der Deutschunterricht* 9/ii (1957): 5–15, as well (in this context) as Ralph W. V. Elliott, "Byrhtnoth and Hildebrand: a Study in Heroic Technique," *Comparative Literature* 14 (1962): 53–70.

Otfrid of Weissenburg

Linda Archibald

THE MOST SIGNIFICANT FIGURE in the early history of German literature is the Benedictine monk Otfrid (sometimes Otfried) of Weissenburg, author of the *Evangelienbuch* (Gospel Book).[1] He lived from
around 800 until around 875 and completed his major work toward the
end of his life between 863 and 871 in the monastery at Weissenburg,
now known as Wissembourg, in the northeast of France. His poetic retelling of the gospel story consists of 7,104 lines of Old High German, pack-
aged in sections with Latin headings taken mainly from the Bible, and
provided with additional introductory pieces, one in Latin prose and three
in Old High German verse. The dialect he used is known as South Rhenish Franconian, a variety that he himself would call *theotisce* (German[ic])
or *frenkisgon* (Frankish). The fact that the poem is free composition and
paraphrase rather than a direct translation from the Latin Vulgate Bible or
any other source makes it particularly interesting for philologists studying
the beginnings of the German language and its literature. Its considerable
length provides a useful range of vocabulary and grammatical features,
showing how the early German language had begun to integrate new
Christian terminology and concepts into its traditions, sometimes using
the old heroic words with slightly different meanings, and at other times
adopting new words from the Greek or Roman Christian domains. Moreover, the *Evangelienbuch* has also survived intact in several well preserved
manuscripts, which makes textual study comparatively straightforward
when one considers the precarious and often fragmentary state of most
other contemporary vernacular texts.

The *Evangelienbuch* is a synthesis of all four Gospel narratives integrated with accompanying homilies and exhortations drawn from Carolingian and earlier Latin commentaries. Though most of the content is
standard Christian material intended to educate and edify the reader,[2] the
style and structure make it one of the most important works in the history of German literature. At the time of writing, Otfrid was concerned
with the immediate task of promoting understanding of the basic Gospel
message in his own country. It is likely that he would have been disap-

pointed to find that the language and format of his work, much more than the messages it contains, have turned out to be what interests most contemporary readers.

In the last quarter of the ninth century the Golden Age of the court of Charlemagne, known to later scholars as the Carolingian (or Caroline) Renaissance, was on the wane, and the great empire was divided between rival branches of the family. There had been a flourishing of learning under Charlemagne and his immediate descendants, but the wealth and stability of that period was beginning to erode. Otfrid grew up in this early period of renewed interest in scholarly activity and spent his younger days learning from the great scholar Hrabanus Maurus (or Hraban) at the monastery of Fulda. It was under Hraban that Tatian's Gospel harmony was translated from a Latin version into Old High German, and Otfrid may have been inspired by this concept, though he appears not to have used the harmony itself as a source, preferring to construct his work according to his own plan. Influences from Hraban's own writing, including his treatise *De inventione linguarum* (On the invention of languages), may account for Otfrid's subsequent enthusiasm for language theory and his favorable opinion of composition in the hitherto relatively untried local languages.

Unlike Hraban, Otfrid was not an important or famous man in his own lifetime. He appears to have spent most of his adult life observing the daily rule of the Benedictine order and working in the scriptorium, where manuscripts were made or copied for internal use and for sharing with other readers in distant monasteries or noble families across the German-speaking area. The library at Weissenburg specialized in biblical writings, mostly copies of famous commentaries, and of course these were written almost entirely in Latin. Later scholars have found Otfrid's handwriting in the margins of several Weissenburg manuscripts, including many Old High German notes and glosses.[3] Indeed the preservation of the *Evangelienbuch* in four high quality manuscripts is no doubt due to the fact that Otfrid was himself in charge of the production of new manuscripts, and could allocate resources and time to the works he judged to be required. Otfrid's own distinctive Carolingian minuscule handwriting, which is also found in the margins of the Vienna manuscript of the *Evangelienbuch,* corrects and clarifies the Latin texts of the Weissenburg library, showing the careful attention of a supervisor monitoring the efforts of the scribes, or adding helpful hints to explain the meanings of key concepts.

The four surviving manuscripts of the *Evangelienbuch* show that this was no afterthought scribbled in the margins of more established authorities, as is the case with much of the surviving material in Old High German, but a substantial and impressive work in its own right. It is laid out with red initial letters at the start of every pair of long-lines, and elaborate headings and sub-headings showing reference points to the reader which would allow comparison with the biblical source and with works of Latin commentary. The Vienna manuscript also contains several full-page illustrations, and the whole work is carefully and neatly laid out. One manuscript reveals Bavarian influences, which are probably due to the origins of the scribe or scribes who were responsible for that copy. The expense and time required for the production and multiple copying of such a long text must have been considerable, an indication of unusual commitment to a vernacular piece.

Otfrid was also a teacher, charged with teaching Christian doctrine to younger monks, and his work reflects a profound knowledge of the Bible, especially of the Gospels and the Psalms, which were the key teaching texts for inexperienced learners. There is also evidence in the introductory pieces that he had a sound grasp of the principles of rhetoric, another of the basic curriculum subjects in this period. Otfrid writes fluently in Latin, as is clear from a letter accompanying the work, and displays virtuoso composition skills when he adorns his Frankish verse dedications with Latin acrostics and telestichs. This complex pattern of spelling out words by means of the initial letters, final letters, and (to the modern mind incredibly) also middle letters in these poems offers a greeting to each of the recipients. This shows beyond doubt that Otfrid was a competent scholar and imitator of Carolingian Latin authors who also favored such literary set pieces.[4] His choice of the vernacular is not due to any failings in his own linguistic competence but is a deliberate strategy that he adopts for the benefit of his readers.

At that time, and for centuries to come, most monastic writings were in Latin, and the dialects of the different Christian tribes and nations were considered barbaric and unsuitable vehicles for the sacred writings of the Church. Otfrid is aware, however, from his daily experience in the monastery, that it is difficult to teach students through the medium of a foreign language. He is concerned that his Frankish-speaking students understand their lessons, and so he makes the radical choice of writing his long poem in their own local language. In a Latin introductory letter to Liutbert, who was Archbishop of Mainz from 863 until 889, Otfrid attempts to obtain official approval for his work and explain the rationale behind his choice of language. He cites a number of factors motivating him, including encouragement from brother monks and a noble woman called Judith to do this, and his own desire that his fellow Frankish speakers should not be afraid of the complexities of Latin but should learn the scriptures in their own language.

With traditionally expressed formulas of deference and humility, Otfrid offers his work to the archbishop, explaining the shortcomings of the German language in comparison with the perfection of the holy Latin language. He explains how the Latin alphabet is ill-suited to represent the uncultivated German dialects, and lists the spellings he has chosen to reflect certain sounds. Likewise, the foursquare perfection of the Gospels is contrasted with the five human senses and the overall five-book structure of Otfrid's vernacular text. In Otfrid's mind, religious theorizing is not separate from literary theorizing. Even terms which have a primarily non-religious meaning are suffused with dogmatic connotations. The evenness of the number four represents sublime perfection, for example, while the unevenness of five means superfluity and excess. The restraining influence of grammar on a language is likened to the purifying effect of religious discipline on life. In an elaborate chain of images begun in the introductory letters and then picked up later in the main text, Otfrid shows how humble human beings using their ordinary local dialect can obtain the rewards of the Christian faith through the reading and following of the Holy Scriptures as presented here in reduced and simplified form.

Most of the literary activity available in German at the time appears — as far as we can tell — to have been heroic and worldly, with themes such as family feuds and epic battles; there was certainly an oral tradition of such material, but little remains of it in writing, and so it is impossible to be sure how much variation there was in its type and form. Otfrid refers to this kind of creative activity as a *cantus . . . obscenus* (obscene song), which indicates that he feels this would be the wrong sort of model to use for holy writings. Judging by the surviving evidence, the standard literary form for Germanic poetry of the period is the alliterative long line. The well-established and Christianized late Latin tradition prefers classical meter for long poetic works. There are also examples of specific forms adapted for religious purposes such as simplified lyrical verses or short liturgical pieces adapted from rhetorical flourishes such as repetition and end-rhyme. These shorter hymns, doxologies, sequences and other liturgical pieces encouraged a move away from strictly metrical patterns and toward more rhythmical approaches. Otfrid appears to find a fusion in his own choice of form: a system based on short rhyming phrases containing two stresses each, arranged in pairs of long lines. It looks like the old alliterative long line but sounds quite different. A comparison with the alliterative Old Saxon Gospel poem known as the *Heliand*[5] makes the stylistic difference clear:

> Hiet im thuo te is handon   dragan hluttran brunnion,
> water an uuegie,   thar hie furi them uuerode sat . . .
> (*Heliand,* vv. 5473–74.)

[He had brought to his hands, drawn from the clear well,
water to the wayside, where he stood by the people.]

This structure has the long line format, with a caesura, a firm break, and the link between the two half lines is alliterative. This is the type of poetry also known in other languages, such as in the Old English *Beowulf.* There is no sustained couplet or stanza structure, and sometimes the new sentence begins in the middle of the line rather than at the start of a line.

In contrast Otfrid narrates this same scene where Pontius Pilate washes his hands thus:

> Tho wúasg er sino hénti;   er wólt es duan tho énti,
> sih wolt er réhto ubarlút   néman ir thera léidunt.
> (*Evangelienbuch* IV, xxiv, 25–26).

[Then he washed his hands; he wanted to make an end,
he wanted to remove quite clearly, their shame from him.]

As in the first example, there is a break between the half lines, but in Otfrid's version the link between each half is in the rhyme, and any alliteration is a coincidental occurrence. The two long lines are linked in sense as a complete unit. Thus Otfrid has constructed a new form which is, as far as we know, original and which allows a four-stress pattern similar to the old heroic line, but at the same time distances itself from the secular connotations of the alliterative form by introducing rhyme as a consistent formal feature. Otfrid's innovative rhymed form has been much studied[6] and it constitutes perhaps his greatest contribution to literary history. But there is more to his work than this feature.

It should be noted here that although the *Heliand,* the earlier Old Saxon Gospel poem, uses the older heroic tradition in form and to an extent in content, it remains, nevertheless, a Christian poem, with a similar balance of narrative and interpretation based on the commentaries of the period. Unlike Otfrid, however, the anonymous Old Saxon poet seems to have used a Gospel harmony as a basis, and there is a clearer primary proselytizing intent.

Besides a concern for the learners in his care, Otfrid also reveals a special interest in everything to do with teaching. In another introductory letter, this time in the same Old High German rhymed verse that is used for the main text, Otfrid writes to Salomo, Bishop of Constance, again in an attempt to gain the approval of a senior figure for his new Gospel book. The poetic letter follows standard classical and early Christian epistolary patterns, starting with a *salutatio* (greeting) followed by the main argument liberally sprinkled with blessings and expressions of humility, and then a formulaic *conclusio* (conclusion). Otfrid depicts Salomo as his wise and admirable teacher, one who takes after his namesake the biblical King Solomon in leading his people. The Benedictine community was built on the foundation of strong teacher-pupil relationships, and Otfrid's own travels exemplify the common practice of younger monks traveling to sister communities for educational purposes, and older monks maintaining these brotherly connections in later life through exchanges of books and occasional visits.[7] Otfrid asks the bishop to read his humble book and see if there is anything good in it — in effect Otfrid is seeking permission and assistance in promoting his writing beyond the confines of the monastery at Weissenburg. In the absence of modern printing and publishing networks this is the way that clerical authors distributed their works and the way that libraries extended their stocks. The approval of a teacher and senior figure in the church hierarchy is the best possible advertisement for Otfrid's work.

In a third dedicatory poem, presumably accompanying a third copy of the *Evangelienbuch,* Otfrid writes to two of his contemporaries Hartmuat and Werinbert of the monastery of St. Gallen. These two monks had known Otfrid from their period of study at Fulda, and their monastery was to become one of the most illustrious of all Benedictine communities at the beginning of the tenth century under Salomo, the nephew of the earlier bishop Salomo mentioned by Otfrid. In fact, much of the groundwork for the later renown of Fulda was done in the mid-ninth century under the abbot Grimald and the two monks Hartmuat and Werinbert. Grimald was previously abbot at Weissenburg from 855 until 872 and would surely have been in contact with Otfrid then. At St. Gallen Grimald was often absent on church business, leaving Hartmuat in charge of the scriptorium. While Weissenburg concentrated on works of exegesis and commentary, St. Gallen specialized in the Bible itself, producing expensive, sometimes illuminated copies of the different books. Werinbert was the *magister scholae* (master of the school) and it seems that they both, like Otfrid, spent their lifetime's work on activities related to copying, studying and teaching the holy Christian texts. In the letter to Hartmuat and Werinbert, Otfrid specifically mentions the important gifts and services, including the exchange of books and prayers, that link the two monastic communities.

A further common factor between Weissenburg and St. Gallen is an emphasis on Augustinian thinking. The central theme of Otfrid's dedicatory letter to Hartmuat and Werinbert is the notion of *caritas* (charity), which is here defined in the sense of brotherly love between monks. Examples are drawn from the Bible to illustrate ideal loving relationships, especially those understood to foreshadow the love between mankind as a whole and God as their savior. There is much emphasis on the word *drut* (loved one) with, for example, Otfrid speaking to God and describing the community of believers in heaven as *druta thina* (your loved ones). The brothers Cain and Abel are mentioned, and the story of Jacob and his brother, though this is a complex and perhaps somewhat negative example, and Esau is not named. Enoch is labeled *druhtines drut* (the Lord's loved one); Noah is *gote drut* (loved one of God) and Abraham, too, is *gotes drut*. Christ is called *thero selbo gotes drut* (the loved one of God Himself) and Otfrid even urges the readers to reflect and do better, so that they too can each become *gotes drut*.

When speaking of love Otfrid uses also the word *minna,* which in a much later period takes on the meaning of courtly love, but Otfrid defines it carefully as meaning *karitas* (charity) and *bruaderscaf* (brotherliness). Both the horizontal dimension, love for each other, and the vertical dimension, love between people and God, are discussed, with Christ playing a pivotal role in both. It is typical that the communal aspect is at the forefront, since monastic love is supposed to be for the whole community, both locally in each monastery, and further afield in the large Christian family that the church represents. Otfrid directs a final exhortation to love one another specifically at the monastery at St. Gall, including Hartmuat, Werinbert, and all the monastic brothers in that community.

An interesting emphasis in the letter to Hartmuat and Werinbert is found in Otfrid's laboring of the concept of the elder brother — a relationship deriving from the Old Testament laws which grant the elder brother or kinsman certain legal privileges and responsibilities toward dependent relatives. This is a powerful relationship that resonates in the all-male environment of the monastery; Otfrid even says that *bruaderscaf* has the power to release believers from Satan. It is clear that Otfrid sees the role of older monks and leaders, as exemplified by David and Moses, as an important one, and the tone of his letter to his contemporaries and brother monks is one of encouragement in the role of spiritual and loving leadership at St. Gallen, just as Otfrid plays this role at Weissenburg.

The final dedicatory piece, a poem addressed to Ludovicus, Ludwig the German, follows the traditional Latin pattern of the praise poem, though it is in the same rhyming and acrostic pattern and Frankish language as the other two poems.[8] Its function is to eulogize the king in deference to his role as leader of the Frankish people. Otfrid highlights two aspects of his character that are etymologically discernible in his name: *hlut* meaning "loud" or "famous," and *wig* meaning "battle." This is no doubt a reference to the turbulent political scene in the second half of the ninth century, in which the descendants of Charlemagne constantly battled for supremacy over vast areas of the formerly unified Carolingian empire. It could also be a reference to the Christian ruler's struggle to lead his people against the tyranny of temptation and sin. The wordplay is again a daring application of subtle literary techniques to the humble vernacular, showing how literary and theological interpretations are merged to create a text with layers of meaning for the adept reader or listener to appreciate.

Echoes of Augustinian thought can be found in Otfrid's depiction of the Frankish realm, and the favored role model for leadership is on this occasion the Old Testament King David — a warrior king who also loved to sing God's praises. One unusual aspect of Otfrid's praise poem is the fact that he addresses himself directly to the Frankish people rather than to Ludwig. In tone it often sounds more like a sermon than a eulogy and this is typical of Otfrid's didactic style. Because of this focus on the Christian nation under their Christian king, some scholars have interpreted the poem as a campaign piece intended to win support for Ludwig the German in his political struggles.[9] This may be reading too much into the piece, however, since, after all, Otfrid wrote three dedications to monastic recipients and only this one piece to a secular authority. Moreover, Otfrid includes the king in his exhortation to read the Gospel story, suggesting that he is addressing him in his exemplary role as leader of all Franks, placing him firmly within the religious framework.

The first chapter of the *Evangelienbuch* proper continues this discussion of nationhood and language again within the context of reading the Gospel and praising God. The chapter title *Cur scriptor hunc libri theotisce dictaverit* (Why the author fashioned these books in German) is the first known author's preface in the German language. It repeats all the arguments of the dedicatory piece and contains the following memorable lines:

> Wánana sculun Fránkon   éinon thaz biwánkon,
> ni sie in frénkisgon bigínnen,   sie gotes lób singen?
>   (*Evangelienbuch* I, i, 33–34).

[Why should the Franks be the only ones unable
to begin in Frankish to sing God's praises?]

This plaintive plea for linguistic freedom has been linked in some studies
with an emerging nationalism in the Frankish realms: an expectation that
the Carolingian era would herald the dawn of a new age in which the
Franks would inherit from the Romans leadership of the Christian world.
Others perceive in Otfrid's praise of the Franks and their language an
attempt to glorify prowess in battle and build alliances for King Ludwig
against other players. It should be noted, however, that Otfrid is writing
from a position of defensiveness: the novelty of his concept makes it suspicious to those in authority. He tempers his extreme deference to authority in the dedicatory pieces with a firm belief in the worthiness of the
humble Frankish language to carry the sacred message of the Gospel.
Just as sinful humans can be saved by the divine words of the Gospel, so
Otfrid believes that with appropriate training, the Frankish language and
people can be brought into the service of God. As one would expect
from Otfrid, there is a biblical underpinning and support in Carolingian
commentaries for this idea that multiple languages are a good thing, so
long as they are dedicated to the singing of God's praises.[10]

Otfrid praises the exceptional literary skills of the Greeks and the Romans: they write so intricately and beautifully that he seeks to imitate
them, not replace them. The imagery he uses betrays his admiration: writings in the classical languages are like fine ivory, by which he means they
are made from a rough natural material (the language) which is refined
and purified by a skilled worker. Again he mentions the discipline that language undergoes: in this case fine prose or detailed metrical patterns.

The topic of Christian literary work in the vernacular was contentious throughout the ninth century, and for many centuries beyond.
Most Christian authors saw the works of pre-Christian Greek and Roman
authors as beautiful but dangerous objects to be admired for their technical and literary merits, but also to be feared because of the idolatrous,
immoral, or heretical content in their stories. Literary composition by
Christian authors in Latin was encouraged, especially when based on religious themes or overlaid with a heavy moralizing tone. There is little
surviving evidence of literary composition in the vernacular and it was
not until well after the Reformation that Christian worshipers could expect to have their ceremonies conducted in their native language, rather
than in Latin. Fragmentary initiatives were begun and attempts to translate the liturgy and change local practices were made in various parts of
the Christian world, but the higher levels of the church always felt uneasy

if the ordinary people had too much grasp of the finer points of theology. It was not so much a fear of education in itself, but a fear that the separate branches of the church would develop into factions and remove themselves from central control in Rome or other key centers. History would prove that this fear was well founded. In 868 Pope Hadrian issued an edict which allowed Slavic Christians to use their vernacular in the liturgy, but Pope John VIII took a much more negative position. Otfrid's defense of the Frankish tongue must therefore be seen against this background, and he marshals his arguments to make his endeavor clear to a suspicious audience.

Otfrid uses illustrations from the Bible in his description of the Franks and their lands and history, He likens their strength in battle to the legendary prowess of the Medes and the Persians. A reference most probably inspired by the book of Daniel[11] describes the divided kingdom of the Greeks and the rising of the great horn, which is interpreted to mean Alexander the Great. There is no doubt that Otfrid merges his depiction of the Franks and their leader with a warning against disunity, as if to forestall any suggestion that his sense of pride in this small nation should be a source of temptation toward rebellious thoughts. As usual in Otfrid's work, both literal and spiritual dimensions are present in his argument and it is hard to tell where quotation and Christian symbolism ends and where contemporary reference begins. This passage can be read as a warning against the consequences of political struggles between different branches of the royal family, or against doctrinal disagreements between different factions of the church. In the Christian perspective, it does not much matter, since both are part of the divine order of things and both levels of meaning can stand together for eager learners to read, decipher and digest.

Otfrid describes again in this chapter the activity of literary composition, but here he leaves behind the linguistic terminology and speaks instead in pictures: he chooses more visual imagery to illustrate his point. Thus he describes the work of Greek and Roman authors as "dark" and "complicated," as if it contains hidden mysteries that the reader must labor to uncover. He evidently aspires to this level of subtlety in his own work, because as he speaks of such things, he himself uses these techniques. Prose is described as something good to drink, and poetry as something good to eat, though more difficult to digest. Food and drink imagery for ideas is common to classical tradition as well as later Christian works, and would be easily recognized by a monastic audience. In another resonant image Otfrid indicates that authors purify their works just as grain is purified, separating the precious wheat from the worthless chaff. On a spiritual plane this is, of course, a reference also to the separa-tion of true teaching from heresy, and of good deeds from bad deeds. This chapter uses many common harvest images for literature and teach-ing: wheat, seeds, bread, storage barns and weighing, for example. The work is not the stirring stuff of legend or epic but the contemplative multiple layering of thoughts so beloved of Christian theological writers. It may be simplified, harmonized, and presented in a more accessible vernacular language, but this is a work of doctrinal importance intended primarily for a monastic audience.

A further section in this chapter on words such as *regula* (rule), *fuazi* (foot), and *zit* (timing) can also be read on multiple levels. It can be inter-preted as a treatise on the literary techniques used for composing the *Evangelienbuch*, since these terms have secondary meanings beyond their literal ones that can be related to the metrical ordering of syllables and stresses common to Greek and Latin poetry. On yet deeper spiritual level, these terms could further be interpreted as a depiction of the measured steps that a Christian is supposed to take on the path to salvation. The Benedictine *regula*, the monastic rule, is perhaps also indicated here, since it is governed by discipline and order, with ritual singing and prayer times throughout the day and a recurring rhythm of festivals over the Christian year. This chapter lays out clearly what is to come in the rest of the *Evan-gelienbuch:* a slow unfolding of the complex allegorical system under-pinning Christian belief. Every literal image has several other possible interpretations and all human experience can be analyzed and explained in several spiritual categories of moral or mystical meaning. It is the commu-nication of this key insight, far more than any immediate historical or po-litical concern, which drives the author of the *Evangelienbuch*.

The narrative of the Gospel itself is presented in chronological order, according to Otfrid's own recollection, he says, with many additional passages of commentary when a topic is considered of sufficient interest to explore further. By no means is every event or parable interpreted by Otfrid, and indeed there appears to be a deliberate shortening of the middle sections dealing with Christ's teaching and a more detailed treatment of events surrounding the nativity, death, and resurrection. The effect of this shift of emphasis is to stress the role of Christ as savior, and to skip over the detail of the preaching and miracles. This does not mean that Otfrid considers these matters unimportant, but is due to the need to keep the manuscript to a manageable length and highlight spe-cific concepts relating to the monastic context such as ways of making sure that the Gospel message is understood in some depth, and passed on faithfully to Frankish-speaking learners. Thus, exhortations to read and digest the text are frequent and the reader or listener is expected to apply these lessons in daily life.

The first book of the *Evangelienbuch* consists of two introductory chapters, including the chapter about the Franks and an invocation to God for inspiration, and then a further twenty-six chapters dealing with the birth of Christ until His baptism, ending with the story of John the Baptist. Otfrid uses the Gospels of Matthew and Luke mostly, and dwells on the symbolism of the wise men and their search for the infant. In a separate chapter (xviii) headed *Mystice* (mystical or allegorical reading), he explains why the magi returned to their homeland by a different path: it symbolizes the human condition, since mortals are destined to wander the earth in suffering because of their sin. The good Christian must choose a different path to find a way back to salvation — the difficult path of service to God, and this is the moral that must be drawn from the story.

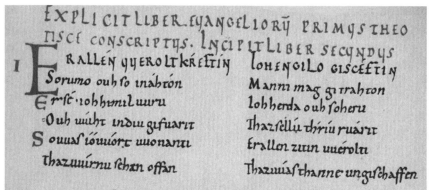

Otfrid's Gospel-book (the Freising text, beginning of book II)

Books II and III of the *Evangelienbuch* narrate the main miracles and teachings of Christ. The title of book II, chapter i: *In principio erat verbum* (In the beginning was the word) signals a shift to the Gospel of John. The second chapter of book II is headed *Recapitulo signorum in nativitate Christi* (Recapitulation of the signs surrounding the birth of Christ), suggesting that the author wishes his readers or listeners to pause and reflect on a series of related symbolic details. This is evidence of Otfrid's teacher mentality: he breaks down the Gospel material into pieces and directs the learner to focus on key images which encapsulate the deeper meanings of the text. Once a certain amount has been presented, there is a revision chapter to ensure that the lessons are not forgotten.

The allegorical nature of Otfrid's work has prompted many useful studies of his key imagery,[12] showing where Otfrid finds biblical starting points and takes ideas from clerical commentaries. He is a compiler rather than an originator, and he is conscious of this debt to scholars who have gone before him. The image of the book, or the written word, is central to the concept of the *Evangelienbuch,* and images for reading or listening to the scriptures abound. There are several words used for food: *gouma, muas, pruanta,* and *zuht,* and these are used interchangeably with an intention to symbolize the taking-in of the Gospel in a spiritual sense. Bread and wine are also powerful symbols and Otfrid uses the changing of water into wine and the feeding of the five thousand to make clear the link between physical and spiritual nourishment. Concrete and abstract concepts are spelled out and every item in the stories is given a spiritual meaning. Thus, tasting water is like uncovering literal meaning while tasting wine is like uncovering spiritual meaning; the jars symbolize the hearts of God's followers because they are full of Holy Scripture. To make the point even more obvious, Otfrid relates the story of Abraham and Isaac, and comments that reading the story can be like drinking pure water, in other words as an example of how a holy man behaves. But it can also be like drinking wine, if its deeper meaning is recognized as well, namely as an Old Testament type (in the technical sense), which prefigures the later coming of Christ in New Testament times. The source of the homily is probably a Latin commentary by Alcuin,[13] but Otfrid gains added value from the telling of it in Frankish because he plays on the similarity between *win* (wine) and *wini* (friend). Otfrid shifts attention from the biblical miracle itself, where the miraculous transformation is the point, demonstrating the divinity of the young Christ, to the notion of tasting and taking-in various levels of meaning. It is not a departure from traditional interpretation so much as a change of emphasis. The ninth-century reader cannot witness the miracle, but is asked to make it real by living out the spiritual meanings it is intended to carry.

This point is labored even more in the following chapter, entitled "Why He made wine out of water and not out of nothing" (II, x). In this non-biblical section Otfrid explains that the use of water signifies the continuity which Christ has with the past and with earthly things. The guests at the wedding are described as *biscofa* (bishops), which is of course something of an anachronism, but Otfrid is speaking again on a figurative level, showing that the bishops of the Christian church select passages from the scriptures and pass them on to believers.

This imagery is recalled again in the third book: III, vi is a narrative chapter dealing with the feeding of the five thousand, and III, vii is a *Spiritaliter* (spiritual interpretation) chapter. Otfrid interprets the meaning of the five loaves and two fishes as being a reminder of God's law, no doubt a passing reference to the five books of Moses in Old Testament Law as indicated in standard Carolingian commentaries. But, perhaps in an attempt to recall his own choice of a five-book structure for the *Evangelienbuch,* he lingers on a long excursus about the physical properties of bread, and the figurative meanings that readers should see in it. The commentators mention the hard outer crust and soft inner part, and Otfrid expands this further, suggesting it signifies the difficulty of the words that must be overcome if one is to reach the inner goodness that will nourish the soul. Parallels with the introductory letter to Liutbert are clear, and the emphasis on the five humble human senses as receivers of the heavenly nourishment is likewise a link with Otfrid's own concept of Christian literary effort. An interesting comment on the baskets used to gather up the crumbs left over from the meal: these are called *scalklichaz faz* (servant vessels, III, vii, 59), which again emphasizes the lowly nature of these containers of Holy Scripture, surely another reference to the Old High German *Evangelienbuch* itself.

This food/teaching imagery is recapitulated in the story mentioned in III, x, *De muliere Chananaea* (The Canaanite Woman). On this occasion Otfrid does not narrate the detail of the story, but simply retells the dialogue and makes explicit the hidden meaning. The biblical text is brief: "But he answered and said, It is not meet to take the children's bread, and to cast it to dogs. And she said, Truth, Lord: yet the dogs eat of the crumbs which fall from their masters' table." (Authorized Version, Matthew 15: 26–27). Otfrid devotes six lines to the woman's response and merges the allegorical with the literal in her very words. She uses the German words *welfa* (young dogs) and *wise* (wise men) to highlight the low and high status of different people, and repeats the vocabulary of the earlier miracles to stress the taking-in of bread and crumbs for spiritual nourishment. In the following chapter III, xi, this time headed *Moraliter* (moral interpretation), Otfrid leans on the ideas of Hraban to reflect on the hierarchy of players in this story.[14] Christ is at the top, as the provider of spiritual food. The "wise men" are seated around the table, which Hraban interprets as the Holy Scripture, and they signify the clergy. The children are believers, and the dogs under the table are heathen nations who, some would say, are not ready to receive the gift of teaching and with it ultimately salvation. Otfrid stresses the woman's patience and faith. Her humility and willingness to take the words of Christ as true are an example for young people to follow: even the least learned or least committed listener can take away valuable lessons from the preaching of the Gospels. Taken together, these three passages on food imagery first spell out the key concepts literally and figuratively, then practice the application of these in daily life, and finally summarize them.

One of the most distinctive features of Otfrid's work is its coherence as a single literary piece. Much of the detail supports the overall concept: for example, as the work draws to its dramatic conclusion with the death and resurrection of Christ, the number symbolism of four and five arises again. Otfrid mentions the four soldiers and, recalling his introductory letters, stresses the fact that this is an even number, and the fact that they had divided the rest of Christ's clothing, but the robe was an extra piece left over. The Bible mentions the seamless robe of Christ and the fact that the soldiers cast lots for it, as being prefigured in the Psalms,[15] but Otfrid takes a leisurely sixty-two lines and constructs a major allegory out of this. His chapter 4, xxviii–xxix are not typical of the rest of the work because they depart from the Gospel narrative to become a treatise on the concept of *caritas,* here used in the specific sense of brotherly love between Christian believers. Otfrid personifies the concept of Christian love, almost in the way that the classical gods and goddesses were turned into idealized human virtues in the Late Latin literary tradition, and says that she wove the seamless robe to tie believers together in unity. The words used to describe the perfection of the robe recalls the vocabulary Otfrid had used earlier to signify the excellent literary works of the Greeks and Romans. This discussion is not an exact parallel, but an echo of earlier metrical and moral connotations, showing that Otfrid expects by now that his readers or listeners will pick up these references without further explanation.[16]

The whole of the *Evangelienbuch* is designed to add relevance to the Gospel narratives for a ninth-century audience. The stress on the five human senses and all of the vivid imagery that is expanded and explained bring it into the range of experience of ordinary human beings. This tactic, along with the decision to deliver the message in the humble vernacular, gives the work immediacy and accessibility, but also runs the risk of turning attention excessively to worldly things. Otfrid counteracts this danger with an emphasis on the life of Christ after death. His entire fifth book is devoted to this part of the Gospel message, and the last nine chapters move away from the four Gospel sources altogether to concentrate on heavenly matters of judgment and salvation. This is a major departure from traditional Gospel harmony tradition, carrying on the chronological story-line by supplementing it with items from the Acts of the Apostles, or from prophetic sayings in both Old and New Testaments. All the sensory imagery that was painstakingly presented in the earlier chapters is now given a further, heavenly dimension. Where hunger, thirst and emptiness were depicted as positive states appropriate to earthly beings on their path to salvation, now in the fifth book there are images of fullness and sweetness, showing the ultimate reward awaiting those who have been purified by their adherence to the gospel teachings. The five senses are not in the least rejected and the long chapter V, xxiii on the trials of earthly life and the perfection of heaven stress the need to have both physical and spiritual dimensions fulfilled. A short chorus, reminiscent of the liturgy, is repeated seven times:

> Biscírmi uns, druhtin gúato,   thero selbun árabeito,
> Líchamon joh séla,   in thínes sélbes era;
> (*Evangelienbuch* V, xxiii, 11–12 etc.)

[Protect us, good Lord, from this same hardship
Body and soul, in your own glory.]

Otfrid's fusion of the physical and the spiritual in the form of a five book German harmony of the four Latin gospels ends with an image of believers gathered together with the heavenly angels to sing God's praises.

In literary histories of German Otfrid has generally fared badly. Critics have found his style repetitive and his frequent asides and explanations intrusive. Few readers would now read the work through for pleasure, and it is most often quoted in the context of describing the early stages in the development of the German language. Much of the work is simple retelling of familiar stories, and there is little in the way of excitement or dramatic development. To compare the *Evangelienbuch* unfavorably with heroic epic, however, is to misunderstand its purpose. While the Old Saxon *Heliand* appears to have drawn some parallels purposely with the feudal traditions of Germanic society, and with the formal literary patterns produced by that culture, Otfrid chooses to depart from these influences altogether. His work is not a poorly executed Christian epic, but a carefully crafted textbook for use in an educational context, and a monastic one at that. The presence of a few musical notes in the margins of one manuscript, and the accent marks indicating stresses have been cited as evidence that the work was intended to be sung, or at least chanted, perhaps in a formal religious setting. Certainly the arrangement into chapters with biblical reference points in the headings and margins would suggest that the book could be used alongside the original Gospel sources, perhaps even with the daily readings from the Bible as prescribed in the Benedictine Rule, but this could happen in the classroom just as well as in any more formal context. The careful red initials, the indenting of lines and the references to critical works and other parts of the Bible indicate that the work was intended to be read and used for study.[17] The narrative is broken up in order to form lessons, at first in small pieces, but as the work develops there are also some longer and more difficult chapters, such as the one on the seamless robe and the long description of heaven. The key to understanding the function of the work lies in the symbolic explanations Otfrid gives us himself, especially in the introductory pieces. The work is intended to aid in the understanding of the gospels: it is designed to explain them, and open up a way for humble Frankish readers to reach the rich spiritual nourishment that the Latin Gospels contain. The four-stress rhyming long line, which Otfrid is at pains to explain as an artificial discipline that he forces the untrained language to obey, is in fact the most distinctive feature of the work, and probably the invention of Otfrid himself. This rhyming Gospel harmony is the first example of a new vernacular verse tradition for the whole of Western Europe and for this Otfrid is to be remembered.

Notes

[1] The standard edition is *Otfrids Evangelienbuch* edited by Oskar Erdmann (1882) and revised by Ludwig Wolff, 7th ed. (Tübingen: Niemeyer, 1973). References are made to book number, chapter number and line number of the *Evangelienbuch*. There is a bibliography of Otfrid by Johanna Belkin and Jürgen Meier, *Bibliographie zu Otfrid von Weißenburg* (Berlin: Schmidt, 1975) and see the collection of essays edited by Wolfgang Kleiber, *Otfrid von Weißenburg* (Darmstadt: WBG, 1978). Partial modern German translation by Gisela Vollmann-Profe, *Otfrid von Weißenburg, Evangelienbuch* (Stuttgart: Reclam, 1987).

[2] The most comprehensive study of Otfrid's source materials beyond the Gospels is still Ernst Hellgardt, *Die exegetischen Quellen von Otfrids Evangelienbuch* (Tübingen: Niemeyer, 1981).

[3] For details of Otfrid's activities in the scriptorium see the excellent study by Wolfgang Kleiber: *Untersuchungen zur handschriftlichen Überlieferung und Studien zum Aufbau des Evangelienbuches* (Munich: Francke, 1971).

[4] See, for example, two works by Hrabanus Maurus: *Hymnus de charitate* (A hymn on charity), *PL* 112, 1666D–1668A, and *De laudibus Sanctae Crucis* (In praise of the Holy Cross), *PL* 107, 133–294.

[5] On the *Heliand*, which is an important work of early German(ic) Christian literature in its own right, see the full discussion by G. Ronald Murphy in the first volume of this literary history. The standard text is *Heliand und Genesis*, ed. Otto Behaghel, 11th ed. by Burkhard Taeger (Tübingen: Niemeyer, 1996). See also G. Ronald Murphy, *The Saxon Savior* (New York and Oxford: OUP, 1989), and Murphy's translation, *The Heliand* (New York and Oxford: OUP, 1992). The Behaghel edition also

contains the fragments of the Old Saxon Genesis, which also survives in an Anglo-Saxon translation, and provides a link, therefore, to insular biblical poetry.

[6] See for example Ulrich Ernst, *Der Liber Evangeliorum Otfrids von Weißenburg: Literarästhetik und Verstechnik im Lichte der Tradition* (Cologne: Böhlau, 1975); Walter Haug, *Literaturtheorie im deutschen Mittelalter — von den Anfängen bis zum Ende des 13. Jahrhunderts* (Cologne, Böhlau, 1975); Rainer Patzlaff, *Otfrid von Weißenburg und die Mittelalterliche versus-Tradition: Untersuchungen zur formgeschichtlichen Stellung der Otfridstrophe* (Tübingen: Niemeyer, 1975); Bert Nagel, *Das Reimproblem in der deutschen Dichtung: Vom Otfridvers zum freien Vers* (Berlin: Schmidt, 1985). There is a translation of Otfrid's important Latin letter in Paul Dutton's reader, *Carolingian Civilisation* (Peterborough, ON: Broadview, 1993), 419–23 (translated by F. P. Magoun, 1943).

[7] For an excellent survey of Otfrid's monastic connections see Wolfgang Haubrichs "Otfrids St. Galler Studienfreunde," *ABäG* 4 (1973): 49–112.

[8] On the praise poem as a genre, including Otfrid's letter to Ludwig, see Annette Georgi, *Das lateinische und deutsche Preisgedicht des Mittelalters in der Nachfolge des genus demonstrativum* (Berlin: Schmidt, 1969).

[9] This is the line taken by Gisela Vollmann-Profe in her *Kommentar zu Otfrids Evangelienbuch* (Bonn: Habelt, 1976).

[10] See for example Apocalypse/Revelation 5: 9: ". . . for thou wast slain and hath redeemed us to God by thy blood out of every kindred, and tongue, and people, and nation." See also Cassiodorus *De institutione divinarum litterarum* (On the teaching of divine letters) *PL* 70, 1149D–1150.

[11] "The ram which thou sawest having two horns are the kings of Media and Persia. And the rough goat is the king of Grecia: and the great horn that is between his eyes is the first king." Daniel 8: 20–21.

[12] See especially Reinildis Hartmann, *Allegorisches Wörterbuch zu Otfrieds von Weißenburg Evangeliendichtung* (Munich: Fink, 1975).

[13] *Commentaria in S. Johannis, PL* 100, 768–70.

[14] *Commentariorum in Matthaeum, PL* 107, 980D.

[15] See Psalm 21: 19 and John 19: 23–24.

[16] For more details see Linda Archibald, "The Seamless Robe and Related Imagery in Otfrid von Weißenburg's *Evangelienbuch*" in *mit regulu bithuungan*, ed. John Flood and David Yeandle (Göppingen: Kümmerle, 1988), 123–32.

[17] See Donald A. McKenzie, *Otfrid von Weissenburg: Narrator or Commentator? A Comparative Study* (Stanford and London: Stanford UP, 1946). This early work is still one of the best appreciations of the function of the *Evangelienbuch*.

The Shorter German Verse Texts

Christopher Wells

COMMONLY, THE OLDEST written documents of any culture are ritual, historical, and legal texts embodying the religious and cultural
concerns of a people. These are often verse texts, reflecting a pre-literary,
pre-textual origin, since rhythm, alliteration, assonance and, later, rhyme,
make the material memorable and carry it from generation to generation
until it is written down. At the same time, their carefully crafted form
lends them a heightened expression and raises them above the everyday.[1]
Early German poetry also comes to us refracted through writing; we
know nothing directly of popular oral poetry and song among the illiterate Germans, and what we know indirectly comes mostly from condem-
natory statements by concerned clerical writers[2] who use vague terms
asymmetrically. The Christian-Latin labels *hymnus* and *(p)salm(us)* are
not applied to secular songs, whereas terms like *carmen, cantica,* and
cantus are used for both Christian and secular song.[3] But, given the
forms of some Christian-German poems, we can reasonably surmise that
features of secular song, folk-songs and native oral traditions have been
borrowed deliberately to work in an idiom known to the secular popula-
tion. That native literary idiom, which must have had variations, was familiar to many monks and nuns who came from noble families and knew
the secular life of the court from childhood. In particular, early German
Christian alliterative poetry seems to represent the adaptation, not the
replication of native traditions, but so, more subtly, does Otfrid, whose
strophes of long, internally rhymed lines eventually gave way to the
short, four-stress rhyming couplets that form the basis of Middle High
German narrative verse. German and Christian Latin culture existed
symbiotically, with the Latin dominant, although some church music, for
instance the so-called sequence, may have been prompted not (or not
solely) by liturgical cadences, but by secular songs.[4]

Shorter Old High German verse texts do not fall into one genre or
category. They are not connected with each other directly, and even a
chronological account proves problematic, since there are few poems from
the tenth and early eleventh centuries — and those are mainly dated ap-

proximately by paleography. At first sight there seems to be little continuity with later vernacular spiritual poetry. However, setting these poems alongside Latin texts as part of a common monastic and clerical culture enables us to make connections. Moreover, the form of the poetry shifts fundamentally, if gradually, from alliteration to assonance and rhyme, with early strophic structures and sometimes musical notation (in the form known as neumes) implying that poems could be accompanied, sung or recited, perhaps as plainchant.

Most early vernacular German verse survives from the ninth century. The *Hildebrandlied,* and also the two earliest short poems considered here, the *Wessobrunner Gebet* and the *Muspilli,* are all alliterative, whereas the surviving High German rhymed texts, including Otfrid's *Evangelienbuch* and the *Ludwigslied,* all fall into the second half of the ninth century. No purely alliterative poems have survived since, except the tenth-century *Merseburg Charms,* collected probably by monks for later use,[5] if not out of anthropological interest, as relics whose form is ancient. The audience for all rhyming poetry, in long lines or in short, was primarily monastic, whether monks or lay brothers, nuns, those in religious training, or under religious protection, like widows and orphans, so that the texts were probably both read and heard, when read aloud or performed for an audience.[6] Some placings of works in their manuscripts suggest one mode, some another. Otherwise, we have a few tiny fragments of verse that are little more than private jottings by scribes affording glimpses of a worldliness more fully evidenced in Latin texts throughout the period, or startlingly, in the *Kassel Glosses* or *Paris Conversations.* Alliteration (*Stabreim* or stave rhyme) as a vehicle for Christian poetry died out by the mid-ninth century; the *Hildebrandlied, Wessobrunner Gebet,* and *Muspilli* all have defective lines, whereas the apparently more technically proficient Old Saxon poetry, the *Heliand* and the *Genesis,* constitute special cases associated with Frankish and Anglo-Saxon missionary initiatives directed at a fierce and backward-looking people in a language whose consonants and syllable structure remained conservative, unaffected by the High German consonant shift.[7] The oldest surviving High German poetry is in long, alliterating lines, a Germanic form more fully represented in Old Saxon and in Old English texts, like *Beowulf* or the *Wanderer,* or by later Norse poetry. The *Hildebrandlied* illustrates the power of this verse form, despite irregularities, where the bipartite Germanic personal names — *Hildebrand enti Hadubrant* — resonate with double alliteration in the half-line. This alliteration is not mere embellishment; with rhythm and stress it binds together the elements of the long line, since only stressed syllables can alliterate, and alliteration itself indicates the prominent stresses. Increasingly elaborate rules govern the meter in Old English and in Icelandic Eddic poems.

We cannot discuss these texts and rules here, but compared with the Old Saxon *Heliand,* the verse technique of the *Hildebrandlied* is uneven, to say the least, while that text's dialectal mixture of Low and High German complicates the picture. Essentially, the Germanic alliterative long line falls into two half-lines, each containing two more or less strongly stressed syllables. The number of unstressed syllables is immaterial, but the first stressed syllable of the second half-line must always alliterate with one or both stressed syllables in the first half-line. The last stressed syllable of the second half-line is generally without alliteration, although all four stressed syllables in the line can share the same pattern of alliteration, and there may even be double alliteration involving alternating (a-b-: a-b-) or embracing patterns (b-a-: a-b-).[8] The alliterative poetry in High German appears, then, to be decaying: but it might be more accurate to say that it was not the chosen vehicle for bringing Christianity to the Germans. Christian literacy acted as a filter or barrier to keep out secular native traditions, although the Irish and Anglo-Saxon missionaries who imported Christianity to replace the German beliefs also spread that Latin-based literacy which preserved what vernacular texts we have. But most German poetic texts, including all the verse considered here, should be seen as innovations, opening up a space between native German oral and Latin Christian written culture in a continuing dialogue. They should be assessed as effective vehicles for spreading knowledge of Christian faith and practice, not bewailed as the sad, fragmentary relics of a Germanic national heritage.

Alliterative verse must have been familiar in a range of shorter genres with various functions in a public setting — for recitation, performance, declamation (perhaps proclamation) and even singing or incantation.[9] Einhard's oft cited statement that Charlemagne wanted to preserve the barbarian (that is, the German) ancient songs celebrating the deeds and battles of old kings implies that the old culture was passing and perhaps was also no longer perceived as a threat.[10] However, his son, Lewis the Pious, repudiated secular songs and did not want them to be heard or taught,[11] which must also have set back attempts to reach the Germans in their own idiom, at least in the Frankish heartlands. Later on, between 860 and 870, Otfrid explicitly seeks to enhance the status of Frankish by writing a life of Christ in it, and in a letter to Archbishop Liutbert of Mainz expresses his desire (discussed in the previous essay) to replace the "obscene lay song in the vernacular" (*laicorum cantus obscenus,* where *cantus* implies singing), which shows the low regard in which German was held. Otfrid exploits the traditional long line, but innovates by using rhyme and assonance at the caesura and the end of the line to link both halves. Late classical Latin verse, arguably the Ambrosian Hymns (these hymns, named after the fourth-century theologian Ambrose of Milan, had four lines, each with the same number of syllables but usually no rhyme), or rhyming hymns developed from them, may have served as models and also, perhaps, earlier vernacular assonanced or rhyming verse. German's weakening inflectional syllables made rhyming easier, but Otfrid alters the grammar for the sake of rhyme,[12] or pads out his poem with tag phrases to help the meter and rhythm. Otfrid conceived his poem as a help for reading the scriptures in Latin, with commentary and interpretation, and his long, internally rhyming line looks forward to the later religious texts in short rhyming couplets aimed at aristocratic lay audiences which will be discussed later in this chapter.

Thus Otfrid's verse combines older and more modern techniques in virtuoso fashion for the needs of a monastic audience whose dominant culture is based on Latin, on book learning and on reading, not directly on oral tradition. Otfrid's long line with internal rhyme or near rhyme at the caesura has been termed the *binnengereimte Langzeile*,[13] but his unit of composition is undoubtedly the two-line strophe, as confirmed by the use of capital letters for the first and indentation for the second line in the manuscripts and by the acrostics and telestichs in the dedicatory sections to his work. Other non-alliterative Old High German poetry also has this or a similar form, although the length of the strophes varies, sometimes within a poem. The status of the internally rhyming long line has been questioned;[14] instead Otfrid is considered to have composed in rhyming couplets organized into strophes. In this view, both halves of the long line are metrically and rhythmically equivalent, and they are syntactically interchangeable, in fact, parallel and often independent, except that they are bound by rhyme, and the rhyming couplet they form is delimited by the syntax — the rhyme is not broken by one of lines belonging to a following (or preceding) syntactic structure. In the present context, the fact that the couplets or long lines coincide with syntactic breaks seems more important than whether the lines are long or short, because the lack of broken rhymes separates earlier verse from Middle High German verse. Long internally rhyming lines would have been indistinguishable from short couplets in oral performance, although the musical accompaniment (which we do not have in interpretable form) might have solved the issue. The manuscripts do not present our texts as short couplets, however. Indeed, they mostly do not present texts in long lines either: often dots are used to mark the half-lines. The

Ludwigslied, however, is clearly set out in long lines with internal rhyme in the manuscript, as is Otfrid's *Evangelienbuch,* although the copyist of one manuscript of the latter did not at first observe the line or strophic division.[15]

Processes of literal copying, rather than performance, may have shaped Otfrid's text, as did the use of literary models for its content and the commentaries. This need not have excluded sung performance, beside private study and reading (out loud),[16] and in Otfrid's own autograph copy (MS V), his notation indicates stressed forms, especially in the earlier sections, not unlike a performance script, while another manuscript, MS P, has two instances of neumed lines, lines with musical notes. But old alliterative patterns still shimmer through, since Otfrid frequently uses formulaic phrasing in his half-lines, fitting them metrically and rhythmically into the new assonanced and rhyming long line.[17] Indeed, one Latin-based cliché about heavenly bliss as life without death and light without darkness occurs in the *Muspilli: thar ist líp ana tód, líoth ana fínstri.*[18]

The earliest Christian poetry in High German before Otfrid employs alliterative verse to present the first and last things of the World, with the aim of supplanting heathen myths by Christian ones. The two poems known as the *Wessobrunner Gebet* and the *Muspilli* are complementary in subject matter and are often interpreted together although they do not represent a distinct genre of German religious poetry.[19] Their differing forms, dialects, and codicological settings suggest quite different functions. The *Wessobrunner Gebet* is carefully written in a Latin codex once at the monastery of Wessobrunn in Upper Bavaria, and was deliberately selected to appear there. The *Muspilli,* on the other hand, scrawled untidily into the margins and text of an imposing manuscript dedicated to Ludwig the German, possibly after 840, looks like a later addition whose content was more important than its form.

The *Wessobrunner Gebet,* the Wessobrunn Prayer, forms the central part of a small quarto manuscript dated in part to 814, which may have been a compendium of information useful for a preacher, mostly from Isidore of Seville's *Etymologies.* The original has been attributed to the later eighth century, ca. 770, presumably part of the ongoing conversion of the Bavarians.[20]

A title along the lines of "Wessobrunn Creation and Prayer" more accurately describes the two sections of the work: a cosmogony of nine alliterative lines that introduce God and his angels (*cootlihhe geista* — "good spirits"), followed by a rhythmical prose prayer asking God for the gift of grace and faith (text: St. II, Braune XXIX). This prayer answers the question implicit in the *firiuuiza meista* (greatest of wonders): who, then, created the world? The title *De Poeta,* like other headings in the manuscript, must apply in some sense to what follows, and God appears in both parts. Although Latin *poeta,* unlike its Greek equivalent,[21] is not attested in the sense of creator as well as poet,[22] a literal equivalence is unnecessary if this is metaphor. Bede's account of the poet Cædmon, who "sang of the Creation," describes God as *conditor* (founder), *Dei Conditoris,* as *creator* (creator) in *potentiam Creatoris,* and, significantly, as *auctorem regni cælestis* (author of the kingdom of heaven).[23] So *auctor* may be the metaphorical link between literary and other kinds of creation. The *Wessobrunner Gebet* follows material on the seven liberal arts,[24] whose subjects include rhetoric and, in the later part, the quadrivium, arithmetic, geometry, astronomy and music, which cover the dimensions of space and time, enumerating the creatures, shaping the territories, measuring intervals in the music of the spheres with their fixed stars. Since the liberal arts were taught as an adjunct to theology, it would not be inappropriate to see God as the rhetorical craftsman, linking poetic creation with the creation of the world — both are acts of the logos, the Word. Otfrid, combining Genesis and John's Gospel, tells how the Word was present before sea, sky and earth or any creature, and how God and the Word together created everything (Otfrid II, 1: *In principio erat verbum*).[25] So our text anticipates but does not influence Otfrid's later analogous version of the Creation, and at the end of the world God "folds heaven like a book" — *ist inan (himil) faltonti . . . so man sinan liuol tuot,* which echoes the rolled-up scroll of Apocalypse (Revelation) 6: 14: *et caelum recessit sicut liber involutus* (and the heaven departed as a scroll when it is rolled together).

Whether the opening lines were of pagan or Christian origin remains unclear. The individual elements — trees, mountains, the earth or sky — have been interpreted as objects of Germanic worship,[26] and the *Wessobrunner Gebet* provides the excuse to deploy arcane sources about Germanic cults. The first section may well be independent of the prayer which shows structural, rhythmical and stylistic affinities to other prayers, confessions of faith, and baptismal vows (*Taufgelöbnisse*).[27]

The poem has no gaps, although defective syntax and alliteration suggest at least two. With the alteration of *stein* to *scein* (v. 4), the poem reads:

DE POETA	ABOUT THE CREATOR
Dat *ga*fregin ih mit firahim firiuuizzo meista.	I learned among men the greatest of wonders:
Dat ero ni uuas noh ufhimil.	that earth did not exist, nor the sky above,
noh paum [? . . .] noh pereg ni uuas.	there was neither tree nor hill

ni [? . . .] nohheinig noh sunna ni scein.	and there was not any [? . . .] nor did the sun *shine*
noh mano ni liuhta noh der mareo seo.	nor did the moon gleam, nor the shining sea;
Do dar niuuiht ni uuas enteo ni uuenteo.	then there was nothing of ends or turnings.
enti do uuas der eino almahtico cot.	And there was then the sole and almighty God,
manno miltisto.	the most merciful of men,
enti dar uuarun auh manake mit inan.	and there were also with him many
cootlihhe geista.	good spirits (angels),
enti cot heilac.	and God the Holy . . .
Cot almahtico, du himil *enti* erda *g*auuorahtos.	God Almighty, Thou who mad'st Heaven and Earth
enti du mannun so manac coot for*g*api.	and Thou Who gav'st men so many good things,
forgip mir in dino ganada rehta galaupa.	grant me in Thy mercy true faith
enti cotan uuilleon.	and a good will,
uuistom enti spahida *enti* craft.	wisdom and discernment and strength,
tiuflun za uuidarstantanne.	to withstand devils
.*enti* arc za piuuisanne.	and to avoid evil/the Evil One
enti dinan uuilleon za *g*auurchanne.	and to work Thy will.

The half-lines of the first, narrative section are linked by alliteration and lead into a rhythmical prayer that can be treated as verse if we follow the manuscript punctuation.[28] Balanced parallel phrases with dependent objects and clauses, alternately double and treble, describe how God created Heaven and Earth and gave good things (two clauses, three objects). He is asked for true faith and good will (two objects with adjectives attached), then for three qualities relating to three lengthening and parallel final clauses with rhyming verbal nouns (gerunds): wisdom to withstand devils, cunning to avoid evil, strength for God's purposes. Verse and prose are not simply juxtaposed, but skillfully blended as in artistic Latin prose. Attempts to reconstruct the original text using numerical symbolism are prone to circular argument.[29]

Formally, then, the *Wessobrunner Gebet* emerges as no mere compilation from disparate sources, but as an artistic unity, tersely raising existential questions to which it provides the Christian answer, like that of Vulgate Psalm 89: 2.[30] Structurally, the *Wessobrunner Gebet* resembles certain German magic charms,[31] which also have a narrative introduction illustrating an instance where the charm worked, and then an incantatory imperative — here the equivalent is a request to be given the right qualities (*forgip mir*, grant me). Conversely, charms can use Christ and Christian figures or formulae (prayers and the *Paternoster*) to focus the magic. There is therefore no need to look for any specific Germanic source for the cosmogony of the poem, nor to invoke number symbolism or the cult of tree, mountain, and stone worship (*pereg*, *paum*, and the manuscript's *stein*) in order to establish the text's pagan credentials. Later, Charlemagne's capitularies and edicts show that the conversion of the pagans still formed part of his political program. Then, the *Wessobrunner Gebet* celebrates the creator as the consummate (liberal) artist, and the compiler of the manuscript perhaps also took aesthetic pleasure in this text and copied it for that reason.

The *Muspilli* (the poem's title was given it by the first editor, J. A. Schmeller in 1832, based on an obscure word in the text) raises problems of dialect, meaning, interpretation, origins, form and function. It is nowadays mostly interpreted as a daunting alliterative sermon on the fate of the individual soul after death viewed against the Last Judgment and intended to convince an aristocratic audience of the inadequacy of their native legal practices to cope with the doom confronting every one of them.[32] Our text has been entered, untidily and at times barbarously, into the fine manuscript of a pseudo-Augustinian sermon, dedicated to Ludwig the German, duke of Bavaria from 825 and later king, from Adalram, bishop of Regensburg from 821. The poem is incomplete, and lines 1–19a are on the first surviving page of the manuscript (fol.61a), the remaining lines at the bottom of 119b, then 120a after the dedication, the rest on the empty leaves 120b, 121a and b. The poem breaks off, presumably shortly before the end. It is unlikely, and certainly not demonstrable, that Ludwig himself wrote the poem down. We do not know when or where it was written. However, the preponderance of Bavarian linguistic features and Ludwig's known connections to persons interested in vernacular writings, like Hrabanus Maurus, Abbot of Fulda, or Walahfrid Strabo, or Otfrid himself, who dedicated his *Evangelienbuch* to Ludwig, make it not implausible that he had some connection with the work. Karl Bertau sees the writing of this text into an ornate MS as a deliberate act, to point up the disproportion between secular pomp and representation and the eschatological perspective of the poem which undermines any human delusions of grandeur.[33]

The beginning is missing, and the text opens by describing what happens when the individual dies. Once the soul leaves the body, two armies fight for it, one from the celestial stars, the other from the fiery pitch of Hell. The individual should lead a blameless life so as not to fall prey to Satan's army. The next section leaps forward to the Last Judgment and what precedes it. According to legal experts, Elias (Elijah), helped by God, will champion eternal life against the Antichrist who will be doomed by his own supporter, Satan. However, many men of God think that Elias himself will lose and be destroyed. Amid the general conflagration (not necessarily caused by Elias's death) no kinsman can help another, all are aghast. The poem returns to the theme of individual responsibility. The sole remedy is to act righteously while alive. When the heavenly horn sounds the Judge comes with his host to the place of judgment, the dead rise from their graves and no one can conceal or deny his deeds. The cross is paraded before them, and Christ shows the wounds which he received to atone for humanity's sins. And here the poem breaks off, probably shortly before the end.[34] The central section (vv. 37–62) concerning Elias's fight with the Antichrist has been called "*Muspilli* II" to distinguish it from the text into which it has apparently been interpolated, "*Muspilli* I." It begins with a formula *Daz hortih rahhon* (I heard tell . . .), and ends in a rhymed couplet, a formal break with the alliterative measure.

Three smaller sections present the court as *mahal*: vv. 31–36 introduce it as a summons no-one can ignore; vv. 63–72 explain that any man involved in court procedures should behave correctly and not accept bribes because the Devil carefully records such misdeeds to hold against him; finally (vv. 90–99), everyone must give a true account of his crimes and nothing can be hidden from the King. The poem repeatedly stresses that Judgment is inevitable, and only making amends beforehand by alms and fasting can help.

The word used for the poem's title (line 57, *uora demo muspille*, against/in the face of the *muspille*) means either the Judgment itself, specifically destruction by fire, or possibly the Judge. A great deal of philological ingenuity has been expended on this word, to little avail.[35] The word may even be a Christian loanword borrowed from Old Saxon and given a mythical significance later. In the Old Saxon *Heliand* the two occurrences both connote the end of the world.[36] So it seems to mean the destruction of the Earth by a spell, or perhaps even "by mouth," or the announcement of the end of the world. Scandinavian, Celtic and even oriental eschatological traditions have been suggested as sources for the term — in northern myth, wolves devour the sun and moon, but the Old High German poem is remarkably sober and factual in discussing legal procedures, and there is no need for mythology, other than Christian,[37] as the auto-destruction of the landscape is terrible enough: the bog swallows itself — *muor versuuilhit sih* (v. 53). Moreover, the Bible has destruction by mouth in the Apocalypse, where the rider on the pale horse bears a sword which proceeds out of his mouth, Apocalypse 19: 15 and 21: *Et de ore procedit gladius . . . in gladio . . . qui procedit de ore eius.* But ultimately it is not the word's origins, but its function in the Old Bavarian poem which matters. Like the word apocalypse itself, originally meaning a revelation of something, then the end of the world, the word *muspilli* had come to signify "fiery doom," or "holocaust," regardless of etymology, pagan or Christian.

The manuscript text is corrupt, and in parts illegible, not least because earlier scholars experimented on it with chemical reagents. But it is all we have, and it is inadvisable to seek to improve on it by omitting or altering verses for linguistic or stylistic reasons.[38] The status of the Elias section as a legal combat by ordeal has been disputed by Heinz Finger in his full-length study in 1977, since in patristic and biblical traditions Elias prefigures Christ's appearance at the Last Judgment. Elias was held not to have died a natural death, but to have been transported to Heaven, like Enoch, with whom some commentators on the Apocalypse link him. So theological, rather than legal, reasons may account for Elias's appearance in the *Muspilli*. Although Elias clearly is a champion — one of the *khenfun* (v. 40) — the theological and the legal aspects merge, because the outcome according to many *gotmanno* (men of God) (does this mean canon lawyers?) undermines the institution of judicial combat if Elias, whose cause is just, does not win. It is only the secular lawyers (if that is how the word should be interpreted), the *uueroltrehuuison*, who thought that he would. These people are shadowy, and Kolb's interpretation as "those skilled in earthly, that is, secular law" is substantiated by sporadic, early and non-German (Anglo-Saxon) sources,[39] so skepticism is in order. Furthermore, if the Antichrist is a *uuarch* (v. 39) and not a human, he has no *locus standi* and is debarred from formal legal process.

The sermon must have been aimed at Bavarian aristocracy, those responsible for law and order who acted as or appointed judges, attended courts and upheld German customary law. At the same time, the striking similarities with the administration document *Capitulare missorum generale* of 802 castigating abuses in the (secular) legal practice in a moralizing, paranetic tone, suggest an author who was a member of a clerical caste responsible alike for theological writings, vernacular poetry and judicial legislation.[40] The message of the *Muspilli* appears to be that not only are the German legal traditions *per se* inadequate to cope with the Last Judgment, but also that common ways of manipulating the system are unavailable to the soul under judgment. Our text is a moralizing sermon rather than a legal treatise.

The poet's wordiness has been criticized, but near-synonymic repetition, here of legal vocabulary — *suannan, arteilen; mahal, ding, mahalsteti, suona, gart, rihtungu*[41] — forms part of alliterative poetic style which binds key words together, even at the expense of the narrative flow. Varying alliterative patterns connect clauses, as when the saved soul finds a lodging without care, a dwelling in paradise and a house in

Heaven: *selida ano sorgun, . . . in pardisu pu . . . hus in himile* (15–17). Again, everyone must account for past crimes: *dar scal denne hant sprehhan, houpit sagen, || allero lido uuelihc unzi in den luzigun uinger* . . . (there the hand shall speak, the head say, each limb down to the little finger . . . vv. 91–92), where confession and symbolic legal gesture are equally involved.

Tense and mood present differing perspectives in what is essentially not a narrative text.[42] Present subjunctives indicate possible, potential, but by no means certain circumstances and outcomes, such as *piqueme* (v. 1) (nobody knows the day or the hour when death may come), and modals in past subjunctive form convey the same level of uncertainty, since they function as present subjunctives (*muozzi*, v. 83; *megi*, vv. 94, 95; *fur[imegi]*, v. 97). The description of the Last Judgment is to be taken as factual, each sinner is obliged and constrained, morally and by circumstances, to be judged. Uncertainties hedge him about, and he has cause for concern.

The *Muspilli* is the longest surviving Old High German alliterative poem, but it is rhythmically and metrically defective;[43] some lines lack alliteration altogether (vv. 13, 48, 74), or have two alliterations in the second half-line and one in the first (vv. 3, [49], 90). Sometimes the sole, and therefore principal alliteration in the second half-line falls awkwardly on the fourth stressed syllable (v. 15b; *siuh*). At the end of the Elias section (vv. 61–62) we have two end-rhymed couplets: *diu marha ist farprunnan,|| diu sela stet pidungan, // ni uueiz mit uuiu puaze: || so uuerit si za uuize* (the boundary is burned up, the soul stands aghast; at a loss to atone, and so it goes to punishment). While it seems unlikely that the "new" Christian end-rhymes are deliberately intended to signal a new Christian message, replacing legal traditions inadequate for the Last Judgment, this powerful poem certainly works as an admonition to repent — a *Bußpredigt*. The older remedies of secular law include letting champions decide an issue by judicial combat, fighting in support of relatives, paying fines, and as a last resort bribing the judge. As a sermon, not a narration about the End of the World, nor a legal treatise, the poem anticipates the didactic religious poetry of the tenth and eleventh century, works like *Ezzos Gesang,* or the *Memento Mori* which are also directed to the spiritual welfare of their audience, so reading the *Muspilli* as a Christian sermon removes it from its isolation and justifies its position codicologically in the manuscript of a pseudo-Augustinian sermon, which treats legal and last things.[44] Formally, too, the use of end-rhyme in an alliterative poem has parallels in the use of alliteration in the later rhyming poems, in *Ezzo,* or the *Memento Mori,* and in Otfrid.

It is convenient to consider here three complementary, though unrelated, shorter texts. First, two texts, known inappositely as the *Gebete des Sigihard* (Prayers of Sigihard) were written into a Freising manuscript (F) of Otfrid's *Evangelienbuch*. We know that the "unworthy cleric," the *indignus presbyter* Sigihardus wrote this copy for bishop Waldo (ca. 902–6?): but the so-called prayers are in a different hand and follow Latin benedictions meant to be read or sung before the evening religious services. Thus they are not actually private prayers, but transpositions into German of blessings to introduce devotional readings, including perhaps passages from Otfrid's poem, with which they are rhythmically and metrically identical.[45] The first asks: *Du himilisco trohtin, Ginade uns mit mahtin // In din selbes riche, Soso dir giliche* (Heavenly Lord have mercy on us (and) take us into Thy kingdom, should it please Thee), and the second blessing takes the same form, this time asking Christ to grant the grace of an eternal life free from all pain.

The Trier verses against the Devil (*Wider den Teufel*), by contrast, are not a benediction, but a malediction,[46] which may be why they were written (perhaps in the eleventh century) cryptographically in the late ninth-century Trier manuscript (MS 564 from the monastery of St. Matthew at Trier, containing notes on the Gospels by Isidore of Seville). The code uses the common device of replacing vowels by following consonants so that the first line runs: *nxvukllkh. bidbn. dfnr khc hbn. Crkst,.* and the whole may be resolved as:

Nu vuillih bidan den rihchan Crist, the mannelihches chenist [ist]
ther den divvel gibant, in sinen namon uuillih gan
nu vuillih then ureidon slahan mitten colbon.

[Now I will await Christ the Almighty, the salvation of everyone, who fettered the Devil. In His name I will walk. Now I will smite the traitor with a club.]

The somewhat inept verses conform to the internally rhyming or assonancing long line. The language represents a form of Middle Franconian, whose weakened inflectional syllables point to the later ninth century. Conceivably this is an exorcistic prayer involving a ritual beating, as such might form part of the tools of the trade of a preacher.[47]

Another rhyme against the devil, from Trier (from St. Maximin?) is the translation of a sentence from Gregory the Great's *Moralia* to the effect that "the devil can only harm those whom God permits him to harm."[48] This Rhenish Franconian text (with Low Franconian features: *use* = our) is not a prayer either, and also dates from the eleventh century. The form might again be in internally rhyming long lines, since the meter is unbalanced: *Nisal nieman then diubal uorhtan, // uuanda her nemach manne scada sin, iz nihengi imo use druhttin.* These lines would certainly not work as couplets, and they differ from the strophic pattern of Otfrid, whether construed as long lines or rhyming couplets.

A true prayer is the also inappropriately named *Augsburger Gebet*. The manuscript is now at Munich (Clm. 3851), and the prayer was written in the late ninth century in Rhenish Franconian, and shows Otfridian influence.[49] This prayer to God to release us from the chains of sin appears with its Latin source, a well-known prayer from Gregory the Great's *Liber sacramentorum,* on the fly-leaf of a manuscript containing penitential and canon law texts. The writer has struggled to set the syntax to the meter, which involved omitting the personal pronoun in the first line and the relative pronoun in the third, while the second line acquired an Otfridian filler phrase *thes bethurfun wir sar.* Since the syntax, particularly in lines three and four, does not preserve the integrity of the half lines, the prayer can be taken as a strophe of four internally rhymed long lines, rather than couplets:

> Got, thir eigenhaf ist, thaz [thu] io genathih bist:
> Intfaa gebet unsar, thes bethurfun uuir sar,
> thaz uns [thio uns] thio ketinun bindent thero sundun,
> thinero mildo genad intbinde haldo.

> [God, whose characteristic it is that [You] are always merciful: receive our prayer (our need is pressing), that the mercy of Your grace should swiftly release us [whom] the chains of sin are binding.]

The versifying is clumsy, but the use of a German prayer to introduce a collection of Latin penitential and legal texts and the Otfridian form are interesting.

The cult of saints has proved of enduring popularity, and their miracles and relics, the places where they were worshipped and their festivals and rituals persist to this day, ideologically and commercially exploited as ever. The foundation of local churches each with their peculiar patron saint provided a physical focus for the cult, while chronologically the Church year is divided up by their festivals which dictate the name-giving practices of the faithful.[50] Since Merovingian times, Latin saints' lives — hagiographies — had become common, and the miracles attributed to saints and prayers invoking them blended with and helped replace pagan magic. Two Old High German texts, the *Petruslied* and the *Georgslied* allow us to glimpse different ways of bringing hagiographical material to congregations. By contrast the *Galluslied*, celebrating the patron saint of St. Gallen is an example of a vernacular life (by the ninth-century teacher Ratpert) which survives only in the Latin translation of Ekkehard IV of St. Gallen, a pupil of Notker Labeo, made sometime before 1022. The Latin text is a learned clerical product, translated apparently to preserve the equally complex melody.[51] In Romance areas, too, we find Latin and vernacular Old French in two different treatments of the life of St. Eulalia — and that in a manuscript preserving the *Ludwigslied*, written it seems by the same hand, where a poem of praise for a Christian military leader composed while he was alive is already merging into hagiographical legend after his (in historical terms hardly exemplary!) death.

The *Petruslied*, the oldest known German hymn, was written on leaf 158 of a manuscript once at Freising (Munich, Clm. 6260, containing Hraban's commentary on Genesis) probably in the early tenth century.[52] The original poem may be much older than that, probably ninth-century. The text consisting of three strophes of three internally rhyming lines, of which the last acts as a refrain, is provided with the indicators of musical notation known as neumes, showing that it was meant to be sung. The first two strophes remind us of St. Peter's God-given powers to bind and loose sinners (Matthew 16: 19) and his role of gate-keeper in Heaven, then we are urged to seek his intercession. We do not know how this intercessional hymn (referred to as *Bittgesang an Sanct Peter* by Steinmeyer, St. XXI) was used, perhaps primarily as a processional hymn for Saint Peter's day, perhaps as a pilgrimage song (to Rome?), or even, as Rudolf Schützeichel suggests, as a battle hymn like the *lioth frôno* in the *Ludwigslied* with the refrain, *Kyr(r)ieleison* which is sung by all Louis's men (v. 46–47).[53] If so, the *Petruslied* would be the oldest example of this genre too. However, the song sounds more like a collective plea for mercy from personal sinners than a battle-song for victory, and surely the word *skerian* (to select) does not imply attribution to a Germanic warband in this context?

The hymn might have been performed antiphonally, with different singers for each strophe, or perhaps the priest (first voice) sang the strophe, while the congregation (soldiery?) (second voice) sang the response with the repeated: *Kirie eleyson Christe eleyson* (Lord have mercy on us, Christ have mercy on us). V. 8 of the poem reads *Pittemes den gotes trut alla samant uparlut. daz er uns firtanen giuuerdo ginaden* (Let us all ask God's favorite to intercede so that He may deign to save us sinners) is also found in Otfrid (I, 7, 28), although it is Mary who intercedes, and St. John the Baptist who is the Lord's favorite — *drúhtines drút*. The text is written in Upper German, specifically Bavarian, linguistically appropriate for the monastery of Freising, near Munich, where MS F of Otfrid's *Evangelienbuch* was produced, a work which might have influenced the *Petruslied,* if the hymn is not the reflex of an older tradition on which Otfrid also drew. The rhythmical fluency, purity of rhyme, even cadences, and the obvious complexity of the musical notation which recalls Gregorian chant show that the *Petruslied* was not a popular product, and it seems unlikely to have predated Otfrid.[54] This does not prove dependence on Otfrid, although the filler-adverb *uparlut* in the line quoted is typically Otfridian. The cult of St. Peter grew under the Carolingians for political reasons (the pope as Peter's successor, and Rome as imperial center), and the foundation of a church to him at Freising under bishop Erchambert (until 854), might have prompted a song like this, or it might reflect the literary patronage of the same bishop Waldo who commissioned the copying of MS F of Otfrid's *Evangelienbuch.*[55]

The fragmentary *Georgslied* is a longer and more elaborate poem celebrating the fictional martyr saint George, whose life exists in many versions in various languages.[56] Our text, which is hymnic, rather than narrative, was entered at some stage, probably in the early eleventh century, on folios 200v–201r of a much older manuscript, now at Heidelberg (Cpl 52 — MS P of Otfrid's *Evangelienbuch*). This manuscript has an interesting history and spent time at the Reichenau and in Rome.[57] The form and language of the text are so bizarre that editing it is difficult, and dating and localizing it controversial. George's healing miracles appear in the manuscript as follows (vv. 18–19):

den tumben. dheter sprekenten. den tohuben. | ohrenten. // den pilnten. deter. sehenten. den halcen. gahn. enten.

And in Friedrich Zarncke's reconstruction as printed in Braune (text XXXV):

den blinton tet er sehentan,   den halzon gangentan,
den tumbon sprehhentan,   den toubon hôrentan

At the beginning, George, a nobleman whose name appears in popular form as Gorio, comes with a great company to an assembly with the features of a Germanic court (*ding, ma (ha)l, ring*). Refusing to renounce his Christianity, George is flung into to prison, where his miracles make him a thorn in the flesh of the Persian (?) tyrant Tacian (Dacian: so far insecurely identified). Strophes of varying length followed by refrains celebrate George's miracles in climactic progression — from sustaining fellow prisoners, healing the blind, halt, deaf, and dumb, and causing a wooden pillar to sprout leaves and fruit. He undergoes a threefold resurrection, foiling the Emperor Dacian's desperate attempts to have him killed: by dismemberment on the wheel, excoriation, pulverization, and by throwing him into a well! Confounding his tormentors, George returns a third time to raise a dead man, Jobel, to convert the Empress Alexandria (Elossandria) and to topple the god Apollinus (Abollin) to hell, at which point the poem breaks off in mid-strophe shortly before the end, as other versions testify.

The work is concerned less with narrating events than with celebrating and emphasizing the triumphs of the indestructible martyr for the benefit of a lay audience who would know the outlines of the story[58] or have had it told to them beforehand. There is ample space in the manuscript at the end of the text, and after an interval the Latin word *nequeo* (I can't do it) and the name *Vuisolf* appear, but in a hand and spelling differing from the *Georgslied,* so that Wisolf is not the hapless scribe responsible. Evidently our version is a transcription in a desperate (though not unsystematic) spelling bordering on the dyslexic. Successive layers of copying and transposition from one dialect to another must account in part for the bizarre form of the text. At an early stage a Romance scribe was probably involved, possibly with imperfect German and perhaps taking down the text at dictation. However, word boundaries are generally observed and words are not run together as might be the case with someone who did not know the language.[59] Subsequently, the text was transposed into Upper German (Alemannic?). Attribution of the poem to area, date and monastery therefore varies according to linguistic layer. Wolfgang Haubrichs makes the case for a Franconian original with northerly and western characteristics and with Romance influence. Largely on circumstantial grounds Haubrichs favors Prüm as a monastic center for our poem, and Romance spellings do occur in that scriptorium — there is some evidence for a George-cult, and the monastery acquired a relic (an arm) in 852. The original, dated perhaps as early as 875, was, Haubrichs thinks, transposed into Upper German in around 950, and then copied a century later by our unknown, but probably Alemannic, scribe.[60] For Haubrichs, either the *Georgslied* preserves an unknown western form of Franconian close to Central German, but with Low Franconian features, or it represents an artificial literary language, based on a Romance-influenced westerly form of Middle Franconian. Some of the curious transposed spellings and omitted consonants (strikingly: *psanr,* vv. 41, 89 for *spran[g],* jumped; or *ehelleunht,* v. 116 for *hellehunt,* devil; or *abcurnt,* v. 117 for *abcrunt,* abyss) also occur in southern German texts and on the Reichenau in lists of names and inscriptions. Hymns and tropes in Latin manuscripts from the Reichenau refer to George, a church was dedicated to him in Reichenau-Oberzell in

888, while his supposed relics (notably his head) were sent there from Rome in 896, all of which implies a lively cult tradition there, possibly stimulated by the rival German *Galluslied* in honor of the patron saint of St. Gallen.[61]

The poem itself is not without sophistication, although hardly of high aesthetic quality. Wilhelm Scherer ascribed it to the wandering journalists of the day, the professional *spilleute,* and read it as a parody, whose religious message was secondary, but it is more likely to have been produced by clerics for an enthusiastic lay audience who could have sung the refrains. The style is simple and unembellished, with few adjective attributes apart from the first refrain *der mâro grâbo Gorio*[62] (noble Count George). Short, parallel sentences without dependent clauses predominate, with frequent anaphora to match the repeated assertions of veracity and jubilant praise. The poem is centrally structured around a system of interrelating strophes and refrains such that the middle strophe (six) and its refrain have the same number of lines (three lines each). From this scheme the hymn would have had eleven strophes, focusing on the indestructibility of the hero, with the long refrains to stress the hero's three-fold resurrection, which links him with Christ and symbolizes the Trinity. The food miracle and other miracles — curing the handicapped, raising Jobel and the like — also deliberately echo Christ, including the harrowing of Hell. The eleven strophes, with breaks before and after, would also make this possibly a processional hymn marking the twelve stations of the Cross.[63] There is no need to normalize strophes and refrains, or look for number symbolism.[64] The refrains reveal a progression from George the noble count (I and II) to George the miracle-worker (III and IV); rising from the dead, preaching and converting the heathen (V, VI and VII), to his becoming *hêrro sancte Gorio* (VIII, IX) — the last two strophes (X and the non-existent XI) presumably had a new refrain. The repetitiousness recalls liturgical texts, rising to the ecstatic at George's resurrection (*ûf erstuont sih Gorio dâr*) repeated six times, and some phrases draw on Latin hymn style, as in v. 5: *firliez er wereltrîhhi, giwan er himilrîhhi.*[65] There are also echoes here of the trial of Christ in John 18: 36. This German hymn nevertheless remains popular in tone, like the saint it venerates, who was taken up as one of the fourteen Holy Helpers, saints to pray to in dire need. In the late Middle Ages he became the patron of the knightly classes and national saint of England. Depictions of him slaying the dragon (= devil) are also later, dating only from the eleventh century, a role perhaps borrowed from the archangel Michael, or an echo of the classical tale of Persius and Andromeda.

We do not know who composed the hymn, nor who wrote it down so bizarrely: as a popular tale of a popular hero, the story must have circulated orally. Nevertheless, the form we have is learned and clerical, and has evident affinities with Otfrid's strophes, with some lines repeated as refrains (as in Otfrid's *De die judicii*) — this might account for the *Georgslied*'s being added to the Otfrid manuscript.[66] But what was the original hymn's relation to Otfrid, if any? The *Georgslied*'s treatment of its material differs from Otfrid's by being much less sophisticated: there is no invitation to go beyond the letter of the text to interpret it mystically, metaphorically or typologically. Like the characters, the text seems one-dimensional, and allegory is nowhere explicitly signaled. Metrically, too, the *Georgslied* might represent a tradition of internally rhymed long lines before Otfrid and which he adopted and developed. Rhythmically as well, the *Georgslied* is freer and, we may say, more folksy than Otfrid in placing the stresses, and it resembles the earlier parts of the *Evangelienbuch*, where Otfrid was acquiring his craft.[67] Finally, it has been suggested that the *Georgslied* is musically close to the Latin sequence of the da capo type with a changing melody to cover the strophes of differing length which would be arranged so that two groups of four strophes (I–IV and VIII–XI) mirror each other, and frame the core block of three strophes.[68] At the same time, the invincibility of George and his military origins might explain why his cult became popular in the late ninth century, a time of incursions by the Northmen and Magyars. The *Georgslied* might have fitted into a political, or at least politico-religious context as being about a warrior saint.

Two biblical or quasi-biblical poems, a fragmentary paraphrase of the dialogue between Christ and the Woman of Samaria in John 4: 6–4: 20 (*Christus und die Samariterin*),[69] and a paraphrase of Psalm 138 are also written in internally rhyming long-lines organized into strophes; whether they too draw on pre-Otfridian poetry or are indirectly influenced by Otfrid, is debatable. They are correspondingly difficult to date and were written down at different times and in different dialects.

Christus und die Samariterin was entered in the mid-tenth century in a mixture of Alemannic and Franconian on leaf 5r of the *Lorsch Annals* (Vienna: Cod. 515), with a missing line facing it on fol. 4v. The poem opens:

> Lesên uuir, thaz fuori   ther heilant fartmuodi.
> ze untarne, uuizzun thaz,   er zeinen brunnon kisaz . . .

[We read that the Savior was travelling, worn out by the journey; come midday he sat down, you should know, beside a well.]

Otfrid's version (II, 14) is more long-winded, taking ten lines[70] to expand on the setting, time and place, following the biblical text, but repeating that Christ was tired, explaining that he was away from home at the hottest and most arduous time of day, about sext, the sixth canonical hour. The diction may be deliberately archaic, like the verse, but the word *fartmuodi* appears to be a new formation. Although alliteration is not prominent, the poet echoes initial sounds in both halves of the line, even if sometimes the mixture of Upper German (Alemannic) and Central German (Franconian?) features obscures this. The vocabulary differs from Otfrid's, so that direct influence of Otfrid appears unlikely. Tantalizingly, the Old Saxon *Heliand* omits this episode. Where the biblical text, Tatian and Otfrid all introduce the direct speech by verbs of saying, *Christus und die Samariterin* gives only the speeches, which has been taken as characteristic of older epic style, even as balladesque. The comment by the Evangelist that Samaritans do not associate with Jews (John 4: 9) is also re-attributed to the Samarian woman.[71] The dialogue strikes the modern reader as lively and humorous in the treatment of the Samarian woman, with her naively inappropriate expletive *wizze Christ,* and the five husbands whom she is said to have had "at her disposal" (the enigmatic *dir zi volliste*, v. 26, perhaps an addition, and perhaps not just for the rhyme). The vocabulary shows variation: asked to fetch her husband (*uuirt*), she replies that she has no *commen* (cf. the Tatian-translation as *gomman*, man): the Latin appears to use only *vir* for husband. Otfrid glosses *brunnen* (well), with *puzzi*, whereas the poem uses *buzza, brunnen,* and the new formation *quec-/keckprunnen* interchangeably and without comment. The contrast between the fountain of life represented by Christ's message and the refreshing, but temporary, slaking of thirst at the well remains implicit in *Christus und die Samariterin*, which uses *quecprunnen* for both, giving point to the misunderstanding in the woman's somewhat literal mind. The strophic pattern here is indicated by capital letters and the half-lines by points in the manuscript, but the strophes are of differing length. Any musical accompaniment would either have to develop across strophes or be linked to the individual long line (or rhyming couplet) as a unit. Since the strophes generally alternate with the speakers, antiphonic recitation with alternate voices, as in liturgical texts, might be conceivable. The linguistic mixture does not seem to be distributed by strophe, nor by speaker, nor by scribe, and two distinct hands have been identified in this short text. Inconsistent transposition from a written original is the most plausible explanation of the mixture, as for other Old High German texts: at all events this is not a characteristic orthography from an identifiable scriptorium. The large number of corrections indicates a barely competent scribe or scribes. It is possible, though not proven, that the text was written at Reichenau; however, the *Georgslied,* which is sometimes cited in corroboration may have been written elsewhere.[72]

The early German paraphrase of Psalm 138 was written in Bavarian on both sides of a single leaf (69r and 69v) added to Cod. 1609, now at the National Library, Vienna. The date and provenance of the poem are unknown, but it was perhaps written in the early tenth century. The manuscript is a formulary once belonging to Bishop Salomo III of Constance, abbot of St. Gallen between 890 and 919, possibly having again come from the monastery of Freising where his brother, Waldo, was bishop (883–906); however, this need not hold for the leaf with our Psalm.[73] The thirty-eight couplets or long lines with internal rhyme are divided into some seventeen strophes of two and three pairs of rhymes by the use of capital letters, but the sequence of the lines is occasionally unclear, implying perhaps a chaotic original. The first two lines introduce the psalm with a rhetorical address to the audience:

> Uuellet ir gihoren Daviden den guoten,
> den sinen touginon sin? er gruozte sinen trohtin . . .

> [Do you wish to learn the hidden significance of the words of that good man David? He greeted his Lord as follows . . .]

This places the poem in context, showing that it was not a fragment from a Psalter, but the point of departure for an independent treatment. By contrast, the interlinear translation of the Ambrosian Hymns from the monastery of Murbach (the *Murbacher Hymnen*)[74] divides the Latin hymns into half-lines and strophes by dots and capital letters, while the German text (which does not rhyme or use assonance) is written word-for-word under the Latin. Our isolated *Psalm 138,* on the other hand, has no obvious link to any text in the manuscript. The poem lacks a title or heading and claims to be an interpretation unlocking the Psalmist's secrets, the *touginon sin* (hidden meaning). Patristic interpretation of this difficult Psalm (by early theologians such as Hilarius, Augustine or Cassiodorus) sees it as Christ addressing God and confessing his humanity[75] — this is also Notker's view. It is used as the introit to the Easter Mass, celebrating the resurrection of Christ, and by identification, of all Christians. Here, in the paraphrase, David stands for the individual soul acknowledging the power and omnipresence of the Lord, but also for the ideal king and ruler, and his submissiveness reflects the early feudal relationship. The German paraphrase omits details in the biblical version and

is less ecstatic, focusing instead on the benefits of accepting God's protection.[76] Indeed, this seems a more controlled account of the submissive
attitude of a vassal for the feudal lord (God). David, who is mounted
(*zoum*, bridle, v. 7), acknowledges the power of God and His ever-
present protection. The soul is in God's hands (compare the feudal ges-
ture of manumission) in heaven and hell (v. 14), repeated by association
in the images of journeying into the dark which God makes light (v. 29),
or in any earthly land — *ne megih in nohhein lant, nupe mih hapet din
hant* (v. 15, repeated v. 35). David rejects murderers and declares himself
the enemy of the enemies of his Lord and seeks protection from them,
seeks to further the reputation of the Lord and to be kept eternally
through God's grace — *gináda* is also a term of homage. The relationship lasts from the beginning until the end of the individual's life: God
has both chosen and looked on David (*gichuri*, line 3), with a play on
chêren, "to turn, wend one's way, convert(?)," since, wherever he
chooses to go, God guides: *daz ih mih cherte after dir* (vv. 6–7). In the
closing lines the pairing returns; he asks God to choose him (?) if he
holds fast to God — *Nu chius dir fasto ze mir, upe ih mih chere after
dir* — and asks God's guidance in the future — *cheri mih framort* (vv.
36–37). The text merges images of life as a journey undertaken with
God's guiding hand[77] and of the individual as a (hunting?) bird, testing
its wings and flying out into the world, but nowhere beyond the reach
and range of God. In this way the poem looks forward to early medieval
spiritual poetry of the twelfth century where the journey theme, com-
bined with the transitory nature of life, is a common topos. Where the
biblical text shows the struggle of the soul with God, the German makes
David (the king) acknowledge the subordination of the individual (and
secular power?) to the divine will. Was this perhaps an appropriate message in the late eleventh century after the Investiture Conflict?

Propaganda of a very different kind is the laudatory poem known as
De Heinrico, preserved in the famous manuscript Gg.5.35 of the University Library at Cambridge in England containing the *Cambridge
Songs*, written possibly at Canterbury by an Anglo-Saxon monk some
time in the eleventh century from a source with northern Rhenish features — a form of High German to the north of Middle Franconian.[78]
This song book contains a mixture of religious and secular material,
mostly in Latin. The *De Heinrico* lacks any title in the manuscript and
follows on directly from a series of alphabet strophes on the vanity and
brevity of life and the need to turn to Christ. Our song, which is of interest in this context because it is in Latin and German (macaronic), also
opens by invoking Christ. It is a *modus* in eight strophes of three and

four lines, the first half-lines in Latin (apart from vv. 1 and 22), with irregular syllables, with the second half-lines in German, probably added afterward, and partly rhyming with the Latin. The song is a eulogy of a former Duke Henry of Bavaria, who met the Emperor Otto and became his prime adviser. But which of the several Ottos and Henrys might be meant eludes us.[79] Since Otto's (Otdo's) greeting in strophe four shows what may be Saxon features, possibly to characterize him, this would argue for Otto I (912–973) who was probably closer to his roots, whereas Otto III (980–1002) was exceedingly urbane. No rift between the emperor and the duke is mentioned, so the text does not necessarily describe reconciliation, although some commentators assume it does, because v. 16 somewhat pointedly stresses that Henry had no aspirations toward royal property (and power). The poem might have been composed during the reign of the later emperor, Henry II (1002–1024) celebrating either his grandfather, brother of Otto I, or his father, the quarrelsome Henry, Duke of Bavaria, who had been banished by Otto II (973–983) and had tried to usurp the power of the infant Otto III.[80] The Henry celebrated here was probably dead when the song was composed, since he *had* preserved (*beuuarode*, v. 4) Bavaria, and this reading would consider the song a piece of propagandist rehabilitation to flatter the emperor by praising his ancestors. In vv. 12–13, Emperor Otto (Otdo) seems to be greeting two Henrys — *uuillicumo Heinrich, ambo vos equivoci, bethiu goda endi mi nec non et sotii* (*socii*), unless the interpretation is that Henry and his men were equally welcome to God and to the Emperor.[81]

The aesthetic and metrical skill of the clerical poet are modest.[82] In the manuscript, the opening line mingles, if not muddles, Latin and German, as does the twenty-second line, although in all other lines we have Latin first, followed by German in the second half-line. We may note that the Latin "rhymes" with the German, as it does in another poem from the same collection (Number 28, known as *Kleriker und Nonne* [Clerk and Nun]). The linguistic mixture common in monastic scriptorium or schoolroom (we may compare Notker's *Mischprosa*) would have been a clerical indicator, a badge of learning and prestige. The *De Heinrico* is less skillful than the famous later thirteenth-century macaronic songs from Benediktbeuern, the *Carmina Burana*. Formally, the text seems more primitive than late Latin poetry, with impure, indeed poor rhymes and assonance, although weakening syllables were not always shown in German spelling, so the rhyming may in fact have sounded better than it looks. Marie-Luise Dittrich, using the imperfect rhymes, reconstructs a Bavarian original (Henry was Duke of Bavaria).[83]

Whatever the propagandistic or political purpose of this encomium, the figure of Henry as the wise counselor to his liege idealizes the role and generalizes it. Some phrases recall medieval German feudal formulae: *fecit . . . ac omisit* (vv. 23–24) corresponds to Middle High German *tuon unde lâzen* (did and did not), and the entry of the messenger and the ensuing gestures of courtesy and greeting, rising, taking hands and going to church, all show familiarity with diplomatic protocol. Friction between Bavaria and the emperor is also a theme in later texts. Our song treats the Bavarians sympathetically, and as a song of praise for a prince accords with other poems in the *Cambridge Songs,* two of which were composed for coronations, three as necrologies and two as memorials or obituaries. The poem also bears comparison with the *Ludwigslied.* Although religion is present, in the opening prayer to the Virgin's Son (itself perhaps a transposition into Christian terms of the invocation of the Muse), in Otto's pious welcome and in the visit to the church, nevertheless the main focus is on Henry's loyalty and advice. In the *Ludwigslied,* God is the principal actor, beside whom all the saints are thanked (v. 56). But both the figures of Louis III and Henry are candidates for a political hagiography, in which religion enhances their status as role models. Presumably, however, any interest for the song in England lay in its melody, not its content.

Aesthetic appreciation of German vernacular verse is evident in the examples given by Notker Labeo of St. Gallen (d. 1022) within his Latin excerpt on rhetoric.[84] Two passages illustrate for Notker the pleasurable effects of repeating and varying sounds and forms:

> Sóse snél snéllemo   pegágenet ándermo
> só uuírdet slîemo   fir-sníten scilt-rîemo

> [When one fierce fighter fights another
> shield-straps will swiftly be slashed to slivers]

A second poem, about a huge boar, makes the same point:

> Der heber gât in lîtun   tregit sper in sîtun.
> sîn bált éllin   nelâzet ín uéllin

> [The boar roams the fells, a spear in his side
> but his great might keeps him upright]

A few lines later, probably the same unknown "German poem about a boar" illustrates the trope known as hyperbole, that is, where "more is said than is meant" (*Nam plus dicitur. et minus intelligitur. Sicut et teutonice de apro*):

Imo sínt fûoze fûodermâze. imo sínt búrste ébenhô fórste.
únde zéne sîne zuuélifélnîge

[His hooves are hefty as wine-tuns, his bristles forest-high, the tusks on
him twelve-ells-long]

Here we glimpse epic vocabulary — *snel* and *balt,* both meaning "bold,"
and also *ellin,* "strength" — which resurfaces in the *Nibelungenlied* in
around 1200.

Notker's own gnomic verses, known as *Sprichwörter,* proverbs, are not
strictly poetry, although their stylized form shows repetition, rhythmical
phrasing and occasionally alliteration. Proverbs have always attracted attention for their pithy content and apt turn of phrase. The twelve or so proverbs drawn from Notker's treatise on logic are sometimes linked, as number
1: *Tár der íst ein fúnt úbelero féndingo, Tár nist nehéiner guot // Unde dâr
der ist ein hús follez úbelero líuto, Tár nist nehéiner chústic* (Take a pound of
dud pennies, none of them is worth a bean. Where you have a house of
rogues, none of them is clean).

Some of his truisms make useful logical examples: if A, then necessarily B, as in number 6, along the lines of "if you feel ill, then it follows
that you don't feel well." Others are inventive and critical: (4) *Dír scólo
scóffizit ío // Vnde dír gouch dér gúccot ío* — (A debtor is always making
up excuses — is as inventive as a penniless poet; and a cuckoo always calls
cuckoo). Immoderate expectations are deflated: (7) "You can't get two
sons-in-law from one daughter, and you can't have a mouthful of flour
and still blow." One couplet (number 5) might be from Notker's (lost)
translation of the *Disticha Catonis* (the Distichs of Cato), a well-known
schoolbook:[85] *Vbe man álliu dîer fúrtin sál, // nehéin só harto só den
mán* (If all animals are to be feared, Man is yet more fearsome).

Another St. Gallen manuscript (MS 111), has two eleventh-century
proverbs in German on the final page, probably again school examples to
teach logic. Notker knows the first: *so iz regenot, so nazscent te boumma,
so iz uuath, so uuagont te bo(u)mma* (when it rains, the trees get wet; and
when it blows, the trees toss.) The second proverb, not in Notker,
teaches that accidents betray essences, and specifically that cowardly behavior shames: *So diz rehpochchili fliet, so plecchet imo ter ars* (When the
young roebuck turns to run, he cannot help but flash his ass.) The diminutive suffix refers to young animals, but has a familiar, contemptuous
tone. The vulgar word *ars* is rare outside glosses, but the saying crops up
in the Latin dialogues between Solomon and Marcolfus, where high sen-
timents are coarsely parodied.[86] Other fragments which it is convenient
to treat here, although they cannot be accurately dated or interpreted,

give great insights into the minds and cultural conventions — sometimes, admittedly, principally of their more recent interpreters! The *St. Galler Spottgedicht* (the St. Gallen lampoon) targets a failed wedding:

> liubene ersazta sine gruz   und kab sina tohter uz
> to cham aber Starzfidere   prahta imo sina tohter widere[87]

[Liubene brewed his beer and married off his daughter; Starzfidere brought her back again and said he didn't want her.]

The obscure joke probably revolves around the names: Liubene (Dear friend, Lovejoy, from *liub + wini*) bestows his daughter, but possibly when *Starzfidere* (Featherbottom?) looked at her sober, he found her wanting, even perhaps not a virgin? The rhyming couplets are metrically well-formed, with a contrast between *úzgeban*, "marry off" (although some Middle High German contexts for the word involve prostitution!) and *widerbringan*, "bring back," or perhaps "make restitution" (the latter nonsensical if the girl had lost her virginity). The name *Starzfidere* seems ridiculous and sounds like a nickname: Bostock, King and McLintock translate it as "Cockstail" and suggest "an obscene significance" in the lampoon, signaling the reason why Liubene's expectations are dashed. Perhaps *-fidere* is an agent noun from the ornative verb *fideren*, "to supply with feathers" (hence Featherbottom, Buttfeatherer, Tailplucker).[88] Whether this little text is influenced by, or independent of Otfrid, or even predates his *Evangelienbuch*, it does show non-alliterative verse, at however trivial a level, outside a religious or theological context.

Other lampoons are very fragmentary — a ninth- or tenth-century St. Gallen MS (MS 105) has two verses, one on the first page reads: *ueru. taz ist spiz, taz santa tir tín fredel ce minnon* (*Veru*, that means a spear: your lover sent it to you for love). Associations with Cupid's dart, or a crass erotic metaphor may be involved, although the Latin word *veru* seems to mean both a spear and a cooking spit, and it rarely occurs outside glosses. Here there is neither rhyme nor alliteration, but the rhythm has a certain ring and the line appears to be neumed. Apparently a gloss is being used for an erotic message. The use of the third person address need not necessarily stem from the lover speaking of himself: it might even be a nun writing to another nun — quite surprisingly, erotic banter is sometimes attested in the convent, even if it is probably fictive, for example in a manuscript perhaps from Regensburg and now at Munich (Clm. 17142).[89]

The other verse in the margin of a medical treatise on fol. 204 of the same MS[90] reads: *churo comsic herenlant aller oter lestilant,* but what this meant is utterly obscure. It may mean "Churo, a man from Rhaetia, came over here, running everybody else down" (perhaps "A Rhaetian bastard came to town/ running other people down!"). The word *lesti-lant,* is indeed (as Wipf translates) a participle of *lestilôn,* modern German *lästern,* "criticize," but metrically the whole thing looks like the familiar internally rhymed long line, precursor of the rhyming couplet.

A scribal verse added in a shaky hand to the last leaf of a late ninth-century manuscript (MS 623) at St. Gallen seems to have been popular there, since it also occurs in another MS (Cod. Sang. 166, St., 402). It plays on the adverb *chûmo,* "barely" (modern German *kaum*), "with difficulty," and *chumor,* its comparative form: *Chumo kiscreib. filo chumor kipeit* (I barely managed to write this out; I could wait even less to finish it!). The scribe who wrote this appears in fact not to have written the whole manuscript, so it may be only a *Federprobe,* a line to practice with the pen.

A strikingly modern line, neither alliterative, nor rhyming, but showing two half-lines, the first with four beats, the dependent second half-line correspondingly shorter, appears to be a statement made by the manuscript book itself about a reader (the scholiast scholia'ed, perhaps!):

> Kícilà diu scónà   mín fílu 1[á]s
>
> [Gisela the fair (the noble?) read frequently in me]

This entry appears in the Heidelberg Otfrid manuscript (MS P, that is, Heidelberg MS Cpl 52) on folio 90r in a hand of the early tenth century. As a line of epic verse, it conforms to the rhythmical pattern of the first three lines of the later *Nibelungenlied* strophe. Who was the fair Gisela, and was this entry by her or by someone else? The inscription cannot be dated: one surmise, placing the entry in the first third of the tenth century, is that Gisela was a member of the Swabian ducal Hunfridinger family.[91] But another suggestion dates it a full century later, identifying the lady with the Empress Gisela, wife of Konrad II, who visited the Reichenau around 1025. The spelling with *K* and the use of *c* for *s* have a wide distribution which does not rule out the Reichenau.[92]

The not necessarily fragmentary lines preserving the immodest proposal of a stag whispering an assignation to a hind[93] suggest the existence of erotic poetry at this period:

> Hirez runeta hintun in daz ora   "uuildu noh, hinta[?]."
>
> [A stag whispered into the ear of a hind:
> "Hind, my dear, are you inclined?"]

The manuscript into which these words were written (Royal Library, Brussels, Cod. 8860–8867, fol. 15v) probably in the late tenth century, was at some stage at St. Gallen, where it appears that a musical notation was added both above our text and above the first lines of a Latin song to St. Peter, which has also been entered immediately beneath it in the same hand, and in the margins of the same leaf and the next. Whether the neumes indicate the transference of a popular melody to a religious text with the intention perhaps of replacing the text with something more edifying is hard to tell. Our text shows both alliteration and rhyme, and has been taken as a long alliterative line followed by a fragmentary half-line (as above), but comparing the form with the song to St. Peter, Ute Schwab shows their similar structure and argues that the German text is a complete strophe of three rhyming lines — the first Peter strophe runs *Solue lingua moras / et beato laudes / refer petro canens.* The German lines might be from a folkloric dance. However, the animality of sex and the seasonality of rutting are universals, and there is no need to invoke stag-cults and ritual to explain our jotting, fascinating though such hermetic knowledge may be.[94]

Another erotic piece is the now barely legible approach by a cleric (?) to a nun in the *Cambridge Songs,* known as *Kleriker und Nonne.*[95] This was obviously felt to be so improper that it has, sadly, been all but scratched out in the manuscript. The traces of some ten surviving strophes reveal another macaronic text, with German and Latin rhyming, like the *De Heinrico,* and there is vernal imagery — *tempus adest . . . gruonot gras* (the time is ripe, . . . the grass is green) — while *philomela,* the nightingale, is singing. The lover, who might be a noble (clerically trained, in view of the Latin-German idiom) seems to win the lady round, but Gustav Ehrismann, in his major literary history, remained adamantly convinced of the nun's resolute virtue — and yet ruled out a clerical author. But Latin poetry has a broad repertoire produced by clerics who knew Ovid's *Amores* and *Metamorphoses,* and the *Carmina Cantabrigiensia* themselves comprise very disparate works reflecting the catholic musical tastes of some Rhenish prelate or of a humanistically inclined cathedral school, or possibly even the court of Henry III (1039–1056) at Cologne.[96]

These glimpses of a counter-culture in which mundane and elemental human emotions surface should be considered as precursors of the *Carmina Burana.* Here we see the complementarity of secular and spiritual, Latin and vernacular. Monastic culture has also preserved for us glosses of a distinctly practical kind listing the terms of art of trades and technical, mechanical arts, botany, husbandry and medicine, including magic charms.

These smaller and smallest disparate texts mark the marginalization of German vernacular verse at this time: they tenuously span the much vaunted gap in the literary record from late ninth-early tenth to the late eleventh century. During this time the monasteries, episcopal and ruling courts reached a high point of Latinity, with many manuscripts of glosses, so that even the (literary) world outside the schoolroom is presented through the language inside it — Latin — the lost German *Galluslied*, the *Waltharius*, the *Ruodlieb* and the glimpse of the *Dancers of Kölbigk*.[97] Until, that is, we find new beginnings in German[98] with transitional texts — *Merigarto, Memento Mori, Ezzos Gesang*, and the *Annolied* and one or two others, including some prose. The *Annolied*, preserved only in Martin Opitz's seventeenth-century edition, must be ruled out of detailed consideration here by its length and importance, and is dealt with elsewhere. These transitional texts seem to emerge at a humbler level, no longer representative of Carolingian or post-Carolingian cultural politics imposed from above, but coming from humbler origins closer to the grass roots, and produced it seems, not only by monks, but also by priests who were catering for the needs of local lay aristocratic audiences who were interested in spiritual matters. Monasteries and religious orders were becoming diverse and new forms of spiritual life inside and outside the religious orders were springing up, creating a demand for vernacular didactic texts.[99] Henceforth, German verse does not dry up, but emerges to become unambiguously flowing rhyming couplets with enjambment, the vehicle for the first great German poetry in the High Middle Ages.

Among the early transitional texts is the *Merigarto*, a fragmentary early cosmographical text preserved in Bavarian on a double parchment leaf from the late eleventh or early twelfth century now at Donaueschingen stuck to bookboards as a cover for another manuscript.[100] The beginning is lost, probably only a few lines, and the text breaks off at the end of the first leaf, while leaf two starts with the "I heard tell" formula: *Daz ih ouh horte sagan*. One or more leaves went missing in between. The familiar couplet or internally rhymed long line is organized into strophes (or sections) of varying length by the use of capital letters. The poetic quality is modest, and the first editor's not inappropriate title means "the sea-girt world." Much of the information about water: seas, rivers and springs, derives directly from Isidore of Seville's *Etymologiae*, perhaps with or by way of Hraban's *De rerum naturis*.[101] The sea changes its characteristics according to geographical region, hence the Red Sea gets its name from the colored sands over which it flows (vv. 30–36). The *lebirmere* or curdled sea (probably the freezing northern Arctic Ocean) which traps ships, lies, alliteratively, away to the west in the world sea, *in dem uuentilmere uuesterot.* In an apparently autobiographical central section, the author, having fled to Utrecht from an episcopal squabble, met a priest called Reginbert who had visited Iceland and tells of the high cost of wood there, of the lack of sun, and of the hardness of the ice, which is even used for heating and cooking (vv. 50–83). Here the author is at pains to establish the credentials of his informant, whereas the material from learned authorities is taken for granted. If the episcopal dispute of 1077–1086 at Würzburg is what is being referred to, then the poem could be dated, but this is controversial.

The second fragment describes remarkable rivers and springs in Tuscany, Rome, Morlant (Ethiopia), Campania, Idumea, and Sardinia and their properties. After an extended account of a river which flows underground in Tuscany, the poem changes style, becoming terser over the last eleven strophes which follow the written sources closely, but selectively.[102] Various streams cure the eyes, make the body beautiful or the voice sweet, make one forgetful, or improve the memory, instill lust, or make fertile or infertile, or render wine's pleasures repellent. In one bathing place, two streams flow, one makes sheep white, and the other black — drinking from both produces speckled wool (echoes of Jacob in Genesis)! In Idumea a spring changes color with the seasons, elsewhere a lake acquires a bitter taste three hours before sunset. In Sardinia, thieves who perjure themselves after drinking a particular spring go blind and cannot even see the path they walk on.[103] Our poet chose from his sources (red citation marks occur in the margin) to present his audience with a "topography of the marvelous."[104] Despite references to God's separating land and sea, instituting tides and setting the limits of the waters after the Flood (Psalm 103: 9), and although divine intervention can release those stuck in the *lebirmere,* the religious message is otherwise low-key. Unlike the significant natural history of the *Physiologus,* where Nature is a book wherein we read the mysteries of God, and animal behavior an index of divine mysteries, here we sense an intellectual curiosity outweighing the spiritual. But this text is far from technical, and the style is personal, rather than abstract, appropriate for reading aloud or singing. Yet details about life in Iceland and the high price of inferior quality wood appear factual, based indirectly on observation. The earlier strophes could have been set down from memory or oral narration, while the later sections look more like copying out; alternatively, more than one poet may have been involved. The text was possibly written by a Bavarian priest at Prül, a monastery near Regensburg and a center of cosmographical and geographical interest at this time.[105]

Completely different in tone, the Alemannic *Memento Mori* dates from about 1070[106] and is preserved in a manuscript from the Upper Swabian monastery of Ochsenhausen. The (modern) title may be too suggestive, for although a penitential sermon (*Bußpredigt*), the poem does not so much condemn the world as criticize preoccupation with its transient pleasures at the expense of future salvation. It tells people how to live, not how to die. The audience is enjoined, women and men both, to think about their future. The temporal world, however sweet, is fragile and unpredictable, and many have passed before who expected to dwell here forever. The preacher is inconsistent: he claims not to know where they have gone, yet he seems convinced that having reached their destination they would gladly change it! Paradise is a distant goal, and no one has ever returned to tell of it. The image of the journey frames the poem and may derive from Gregory the Great into a copy of whose celebrated *Moralia in Job* our poem has been written, and echoes from the Book of Job itself are frequent,[107] but other, biblical, topoi occur — of transitoriness, of Death as a thief, or as a leveler whom no amount of treasure can buy off (v. 93–94):

> er ist ein ebenare: necheiman ist so here,
> er ne muoze ersterbin: tes ne mag imo der skaz ze guote
>   werden

> [he is a leveler. No man is so great that he will not have to die, nor will his wealth be of any use to him]

The image of the man who rests under a tree on the journey and awakens too late is explicated in strophe 17 — the audience is the man, the tree represents the world and its attractions, and they have tarried too long. The last two strophes differing in style and tone from the rest have been regarded as late additions;[108] they address an inclusive audience (*uns*) as opposed to *ir* otherwise. But, including them, the poem divides into three, with three pairs of strophes (1–6) whose themes are mirrored in reverse order in the last section (strophes 14–19).[109] The central section contained three pairs of strophes, or two, depending on whether a gap is postulated in strophe 8 which reminds the rich and powerful of their obligations to the poor, since all men are created equal in God. The word *reht* in this passage is open to interpretation and possibly alludes to simony, a topical abuse;[110] many Latin writings pillory the selling of ecclesiastical office. The transitoriness of this world and man's status as traveler combine, which is commonplace in the Bible, theological texts, sermons and Latin hymns, and in patristic commentaries by Augustine,

Gregory the Great, and later writers such as Haimo of Halberstadt and Alcuin. Such material formed the intellectual and spiritual background to our text whose dark, negative tone suits the genre of the penitential sermon and draws on old traditions long before any so-called Cluniac religious reforms, while its centrally structured composition (like *Ezzo's Hymn* and the *Georgslied*) looks forward to Early Middle High German religious poetry.[111]

The author of the *Memento Mori*, Noker, is unlikely to be abbot Notker (Noggerus) of Zwiefalten, not least because the manuscript might be as late as circa 1130 and he died in 1095. The poem might be part of a new wave of lay piety in southwestern Germany associated with the reforming monasteries of Hirsau and St. Blasien, where lay people were trying to live in the simple ways of the primitive church.[112] However, there is nothing to link the *Memento Mori* with one of these centers. It is best seen as a vernacular verse sermon for laymen who knew no Latin and could not read. Religious reform was not uniform, and the influence of a single center, Cluny, on German areas should not be exaggerated — nor was Cluny hostile to the world, the monastery was lavish, and its monks cultivated architecture and music and furthered among the nobility an ethos of Christian chivalry. In this respect, *Ezzo's Hymn*, which reflects the new piety, the idea of the holy war and the "peace movement" might have been influenced, indirectly, by Cluny. Both the *Memento Mori* and *Ezzo's Hymn* have been transmitted in the same manuscript: they may seem opposites, and yet they are complementary, both drawing on Job. Reform of the nobility entailed both taking nobles into the monastery as lay brothers, and also giving them a role as Christian warriors outside it, eventually a holy war to free Jerusalem. Both currents are present throughout the eleventh century.

The eleventh-century song in praise of Christ known as *Ezzo's Hymn* (*Ezzos Gesang, Ezzolied*) exists in two versions, an incomplete text from Strasbourg (MS S = *Codex Germ.* 278, which also contains the *Memento Mori*) and the later redaction from the monastery of Vorau in Carinthia, whose famous *Vorauer Handschrift* (V) preserves an important collection of eleventh- and early twelfth-century religious poetry. Manuscript V of *Ezzo's Hymn* has elaborated on its source in a more modern form of German with reduced inflectional syllables, although both versions show assonance beside pure rhyme. *Ezzo's Hymn* is often claimed as the "first Middle High German poem," but its themes and presentation are traditional. The strophes are usually printed in couplets in modern editions, which overemphasizes the formal break with other Old High German texts: in default of the melody, long internally rhymed lines remain a possibility, at least for MS S, which marks them by dots in the manuscript. Since MS S contains only seven strophes, any attempt to structure the poem involves the always tenuous undertaking of reconstructing the original *Ur-Ezzo*. A plausible structure centers the poem around the birth of Christ, with seven pairs of strophes of twelve lines treating creation, fall, Old Testament, then Christ's birth, life, crucifixion and resurrection, framed by a prologue of two strophes and conclusion of three.[113] A certain amount of re-organization is necessary to achieve this pattern, which follows medieval modes of spiritual interpretation, with number symbolism, allegory, and symmetry. But the older fragment S might have had a different focus and emphasis. In V, the last three strophes celebrate the cross allegorically, like a crusading hymn,[114] where Christ's cross is the mast-tree, the world is the sea, God is the sails and helmsman, good works the tackle, the sails are true faith and the Holy Ghost the wind blowing men back to their homeland in heaven. While this is typical of sermons, V may have encumbered the simpler structure of S with significant details, in the spirit of vv. 335–36: *Daz was allez geistlich, daz bezichnot christenlichiu dinc* (That was all spiritual, that all signifies Christian things). For instance, the Old Testament is linked typologically to the New, so that the parting of the Red Sea which saves the Israelites (Exodus 14: 5–14: 31) becomes the blood of Christ, who harrows Hell: the Devil and all his host are swallowed in *daz rote toufmere* (the Red Sea of baptism), a contrast with the "factual" explanation of the redness of the sea in *Merigarto*. The first strophe, added in V, tells us that Gunther, Bishop of Bamberg from 1057–1065, commissioned the song, Ezzo wrote it, while Wille composed the tune, whereupon they joined the monastery as regulated canons of St. Gangolf in 1063. The *Vita* of Bishop Altmann of Passau, circa 1130, informs us that Gunther and Ezzo scholasticus set out on a pilgrimage to the Holy Land in 1065 because many believed the Last Judgment was nigh. Moreover, Ezzo composed a *cantilena de miraculis Christi* (song of Christ's miracles) in the vernacular; this title does not strictly accord with the content of fragment S, although Ezzo may have composed more than one song.[115] Even if *Ezzo's Hymn* was originally written for a church festival to celebrate those entering regular orders, it might still have been sung on the pilgrimage, and even have been recycled as crusading propaganda in an adaptation like that in the Bavarian manuscript V: the first crusade took place only in 1095. Version V also seems to be directed to a wider and probably lay audience: v. 13 *iv eben allen* (all of you), whereas the S-text may possibly be more narrowly clerical, and is addressed to the [*chor?*]-*herron* (canons). It celebrates the beginning of the world (*anegenge*), exploring the interplay between the Light and Darkness (a concept deriving again from Gregory the Great's *Moralia*)[116] associating the darkness with the Devil and the fall, while the stars prefigure the exemplary figures of the Old Testament, beginning with Abel, who shed his light so that we might die justly. Enoch, Noah and the Ark, and Abraham and David all signify stages on the Christian's path to salvation, at which point S breaks off. Possibly it, too, might have explored the theme of the cross, as in earlier Latin poems, including one by Hraban, which link the cross with the Tree of Life and with the genealogical tree of Jesse. A wider audience might have needed the exegetical and allegorical hints to be made explicit; professional clerics doubtless grasped the references.

All the poetry discussed in this chapter has been preserved through the mediation of clerics, and apart from the small trifles, it can all be interpreted as having a religious purpose. Both themes and forms show the symbiosis of Christian, Latin religion, and vernacular language. The newer assonanced or rhyming verse blends with the alliterative long line which seems to be the old form, eventually to emerge as rhyming couplets, the dominant form of medieval German religious and secular texts from the eleventh century on. The combination of alliteration and rhyme is also found in non-vernacular secular writing preserved in monasteries, Virgil uses alliteration in his poetry. At any event, the transition is fluid, and Old High German texts inevitably anticipate later works in theme and treatment. Some texts, like *Ezzo's Hymn,* or the *Merigarto* or *Memento Mori* are treated in literary histories of German as early Middle High German texts, and are markedly transitional, and already in the last decades of the nineteenth century Wilhelm Scherer saw *Memento Mori* as a link between tenth-century monastic literature and the spiritual poetry of the eleventh and twelfth, although he also invoked the Cluniac asceticism of the monastery of Hirsau.[117] But neither in respect of literary form, nor of linguistic developments can we discern any clear break, nor, consequently, any new beginning circa 1050.[118] True, few German texts have come down from the eleventh century, but this may reflect, as stated above, a higher level of *Latin* literacy among clerics or in the audiences they were addressing. Linguistically, there is equally no clear break. The influence of monastic reforms in the eleventh century and the supposedly new ascetic spirit linked with the French and Lothringian centers of Cluny and Gorze and their dependent monastic houses like Hirsau and St. Blasien has been over-emphasized, particularly in the influential literary history of Helmut de Boor.[119] Stressing the transitory nature of human existence and the inferior quality of its pleasures compared to everlasting bliss is entirely compatible with a more positive view of God's creation. Moreover, the early Middle High German poetry, which cannot concern us here, is usually taken to reflect increasingly the proselytizing and pastoral efforts of priests in the lay community, not of cloistered monks. As Heinz Rupp has argued,[120] the earlier Old High German texts are almost exclusively produced in monastic scriptoria; Otfrid, Williram and Notker were monks, but later, eleventh-century texts address the laity and it seems that secular priests and clerics were largely responsible for them. They took over and continued the tradition of mediating the Christian message in comprehensible, vernacular form. At the same time, they took their audiences beyond the literal meaning of the Christian texts and interpreted their inner meaning and significance, particularly within the framework of a history incorporating men's daily lives into a divine framework (the *Heilsgeschichte*) running from the Creation to the End of the World. This structure, with typological recapitulations and echoes between the Old and New Testaments, was later used for a number of medieval works, particularly the Arthurian court epics. Possibly the monastic reforms, far from promoting ascetic and cloistered values in the community at large, constituted a withdrawal of the monks into their orders, leaving lay clerics — priests and clerically trained laymen — to develop a vernacular sermon and a pastoral literature. So even the shorter Old High German verse texts can be taken as synthesizing apparently disparate elements of vernacular, classical, and religious tradition that must have been aimed at an audience that was illiterate or semi-literate but politically powerful. Indeed, in this respect, we may cite again the co-existence in the same manuscript (from Ochsenhausen) of *Memento Mori,* with its negative, indeed revolutionary egalitarian view of man's predicament, and *Ezzo's Hymn,* which even in fragmentary form seems much more positively confident in the eventual salvation of the individual, the purpose of history. Ezzo indeed already represents, according to MS V, a *phaphe* or priest who later became a monk, shaping his own life to a spiritual end, and, as an individual, endorsing at the same time a collective ideology.

The Strasbourg manuscript version of Ezzo's Gesang.

Notes

[1] Gustav Ehrismann, *Geschichte der deutschen Literatur bis zum Ausgang des Mittelalters, 1: Die althochdeutsche Literatur,* 2nd ed. (Munich: Beck, 1932; repr. 1954), 1–14 discusses such mnemonic poetry (*Dichtung*) in relation to mythology, law and personal names. Jacob Grimm was drawn to the poetry in often alliterating formulas of German customary law — *Haus und Hof, mit Haut und Haar* — corporal punishment, including death penalty, *mit Kind und Kegel* — "offspring, legitimate *and* illegitimate," and many others. See also Rudolf Koegel, *Geschichte der deutschen Litteratur bis zum Ausgange des Mittelalters, 1. Bis zur Mitte des elften Jahrhunderts: Erster Teil: Die stabreimende Dichtung und die Gothische Prosa* (Strasbourg: Trübner, 1894), 206.

[2] Koegel, *Geschichte*, 1/i, 24–34.

[3] See Michael Richter, "Vortragsformen und Vortragsbedingungen in einer mündlichen Kultur im Frühmittelalter," in *Theodisca: Beiträge zur althochdeutschen und altniederdeutschen Sprache und Literatur in der Kultur des frühen Mittelalters,* ed. Wolfgang Haubrichs et al. (Berlin and New York: de Gruyter, 2000), 1–9.

[4] Peter Dronke, *The Medieval Lyric* (London: Hutchinson, 1968, 3rd ed. 1996), 38–39, n. 1: "As none of the 'archaic' sequences show a connection with a liturgical Alleluia, or show any trace of having grown out of earlier liturgical compositions, the widely held view that the sequence originated in the liturgy and was first developed out of *Alleluia* melodies is at the very least questionable." See also Peter Dronke, "The Beginnings of the Sequence," *PBB/T* 87 (1965): 43–73, and cf. Karl Langosch, *Mittellatein und Europa: Führung in die Hauptliteratur des Mittelalters* (Darmstadt: WBG, 1990), xii.

[5] Koegel, *Geschichte,* 1/i, 84 and 208, considers that the Church had given up trying to stamp out magic by this time, and that the monks who copied it believed in its powers, like the laity.

[6] Dieter Kartschoke, *Geschichte der deutschen Literatur im frühen Mittelalter, 1* (Munich: dtv, 1990), 84–86.

[7] Koegel, *Geschichte* 1/i, 201 discusses the implications of linguistic changes for alliteration.

[8] See Werner Hoffmann, *Altdeutsche Metrik* (Stuttgart: Metzler, 1967), 20–27; J. Sidney Groseclose and Brian O. Murdoch, *Die althochdeutschen poetischen Denkmäler* (Stuttgart: Metzler, 1976), 21–23, and esp. McLintock's chapter on alliterative verse in J. Knight Bostock, *A Handbook on Old High German Literature*, revised by Kenneth C. King and David Robert McLintock [1954] (Oxford: Clarendon, 1976), 302–26.

[9] Andreas Heusler, *Die altgermanische Dichtung* (Berlin-Neubabelsberg: Athenaion, 1923), 182–84.

[10] *Barbara et antiquissimia carmina, quibus veterum regum actus et bella canebantur, scripsit memoriaeque mandavit.* Cap. 29: Einhardi *Vita Karoli Magni,* ed. after G. H. Pertz by G. Waitz, 6th ed. (Hanover and Leipzig: Hahn/MHG, 1911, repr. 1947), 33.

[11] See Koegel, *Geschichte* 1/i, 206. *Poetica carmina gentilia, quae in juventute didicerat, respuit nec legere nec audire nec docere voluit,* quoted from Thegan, chap. 19, by Koegel, 122–23 and 206. But this might refer to Virgil and classical authors, not German poetry. For Thegan's work, see *Thegan: Die Taten Kaiser Ludwigs; Astronomus: Das Leben Kaiser Ludwigs,* ed. trans. Ernst Tremp (Hanover: Hahn/MGH, 1995).

[12] Hoffmann, *Metrik,* 32.

[13] Friedrich Maurer, "Über Langzeilen und Langzeilenstrophen in der ältesten deutschen Dichtung," in Friedrich Maurer, *Dichtung und Sprache des Mittelalters: Gesammelte Aufsätze* (Bern and Munich: Francke, 1967, 2nd ed. 1971), 174–94.

[14] Werner Schröder, "Zum Begriff der 'binnengereimten Langzeile' in der altdeutschen Versgeschichte," in *Festschrift Josef Quint,* ed. Hugo Moser, Rudolf Schützeichel and Karl Stackmann (Bonn: Semmel, 1964), 194–202.

[15] Karin Pivernetz, *Otfrid von Weißenburg: Das Evangelienbuch in der Überlieferung der Freisinger Handschrift (Bayerische Staatsbibliothek München, cgm.14). Edition und Untersuchungen* (Göppingen: Kümmerle 2000).

[16] Dennis H. Green, "Zur primären Rezeption von Otfrids Evangelienbuch," in *Althochdeutsch,* ed. Rolf Bergmann et al. (Heidelberg: Winter, 1987), 1, 737–71.

[17] Elfriede Stutz, "Spiegelungen volkssprachlicher Verspraxis bei Otfrid," in Bergmann, *Althochdeutsch,* 1, 772–94. Debate about whether we should regard Otfrid's measure as rhyming couplets or an internally rhyming long line does not affect the issue of whether the half line (or half couplet) derives from alliterative traditional verse. At the same time, we may recall Jacob Grimm's formulae from legal texts, both alliterating, rhyming, tautologous, and metaphorical and otherwise strikingly wrought "solemn concepts" in the first two chapters of his *Deutsche Rechtsaltertümer,* 4th ed. by Andreas Heusler and Rudolf Hübner (1899, repr. Darmstadt; WBG, 1989).

[18] Otfrid's *Evangelienbuch* I, xviii, 9. The form given in the sixteenth edition of Braune's *Lesebuch,* 108, is *líoth;* the line lacks assonance or rhyme and stands out for this. Moreover, the phrase translates the Latin cliché *vita sine morte, lux sine tenebris,* so the German rendering in each text may be purely coincidental: Heinz Finger, *Untersuchungen zum Muspilli* (Göppingen: Kümmerle, 1977), 177–82, notes that the *Muspilli* manuscript actually has the form *lihot* which occurs in the Otfrid MS F, so labeled after the monastery of Freising.

[19] A fuller treatment of these two poems is Bostock, *Handbook;* Ehrismann sets out in his literary history the linguistic features of the texts; Glenys A. Waldman, *The Wessobrunn Prayer Manuscript Clm 22053: A Transliteration, Translation and Study of Parallels* (Diss., University of Pennsylvania, 1975; Ann Arbor, MI: Xerox University Microfilms, 1988) treats the scholarship up to 1975 and examines the manuscript and its sources and analogies; Hanns Fischer, *Schrifttafeln zum althochdeutschen Lesebuch* (Tübingen: Niemeyer, 1966) has facsimiles, partial in the case of the *Muspilli,* where an accessible full-length facsimile is urgently required to rein in philological flights of fancy from non-existent or illegible forms. See most recently Cyril Edwards, *The Beginnings of German Literature: Comparative and Interdisciplinary Approaches to Old High German* (Rochester, NY: Camden House, 2002), 11–77 on both works.

[20] Koegel, *Geschichte,* 1/i, 270–71.

[21] Johannes A. Huisman, "Das Wessobrunner Gebet in seinem handschriftlichen Kontext," in Bergmann, *Althochdeutsch,* 1, 632–33, noting some Greek in the manuscript, confidently interprets *poeta* as the Latinized form of the Greek for "Creator of Heaven and Earth."

[22] Bostock, *Handbook,* 128.

[23] Bertram Colgrave and R. A. B. Mynors, *Bede's Ecclesiastical History of the English People* (Oxford: Clarendon, 1969; repr. 1991): see book 4, chap. 24 [22].

[24] Ehrismann, *Geschichte,* 139.

[25] Otfrid repeats the refrain five times: *So uuas er io mit ímo sar, mit imo uuóraht er iz thar:‖ so uuás ses io gidátun, sie iz allaz sáman rietun* (So He was always with it (the Word) from the outset [*sar*]), and through it He wrought it all; whatever they ever did, they always agreed it together).

[26] See Carola L. Gottzmann, "Das Wessobrunner Gebet. Ein Zeugnis des Kulturumbruchs vom heidnischen Germanentum zum Christentum," in Bergmann, *Althochdeutsch,* 1, 637–54.

[27] See Leslie Seiffert, "The metrical form and composition of the Wessobrunner Gebet," *Medium Ævum* 31 (1962): 1–13.

[28] Peter F. Ganz, "Die Zeilenaufteilung im *Wessobrunner Gebet*," *PBB*/T (1973 = *Festschrift für Ingeborg Schröbler zum 65. Geburtstag*): 39–51.

[29] Huismann, "Das Wessobrunner Gebet," 635.

[30] *Priusquam montes fierent aut formaretur terra et orbis, a saeculo et usque in saeculum tu es, deus* (in the Authorised Version of Psalm 90: "Before the mountains were brought forth, or ever thou hadst formed the earth and the world, even from everlasting to everlasting, thou art God"). See Koegel, *Geschichte*, 1/i, 274.

[31] Hans-Hugo Steinhoff, "Wessobrunner Gebet," in *VL* X, 961–65.

[32] Herbert Kolb, "dia weroltrehtwîson," *Zeitschrift für deutsche Wortforschung* 18 (1962): 88–95.

[33] Karl Bertau, *Deutsche Literatur im europäischen Mittelalter* (Munich: Beck, 1972), 1, 69, and see Peter Nusser, *Deutsche Literatur im Mittelalter: Lebensformen, Wertvorstellungen und literarische Entwicklungen* (Stuttgart: Kröner, 1992), 34. Contrast for example the views of Eugen Joseph (in *ZfdA* 1898), who feels that Ludwig must have felt a pang of conscience when he read of the dissension among the sons of Lewis the Pious — taking v. 60 to mean "fighting against relatives."

[34] See Wolfgang Mohr and Walther Haug, *Zweimal "Muspilli"* (Tübingen: Niemeyer, 1977), 6–7.

[35] Dieter Kartschoke, *Altdeutsche Bibeldichtung* (Stuttgart: Metzler, 1975), 31 gives a clear overview.

[36] V. 2591: *anttat mûdspelles megin obar man ferid, endi thesaro uueroldes* (until mudspell's forces come over men, the end of the world); and v. 4358: *Mûtspelli cumit an thiustrea naht . . .* (Mudspell comes in the dark night (like a thief hiding his deeds)). Rudolf Schützeichel, *Das alemannische Memento Mori: Das Gedicht und der geistig-historische Hintergrund* (Tübingen: Niemeyer, 1962), 56–57 gives biblical quotations and other sources that equate the Day of Judgment and Death with a thief in the night; see also Heinz Rupp, *Deutsche religiöse Dichtungen des 11. und 12. Jahrhunderts* (Freiburg/Br.: Herder, 1958), 10, and Finger, *Muspilli*, 142–44.

[37] See Jacob Grimm, *Deutsche Mythologie*, 3rd ed. (Göttingen; Dietersche Buchhandlung, 1854), 224–25, and 674 on the wolves. For Christian sources on the Last Judgment other than the Apocalypse, see Ehrismann, *Geschichte*, 145.

[38] See Mohr and Haug, *Zweimal "Muspilli,"* 24–54, and Cola Minis, *Handschrift, Form und Sprache des Muspilli* (Berlin: Schmidt, 1966).

[39] Both *uilo gotmanno* and *uueroltrehtuuison* are suspect: the former cannot grammatically mean "many men of God," since the verb *uuanit* is singular (or is it an impersonal construction?) — on the other hand, it might mean "the man of God" — i.e., every man of God? Or is *vilo* an abstract noun = "die Vielheit der Gottesmänner"? In any case, the ms. has *uula*. Compare line (89) *quimit . . . vilo*. The word *uueroltrehtuuison* represents a compound noun with three elements, improbable even at this late date (around 840). On the other hand, taking *uuison* as a verb would require the final *-t* of the third person ending to have been omitted: *dia uueroltreht*

uuison(t) — "those who practice, teach earthly law." See Finger, *Muspilli*, 56–58 and 69–72.

[40] Finger, *Muspilli*, 111.

[41] These words probably indicate differences in the judgment, from place to process, trial to assembly to time for the court appearance, they are also part of a thoroughgoing distinction between earthly courts and process — *mahal* and penalties (*uuize*), and the Christian *suona* and *puaze* (Bostock, *Handbook*, 152). But far from the texts having an impoverished vocabulary, "dürftigen Wortschatz" (St., 77), Ruth Schmidt-Wiegand shows a wide southern-based German legal vocabulary, but with some possibly Franconian features — *arteilen* — showing full familiarity with legal procedures: "*Muspilli*," in *Handwörterbuch zur deutschen Rechtsgeschichte*, ed. Adalbert Erler et al. (Berlin: Erich Schmidt, 1984) III, 795–98. On the wordiness, see St., 77–78.

[42] Wolfgang Brandt, "Zukunftserzählen im *Muspilli*," in Bergmann, *Althochdeutsch*, 1, 720–36.

[43] See for example Koegel, *Geschichte*, 1/i, 327; *uuerde*, v. 49, not in the MS, is supplied by editors.

[44] On the penitential sermon, see Mohr in Mohr and Haug, *Zweimal "Muspilli,"* on the MS position, see Ehrismann, *Geschichte*, 147.

[45] Achim Masser, "Sigiharts Gebete," in *VL* VIII, 1242–43.

[46] St. LXXX; Rudolf Schützeichel, *Textgebundenheit: Kleinere Schriften zur Mittelalterlichen deutschen Literatur* (Tübingen: Niemeyer, 1981), 68–76; Hans-Hugo Steinhoff, "Trierer Teufelssprüche," in *VL* IX, 1058–59; M. Lundgreen, "Kleindichtung," in *Reallexikon der germanischen Altertumskunde von Johannes Hoops*, 2nd ed. (Berlin and New York: de Gruyter, 2000), XVI, 627–34.

[47] Wolfgang Haubrichs, *Die Anfänge: Versuche volkssprachiger Schriftlichkeit im frühen Mittelalter (ca. 700–1050/60)* (Frankfurt am Main: Athenäum and Tübingen; Niemeyer, 1988), 419.

[48] St. LXXXI; Groseclose and Murdoch, *Denkmäler*, 101.

[49] Text in Schlosser, 226–27. See Groseclose and Murdoch, *Denkmäler*, 99, and Haubrichs, *Anfänge*, 299–300.

[50] Haubrichs, *Anfänge*, 290–412; see David Hiley, *Western Plainchant: A Handbook* (Oxford: Clarendon, 1993).

[51] Haubrichs, *Anfänge*, 401–4.

[52] Helmut Lomnitzer, "*Petruslied*," in *VL* VII, 521–25; Pivernetz, *Otfrid von Weißenburg*, 125–26.

[53] Schützeichel, *Textgebundenheit*, 29–44.

[54] See Ehrismann, *Geschichte*, 204, note 1 on the possibly of a shared source. Paul Habermann, *Die Metrik der kleineren althochdeutschen Reimgedichte* (Halle/S.: Niemeyer, 1909), 33 thinks that each strophe had its own melody.

[55] Pivernetz, *Otfrid von Weißenburg*, 124–29.

[56] Wolfgang Haubrichs, *Georgslied und Georgslegende im frühen Mittelalter: Text und Rekonstruktion* (Konigstein/Ts: Scriptor, 1979), 206–17 reconstructs the outlines of

this tale of most sadistic judicial tortures, whose oldest form lacks what became its dominant motif, George's fight with the dragon.

[57] Rudolf Schützeichel, *Codex Pal. Lat. 52: Studien zur Heidelberger Otfridhandschrift, zum Kicila-Vers und zum Georgslied* (Göttingen: Vandenhoeck and Ruprecht, 1982).

[58] Koegel, *Geschichte* 1/i, 107.

[59] For detailed analysis of the textual, orthographical linguistic and codicological features of the text, and for the older literature, see Haubrichs, *Georgslied,* and Schützeichel, *Codex Pal. Lat. 52.* Schützeichel shows that the supposed indicators of Middle Franconian have a wider distribution, leaving the issue of localization unresolved.

[60] Haubrichs, *Georgslied,* 144–50. But puzzles remain, for instance the apparent coexistence in our text of Germanic unshifted post-vocalic /k/ (e.g., *mikilemo,* vv. 2, 4) and of shifted post-vocalic /p/ and /t/ *uhffherstuont* (vv. 66, 67, 84 etc) *ze* and *ce* (vv. 1, 5, 20, 32, 63), or the occurrence of the lexical indicator of Middle Franconian *bit* (MS: *bet*) = *mit,* with, beside so-called relic words that normally remain unshifted in Middle Franconian (*up, that, it*) but are shifted (*uf, thaz, iz*) in the *Georgslied.*

[61] Schützeichel, *Codex Pal. Lat. 52,* 75–76.

[62] Wilhelm Scherer, *Geschichte der deutschen Literatur* (Berlin: 1880/83 [repr. Berlin: Knaurs Nachf. n.d.], 81. The text here recalls the Merovingian chancery formula "*NN vir inluster . . . comes,*" where *mâro* means illustrious, and *grâbo* is the equivalent of Count (*Graf*).

[63] These points are derived here from lecture notes from the late Ruth Harvey, who observed that in his Middle High German *Ritterroman,* Reinbot von Dürne's "rehashing of the George legend into courtly style still nonetheless retains the Christ analogy."

[64] Haubrichs, *Georgslied,* 153–57; Murdoch and Groseclose, *Denkmäler,* 89.

[65] Schmidt-Wiegand, *Rechtsgeschichte,* col. 1214.

[66] Schützeichel, *Codex Pal. Lat. 52,* 61, interprets the verse form as couplets and rejects the *Langzeile* as a unit.

[67] See Haubrichs, *Georgslied,* 161–63.

[68] Haubrichs, *Georgslied,* 153–64; *Anfänge,* 405–6; see p. 407 of the latter work on the political possibilities.

[69] See on this text especially Kartschoke, *Bibeldichtung* and also *Geschichte;* David R. McLintock, "*Christus und die Samariterin,*" in *VL* I, 1238–41, and Groseclose and Murdoch, *Denkmäler,* 81–82. On the possible influence of this and the Psalm version by Otfrid see Haubrichs, *Anfänge,* 377. The text is St. XVII. The Psalm is St. XII.

[70] Compared in Kartschoke, *Bibeldichtung,* 72–74, and *Geschichte,* 161–62 as well as by McLintock. The 16th ed. of Braune gives several versions, enabling a stylistic comparison — the Tatian translation 87, 1–5, with a Latin version (not the source text) — at XX/7, 51–54; Otfrid's version is at XXXII, 111–13 (II, 14 of the *Evangelienbuch*). Brian O. Murdoch, *Old High German Literature* (Boston: Twayne, 1983), 83 defends Otfrid, who stresses Christ's humanity by the opening detail.

[71] Walter Haug and Benedikt Konrad Vollmann, *Frühe deutsche Literatur und lateinische Literatur in Deutschland 800–1150* (Frankfurt am Main: Deutscher Klassiker Verlag, 1991), 1129.

[72] See Fischer, *Schrifttafeln*, 24* for an illustration of the MS; on its provenance, see for example Haug and Vollmann, *Frühe deutsche Literatur*, 1128.

[73] Kartschoke, *Bibeldichtung*, 75–77; Groseclose and Murdoch, 1976, 81–82; Fischer, *Schrifttafeln*, 23, 25*.

[74] The Murbach Hymns may have been intended to teach German if they are indeed the *carmina ad docendum Theodiscam linguam* (songs to teach German) of the catalogue of Reichenau library where they were held originally in the early ninth century, before passing to the daughter foundation at Murbach: see Max Wehrli, *Geschichte der deutschen Literatur vom frühen Mittelalter bis zum Ende des 16. Jahrhunderts* (Stuttgart: Reclam, 1980), 51–53. Rhythm, alliteration, rhetorical skill and the use of Germanic poetic vocabulary seem to raise the text to poetry in places.

[75] Haubrichs, *Anfänge*, 324 and 379–83.

[76] Otto Ludwig, "Der althochdeutsche und der biblische Psalm 138. Ein Vergleich," *Euphorion* 56 (1962): 402–9, and David R. McLintock, "Psalm 138," in *VL* VII, 876–78.

[77] Vocabulary associated with the journey includes *giuuanchon*, deviate (v. 5); *stiga*, paths, *gingo* (for *gingi*, perhaps from the verb *gan*, to go, changed to *ginigo*) (v. 6); *cheren* (vv. 7–8); *uuech* (v. 8) *furi uuor(h)tostu*, guided on (a mistake or a deliberate word-play on *forhta*, fear?) (v. 8); *intrinnan* (v. 112); *Far* (vv. 13, 29): *fart* (v. 14).

[78] David R. McLintock, "*De Heinrico*," in *VL* III, 928–31. See *The Cambridge Songs (Carmina Cantabrigiensia)*, ed. and trans. Jan M. Ziolkowski (New York and London: Garland, 1994, also Tempe, AZ: Medieval & Renaissance Texts & Studies, 1998).

[79] Marie-Luise Dittrich, "*De Heinrico*," *ZfdA* 84 (1952/53): 274–308 favors Otto III and Heinrich der Zäncker (Henry the Quarrelsome); while Willy Sanders, "*Imperator ore iucundo saxonizans. Die altsächsischen Begrüßungsworte des Kaisers Otto in De Heinrico*," *ZfdA* 98 (1969): 13–28 favors Otto I, not least because of his "Saxon" welcome to Henry, which may be an attempt at characterization by the poet, since Saxon dialect features are concentrated in strophe 4.

[80] Murdoch, *Old High German*, 101–2.

[81] Some, including Dittrich, "*De Heinrico*," argue for identifying the two Henrys as Heinrich der Zäncker and Heinrich Duke of Carinthia. Presumably Henry and his colleagues are all Bavarians and share at least that name? Elsewhere, *aequivocus* is a philosophical term usually rendered by Notker as *ginamno* (*kenammen*) — "sharing the same name although different in essence." See Stephan Müller, *Die Sprache der Logik bei Notker dem Deutschen: Überlegungen zur Vorgeschichte einer deutschen Wissenschaftssprache* available on the website Rumolts Artikelpool (http://www.rumolt.com/notker.htm.) Notker's work on the *Categories* of Boethius opens with a discussion of the difference between the same name (*aequivocus*) and one name (*univocus*). See Notker's *Werke: 5. Boethius' Bearbeitung der Categoriae des Aristoteles,* ed. James C. King (Tübingen: Niemeyer, 1972), 1–7.

[82] Dittrich, "*De Heinrico*," 292, 295–97.

[83] Dittrich, "*De Heinrico,*" 291–92.

[84] Notker's *Werke: 7. Die kleineren Schriften,* ed. J. C. King and P. W. Tax (Tübingen: Niemeyer, 1996), 160–64.

[85] Ehrismann, *Geschichte,* 421–22.

[86] See Stefan Sonderegger, "St. Galler Sprichwörter," in *VL* II, 1051–53.

[87] For an illustration from the first leaf of Codex Sangallensis 30, a Bible, filled with various scribal doodling, alphabets and so forth, including the lampoon, see Edwards, *Beginnings,* 116; see also Ute Schwab, "Das althochdeutsche Lied *Hirsch und Hinde* in seiner lateinischen Umgebung," in *Latein und Volkssprache im deutschen Mittelalter 1100–1500,* ed. Nikolaus Henkel and Nigel F. Palmer (Tübingen: Niemeyer, 1992), 120. For *grúz,* cf. Old English *grút* f., dregs; therefore *grúz ersetzen* perhaps means "brew new beer"? Matthias Lexer's *Mittelhochdeutsches Handwörterbuch* [1872] (Stuttgart: Hirzel, 1992), II, 2022 gives *úzgeben* as "ausstatten, verheiraten."

[88] See Bostock, *Handbook,* 21. Adolf Socin, *Mittelhochdeutsches Namenbuch* (Basel: Helbig und Lichterhahn, 1903), 466, has some examples of speaking names with the verb in second element, e.g., *Gernaz* (Gladly-ate); *Nievergalt* (Never-settle-up); *Orapbeis* (Lug-chomper): they are rare, but comic. Otherwise, *Starz-* would be verbal, meaning something like "to erect, prick up."

[89] Dronke, *Medieval Lyric,* 221–38. This interpretation would make *veru* some kind of fetishistic love-toy, and possibly the verse a malicious jibe from one nun to another. See Edwards, *Beginnings,* 199. The word *fredel* can apply to either sex; the use of the preterite *santa* surely implies that the writer is not the same as the lover? Facsimile in Schwab, "Das althochdeutsche Lied," 121.

[90] Published by Karl Müllenhoff, "Ein Vers aus Sangallen," *ZfdA* 18 (1875): 261–62. See Wipf, 264.

[91] Haubrichs, *Anfänge,* 376 and 411–12.

[92] See Schützeichel, *Codex Pal. Lat. 52.*

[93] See Stefan Sonderegger, "*Hirsch und Hinde,*" in *VL* IV, 47–49.

[94] Schwab, "Das althochdeutsche Lied," 88–92, with excellent facsimiles; also Edwards, *Beginnings,* 118.

[95] Fidel Rädle, "*Kleriker und Nonne,*" in *VL* IV, 1213–15, and Peter Dronke, *Medieval Latin and the Rise of European Love-Lyric* (Oxford: Clarendon, 1966, 2nd ed. 1968), 1, 277–81 and 2, 353–56.

[96] See F. J. E. Raby, *A History of Secular Latin Poetry in the Middle Ages* (Oxford: Clarendon, 1934); Dronke, *Medieval Lyric,* 30; 281; Ziolkowski, *Cambridge Songs.*

[97] Schwab, "Das althochdeutsche Lied," 104–6.

[98] Haug and Vollmann, *Frühe deutsche Literatur,* 553–679; see Haubrichs, *Anfänge* and Gisela Vollmann-Profe, *Wiederbeginn volkssprachlicher Schriftlichkeit im hohen Mittelalter (1050/60–1160/70)* (Königstein/T.: Athenäum, 1986).

[99] Vollmann-Profe, *Wiederbeginn,* 25–33.

[100] Braune, 140–42; see Helmut de Boor, *Die deutsche Literatur von Karl dem Großen bis zum Beginn der höfischen Dichtung (1770–1170)* (Munich: Beck, 1949, 5th ed.

1962), 153–54; N. Th. J. Voorwinden, *Merigarto: Eine philologisch-historische Monographie* (Leiden: Leiden UP, 1973); Fidel Rädle, "*Merigarto,*" in *VL* VI, 403–6.

[101] Voorwinden, *Merigarto;* Wipf, 256–58.

[102] Voorwinden, *Merigarto,* 68–71, 75–76.

[103] This episode derives from Solinus's *Collectanea rerum memorabilium* and recurs in Hugo von Trimberg's vast *Der Renner* (ca. 1300, vv. 20, 237–42: see Voorwinden, *Merigarto,* 85.

[104] Vollmann-Profe, *Wiederbeginn,* 79.

[105] Voorwinden, *Merigarto,* 126.

[106] Braune, 142–44, no. XLII: There are no gaps in the poem in the MS, but on grounds of strophic structure and meaning (a wise and discerning man is damned: see Schützeichel, *Memento Mori,* 66) a gap is postulated at strophe 8–9. Similarly, strophe 17 (vv. 123–37 in the edition which counts hemistichs), vv. 128–29 and 134–37 are regarded as interpolations. Removing them creates a strophe of four long lines, internally rhyming. See on the modern title Schützeichel, *Memento Mori,* 34.

[107] See Schützeichel, *Memento Mori,* 38 on Gregory, and on Job, see Hugo Kuhn, *Dichtung und Welt im Mittelalter* (Stuttgart: Metzler, 1959, 2nd ed. 1969), 126–27, note 44.

[108] Schützeichel, *Memento Mori,* 92–93.

[109] Rupp, *Deutsche religiöse Dichtungen,* 5–9.

[110] Schützeichel, *Memento Mori,* 80–84, and *Textgebundenheit,* 107–10.

[111] Rupp, *Deutsche religiöse Dichtungen,* 19–20 and 24–25.

[112] Schützeichel, *Memento Mori,* 101–8; *Textgebundenheit,* 115–17.

[113] Text in Hans Joachim Gernentz, *Kleinere deutsche Gedichte des 11. und 12. Jahrhunderts: Nach der Ausgabe von Albert Waag* (Leipzig: Bibliographisches Institut, 1970; 3rd ed. 1977), 32–33; see Schützeichel, *Textgebundenheit,* 77–101, esp. 98–99. Text also in Braune XLIII.

[114] Friedrich-Wilhelm Wentzlaff-Eggebert, *Kreuzzugsdichtung des Mittelalters: Studien zu ihrer geschichtlichen und dichterischen Wirklichkeit* (Berlin: de Gruyter, 1960), 36–38, and Bertau, *Deutsche Literatur,* 1, 137–40.

[115] Hugo Kuhn, *Dichtung und Welt im Mittelalter* (Stuttgart: Metzler, 1959; 2nd ed. 1969), 113–14, and Bertau, *Deutsche Literatur,* I, 140.

[116] Kuhn, *Dichtung und Welt,* 126.

[117] Wilhelm Scherer, "*Memento Mori,*" *ZfdA* 24 (1880), 426–50; see p. 449.

[118] See Rupp, *Deutsche religiöse Dichtung,* 300–307, and the introduction to Gernentz's edition of eleventh and twelfth century poems, 9–11.

[119] See C. Soetemann, *Deutsche geistliche Dichtung des 11. und 12. Jahrhunderts* (Stuttgart: Metzler, 1963) and Rupp, *Deutsche religiöse Dichtungen,* 281–86.

[120] *Deutsche religiöse Dichtungen,* 307–10.

Historical Writing in and after the Old High German Period

R. Graeme Dunphy

Medieval Historiography

MEDIEVAL HISTORICAL WRITING did not arise in a vacuum. The classical Greek and Latin historians had already established a tradition with its own standards and norms, which were to continue to be influential well into the modern era. However, in the late classical period a process of selection took place that determined which ancient writers would be available to the medieval reader. Some of those whom we regarded as the greatest Greek and Latin historians (from the fifth century B.C. to the first of our era) were all but forgotten in the Middle Ages. Herodotus, Thucydides, Plutarch, and Tacitus were virtually unknown, and even Julius Caesar received remarkably little attention as a historian when one considers the great interest shown in him as an object of historical study. But others were read. The Greek works of Josephus (first century A.D.) were popular in Latin translation, and the monumental *Ab urbe condita* (From the foundation of Rome) of Livy (59 B.C.–A.D. 17) was enormously influential, though it was almost exclusively read in a summary version. Sallust, Lucan, and Suetonius (from the first century B.C. to the second century A.D.) were also familiar, as was Justinus's abridgement of Pompeius Trogus, a third-century version of a universal history written at the time of Augustus. These were important as sources of historical material, but also as roots of the historiographic tradition itself.[1]

The most incisive caesura marking the transition from late classical to early medieval historical writing was the development of a specifically Christian worldview centering on a historical event, the incarnation of Christ, and incorporating a series of theological concepts that impinge on the way history must be presented. Foremost among these are the doctrine of creation as a divine act, which gives history a definite beginning, and the literal belief in the Biblical end-times — the apocalypse, the Antichrist, and the Last Judgment — a complex of eschatological ideas which means that the end of history is as clearly conceived as its beginning. Then there is the status of biblical narrative as revealed truth, including the descent of all humanity from the protoplasts Adam and Eve, which gives ancient history so much of its content. The concept of regress, meaning that since the golden age of paradise the human condition has been one of inevitable decline, results in a linear historiography and a reverence for antiquity. Finally, the notion of the divine economy of history, the belief that every historical event has a purpose in God's plan, means that history teaches moral lessons. Taken together, these ideas ensured that the history emerging from Christian intellectual circles from the fourth century on was strikingly different from that which had gone before.[2]

The pioneers of Christian historiography in the fourth and fifth centuries were Sextus Julius Africanus, Jerome, Eusebius, Orosius, and Augustine, and in the sixth to eighth centuries Isidore of Seville and the Englishman, Bede. In addition to defining the theological character of Christian history, they also did much work on practical questions, resolving difficult problems of chronology and suggesting patterns into which historical events could be grouped to give history a clearer shape. Two constructs in particular were to have immense influence, developed by the fathers Jerome and Augustine respectively. Jerome worked out the concept that non-biblical history could be understood as a series of four empires characterized by Daniel's dream of the four beasts (Daniel 7), with the parallel dream of the statue (Daniel 2) providing confirmation. The four empires were usually identified thus:

Lion with eagle's wings	Babylon
Bear	Medo-Persia (Cyrus, Darius)
Winged leopard	Greece (Alexander)
Beast (boar) with iron teeth and ten horns	Rome

But the interpretation could vary, as we shall see.[3] A problem for the chroniclers of the later Middle Ages was that, unlike Jerome, they were no longer living under the Roman Empire, and continuities with the Carolingian, Salian, and Staufen dynasties had to be postulated so that the historiographical category "Rome" still applied. From the beginning of the twelfth century this was formalized in the *translatio imperii* doctrine, which held that the Roman Empire did not fall, but was merely transferred to the Franks; the term Holy Roman Empire (*sacrum Romanum imperium* or *S.R.I.*), used from the mid-thirteenth century, reflects this.[4] Quite separately, Augustine worked on the approach that world history could be divided into six ages, *sex aetates mundi,* which were parallel to the six days of biblical creation. These ages of the world could also be seen as parallel to the six ages of human life (infancy, childhood, adolescence . . .), so that history could be seen as the story of the world growing old, inevitably a narrative of decline. As divisions of the ages, Augustine took the major turning points in biblical history. Like the four empires, these could vary slightly in later writings, but the standard pattern was:

aetas I:	from Adam to the flood	*infantia*
aetas II:	from the flood to Abraham	*pueritia*
aetas III:	from Abraham to David	*adolescentia*
aetas IV:	from David to the Babylonian captivity	*iuventus*
aetas V:	from the Babylonian captivity to Christ	*gravitas*
aetas VI:	from Christ to the Second Coming	*senectus*

Since the sixth *aetas* begins with the birth of Christ, Christians are living in the final age, which links well with the apocalyptic element in the presentations of the end of history.[5] Although the *aetas* divisions do not coincide with the rise and fall of Jerome's empires, the two systems were seen as simultaneously valid, and either (or a combination of both) could be used as a structuring principle. Other patterns could also be relevant. Augustine's doctrine of the two cities led to the notion of a dynamic tension between sacred and secular threads running throughout history. Bede's application of the system of counting years from the birth of Christ led to a complementary division of history into two parts, B.C. and A.D., which would survive the Middle Ages and be prescriptive also for the modern world. While many medieval writers still preferred to cite dates by year of the reign of a current ruler, the citation of dates A.D. becomes increasingly common as the Middle Ages progress, especially in annals. The retrospective numbering of years B.C., however, only became standard practice in the fifteenth century, though some have argued that it too was known in embryonic form as early as Bede.[6]

Medieval historical writing was intended to serve a number of purposes. It could be apologetic, presenting the Christian worldview in the earlier period of the Church's expansion or supporting a stance in a later theological or political dispute. It could be philosophical, seeking meaning in history, or hermeneutic, drawing lessons for the pulpit. It could be didactic, for the instruction of young monks, later of young noblemen. In the closing centuries of the Middle Ages it was often intended to develop the sense of identity of a particular group such as the nobility or the patricians who wished to see themselves in history, or to encourage a sense of local patriotism. And in the case of imperial or urban histories, it could have legal importance, recording prerogatives and precedents.

To meet these ends, several discrete literary forms emerged. We may distinguish the annal from the chronicle, though the distinction is often imprecise. The theoretical difference is that an annal is the record of an institution or court, kept like a diary with regular annual entries by a succession of writers, while a chronicle is conceived and executed retrospectively by a single author as an integrated whole. But in the practice of medieval writing, it is seldom so simple. Among the various types of chronicle, the world chronicle stands apart from local or Church chronicles in its attempt to give comprehensive coverage of all of world history. Chronicles that are not universal in this sense have instead a thematic focus. Alongside these obvious forms we must also consider biographical works or accounts of particular events such as battles, which may not seek to elucidate wider historical contexts, but do nevertheless record historical data, and feed both from and into the larger forms. We might also mention in passing that such diverse forms as biblical epic (the *Heliand,* Otfrid, the Genesis poems) or fictional works based on historical constellations, the medieval equivalent of our historical novel, are also in a sense historical writing, and are relevant here at least in so far as a constant borrowing took place in both directions between these and the great chronicles. In the latter category we are thinking especially of the early courtly novel when it deals with such figures as Alexander or Charlemagne, but also works of the heroic tradition such as the *Hildebrandlied,* which presents in part the folk-memory of historically verifiable figures. Furthermore, cosmographies (geographical texts) and legal compilations also contain historical material. And finally, the computus, a form of handbook on the method of calculating Church festivals, and other theoretical discourses or practical reference charts on questions of chronology, also belong under the rubric of historiography. Taken together, these forms represent the work of many hundreds of writers.[7]

Thus, when historical writing first emerged in Germany, in the ninth century in Latin and later in German, it was part of a European tradition rooted in antiquity that already had a clear theoretical framework. Within this framework it would continue to develop, innovative both in form and style. The framework itself, however, was fixed with all the rigidity of Christian dogma.

Annals

Although the term "annals" was used in classical times (the *Annals* of Tacitus are a familiar example), the form as we know it in the West in the Middle Ages seems to originate no earlier than the eighth century. Apparently, it first arose out of marginal notes in Easter tables — charts giving the dates of Easter — of the type which late seventh-century Anglo-Saxon missionaries introduced into Frankish monasteries. These Easter annals soon outgrew the space available in the margins of manuscripts and took on a life of their own, influenced perhaps also by other sorts of historical listings. Their heyday in Germany is the ninth to eleventh centuries, after which they begin to decline, the chronicle then becoming the preferred form. Any year-by-year account in which entries are headed by the year number as counted from the incarnation can be regarded as an annal. Ideally we think of them as written progressively, the information on any given year being set down in that year, but of course they could also be composed retrospectively, and when copied they were frequently modified, expanded or conflated. At any rate, annals were primarily conceived to record contemporary or recent events, as the form does not lend itself to surveys of great swathes of human history.

Court annals in Germany date from the time of Charlemagne. The most important early example, the *Royal Frankish Annals* (*Annales regni Francorum*) were begun in the late eighth century and cover the years 741–829, composed by writers associated with the royal chapel.[8] A second generation of Carolingian annals can be epitomized by those of Fulda (*Annales Fuldenses*) and of St. Bertin (*Annales Bertiniani*). These represent the turbulent period after the Frankish kingdom was split, and whereas the Fulda annals present the political wrangling of the years 838–901 from the perspective of East Francia (what became Germany), the St. Bertin account focuses on West Frankish (French) affairs from 830–882. These and similar works, all written in Latin prose, are our principal source of information on Carolingian history. The titles of many of the early annals link them with towns or monastic institutions (Fulda, St. Bertin, Lorsch, Xanten, Metz, Corvey, Salzburg, Hildesheim, St. Vaast), but these names are often misleading, reflecting merely the library in which the manuscript was preserved or an erroneous attempt by scholars of the humanist period to ascribe authorship. Nevertheless, there is frequently a regional focus in the reporting that makes comparisons between them particularly interesting for the modern historian. While the larger works were commissioned by court circles, the smaller ones are usually monastic in origin.

The *Annals of Fulda* will serve well to illustrate the nature and interest of the genre.[9] The work begins and ends abruptly, with neither prologue nor epilogue, nor any attempt at a theoretical systematization of the history to be recorded. The manuscripts ascribe authorship to a certain Rudolf, but nothing is declared about patronage, purpose or circumstances of writing. Each entry is headed by a year number and launches straight into the events of that year. One randomly selected entry will demonstrate the style of reporting:

> DCCCXLIII. Descripto regno a primoribus et in tres partes diviso apud Viridunum Galliae civitatem tres reges mense Augusto convenientes regnum inter se dispertiunt: et Hludowicus quidem orientalem partem accepit, Karlus vero occidentalem tenuit, Hlutharius, qui maior natu erat, mediam inter eos sortitus est portionem. Factaque inter se pace et iuramento firmata singuli ad disponendas tuendasque regni sui partes revertuntur. Karlus Aquitaniam quasi ad partem regni sui iure pertinentem affectans Pippino nepoti suo molestus efficitur eumque crebris incursionibus infestans, grande detrimentum proprii saepe pertulit exercitus.
>
> Gregorius papa obiit, in cuius locum subrogatus est Sergius. Et Mauri Beneventum occupaverunt.
>
> [843. After the kingdom had been surveyed by the leading men and divided into three parts, the three kings met in the month of August at Verdun, a city in Gaul, and divided it amongst themselves. Ludwig received the eastern part; Charles held the western part; Lothar, who was the oldest, obtained the part which lay in between. After peace had been made between them and confirmed by oath, each set off to govern and defend the lands of his own kingdom. Charles, who claimed Aquitaine as if belonging to his portion of the kingdom by right, made difficulties for his nephew Pippin by frequent attacks; but often his own army suffered severe loss. Pope Gregory died, and in his place Sergius was chosen. The Moors occupied Benevento.]

This entry for the year 843 is typical in length, though some others are far fuller; the entry for 858 is roughly eight times as long. The main focus is on East Frankish royal affairs, and these are recounted in longer paragraphs of continuous text, as with this account of the peace of Verdun; such passages form the bulk of each entry, highlighting especially military maneuvers, ongoing struggles with the Scandinavian invaders, and disputes over titles and territories. As this is contemporary history, almost journalistic shortcuts are taken in the forms of reference. Little attempt is made, for example, to explain precisely who the protagonists are: the reader's familiarity with the constellation is assumed. West

Frankish affairs are also covered, but in far less detail. The battle of Saucourt, a decisive West Frankish victory over the Vikings in 881, is mentioned in a single sentence:

Nepos vero illius cum Nordmannis dimicans nobiliter triumphavit; nam
novem milia equitum ex eis occidisse perhibetur.

[His nephew fought with the Norsemen and triumphed nobly; for he is
said to have killed nine thousand of their horsemen.]

Even here, the initial "his" refers to the East Frankish king. Contemporary events beyond the boundaries of the Frankish kingdoms are mentioned in brief sentences, usually at the beginning or end of an entry, as
with the reference in the passage above to the death of Pope Gregory or
the Moorish occupation of Benevento.

The apparently detached tone of reporting is deceptive. The authors
have clear sympathies, and these occasionally find voice in value judg-
ments. The Bohemian revolt of 849 is introduced with the words *Boe-
mani more solito fidem mentientes* . . . (The Bohemians in their usual
fashion denied their loyalty . . .). A synod of 868 was called to produce a
suitable response to the *Graecorum ineptiis* (the stupidities of the
Greeks). The outcome of battles may be identified as God's vengeance,
while political figures may be likened to Bible characters. In the entry for
875, Charles the Fat, king of the West Franks, is described as *Galliae
tyrannus* (the tyrant of Gaul), and his coronation as emperor is described
as a piece of wanton thuggery, the slanted account wrongly suggesting
that the pope acted under coercion.

Great interest is also attached to natural phenomena, especially astral
phenomena. There are four descriptions of comets, two of eclipses, two
of shooting stars, nine of earthquakes, we read of lightning striking a
church (855), a particularly hard winter (874), unusually heavy rain
(868) or hail (872). Among these are unnatural events such as red snow
(860), or blood raining from heaven, which coincides with a plague of
insects (873). The effects of these events on crops are invariably noted,
and if these portents coincide with high points in the church calendar or
significant occurrences in human life, this is made explicit, as when a
comet appeared on Christmas day (841), was followed by a flood in
which eighty-eight people died (857), or presaged the death of the king
(882). These reports must be understood in the context of the general
expectation that the world would end with the millennium, which led
historians to seek the portents promised in the New Testament (Matthew 24: 7). Events that are more down-to-earth are also occasionally
included, such as a theft from a monastery in 853, or, in 870, the moral

story of the woman who baked on a religious festival in defiance of piety, only to find the bread was burned.

In the later Middle Ages, monastic and imperial annals continue to be written, though the Easter annal gradually disappears. From the late ninth century, a form of annalistic chronicle begins to develop, which complicates the genre question by drawing for its inspiration on both annal and chronicle traditions. The most important work here is the *Annales* of Lampert of Hersfeld, written around 1077–79. It begins with a chronicle-type survey of world history, going over to the annalistic form from 708; this early material is borrowed from Isidore and Bede, and the annals of Hersfeld and Hildesheim (the former now lost). From 1040, Lampert's annual entries become longer as he begins to record his own memories, so much so that from 1063 the annalistic form is lost sight of, and the work again resembles a chronicle. This use of annalistic elements in a work that, despite its name, is not strictly an annal, represents a particular sophistication as the golden age of the form draws toward its close.

Chronicles

Although the chronicle is actually the older form in Latin historiography, it reached the highest point of its development in Germany later than the annal. The tradition of chronicle writing in Germany began to produce large numbers of significant works beginning in the eleventh century. Unlike the annal, it made the leap into the vernacular in the twelfth century, and it continued in an unbroken line down to the humanist period. In contrast to the annal, with its limited geographical coverage and its focus on recent events, the chronicle is a form of historical writing that, although it does present events chronologically, is free of the constraint to give comparable weight to every year, and thus lends itself to the exploration and interpretation of larger historical contexts.

The world chronicle, or universal chronicle, with its aspiration to completeness, was especially popular in the Middle Ages, partly because it satisfied the medieval penchant for amassing information, and partly because it so neatly reflects the pattern of salvation history that lies at the heart of all Christian thinking.[10] World chronicles can be divided, with all the usual caveats, into three groups. The *series temporum* (sequence of dates), the major form of the eighth to eleventh centuries, is a chronological listing, with brief records of events which are simply noted, seldom evaluated. To this extent it most closely resembles the annal. The *mare historiarum* (the expanse — literally "the sea" — of histories) has less emphasis on chronology and more narrative, and thus lends itself to vernacular verse renditions which can draw on the tradition of courtly literature. Finally, the *imago mundi* (mirror of the world) type is interested in the encyclopedic assembling of all knowledge, and is likely to combine a chronicle with geographical or scientific texts. Chronicles of the second or third type, and especially those that combine the narrative and the cosmological approaches, can grow to immense proportions, and these are typical of the later Middle Ages. The ultimate ambition of the world chronicle is to elucidate the divine plan in history, and to interpret the present in terms of this.

By contrast, chronicles which are not world chronicles, all those which, rather than aiming at universality, focus instead on a specific period or locality, or are otherwise restricted in their coverage, can be grouped under the heading of thematic chronicles. Since the majority of early medieval chronicles were world chronicles, as were a sizeable proportion of later ones, it is useful to class chronicles under two headings: world chronicles and other types, but the latter form a disparate group. The thematic element that characterizes them may be local or national sentiment, or the interests of a ruling house or institution. We are thinking, then, primarily of histories of the church or of particular orders or monastic establishments, and of secular histories of political entities, regions, ethnic groups, and cities. Whereas in France and England the centralized royal houses led to the growth of national chronicles, the fragmented nature of the political structures of the empire resulted in a greater focus on regional affairs, though there were also several chronicles of emperors.

Among the earliest chronicles in Germany was the *Chronicon* of Regino of Prüm, composed in Lorraine in the early tenth century, and which runs from the birth of Christ to 906; it later was extended to 967 by Adalbert of Magdeburg. This kind of *continuatio* is a common phenomenon in the manuscript tradition of medieval chronicles, often added when a work is copied to bring the new version up to date. In the eleventh century, the polymath Hermann of Reichenau (Herimannus Contractus, "Hermann the Lame") produced the first attempt by a German writer at a precise chronological account of the Christian era, his *Chronicon*, running from the birth of Christ to 1054; he also wrote a *computus* which was relatively widely used in the following two centuries. Hermann's chronicle, as continued by Bertold of Reichenau, was used by Bernold of St. Blasien and others, and thus had a profound if often indirect influence on the German historiography of the twelfth century. An extremely important late eleventh-century church chronicler is Adam of Bremen, whose *Gesta Hammaburgensis ecclesiae pontificum* (ca. 1076) is a history of the see of Hamburg and of Christian missions in the north from 788 to 1072. Among the most important names of this period is Marianus Scotus (1028–82), actually Moelbrigte, an Irish monk who was active in Fulda and later in Mainz, whose world chronicle was apparently written in the years 1072–76. Marianus wished to correct the traditional dating for the birth of Christ, and is therefore an innovative as well as an influential historian. Among the major twelfth-century contributions to the form are the *Chronicon universale* of Frutolf of Michelsberg (died 1103), continued to 1107 by Ekkehard of Aura, and the (Latin) *Kaiserchronik*, commissioned by Emperor Henry V. Otto of Freising, whose monumental *Historia de duabus civitatibus* was penned in the years 1143–46, was an uncle of the emperor Frederick Barbarossa, and his history is interesting for its defense of Staufen legitimacy, as well as for its innovative use of the two-cities motif as a historiographic schema. All these works are in Latin prose.

If one had to select a single Latin chronicle for fuller treatment, it should perhaps be one that reflects the breadth of material which could be amassed in a relatively concise volume, a compendium not only of historical knowledge. The *imago mundi* type of world chronicle takes its name from a vastly influential work by Honorius Augustodunensis, first composed around 1110 and reissued several times over the following thirty years in new versions by the same author.[11] Honorius was probably German by birth, and apart from some time in England as a young man, he spent his active life in Regensburg. His *Imago mundi* is constructed in three books, only the third of which is a chronicle; the first two deal with the cosmos and with the computation of time respectively. The three books are divided into chapters, each with a number and title, which vary in length from twenty words to several hundred. The *Imago mundi* breaks little new ground, in fact, it is decidedly conservative, reflecting the cosmography of the Carolingian period, but perhaps precisely for this reason it was extremely widely read, and must therefore rate as one of the most important German chronicles of the Middle Ages.[12] It would be a mistake to isolate the third book and treat it separately as historiography, for the three parts are clearly to be seen as an encyclopedic whole. Indeed, the construction of the work is entirely logical. The first book is a cosmographical survey, covering the basics of geography, physics and astronomy, that is, it begins with the world as we live in it, goes on to examine the nature of the world, and then moves as one might expect in medieval thinking to the nature of the heavens. The second book explores the nature of time, which of course is based on the heavenly bodies and therefore follows easily from the end of book one, and this analysis of chronological systems leads effortlessly into a survey of historical time, the chronological account of world history which fills the third book.

The geographical survey in the *Imago mundi* was particularly popular as a source for the cosmographical digressions of later chronicles. The first nine chapters deal with the creation and divisions of the world, and the rivers of paradise, and this is followed by twenty-six chapters on continents and countries. The description of the south of Germany is an interesting example:

> 23. De Germania Superior.
>
> A Danubio usque ad Alpes est Germania Superior, qui a germinando populos dicitur, versus occasum Rheno, versus aquilonem Albia fluvio terminatur. In hac est regio Suevia, a monte Suevo dicta. Hec et Alemannia, a Lemanno lacu appellata. Hec et Retia dicta. In hac Danubius nascitur, et .lx. precipuis fluviis augetur, et in .vii. ostia ut Nilus divisus Ponticum mare ingreditur. Est in ea Noricus que et Bawaria, in qua est civitas Ratispona. Est et Orientalis Francia, cui coniungitur Turingia, quam sequitur Saxonia.

> [23. On Upper Germany.
>
> From the Danube to the Alps is Upper Germany, so called because of the proliferation of its peoples, which is bounded to the west by the Rhine, to the north by the river Elbe. In it is the land of Swabia, named after Mount Suevo. Here is also Alemannia, named after Lac Léman [Lake Geneva]. It is also called Raetia. The source of the Danube is in Upper Germany, it is fed by sixty large rivers, and it flows out into the Black Sea, divided like the Nile into seven mouths. Noricus, which is Bavaria, is situated here, in which is the city of Regensburg. East Franconia is also here, bordered by Thüringen, beyond which is Saxony.]

The focus is clearly on place names, their etymology, and their relative geography. The etymologies, like Germania from *germino* (to beget) and Swabia from the otherwise unknown Mount Suevo, which of course are entirely dubious from the viewpoint of modern philology, are taken from Isidore of Seville. A similar listing of facts is typical of the following chapters, with such titles as *De inferno* (On hell, 36), *De estu* (On tides, 40), *De terre motu* (On earthquakes, 42), in which all kinds of geological and meteorological phenomena are described and explained. The chapters on the planets (73–81) deal with the astrologically significant seven "wandering stars" (five planets, the sun and the moon) after which the days of the week take their names; many medieval chronicles give an account of these. Then there is a long section on constellations, before a brief mention of the waters above the firmament and the habitation of angels, and finally 1.147: *Huic longe supereminere dicitur celum celorum, in quo habitat rex angelorum. Explicit liber primus. Incipit liber secundus* (Far above this, it is said, is the Heaven of Heavens, in which dwells the King of Angels. End of book one. Beginning of book two).

The second book is similar in tone, defining time and eternity, hours and days and their relationship to the zodiac, the names of days and months, the cycles of the planets, and the dates of church festivals. It is not surprising, then, that when Honorius turns to history in the final book, we have again a minimalist accretion of basic data. Of Adam, for example, we read (3.1):

> Adam primus homo ad imaginem Dei in Hebron formatus, in paradyso cum Eva septem horis commoratus, ob mandati transgressionem huius mundi exilium subiit, in quo .xxx. filios et totidem filias absque Abel et Cain genuit. Ipse vero post .dcccc.xxx. annos in Ierusalem obiit, in loco Calvarie sepultus, aliquamdiu requievit, deinde in Hebron translatus, in terram de qua assumptus est rediit.

> [Adam, the first man, was formed in Hebron in the image of God, sojourned in Paradise with Eve for seven hours; for his breach of the commandment he was subjected to the exile of this world, in which he fathered thirty sons and as many daughters, not counting Abel and Cain. After 930 years he died in Jerusalem, being buried at Calvary he rested for a while, then being moved to Hebron he returned to the soil from which he was first taken.]

The historical data are arranged strictly according to the *sex aetates* principle. Honorius shows little interest in narrative; a story that other chroniclers might tell in lengthy accounts is dispatched with the words: *Noe vixit .dcccc.l. annos. Huius tempore extstitit diluvium* (Noah lived 950 years. In his days there was a flood). Lists of rulers fill many of the chapters, for most of whom the only information given is the length of their reign. Roman consuls and dictators are listed with their dates according to the Roman system, *annos urbis condite*. Later Roman history is charted under a scheme of ten persecutions of the Church. After the fall of the Roman Empire, only lists are provided, tracing both papal and imperial succession at breathtaking speed right down to the date of writing. The chronicle ends with the words: *Reliquium sexte etatis soli Deo patet* (Only God knows the remainder of the sixth age).

As chronicle writing was to a far greater extent than narrative or poetic literature the province of the scholar, its home in the monastic library or occasionally in the royal chancellery, it followed that the switch from Latin to German came later here than with the more obviously literary forms. It is only in the early Middle High German period that vernacular chronicles appear at all in Germany, and by the end of the twelfth century there were still only two works in the language that were more or less chronicle in their form, the *Annolied* (Song of Anno, late eleventh century) and the (German) *Kaiserchronik* (Chronicle of the emperors, mid-twelfth century).

The *Annolied* is something of a curiosity, unusual both in form and in purpose. We generally consider it the tentative beginning of German-language chronicle writing, but in some respects it stands aside from the broader developments in the tradition. Like most chronicles in German before the fifteenth century, it is fashioned in rhyming couplets, but unusually these are grouped into forty-nine strophes varying from six to twenty-six lines in length. For a world chronicle, then, this is a short work, which bounds through the historical continuum, dispatching whole swathes of history in cursory summaries or omitting them altogether, then landing on an event that is narrated more fully. Daniel's dream, for example, provides the structural framework for the history of empires, but the first empire is dealt with in just three rhyming couplets:

> Diz eristi dier was ein lewin,
> Si havite mennislichin sin,
> Diu beceichenit vns alle Küninge
> Die der warin in Babilonia,
> Dere crapht unt ire wisheit
> Gidadun ire riche vili breiht.
> (*Annolied* 12, 1–6)[13]

> [The first creature was a lioness
> which had human understanding.
> She represents all the kings
> who were enthroned in Babylon.
> Their power and their wisdom
> made their empires very large.]

When it comes to the third Empire, four tales of Alexander the Great are recounted. These stories were well known in the Middle Ages, and the poet can count on the reader to fill in the details. Occasionally the terse style of this poem is turned into a poetic virtue, as when reporting how Ninus equipped the first army. Here, the repeated insertion of one-liners has been seen as a chaotic string of non-sequiturs, but in fact produces a sophisticated effect which may become clearer if we add modern punctuation:

Her saminodi schilt unti sper
(Des lobis was her vili ger)
Halspergin unti brunievn
(Dü gart er sic, ciih sturm)
Die helmi stalin heirti
(Du stifter heriverti).

(Annolied 8, 7–12)

[He gathered shields and spears
(he longed for glory)
hauberks and byrnies
(he girded himself for battle)
and helmets of hard steel
(he marched out to war).]

However, the historical sections of the *Annolied* are probably at their best in those narratives in which the poet can root his own people in history, particularly in the account of Julius Caesar (the fourth empire), where the *Bellum Gallicum* is transformed into a *Bellum Germanicum*, and the Germans then join Caesar to become the real victors of the *Bellum Civile*.

What makes the *Annolied* stand out from other chronicles, however, is its combination of history and hagiography, which defies the usual genre classifications. It was probably written at Siegburg in 1080 by an adherent of the recently deceased Archbishop of Cologne Anno II, with the intention of presenting this politically controversial figure as a saintly benefactor of city, Church, and empire. It falls naturally into three sections, the third of which is a life of Anno, on the face of it a fairly traditional *vita*. However, the first section is a history of the sacred world from Adam to Anno, focusing on biblical prophets, the early Church, the mission to the Germans and the martyrs of the Rhineland, while the second charts the history of the secular world from Ninus, the founder of the first city, to Anno, the finest ruler of the greatest city, with particular interest in the ancient empires, especially Alexander and Julius Caesar, and in the origins of the German tribes and their cities. Clearly the historical sections are designed as a two-pronged introduction to the life of Anno in the final part of the poem, showing sacred and secular history as separate chains of events, both leading up to the life of *Godis drüt* (God's favorite, 43, 6). This complex form is foreshadowed in the second strophe, where we are told how God created two worlds:

Dü deilti Got sini werch al in zuei,
Disi werlt ist daz eine deil,
Daz ander ist geistin:
Dü gemengite dei wise Godis list
Von den zuein ein werch, daz der mennisch ist,
Der beide ist corpus unte geist,
Dannin ist her na dim engele allermeist.

(Annolied 2, 5–12)

[God divided all His work in two.
This world is one part,
the other is spiritual.
Then God in His wisdom and skill
blended the two to make a single work, the human being,
who is both body and spirit,
and for this reason is closest to the angels.]

One world is physical, the other spiritual, and by mixing them, God creates a third world, the human being, who is both. This tripartite theology of creation prepares the reader for the triple pattern in the poem, the parallel sacred and secular histories which meet and blend in the person of the perfect man. Thus, the three parts of the poem are closely integrated into a hagiographical construction, and an interesting numerological pattern underlines this, placing Anno at the end of history in the strophes with theologically significant strophe numbers, seven and thirty-three. Nevertheless, this poem cannot be seen just as a vita, a saint's life with an added historical preamble, as the chronicle sections fill thirty-three of the forty-nine strophes and are therefore the dominant part of the work. Insofar as the *Annolied*'s chronicle can be seen to have an independent life, it fulfills all the criteria for a world chronicle, albeit a concise one. The twofold trawl through history is a most unusual feature, but in different ways, other world chronicles also separate sacred from secular.

The Middle High German *Kaiserchronik*, which must be distinguished clearly from the Latin *Kaiserchronik* of Henry V,[14] was apparently written in Regensburg in the years 1130–50, and thus is treated here on grounds of context and continuity, even though it is at the very edge of the chronological parameters of this volume. Consisting of 17,283 lines of rhyming couplets, this work is the first large-scale world chronicle in the German language. In contrast to the *Annolied*, its accounts are full and vivid, with much use of dialogue and other techniques familiar from narrative fiction. The author, or possibly the two authors, can be assumed to be monastic, though the work was very likely commissioned for a secular, that is, a courtly audience.[15] The *Kaiserchronik* is to be understood as the history of the Roman Empire from its foundation through the classical period and in its medieval continuation on through the Carolingian and Salian periods as far as Konrad III. The structural mechanism is the sequence of thirty-six Roman and nineteen German emperors, the reigns of the Roman emperors comprising four fifths of the work (down to line 14,281), but these are so depicted as to highlight larger patterns both in the spiritual realm, as Christianity gradually wins the "heathen" empire, and the political, as the empire passes from Rome to the Carolingians and their heirs, the first expression of the new "*translatio imperii*" doctrine in the German language. The account of each reign concludes with chronological data in a fairly standardized formulation, for example Lewis the Pious:

> Ludewîc rihte daz rîche,
> so iz den vursten wol mahte lîchen, —
> daz saget das buoch vur wâr —
> sehs unde drîzech jâr
> unt drîer mânode mêre.
> die vursten clageten in sêre.
> Alse Ludewîch von der werlte versciet . . .
> . . . Karl daz rîche besaz.
> (*Kaiserchronik* 15388–94; 15400)[16]

> [Lewis ruled the empire
> much to the liking of the princes
> (so indeed says the book)
> for 36 years
> and three months.
> The princes grieved for him greatly.
> When Lewis had departed from the world
> . . .
> Charles took possession of the empire.]

This gives the impression of great precision, almost of pedantry in cases where even days are counted, but in fact the figures are often random and even the order of the reigns is occasionally confused. The effect is to place the lives of the individual emperors in the center and subordinate all other narrative to this context.

But this does not mean that the poet is always concerned primarily with the emperor himself. The catch-phrase *Sage und Legende* (Saga and legend), used as the title of Friedrich Ohly's classic study of the poem's sources,[17] sums up the wealth of narrative material which is inserted into the fifty-five reigns: tales and legends, with the word *legend* being used here strictly in its medieval sense, meaning miraculous stories about saints, while tales (*Sagen*), include everything else which modern usage might loosely class as legendary. Good examples are the legends of Faustinian, Silvester and Crescentia, or the tales of the rape of Lucrece and the chastity of Tharsilla. Though the tales are not specifically spiritual, their purpose is not merely to entertain, as is the case with the anecdotal material in some later patrician chronicles, which can have a similar tone. All the inserted material — we might say the ahistorical material, though the Middle Ages were less inclined to make such a distinction — is included for its exemplary value as models of right or wrong conduct. The women are mostly chaste and one-dimensional; the most interesting men are villains who either become saints or come to an unpleasant end; the emperors are torn back and forth between heathen and Christian perspectives until gradually the Gospel is brought to the empire and to the whole world. An unusual feature in a chronicle, though familiar in other forms, is the integration into the narrative of lengthy accounts of three formal disputations between Church Fathers and their non-Christian adversaries, which allow theological ideas to be explored in far greater detail than would normally be possible in a narrative text. One of these, for example, is a debate on astrology, a problem for the early Church that enjoyed a resurgence at the beginning of the twelfth century. Obviously, the disputations end in victories for the champions of Christ, and being associated with the stories of Faustinian, the (fictional) first Christian emperor, and Constantine, who made Christianity the religion of the establishment, they are so placed in the historical continuum that they can symbolize the whole conflict of new and old ways, and mark important stages in the progress of the Christian mission.

A great deal of scholarly attention has been devoted to the relationship between the *Kaiserchronik* and the *Annolied*, which have some 200 verses in common. These are the *Annolied*'s account of Daniel's dream, including material on Alexander, and on Caesar and the Germans, which the *Kaiserchronik* adapts as a series of inserts throughout its first thousand lines. In this way the poet acknowledges the scheme of successive empires, and covers Alexander so to speak in a flashback, without Jerome's doctrine becoming a structural principle: the poet is concerned only with the final empire, and at most wishes to place this briefly in the context of the dream. Interestingly, however, the verses are rearranged to change the sequence of empires. Here we have first Alexander (winged leopard), then three unnamed kingdoms (bear), next Julius Caesar and by implication the whole Roman history (boar), and finally in a passage parallel to *Annolied* 12.1–6 which was cited above, but conflated with *Annolied* 17.9–12, the fourth beast is the Antichrist.

If the *Annolied* was remarkable for the role it ascribed to the Germans in the history of Caesar, the *Kaiserchronik* takes this even further. A whole series of Roman emperors are seen to be dependent on their links with Germany, and the virtues of the Germans appear in stark contrast to the moral inadequacies of the Roman and Greek populations. In this way the path is carefully prepared for a natural *translatio imperii*, a doctrine that the *Annolied* poet would have appreciated, but which the *Kaiserchronik* poet certainly knew. In terms of the number of verses actually adopted, the *Annolied* is but a minor source. If, however, it helped to inspire the patriotism of the *Kaiserchronik*, its influence may be far greater than it first appears.

The *Kaiserchronik* is often regarded as a world chronicle in its breadth and scope, but the fact that it begins, as Livy's work had done, with the foundation of Rome, means that elements of the Christian historiography are neglected. This lacuna was obviously felt in the Middle Ages, for two separate attempts to fill the gap can be observed. The important Vorau manuscript combines the *Kaiserchronik* with the *Altdeutsche Genesis* (also known as the *Wiener Genesis*, the Vienna Genesis)[18] and other verse renditions of biblical narratives, which however it precedes, though one might expect these to come first; and the *Prosakaiserchronik*, a prose reduction which was used in the late thirteenth century as a historical preamble to the *Schwabenspiegel*,[19] was prefaced with a *Buch der Könige*, covering the kings of Old Testament history.[20] In both cases, the compilation becomes a world chronicle in the fullest sense.

With the success of the *Kaiserchronik*, the floodgates opened for a wave of vernacular chronicle writing in the thirteenth century and beyond. Although this takes us beyond the scope of the present volume, it has to be noted that the late Middle Ages were the heyday of the German world chronicle. In the mid thirteenth century we have Rudolf von Ems's *Weltchronik*, and the anonymous *Christherre-Chronik* and the Low German prose *Sächsische Weltchronik*. The later thirteenth century saw the composition of the Viennese *Weltchronik* of Jans Enikel and Jacob van Maerland's Middle Dutch *Spiegel historiael*. In the fourteenth century these works were adapted into the great compilation chronicles of Heinrich von München, some versions of which are also associated with the name of Hans Sendlinger. This medieval tradition may be said to culminate at the end of the fifteenth century with Hartmann Schedel's prose *Weltchronik,* which appeared simultaneously in Latin and German versions in 1493. As the first German world history written for the printed medium, it points forward to the modern age. Likewise, the local or town chronicle became established in the vernacular in the thirteenth century.[21] Important early examples are Enikel's *Fürstenbuch,* a fragmentary history of Vienna, and the anonymous *Braunschweigische Reimchronik,* a history of the ruling house of Saxony, both dating from the late thirteenth century. The fourteenth century saw a vast expansion of this form, and we can do no more here than mention a few famous but random examples: the *Österreichische Reimchronik* of Ottokar of Styria, Levold of Northof's *Chronik der Grafen von der Mark,* Leopold of Vienna's *Österreichische Chronik von den 95 Herrschaften* or the *Limburger Chronik* of Tilemann Elhen von Wolfhagen. Church chronicles remain overwhelmingly in Latin, but *Klostergründungsgeschichten* (Histories of monastic foundations) begin to appear in the vernacular. An unusually early example is Eberhard of Gandersheim's *Gandersheimer Reimchronik,* written in 1216, which also has the distinction of being the first work of significance in Middle Low German; this form too really only establishes itself in the fourteenth century, with such pieces as *Karl der Große und die schottischen Heiligen* (Charlemagne and the Irish saints), the history of the foundation of three Irish-Scottish monasteries in Regensburg and Würzburg. It is perhaps significant that the explosion of vernacular chronicle writing begins in the wake of the so-called Golden Age of Middle High German writing, the *Mittelhochdeutsche Blütezeit,* around 1200, a pivotal date for all medieval German literature; for it may well be that the golden age of courtly literature was first needed to create a climate and a confidence in which forms already so well established in Latin could finally become familiar in the language of the people.

Biography

Biography as a historical form has a proud tradition in classical writing, and since it does not take its shape from a theory of history to the extent that the chronicle does, there is a far greater continuity from late classical to medieval writers. Thus medieval lives of emperors, for example, resound with echoes of Suetonius and his *Twelve Caesars.* The vita tradition falls into two main groups, the lives of kings and of saints. Biographies of kings begin in Germany with Charlemagne, whose life was first recorded by his friend and confidant Einhard in his *Vita Karoli Magni,* and later in the ninth century, nostalgically in Notker I of St. Gallen's *Gesta Karoli Magni Imperatoris* (Deeds of the Emperor Charlemagne). Charlemagne's son, Lewis the Pious, is remembered in two contemporary biographies, the *Gesta Hludowici imperatoris* of Thegan, written in 836–837, and, with more historical value, the *Vita Hludowici imperatoris* by an anonymous ninth-century writer referred to as the Astronomer. Such biographies generally present their subject as an ideal ruler, often with a political slant that can be understood as apologetic either with respect to the controversies of the reign of the subject, or to those of the author's contemporary world. This tradition continues throughout the period, finding a fitting climax in the life of Frederick Barbarossa, which Otto of Freising wrote some ten years after his chronicle. Lives of saints often focus on the missionaries and martyrs who adorn the German church. About 1073, for example, several years before the composition of his *Annales,* Lampert of Hersfeld wrote a life of the Anglo-Saxon missionary Lul, who was bishop of Mainz until he died in 786; this *Vita Lulli* can stand as a fine representative of the form. When it comes to the politically weighty bishops of the great cities of the empire, such figures as Anno II of Cologne, political and religious interests coincide. The *Annolied,* which we have already discussed as the earliest vernacular chronicle, is also one of the earliest examples of hagiography in the vernacular, and provides interesting points of comparison with the very much longer Latin life, the *Vita Annonis.* In both of these works, Anno is presented in equal measure as a saint and as an exemplary ruler, and here the distinction between sacred and secular biography reaches the limits of its usefulness.

As the beginning of this tradition, Einhard's *Vita Karoli Magni* bears closer inspection. Suetonius is clearly the model for the overall style and structure. Like its predecessor, Einhard's biography is arranged in prose chapters usually 150–300 words in length: that there are thirty-three of these, a number laden with religious significance (as the traditional age of Christ), is no coincidence. The work opens with a brief account of the fall of the previous royal house:

> Gens Meroingorum, de qua Franci reges sibi creare soliti erant, usque in Hildricum regem, qui iussu Stephani Romani pontificis depositus ac detonsus atque in monasterium trusus est, durasse putatur.

> [The Merovingian dynasty, from which the Franks habitually chose their kings, is said to have ruled until the reign of Hilderich, who was deposed by the command of the Roman Pontiff Stephan, and was shaved and sent to a monastery.]

Already in these words we sense the style and even some of the typical vocabulary of classical biography. Einhard now moves quickly into a sixteen-chapter narrative of Charles's rise to power and his battles and conquests, the emphasis being firmly on his generalship, again as we might expect from the life of a Caesar. Then come more cultural accomplishments. In chapter 17 we read of Charles's building works, in chapter 25 of his command of languages and rhetoric, and in chapter 29 he is portrayed as a lover of literature, committing to writing the ancient heroic songs and the legal codes of Germany, and commissioning the first German grammar book. At this point, the names he gave to the months and to the winds are listed in full. His support of the poor, a stock piece in medieval biography, and his openness to foreigners are also major themes. The final chapter, the longest, is devoted to the contents of his will. Einhard is at great pains to show Charles in a good light, and with some delicacy glosses over the scandals surrounding his daughters. The account is not at all anecdotal, as that would be trivial; rather, it moves with dignity and single-mindedness through its clearly planned program. Einhard's biography was widely read, surviving in eighty manuscripts and in a Middle High German translation. It not only marks the beginning of a genre in the literature of Germany, but also sets a high standard for its imitators.

Long before German-language chronicles first appeared, the smaller forms of historical writing first made the transition into the vernacular. Old High German and Old Saxon boast a number of important retellings of biblical narrative, produced as a programmatic part of the Church's mission. These range from close translations of Bible texts to the *Heliand*'s epic life of Christ. Otfrid's Gospel Harmony marks a high point, while in the eleventh and twelfth centuries the Early Middle High German Millstätt and Vorau Books of Moses appear to be the springboard to a fuller tradition of biblical narrative and eventually biblical drama in the later Middle Ages. Biography also appears in the vernacular in the Old High German period, as does the reporting of contemporary events. In addition to Ratpert's biography of St. Gall, which was written in Old High German but survives only in a Latin translation, we might note once again three works which are considered in detail in other chapters: the Alemannic *Georgslied*, the interesting macaronic piece *De Heinrico* on an incident involving a Duke Henry of Bavaria, and the *Ludwigslied*.[22]

Both biography and the reporting of events are epitomized, finally, in the *Ludwigslied*, the earliest surviving German-language account of a battle, a work discussed already, significantly under a number of different heads. It tells how the king of the West Franks (in retrospect, Louis III of France), a grandson of Lewis the Pious, defeated the Vikings at Saucourt, Picardy, in 881. It opens with an eight-line account of the king himself, focusing on his fatherless youth and piety, then describes the onslaught of the Northmen as the scourge of God for the sins of the Franks. Penance is done and God's anger turns back on the heathen, the Franks singing the *Kyrie,* the liturgical "Lord have mercy on us," as they march into battle. The poem concludes by praising God for the victory. Of interest for the present analysis (the work is of interest, too, in terms of heroic poetry, and for its metrical form) is the fact that historical events are not only described but also are interpreted in terms of Christian historiography. In particular it is the providential element of the divine economy that determines the theological character of the poem, with God steering the course of history, employing both the good and the evil as his tools and revealing himself to his people in their defeats and in their victories alike. It was God who had sent the *heidine man* across the sea to test Louis and to punish his subjects (9–12), but equally, it was he who called Louis back from other battlegrounds to save them:

> Thoh erbarmedes got,   Uuisser alla thia not:
> Hiez her Hluduigan   Tharot sar ritan:
> "Hluduig, kuning min,   Hilph minan liutin!"
>   (*Ludwigslied,* vv. 21–3)

> [But God had mercy on them,   he knew all these sufferings.
> He commanded Louis   to ride there at once:
> "Louis, my King,   help my people!"]

And the victory, praise to the power of God, is his, *gilobot si thiu godes kraft!*

Notes

[1] On the influence of classical historiography in the Middle Ages see the entries on individual classical writers in the *Lexikon des Mittelalters* (Zurich: Artemis, 1976–99). Also Eva M. Sanford, "The Study of Ancient History in the Middle Ages," *Journal of the History of Ideas* 5 (1944): 21–43. An impression can also be gleaned from manuscript catalogues which reveal the frequency with which classical works were copied in the monasteries; for example Birger Munk Olsen, *L'étude des auteurs classiques Latin aux XIe et XIIe siècles* (Paris: CNRS, 1982), lists 175 manuscripts of Sallust which were produced in these two centuries, but only three of Tacitus.

[2] General literature on medieval historiography: C. A. Patrides, *The Phoenix and the Ladder: The Rise and Decline of the Christian View of History* (Berkeley and Los Angeles: U of California P, 1964); Werner Kaegi, *Chronica Mundi: Grundformen der Geschichtsschreibung seit dem Mittelalter* (Einsiedeln: Johannes, 1954); Antonia Gransden, *Historical Writing in England,* vol. I: *c. 550–1307* (London: Routledge,

1974); Herbert Grundmann, *Geschichtsschreibung im Mittelalter* (Göttingen: Vandenhoeck and Ruprecht, 1965); Beryl Smalley, *Historians in the Middle Ages* (London: Thames and Hudson, 1974); Denys Hay, *Annalists and Historians: Western Historiography from the Eighth to the Eighteenth Century* (London: Methuen, 1977); Franz-Josef Schmale, *Funktion und Formen mittelalterlicher Geschichtsschreibung: Eine Einführung* (Darmstadt: WBG, 1985); Martin Haeusler, *Das Ende der Geschichte in der mittelalterlichen Weltchronistik* (Cologne and Vienna: Böhlau, 1980); Ulrich Knefelkamp, ed., *Weltbild und Realität: Einführung in die Mittelalterliche Geschichtsschreibung* (Pfaffenweiler: Centaurus, 1992).

[3] The Bible does not identify the fourth beast (Daniel 7: 7), but Jerome, following Jewish tradition, links it to the boar of the forest in Psalm 79: 14 (= Ps 80: 13). Literature: Edmund Kocken, *De Theorie van de vier wereldrijken en van de overdracht der wereldheerschappij tot op Innocentius III* (Nijmegen: Berkhout, 1935); J. W. Swain, "The Theory of the Four Monarchies," *Classical Philology* 35 (1940): 1–21; Christian Gellinek, "Daniel's Vision of Four Beasts in Twelfth-Century German Literature," *Germanic Review* 41 (1966): 5–24; Annegret Fiebig, "*vier tier wilde.* Weltdeutung nach Daniel in der *Kaiserchronik*," in *Deutsche Literatur und Sprache von 1050–1200: Festschrift für Ursula Henning zum 65. Geburtstag*, ed. Annegret Fiebig and Hans-Jochen Schiewer (Berlin: Akademie, 1995), 27–50.

[4] Literature on the *translatio imperii* and the Empire: Werner Goez, *Translatio imperii: Ein Beitrag zur Geschichte des Geschichtsdenkens und der politischen Theorien im Mittelalter und in der frühen Neuzeit* (Tübingen: Mohr, 1958); Eberhard Nellmann, *Die Reichsidee in deutschen Dichtungen der Salier- und frühen Stauferzeit: Annolied, Kaiserchronik, Rolandslied, Eraclius* (Berlin: Schmidt, 1963); Friedrich Heer, *The Holy Roman Empire* (New York: Praeger, 1968); Robert Folz, *The Concept of Empire in Western Europe from the Fifth to the Fourteenth Century* (London: Arnold, 1969); D. J. A. Matthew, "Reflections on the Medieval Roman Empire," *History* 77 (1992): 363–90.

[5] Literature on *sex aetates*: Hildegard Tristram, *Sex aetates mundi: die Weltzeitalter bei den Angelsachsen und den Iren* (Heidelberg: Winter, 1985); Roderich Schmidt, "Die Weltalter als Gliederungsprinzip der Geschichte," *Zeitschrift für Kirchengeschichte* 67 (1955/6): 288–317.

[6] The counting of dates by the year of the incarnation begins with the Easter calculations of Dionysius Exiguus in the 6th century, but Bede in the early eighth was the first to put it into practice in a history, the *Historia ecclesiastica gentis Anglorum*. The general use of dates before the Common Era probably begins only in 1474 with the Cologne writer Werner Rolevinck. However chapter 1.2 of Bede's ecclesiastical history contains what could be read as the date 60 B.C. For Roman history, dates are occasionally still cited *anno urbis conditae* (year from the foundation of Rome) but seldom after the eighth century. Jewish writers, of course, used their own calendar. The student's first port of call on all questions of chronology and dating systems is P. Grotefend, *Taschenbuch der Zeitrechnung* (Hanover: Hahn 1898; 13th ed. 1991). Other literature: Gerald J. Whitrow, *Time in History: The Evolution of our General Awareness of Time and Temporal Perspective* (Oxford: OUP, 1988); Arno Borst, *Computus: Zeit und Zahl in der Geschichte Europas* (Berlin: Wagenbach, 1990); Arno Borst, *Die karolingische Kalenderreform* (Hanover: Hahn, 1998); Anna-Dorothee

von den Brincken, "Beobachtungen zum Aufkommen der retrospektiven Inkarnationsära," *Archiv für Diplomatik* 25 (1979): 1–20; Frank Shaw, "Chronometrie und Pseudochronometrie in der Weltchronistik des Mittelalters," in *Die Vermittlung geistlicher Inhalte im deutschen Mittelalter,* ed. Timothy Jackson et al. (Tübingen: Niemeyer, 1996), 167–81; Hans Maier, *Die christliche Zeitrechnung* (Freiburg: Herder, 1980); Gertrud Bodmann, *Jahreszahlen und Weltalter: Zeit- und Raumvorstellung im Mittelalter* (Frankfurt and New York: Campus, 1992).

[7] The essential reference work for orientation is the series founded by Wilhelm Wattenbach: *Deutschlands Geschichtesquellen im Mittelalter;* for Austria, Alphons Lhotsky, *Quellenkunde zur Mittelalterlichen Geschichte Österreichs* (Graz: Böhlau, 1963). See also the catalogue and website of the *Monumenta Germaniae Historica,* the great collection of German historical documents begun in the 1820s, as many of the most important annals and chronicles are published in the MGH series: see Harry Bresslau, *Geschichte der Monumenta Germaniae historica* (Hanover: Hahn/ MGH, 1921), and the entries on individual works in the *Verfasserlexikon (VL)* and the *Lexikon des Mittelalters.*

[8] Fredrick Kurze, ed., *Annales regni francorum inde ab a. 741 usque a. 829, qui dicuntur Annales Laurissenses maiores et Einhardi* (Hanover: Hahn/ MGH, 1893).

[9] Fredrick Kurze, ed., *Annales Fuldenses* (Hanover: Hahn/ MGH, 1891); translation cited here: *The Annals of Fulda,* ed. Timothy Reuter (Manchester: Manchester UP, 1992). In the manuscripts it is preceded by a separate annalistic account for the years 714–838, which is ascribed to Einhard; the author of the main section is named as Rudolf.

[10] Anna-Dorothee von den Brincken, *Studien zur lateinischen Weltchronistik bis in das Zeitalter Ottos von Freising* (Düsseldorf: Triltsch, 1957); Claudia Ondracek, "Die lateinischen Weltchroniken bis in das 12. Jahrhundert," in Knefelkamp, *Weltbild und Realität,* 1–14; Franz-Josef Schmale, "Die Reichenauer Weltchronistik," in *Die Abtei Reichenau: Neue Beiträge zur Geschichte und Kultur des Inselklosters,* ed. Helmut Maurer (Sigmaringen: Thorbecke, 1974), 125–58.

[11] Text: Valerie I. J. Flint, "Honorius Augustodunensis: Imago Mundi," *Archives d'histoire doctrinale et littéraire du Moyen Âge,* 57 (1983): 7–153; see also Valerie I. J. Flint, "The Place and Purpose of the Works of Honorius Augustodunensis," *Revue Bénédictine* 87 (1977): 97–127.

[12] Honorius's influence was immense. In the later German chronicle tradition, he is an important source for Rudolf von Ems. The *Imago mundi* is reworked in a French cosmography, Gossouin's *Image du monde,* which then appears in English translation as Caxton's *Mirrour of the World.* But beware: nineteenth-century scholars did have a tendency to exaggerate the influence of Honorius on insufficient evidence, so that he is sometimes cited as the source for works which did not in fact use him.

[13] Cited from Graeme Dunphy, *Opitz's Anno* (Glasgow: SPIGS, 2003); dittography in line 4 has been suppressed here: the text has *warin* twice.

[14] Confusingly, there is also a slightly later Latin translation of the Middle High German *Kaiserchronik.*

[15] At any rate, the poet of the *Rolandslied,* Pfaffe Konrad, was not involved, despite much speculation to this effect in the scholarship of the years between 1874 and 1924.

[16] Cited from the first of the *Deutsche Chroniken* in the MGH series: *Die Kaiserchronik eines Regensburger Geistlichen,* ed. Eduard Schröder (Hanover: Hahn/ MGH, 1892).

[17] Friedrich Ohly, *Sage und Legende in der Kaiserchronik* (Münster, 1940; reprint Darmstadt: WBG, 1968).

[18] The work should not be confused with a famous early Greek illustrated manuscript of the biblical Genesis, which is also in the library in Vienna, and also known as the Vienna Genesis. There are editions by Viktor Dollmayr, *Die altdeutsche Genesis* (Halle: Niemeyer, 1932) and more recently by Kathryn Smits, *Die frühmittelhochdeutsche Wiener Genesis* (Berlin: Schmidt, 1972).

[19] This was an important vernacular codification of law, based on the earlier *Sachsenspiegel.*

[20] These two texts are sometimes known collectively as *Das Buch der Könige alter ê und niuwer ê.*

[21] See the 37-volume series *Chroniken der deutschen Städte vom 14. bis ins 16. Jahrhundert* (Leipzig: Hirzel, 1862–1968, repr. Göttingen: Vandenhoeck and Ruprecht, 1961–69).

[22] The three texts are in Braune XXXV, XXXIX, and XXXVI.

Late Old High German Prose

Jonathan West

THE LITERATURE of the late Old High German period is characterized by the fractured nature of the tradition. Between Otfrid von
Weissenburg (ca. 800–ca. 867) and Notker of St. Gallen (ca. 950–1022),
who dominates the end of the OHG period, and who was probably the
most prolific author of period as a whole,[1] there is almost a century to
which no substantial text of certain date can be assigned. Moreover, after
Notker's death, there is a similar forty-year lacuna in the evidence for
German-language production before Williram of Ebersberg (ca. 1015–
1085) and his paraphrase of the biblical *Song of Songs* (ca. 1060), the
Physiologus (ca. 1070), the *Ezzolied* (ca. 1065), the *Annolied* (ca. 1085)
and the eschatological prose piece *Himmel und Hölle* (Heaven and Hell,
ca. 1070–80). Indeed, it is only from the twelfth century on that literature in German begins to flourish in what Horst Dieter Schlosser[2] calls
the Early Middle High German Renaissance. Of course, much may have
been lost, but, in view of the fact that Latin manuscripts survive from the
same period, admittedly fewer than one might expect in comparison with
earlier centuries,[3] it is unlikely that the absence of German writing can be
attributed solely to the ravages of time. After all, the works of Hrotswitha (Hrotsvit/Roswitha) of Gandersheim (ca. 935–ca. 973),[4] saints'
lives in Latin hexameters, plays redolent of the classical Latin dramatist
Terence — whom Hrotswitha wished to expunge from the curriculum —
and epic works, are preserved in manuscripts from this period,[5] as are the
Latin sequences of Notker Balbulus "the stammerer"[6] (ca. 840–912),
whose writings tell us a good deal about the educational program of the
monastery school at St. Gallen, and the saga of *Waltharius* in Latin hexameters.[7] Thus, it is also unlikely that the lack of German texts is due to
the less vibrant cultural policy of the Ottonian emperors,[8] or the effects
of the Cluniac monastery reforms.[9] The situation seems to be that the
Carolingians, whatever the status of their spoken language may have
been,[10] had instituted under Alcuin at the end of the eighth century a
successful policy of restoring perceived classical Latin norms of the period, in both pronunciation and writing, to the extent that they could be

said to have "invented" medieval Latin.[11] The use of Latin grammars based on that of the fifth-century grammarian Priscian[12] rather than on elementary grammars of the insular type reinforces the impression of a high standard of Latin literacy in a situation where it exists side-by-side with another language, with either Frankish-German or Gallo-Romance.[13] While there seems to be little direct evidence of any actual prohibition of the vernacular, the tension between Latin literacy and German oral language is evident in Otfrid's characterization of it in his preface to his ecclesiastical superior, Liutbert, Archbishop of Mainz, as barbarous, uncultivated, lacking in discipline, a peasant language, but one in which it is still possible to praise God.[14]

Notker also wrote such a letter,[15] in his case to Bishop Hugo von Sitten (of Sion, in Switzerland, 998–after 1017) justifying his work as a new beginning, and his writings do mark him as an innovator. He writes[16] of the need to read ecclesiastical books in the monastery school and, because he wants his pupils to have access to these works, he has, he says, dared to do something out of the ordinary (*rem paene inusitatam*), namely to translate Latin texts into German and comment on them. He is aware of the unusual nature of his enterprise and admits that this could put Hugo off, but he thinks that Hugo will like his translations after a while, and be in a position to read and understand them, and appreciate how quickly one can grasp in one's native language concepts that might often be difficult or inaccessible in Latin.[17] Notker's concern to comment on and explain the texts he translates is consonant with that of earlier glossators whose work was described in the opening essay in this volume; he sees himself as part of an unbroken tradition, and mentions in his letter authorities such as Cicero, Aristotle, and Augustine, even though he used the work of other writers, such as Cassiodorus, as well.[18] The original text is occasionally simplified in its Old High German form to aid understanding, but this does not mean that Old High German was the language in which it was supposed to be read, as some scholars assume.[19] Notker's pains to describe the features of German are more a strategy to gain acceptance for his commentaries and to highlight the difficulties encountered by German learners of Latin. His *real* aim is to further understanding of Latin texts, which are to be read and interpreted, and so to further the tradition he represents. Notker's work is indebted to the scheme of the seven liberal arts, which Boethius had divided[20] into *trivium*: (grammar, philosophy, and rhetoric) and *quadrivium* (arithmetic, music, geometry, and astronomy),[21] but he regarded these as servants of theology or preparatory instruction, whereas Hugo had obviously tried to make him use them as an end in themselves. Notker also used accents to indicate pronunciation — either acute or circumflex — which, he averred, should be added to all German words except the article, which alone was to be pronounced without some sort of accent. In fact, Notker's works are among the few to show vowel length in unstressed position and are therefore of crucial importance for our knowledge of Old High German phonology.

Interestingly, Notker names almost all of his works in his letter to Bishop Hugo.[22] He first mentions his translation and commentary on Boethius's *De consolatione philosophiae*, a standard medieval schoolbook, of which his commentary on Books I–V was probably based partly on the commentary by Remigius of Auxerre (841–908) with interpolations of his own and from another, as yet unidentified source.[23] In addition, there was in all likelihood (as this work is now lost) either another of Boethius's works, *De sancta trinitate*,[24] or possibly Remigius's commentary on the same work.[25] He then lists the *Disticha Catonis* (The sayings of Cato, a late third-century collection); his version is now lost, but there are extant translations into German from the thirteenth century down to Martin Opitz's redaction in the seventeenth. This text was also a common schoolbook throughout the Middle Ages, erroneously ascribed to Cato the Elder (234–149 B.C.).[26] Notker's treatment of Virgil's *Bucolics* is now lost, as is his version of Terence's play, the *Andria*. Then there is a translation and commentary of Martianus Capella's *De nuptiis Philologiae et Mercurii*, a two-volume allegorical introduction to his nine-volume encyclopedia of the seven liberal arts. Notker acknowledges his debt to Remigius of Auxerre in the introduction to this. We hear too that he translated and commented on Aristotle's *Categories* and *Hermeneutics*, both via Boethius's Latin translation with its commentary.[27] His *Principia arithmeticae*, probably again derived from Boethius, which he lists, is now lost. Finally there is his translation and commentary on the sixth-century theologian Gregory the Great's *Moralia in Iob* (Moral-allegorical interpretation of the book of Job), which he finished on the day of his death according to Ekkehard IV of St. Gallen.[28] This work too is now lost, but Ekkehard reports that Gisela, wife of Emperor Conrad II, had it copied, along with the Psalter, on a visit to St. Gallen with their son, later Henry III. Notker's surviving Old High German-Latin work *De musica* is not mentioned in the letter to Hugo, and was apparently composed initially in German.[29] Notker also listed Latin works, including a *computus*,[30] a new work on rhetoric[31] and other smaller works on aspects of logic and rhetoric, such as *De partibus logicae*[32] and *De definitione*,[33] *De arte rhetorica* (which also contains Old High German words and examples), and *De syllogismis*,[34] an Old High German-Latin dual language text.

Because of the way in which Notker translated Latin texts and their commentaries for his own pedagogical needs, he has been categorized as a mere pedagogue rather than an original thinker, but in view of the unique nature and importance of his work as a whole, this judgment seems harsh.[35] Although the real value to the study of language of considering the earliest written occurrences of individual words is limited, a comparison of Rudolf Schützeichel's Old High German dictionary, the *Althochdeutsches Wörterbuch*, which lists the texts in which words are attested, with the thesaurus of Middle High German, the *Findebuch zum mittelhochdeutschen Wortschatz*,[36] results in the following list of words first attested in Notker's writings which survive into Middle High German and beyond with the same meaning. It is a long list, and it includes such words as *âbentsterno* "evening star," *affo* "monkey, ape," *beidenhalp* "on both sides," and *boumgarto* "orchard," but it is extremely important for the development of the language as a literary vehicle and gives an indication of Notker's effect on the language.[37]

Some of "Notker's" words no doubt figure here simply because he wrote so much so early and it is an accident that they are not attested elsewhere — doubtless words like *albiz* "swan," *pero* "bear," and *blâo* "blue" all fall into this category. But others do seem particularly characteristic of his writings. The word *berehaft* "fruitful," for example, is accompanied by *berohafti* "nature" and *(ge)ber(e)haftôn* "to make fruitful," which are attested nowhere else; Notker's formations on the basis of *bild-* and *biegen* (there is also *umbebiegen* "to bend around") are also noteworthy in this respect. With some words, he appears to be experimenting: *brantopfer* appears beside *ferbrenneda* and *brennefuscing*, all meaning "burnt offering," but the first survives even into relatively modern German.[38] One recent study, by Helge Eilers, has also drawn attention to Notker's skill as a translator and commentator.[39] Eilers's comparison of the original and Notker's text reveals his innovative use of subordinate clauses to convey Latinate constructions that do not have an exact German equivalent.

The pagan name that Notker bore (it means something like "spear for trouble") appears not to have been uncommon. Our Notker is called either Notker III or he is given the soubriquet *Labeo* "thick-lipped," or *Teutonicus* "the German" to distinguish him from two others at St. Gallen. Notker I, otherwise known as Notker *Balbulus* "the stammerer" or as *poeta* "the poet," has been referred to already as a Latin poet of some note, and Notker II (d. 975) was a doctor, also called *piperis granum* "grain of pepper, peppery" because of his reputation as a strict disciplinarian. Our Notker earned that designation of Teutonicus because of his contribution to and enthusiasm for the German language,[40] of which his knowledge was indisputably profound, whether it was in terms of the pronunciation of German, or the inclusion of German words, illustrations and proverbs in his Latin texts.[41] He is also widely credited with being the first to use the word *deutsch* in his writings, but Hans Eggers shows that the word was not yet sufficiently current for him to use it as frequently as he could have done, so it may not have been either natural or familiar at this time.[42] He taught at the monastery school at St. Gallen and was librarian for many years. He died on 28 June 1022 aged about seventy-two, having succumbed, along with nine of his fellow monks, to the plague which the army of Henry II had brought back with them after a campaign in Italy.[43]

Notker's "canon" (Notker's *Auslautgesetz*, his "Law of Consonants in Final Position")[44] is one indication of his acute ear for his native language. In the early manuscripts, the letters *b*, *d*, and *g* alternate with *p*, *t*, and *k* respectively, so that *p*, *t*, and *k* appear first at the beginning of a sentence or clause, second at the beginning of a word within a sentence or clause which follows a voiceless segment, and third at the beginning of the second element of a compound word, when the end of the first element was voiceless. The operation of the rule may be seen in the opening few lines of the prologue to Boethius:[45]

> Sanctus Paulus kehîez tîen die in sînên zîten uuândon des sûonetagen, táz er êr nechâme, êr romanum imperium zegîenge únde antichristus rícheson begóndi. Uuér zuîuelôt romanos íu uuésen állero rícho hêrren, únde íro geuuált kân ze énde dero uuérlte?

> [Saint Paul taught those who hoped for the day of judgment in their time, that it would not come before the Roman Empire had passed away and Antichrist had begun to rule. Who doubts that the Romans were already lords of all the kingdoms and that their power runs to the end of this age?]

In this extract, for example, the form *kehîez* (after Paulus) contrasts with *geuuált* (after *íro*); the forms of the definite article with initial *t-* (*tîen, taz*) contrast with those showing initial *d-* (*die, des, dero*); *kân* is the infinitive *gân* "to go" in its form after *geuuált*.[46] Traces of this important set of rules elsewhere in Old High German texts usually point to the written usage of St. Gallen, and this influence applies to Notker's accent system as well. Although vowel length is not generally marked in Old High German texts, it is not surprising that attempts to differentiate long and short vowels in writing appeared early on. Doubling of vowel symbols to indicate length appears as early as in the Benedictine Rule translation (e.g., *habeen* "to have"[47]), but the usage does not spread. The circumflex is probably clearer as an indication of length, but Notker is the first writer to use it in a systematic way. In fact, every accented *long* vowel is given a circumflex accent (a stroke with a hook where the pen leaves the parchment), and every accented *short* vowel an acute accent.[48] Of the many later writers who show traces of this system, Williram of Ebersberg demonstrates it most consistently in his commentary on the *Song of Songs*. This agreement makes it likely that Williram was familiar with Notker's work, although Notker was probably not a direct source, as we shall see.[49]

However that may be, there is evidence from contemporary texts that Notker's work, especially his commentary on the Psalter, had an immense influence on his fellow countrymen, including the Empress Gisela, and later scholars alike. The *Annals of St. Gallen* call him "Notker of our memory, the most learned and kindest of men."[50] There are a number of words in the list above (e.g., *anesage, anesiht, arbeitsamo, blecchezen*) which indicate a probable influence of Notker on the later Millstätter and Mahrenberger Psalters, and although Klaus Kirchert regards the direct influence of Notker on another later version of the Psalter, the Windberg Psalter, as insignificant, he does recognize possible transmission in the case of one of his texts, and it is likely that Notker influenced the choice of words.[51] In any case, Notker's principle of having a dual language text for instruction is mirrored later on, if not directly continued. The amount and quality of copying of Notker's material is also revealing. The manuscripts now in St. Gallen are copies from the period after Notker's death, yet they almost all belong to the eleventh century. There are manuscripts from St. Gallen now in Zurich, and there is both a Bavarian tradition of copying Notker (especially in the case of the Psalter) and a west-central German tradition, exemplified in the Brussels manuscript Bibliothèque Royale 10615–729 (from the mid twelfth century), which came from Trier and was copied from an exemplar from Lorraine.[52] Apart from Notker's text of the Psalter, which also contains translations of the Old Testament and New Testament Canticles as well as catechetic pieces such as the Lord's Prayer and the Apostolic and Athanasian Creeds, there is also a later Bavarian version, slightly abridged, which was probably made at the end of the eleventh century in the monastery of Wessobrunn. This is now referred to as the *Wiener* ("Viennese") *Notker*, as it is now in the Austrian National Library as Vienna Codex 2681 (twelfth century). The only complete version of

Notker's Psalter is in St. Gallen manuscript 21 (termed R), which came originally from the monastery of Einsiedeln in Switzerland, and was probably written there in the middle of the twelfth century. It was copied from a lost manuscript presumably of the mid eleventh century which is mentioned by many secondary sources, and from which about 100 quotations are found in sixteenth-century manuscripts and printed texts. Furthermore, the St. Gallen version is known too from seventeen fragments, mostly from the eleventh century. Another indication of the importance of the Psalter commentary is the glossing activity associated with St. Gallen manuscript Codex. 21, which encompasses as many as 7000 words. The manuscript also contains the so-called *Wessobrunner Predigt,* on the passage of Matthew (20: 1–16), which tells of the keeper of the vineyard.[53]

Another possible link in the chain of Notker reception and an indication of his importance is the work, referred to already, of Williram of Ebersberg,[54] who came from a well-connected Rhenish noble family (the so-called Konradiner[55]). Williram became a monk in Fulda around 1020, and was appointed to head the school in the Bamberg monastery of Michelsberg, which had maintained close ties to Fulda ever since its foundation in 1015. It is likely that he knew both the second abbot Heinrich (1020–46) and his successor Suidger (1046–47), later Pope Clement II. On the evidence of one of his Latin poems, it is possible that Williram belonged to the clergy of Henry III's private chapel during his time in Bamberg. It was Henry III who made him abbot of Ebersberg in Upper Bavaria. This was not one of the great church offices, but perhaps it represented banishment from Bamberg, or on the other hand perhaps was a stepping stone to the bishopric that, on the evidence of the dedication of his paraphrase of the *Song of Songs* to Henry IV (1056–1105), he coveted.[56] As Abbot of Ebersberg, however, Williram continued the literary activities that had made him famous already in Bamberg, and maintained contact with other great figures of the age such as the theologian Otloh of St. Emmeram, who made him a present of a book around 1067.[57] In contrast to his professional setbacks during his lifetime his literary activity — especially his paraphrase of the *Song of Songs*[58] — was crowned with success. It was not an original work, in the sense that its main source was a similar commentary by Haimo of Auxerre (writing around 840–60), possibly supplemented by Angelomus of Luxeuil (who died in 855). However, its declared aim, to explain the text to the laity, by which he surely means his noble friends and relatives, as well as to an ecclesiastical audience in what is in essence a sacred drama,[59] was innovative. He had a high opinion of himself: he closes the Latin introduction to his work with the thought that the merciful God who showered gifts of eloquence on Solomon has also allowed a few drops to fall on Williram himself, for when he reads his lines again he is so pleasantly moved. This was not without some justification, for Williram's paraphrase is the most richly attested German-language work of the early Middle Ages. Over forty manuscripts and several adaptations of it show that it continued to be used into the early modern period. A Latin printed text appeared as late as 1528, but the early copies of the manuscript, whose production he himself supervised, are designed to impress. The text is arranged in three columns on costly vellum,[60] of which the middle column in larger red letters contains the biblical Latin text. To its left is a commentary in rhyming Latin hexameters, which is clearly intended to show Williram's mastery of the material and the medium in the best possible light, and to its right is placed the German-Latin prose commentary. This bears witness to Williram's eloquence in German as well as Latin, as it does not translate the Latin text directly but expresses the ideas using other means. His work stands in the tradition of the so-called *opus geminatum*, a double work, the Latin and German commentaries being the "belt," as he put it, around the body of the original text. Although the eyes of those concerned with German language and literature naturally fall on the prose commentary, it is misleading to extract this from its natural biblical and Latin context. St. Jerome recommended that the *Song of Songs* should be the *last* text on the monastic curriculum, only to be read when the pupils were already versed in biblical exegesis and could understand that the text was not to be understood literally as a love poem, but as an allegory of the mystical union of Christ the bridegroom with His Church the bride, while the synagogue, signifying the old Jewish religion, shunned and forlorn, looks on. Williram uses this tripartite arrangement in the commentary as well. The voice of the synagogue begins[61]

> Cússer míh. mít cússe sînes múndes. Dícco giehîez ér mír sîne cúonft per prophetas. nu cúme ér sélbo. unte cússe míh mit déro sûoze sînes euangelii. Uuanta bézzer sint dîne spúnne démo uuîne. sîe stínchente mit den bézzesten sálbon.
>
> Díu sûoze dînero gratiae ist bézzera. dánne díu scárfe déro legis. áls iz quît. Lex per moysen data est. gratia et ueritas per ihesum christum facta est. Díu sélba gnâda ist gemísket mít uariis donis spiritus sancti. mít den du máchost ex peccatoribus iustos. ex damnandis remunerandos.
>
> [May he kiss me with the kiss of his mouth. Often he has promised me his coming through the prophets, now may he come himself and kiss me with the sweetness of his Gospel. For your breasts are better than

wine, they smell of the best ointment. The sweetness of your grace is better than the sharpness of the Law, so it is written: the law is given by Moses, but grace and truth are made by Jesus Christ. This same grace is mixed with various gifts of the Holy Spirit, with which you make right-eous men out of sinners, and ransomed souls from the damned.]

The images are striking for us today, but are explained in Haimo's commentary in an attempt to reconcile the Song of Songs with medieval Christianity:

Per ubera Christi, dulcedo Evangelii intelligitur, quia eo veluti lacte nu-tritur infantia credentium. Vinum autem austeritatem legis significat; sed ubera Christi meliora sunt vino, quia dulcedo Evangelii melior est austeritate legis.[62]

[By the breasts of Christ we are to understand the sweetness of the Gospel, because the childhood of the faithful is nourished by it like milk. But the wine signifies the sharpness of the Law; but the breasts of Christ are better than wine because the sweetness of the Gospel is bet-ter than the sharpness of the Law.]

Here we see the rhetorical device called *expositio intra* at work, distilling the meaning from the words of the original text, rather in the manner of a modern close-text reading. Unlike Notker, whose *lingua mixta* gives the impression of being the sort of language used informally in class, Wil-liram leaves key terms untranslated, and shows that it is Latin that is the clear focus of his work. Therefore, in the passage above, he prefers Latin *gratia* to German *genade* to express the concept of "grace." In chapter 106, for example,[63] where the Synagogue is speaking about the Church, in answer to the question *Wer ist disiu* . . . (Who is this, who goes ahead like the breaking dawn . . . ?) she answers: *Ecclesiam Christi, die ich ê de-testabar per ignorantiam, dero ne mag ih mih nû vollewunteran, wie hevig siu ist unte wie siu dîhet allizana de virtute in virtutem* ([It is] the Church of Christ, which before I rejected in my ignorance, now I cannot cease marveling, how exalted it is and how it strides from one virtue to the next). The central concepts in the passage are all in Latin — *tenebrae infidelitatis* "the darkness of unbelief," *verum lumen* "the true light," *pulchritudo virtutum* "the beauty of virtues," *sol iustitiae* "the sun of righteousness" — even though suitable words were available in Old High German. There is no experimentation here. This contrast has led linguists like Hans Eggers,[64] for example, to see Notker as a much more original thinker than Williram, even if he lacks the rhetorical and presen-tational skills of the latter. Eggers makes the point that for Williram to be in such command of his medium, he must have had a pattern, and, as

Notker was undertaking "something quite unusual" (*rem paene inusitatam*), it is likely that Notker himself was working from first principles. So if Notker himself was not the direct model that Williram used, the only other possibility would be that there must have been imitators of Notker of whom there are no traces, and this seems, even accounting for the probability that texts have been lost, unlikely. It is similarly improbable that Williram, in view of his social standing, and his position in Bamberg, then one of the literary and political centers of the Empire, was unacquainted with Notker's work. The fact that he uses Notker's accent system seems to be the clinching argument. If the form and content of his work are derivative, though, there is also no experimentation with the German language.[65] Again in contrast to Notker, there are few clear examples of possible neologisms, and little in the way of vocabulary that could not have occurred in Notker's writings or those of his contemporaries. Adjectives such as *muoterlîch* "motherly" and *manlîch* "manly," which seem unattested before Williram, prove little, as they represent a common word formation pattern, which was probably entering a period of productivity. The same applies to nouns in *ge-* such as *gegademe* "chamber," *geverte* "journey." Williram also uses archaic vocabulary which Notker seems to avoid (such as *drâhen* "to smell," *bouchen* "sign" and *feichen* "deception"), and this possibly suggests that he was less sensitive to the trends in the language than his predecessor was. One feature of his personal style which could be seen as innovative and forward looking is his creation of compounds. The Latin phrase *ligna silvarum,* for example, is translated as *waltholz,* which is also attested, naturally enough in the later St. Trudpert *Song of Songs,*[66] but not elsewhere. The same applies to *wurzbette* for *areola aromatum.* Alternatively, *waltholz* may be an adaptation of Notker's neologism *waldpoum* "lignum silvae."[67] On the other hand, *veltbluome* for Latin *flos campi,* is now a part of the language, although it would be difficult to ascribe this to Williram alone, and *salbwurz* for *nardus,* as well as *zartlust* for *deliciae* contrast well with the alternative translations we find (Notker's *lustsami,* for example).

Another scholar of note was Otloh of St. Emmeram[68] (ca. 1010–70), who was born in Freising, went to school at Tegernsee, and lived and worked in St. Emmeram (in Regensburg), Fulda, Freising and finally St. Emmeram again. He was reluctant to become a monk, preferring to become a secular priest instead, but finally took his vows as the result of a vision. The vast majority of his writing was in Latin, but his immediate importance to Old High German letters is his prayer, known simply as *Otlohs Gebet,* which follows a Latin version in the manuscript, of which other prose versions and a metrical version exist. Indeed, the German version of his prayer is not taken directly from the Latin, despite the rubric "German prayer, from the above." The wording of the initial section, with its listing of alternative faults (e.g., *leski, trohtin, allaz daz in mir, daz der leidiga viant inni mir zunta uppigas enta unrehtes odo unsubras* (Extinguish, O Lord, all that in me which the hated enemy [i.e., the devil] has kindled in me which is vain and false or unclean)[69] recalls the confessional formulas attested sporadically throughout the period.[70] This is followed by an attempt to enlist the help of a long list of saints, and the prayer concludes with a plea for God's mercy on the monastery, which had been burned in 1062: *Dara nah ruofi ih zi dinen gnadun umbi unser munustruri das zistorit ist durh unsre sunta . . .* (Thereafter I call on your mercy for the sake of our monastery, which has been destroyed through our sinfulness . . .).[71]

Allegorical interpretation of difficult biblical passages was one of the main tasks of higher learning in the Middle Ages. The Greek word *physiologos* means "an enquirer into nature," and in its Latinized form, *Physiologus* was the title of the Latin translation of a second-century Greek tract on natural science which described animals both real and fantastic and their allegorical or spiritual meanings with reference to Scripture. It was used as a schoolbook, the most widespread versions being *Dicta Chrysostomi* (ca. 1000) and *Physiologus Theobaldi* (ca. 1200).[72] The Old High German text (called *älterer Physiologus* because there is also the more complete *jüngerer Physiologus*[73] as well as a rhyming version, the *Milstätter Physiologus*) is found in an eleventh-century manuscript now in Vienna (ÖNB 223) believed to have been written in Hirsau[74] and is based on the *Dicta Chrysostomi*, of which the Middle English bestiary is, by contrast, a free adaptation. Twelve of the original twenty-seven commentaries have survived: lion, panther, unicorn, hydra, sirens and centaurs, hyena, the wild ass, the elephant, *autula* (ibex?), *serra* (winged fish), viper, and *lacerta* (lizard/dragon?). For example, Leo, the lion, signifies Christ because of his strength, and, because of that the lion is often named in Holy Scripture. The German text then refers to the first of these, from Genesis 49: 9, where Jacob refers to his son Judah as a lion's whelp. Three features of the lion are listed

> . . . which signify Our Lord. One is that when he is walking in the forest and he smells the hunters, he then wipes out his spoor with his tail so that they will never find him. That is what Our Lord did when He was in the world among men, so that the enemy would never understand that He was the Son of God. Then, whenever the lion sleeps, his eyes keep watch, without their being open. With this he signifies Our Lord, as He said Himself in the book Song of Songs: I sleep, yet my

heart keeps vigil, because He remained in His human body and He kept vigil in the Godhead. When the lioness gives birth, the cub is dead and she keeps it until the third day; then the father comes and blows on it and it is brought to life. In this way, the Almighty Father woke His only Son from death on the third day.

Similarly, another animal is called rhinoceros (either a confusion or a misreading of Greek mono-ceros),

that is unicorn, and it is very small and is so swift than no one can follow it, neither can it be sensed in any way. When a maiden sits down in the creature's path, when it sees her it will run up to her and, if she is really a maiden, it will jump into her lap and play with her. Then the hunter comes and catches it. That signifies our Lord Jesus Christ, who became little through the modesty of human birth. The one horn signifies one God. Just as no one can follow the unicorn, so no man can comprehend the secret of Our Lord, nor could He be seen by any human eye, before He, though maidenly love, took the form of a human body by means of which He redeemed us.

In terms of literary output, prose writing remains unusual in German until the sixteenth century. But the tradition of prose writing begun by Notker, and continued by Williram and others becomes the norm for legal texts, chronicles, and religious works, which often continue to mix Latin and German in a similar fashion, using German as a framework for a sentence with Latin words and expression being inserted for key concepts. Humanist writings[75] and Luther's *Tischreden*[76] have received most attention in this respect, but it is worth bearing in mind that the expansion of abstract vocabulary found in the writings of medieval German mystics would not have been possible without Latin models.[77] The German translation of Thomas Aquinas's *Summa Theologica*[78] shows this clearly, and further evidence is found in the German writings of Mechthild of Magdeburg (ca. 1207/1210–ca. 1282 or 1294),[79] and David of Augsburg (ca. 1200–1272),[80] whose works are known in hundreds of manuscripts, not to mention the great number of neologisms in the works of Johannes Tauler (ca. 1300–1361),[81] Meister Eckart (ca. 1260–1328)[82] and his pupil Heinrich Seuse (Suso, 1293–1366). In other words, the glossing activity of the early period, which carries on right through the Middle Ages, feeds into the commentaries and mixed prose of Notker and Williram, which itself nourishes the theological writing of the later medieval period. Consequently, rather than dismissing Old High German writing as a series of scrappy, disjointed and unrelated activities, the literary production of the period is seen to cohere, and feeds into the writing of the later period using vehicles as such as encyclopedias (such as the *Catholi-*

con), the significance of which for the literary and linguistic history of German remains unresearched.

A major feature of Old High German glossarial production, then, is the way in which it continues throughout the Middle Ages — the *Summarium Heinrici* is a good example[83] — showing that scholars were engaging with Old High German tradition for a very long time. Does this perhaps mean that writers of the twelfth century would not have regarded themselves as living in a "new" period, in the same way as modern Germans might still think of themselves as being in the same linguistic period as Goethe and Schiller? Language periodization is a topic that has engendered fierce debate over the years, the issues being determined largely by the criteria used to characterize the period in question.[84] A linguistic approach naturally gravitates to isolating features of the language characteristic of the period, while recognizing that language is never static. Stefan Sonderegger[85] therefore emphasizes the Second or High German Sound Shift and the Old High German monophthongization and diphthongization to mark the beginning of the Old High German period. Similarly, the use of full vowels in unaccented syllables, especially of the inflectional type, contrasts with their disappearance in and toward the Middle High German period, and the use of the neutral sound, the schwa (as in the final sound of modern German *Lampe,* for example) in these unaccented positions in Middle High German. In fact, the beginnings of Old High German are in one sense relatively unproblematic to fix, as there is little written evidence of consequence before the first manuscripts containing significant writing in Old High German (see the opening essay in this volume). If we can trust the evidence of the orthography (and here we must be careful to avoid the snare of the normalized Middle High German, the "standard form" that is to be found in the vast majority of out scholarly editions), the weakening or loss of full vowels in unstressed syllables emerges as the single most important criterion to distinguish core Old High German from Middle High German, and it has important consequences, such as the coalescence into one class of the three separate original classes of weak verbs (Class I: *suochen — suochta / nerien — nerita*; Class II: *salbôn — salbôta*; Class III: *habên — habêta*), but there are also powerful continuities. It used to be a commonplace of histories of German that umlaut "spread" in the Middle High German period, but we now know that indications of umlaut and vowel length became established much more gradually than was realized hitherto. Even in Early Modern texts, spelling is still not an infallible guide to pronunciation. In terms of vocabulary, too, the foundations of the Old High German period are still visible; and the position of

Latin as the only standard supra-regional written language of the day contrasting with non-standardized, regional and primarily oral German remains as clear at the end of the Middle High German period as it was when the first Latin word was glossed in German.

Notes

[1] Eckhard Meineke and Judith Schwerdt, *Einführung in das Althochdeutsche* (Paderborn: Schöningh, 2001), 157–61; Brian Murdoch, *Old High German Literature* (Boston: Twayne, 1983), 112–17; Gustav Ehrismann, *Geschichte der deutschen Literatur bis zum Ausgang des Mittelalters, 1: Die althochdeutsche Literatur* (Munich: Beck, 1932, repr. as 2nd ed. 1954), 416–58. S. Sonderegger, "Notker III von St. Gallen," *VL* VI, 1212–36, contains a useful bibliography; as does also Evelyn Scherabon Firchow, *Notker der Deutsche von St. Gallen (950–1022). Ausführliche Bibliographie* (Göttingen: Vandenhoeck and Ruprecht, 2000); see also the review by John M. Jeep, *ABäG* 55 (2001): 239–47.

[2] Horst Dieter Schlosser, *dtv-Atlas zur deutschen Literatur: Tafeln und Texte,* 4th ed. (Munich: dtv, 1990), 42–43.

[3] Some figures for manuscripts in the Cathedral Library in Cologne, which contains probably the oldest Latin document in Germany (http://www.ceec.uni-koeln.de./) listed by century readily support this view: 6–7c: 2 mss.; 7c: 2mss.; 7–8c: 1ms.; 8c: 8 mss.; 8–9c: 15 mss.; 9c: 48 mss.; 9–10c: 8 mss.; 10c: 24 mss.; 10–11c: 9 mss.; 11c: 25 mss.; 11–12: 5 mss.; 12c: 31 mss.

[4] *Biographisch-bibliographisches Kirchenlexikon,* ed. Friedrich Wilhelm Bautz (Herzberg: Bautz, 1970–98) II, 1095–97.

[5] Electronic version at: http://www.fh-augsburg.de/~harsch/hro_intr.html.

[6] *Biographisch-bibliographisches Kirchenlexikon* VI, 1032–35; Linda Archibald, "Notker Balbulus," in *German Writers and Works of the Early Middle Ages: 800–1170,* ed. Will Hasty and James Hardin (New York: Gale, 1991), 92–95; Dieter Kartschoke, *Geschichte der deutschen Literatur im frühen Mittelalter* (Munich: dtv, 1990), 190.

[7] See Karl Langosch, *Waltharius, Ruodlieb, Märchenepen: Lateinische Epik des Mittelalters mit deutschen Versen,* 2nd ed. (Berlin: Rütten and Loening, 1956).

[8] Schlosser, *dtv-Atlas,* 35.

[9] Schlosser, *dtv-Atlas,* 41.

[10] Nicola Quatermaine, "The Language of the Franks in Gaul" (Diss., Manchester, 2002).

[11] Rosamond McKitterick, *The Carolingians and the Written Word* (Cambridge: CUP, 1989), 10–13, based on Roger Wright, *Late Latin and Early Romance in Spain and Carolingian France* (Liverpool: Cairns, 1982).

[12] See Francis P. Dinneen, *An Introduction to General Linguistics* (New York and Chicago: Holt, Rinehart and Winston), 1967, 114–23.

[13] McKitterick, *The Carolingians,* 19–22.

[14] Braune, XXXII, no. 2.

[15] Probably written around 1020, as it describes his last work, a treatment of Gregory's *Moralia in Iob*, as being about a third finished (if that is what he meant): see Brian Murdoch, "Using the *Moralia*. Gregory the Great in Early Medieval German," in *Rome and the North*, ed. Rolf H. Bremmer, Kees Dekker, and David F. Johnson (Louvain: Peeters, 2001), 189–205. On the letter, see Ernst Hellgardt, "Notkers des Deutschen Brief an Bischof Hugo von Sitten," in *Befund und Deutung: Zum Verhältnis von Empirie und Interpretation in Sprach- und Literaturwissenschaft*, ed. Klaus Grubmüller et al. (Tübingen: Niemeyer, 1979), 169–92; text also in Notker der Deutsche, *Die kleineren Schriften*, ed. James C. King and Petrus W. Tax (Tübingen: Niemeyer, 1996).

[16] Ehrismann, *Geschichte der deutschen Literatur*, I, 142ff.

[17] Anna A. Grotans, "Utraque lingua: Latein- und Deutschunterricht in Notkers St. Gallen?" in *Theodisca: Beiträge zur althochdeutschen und altniederdeutschen Sprache und Literatur in der Kultur des frühen Mittelalters*, ed. Wolfgang Haubrichs et al. (Berlin, New York: de Gruyter, 2000), 267–71.

[18] Gerhard Lohse, "Tituli Psalmorum. Die Überschriften in Notkers Psalter und ihre Erläuterungen," in *Althochdeutsch*, ed. Rolf Bergmann, Heinrich Tiefenbach, and Lothar Voetz (Heidelberg: Winter, 1987) I, 882–94.

[19] As Meineke and Schwerdt, *Einführung*, 157–58.

[20] R. H. Robins, *A Short History of Linguistics* (London: Longman, 1979), 69.

[21] Peter Ochsenbein, "Lehren und Lernen im Mittelalterlichen Galluskloster," in *Cultura Sangallensis: Gesammelte Aufsätze: Peter Ochsenbein zu seinem 75. Geburtstag*, ed. Ernst Tremp (St. Gallen: Klosterhof, 2000), 111–15. See also my chapter "Into German" in the present volume.

[22] Ingeborg Schröbler, "Zum Brief Notkers des Deutschen an den Bischof Hugo von Sitten," in *ZfdA* 82 (1948–50): 32–46.

[23] J. Knight Bostock, *A Handbook on Old High German Literature*, 2nd ed. by K. C. King and D. R. McLintock (Oxford: OUP, 1976), 285.

[24] Hellgardt, "Brief," 186–89.

[25] Kartschoke, *Geschichte*, 196, Ehrismann, *Geschichte*, I, 430.

[26] Michael Baldzuhn: "*Disticha Catonis*" in the *Datenbank der deutschen Übersetzungen*: see http://www.rrz.uni-hamburg.de/disticha-catonis/. The work is also known under the titles *Liber catonianus* and *Auctores octo*).

[27] Bostock, *Handbook*, 284.

[28] Sonderegger, "Notker III," *VL* VI, 1214, 1222; Ehrismann, *Geschichte*, I, 448.

[29] Bostock, *Handbook*, 284.

[30] Notker, *Die kleineren Schriften*, 315–28.

[31] Notker, *Die kleineren Schriften*, 105–86.

[32] Notker, *Die kleineren Schriften*, 187–96, with OHG proverbs.

[33] Notker, *Die kleineren Schriften*, 311–14 with OHG explanations.

[34] Notker, *Die kleineren Schriften*, 266–309.

[35] Bostock, *Handbook*, 281.

[36] R. Schützeichel, *Althochdeutsches Wörterbuch* (Tübingen: Niemeyer, 1969, 5th ed. 1995); Kurt Gärtner, Christoph Gerhardt et al., *Findebuch zum mittelhochdeutschen Wortschatz* (Stuttgart: Hirzel, 1992).

[37] This list is lengthy, but it is appropriate to give it here: *âbentopfer* "evening sacrifice," *âbentsterno* "evening star," *abanemunga* "retraction of an accusation," *affo* "monkey, ape," *afterchomo* "follower," *afterchumft* "following," *ach* "oh," *ahsa* "axle, axis," *âhte* "persecution" (*achadêmisg* "academic" was re-coined in modern German), *ahtunga* "opinion," *ac(c)herman* "farmer," *alegemachsamo* "quietly," *albiz* "swan," *algelîhho* "similarly," *allîhheit* "entirety," *alsus* "as follows," *gealtera* "woman of the same age" (cf. Middle High German *gealter* "man of the same age"), *ambahtare* "servant," *ambahtman* "official," *amma* "wet nurse," *anafehta* "temptation," *anasaga* "spoken contribution," *anasiht* "look," *anderêst* "twice," *andereswâr* "elsewhere," *anderhalb* "one and a half," *antfahs* "long-haired," *antlâzîg* "giving, weak," *antsegida* "justification," *arabisg* "Arabian," *arbeitsamo* "painful," *argerôn* "to spoil," *argerunga* "despoilation," *arglist* "guile," *argwillîg* "guileful," *armelîhho* "humbly," *erarmen* "to impoverish," *armôte* (a neuter noun; there is also Otfrid's feminine *armôti*) "lowliness, poverty," *âwekkôn* "to err," *âwizzôn* "to be mad," *geâzzen* "to feed," *bâbes* "the Pope," *bahen* "to toast," *pacchen* "to bake," *balla* sf. "orb," *bang* "bank," *erbarmelîh* "miserable" (Middle High German *erbarmeclîch* arises by analogy), *irbâren / irbarôn* "to reveal," *barlîhho* "simply," *parta* "axe," *beidenhalp* "on both sides," *beizen* "to prick, spur," *irbeizen* "to dismount," *belgen* "to anger," *bellen* "to bark," *bendel* "band," *berehaft* "fruitful," *pero* "bear," *anabetên* "to pray to," *petinbrôt* "gospel," *bettechamere* "bedchamber," *gebezzerôn* "to better," *bezzerunga* "betterment," *pigihtare* "one who confesses," *piledîg* "imaginable" (this survives in *bildecheit* and *bildegunge* "picture"), *bildlîhho* "correspondingly," *ferbil(i)dôn* "to deform," *forebildôn* "to prefigure," *bildunga* "mental picture," *binda* "tie," *ferbinden* "to tie together," *binez* "reed," *niderbiegen* "to bend down" (Tauler), *ûfbiegen* "to bend upwards," *bietunga* "premise," *blâo* "dark, blue," *geblâsen* "to draw breath," *bleihhi* "light color," *blecchezen* "to sparkle," *blenden* "to shine," *erblenden* "to blind," *blesten* "to fall," *blez* "piece of cloth," *ferblîhhen* "to grow pale," *blindên* "to blind," *erblinden* "become blind," *blîwîn* "of lead," *bloh* "wooden block," *bôse* "low, worthless," *pôsewiht* "scoundrel," *ferbôsôn* "destroy," *bougen* "to bow down," *kebougen* "to bend," *boumgarto* "orchard," *brahten* "to wail," *prant* "fire" (*brantopfer* "burnt offering" re-surfaces in modern German), *durhprehhen* "to break through," *bresto* "lack," *bret* "plank," *briefpuoh* "letter-book" is reflected in a later diminutive *briefbüchli*, *gebriefen* "to write down," *follebringen* "carry out," *niderbringen* "to throw down," *ûzbringen* "produce," *brôde* "weak," *bruh* "break," *prûh* "use," *bruccôn* "to make a bridge."

[38] P. Dietz, *Wörterbuch zu Dr Martin Luthers deutschen Schriften* (Leipzig: Vogel, 1870–72, repr. Hildesheim: Olms, 1997), 1, 491.

[39] Helge Eilers, *Die Syntax Notkers des Deutschen in seinen Übersetzungen: Boethius, Martianus Capella und Psalmen* (Berlin, New York: de Gruyter, 2003).

[40] Bostock, *Handbook,* 282, reproduces a Latin verse from the collection *Ad picturas claustri Sancti Galli* characterizing the three Notkers: "The book is opened: Notker explains the signs, having observed the seven secrets with his piercing little eyes. How good they taste, because they do not obstruct the fourth vessel [i.e., the German

language, the first three being Hebrew, Greek and Latin]. That Notker was a stammerer; the next was (like) a grain of pepper; the third got the name *Labeo* because of his broad lip — none could be broader —and he bore in his heart a mission that was just as broad. See the honeycombs and the honey that that broad lip distils for you."

[41] Stefan Sonderegger, *Althochdeutsche Sprache und Literatur* (Berlin: de Gruyter, 1974), 107. Notker also included Latin material in his German texts.

[42] Hans Eggers, *Deutsche Sprachgeschichte* (Reinbek bei Hamburg: Rowohlt, 1963–77) I, 45. See also Gerhart Wolff, *Deutsche Sprachgeschichte,* 3rd ed. (Tübingen and Basle: Francke, 1994), 57–58.

[43] Bostock, *Handbook,* 281: the relevant passage translates as: "Henry returned to Germany the victor; but the plague arose in his army and killed many, among them Ruodhard the Bishop of Konstanz and our Burkhard passed away; also Master Notker and other excellent brothers in St. Gallen departed this life."

[44] Also called *Notkers Anlautgesetz* (Initial Consonant Rule): Murdoch, *Old High German Literature,* 113.

[45] We may note that the voiceless versions are also indicated by *b, d,* and *g,* which one might assume to be *voiced* from the spelling. However, the operation of Notker's law indicates that these sounds were probably partially de-voiced in initial position, as they are in Modern German. The voiced segments comprise all the vowels and the liquids and nasals indicated by *l, r, m, n.* The Boethius passage is cited from Braune, XXIII.

[46] It should be noted that this rule applies to Old High German /d/ when it derives from Germanic þ, but not when it comes from ð, so it is *súonetagen* in the first extract, not *súonedagen.* Notker's canon is reflected in modern Swiss-German dialects: see Friedrich Wilkens, *Zum hochalemannischen Konsonantismus der althochdeutschen Zeit* (Leipzig: Fock, 1910), 24.

[47] Braune, XV.

[48] Wilhelm Braune, *Althochdeutsche Grammatik,* 14th ed. by Hans Eggers (Tübingen: Niemeyer, 1987), §8, note 2.

[49] Meineke and Schwerdt, *Einführung,* 163.

[50] Bostock, *Handbook,* 282.

[51] Klaus Kirchert, *Der Windberger Psalter* (Munich: Artemis, 1979).

[52] Hellgardt, "Brief," 174–80.

[53] Murdoch, *Old High German Literature,* 120–21.

[54] Meineke and Schwerdt, *Einführung,* 162–65. See Volker Schupp, *Studien zu Williram von Ebersberg* (Bern and Munich: Francke, 1978); Wolfgang Haubrichs, *Die Anfänge: Versuche volkssprachiger Schriftlichkeit im frühen Mittelalter (ca. 700–1050/60)* (Frankfurt am Main: Athenäum and Tübingen; Niemeyer, 1988), 226–29; *Biographisch-bibliographisches Kirchenlexikon* XVII, 1560–61.

[55] *Lexikon des Mittelalters* (Zurich: Artemis, 1976–99), V, 1369.

[56] Meineke and Schwerdt, *Einführung,* 162, 165: He had originally intended to present his work to Henry III, and he complains about the meager income which the abbey provides; in fact, the early death of Henry III in 1056 appears to have foiled

his ambitions, as Henry IV refused him permission to return to Fulda, despite his flattering dedication, and he remained in Ebersberg until his death.

[57] Haubrichs, *Anfänge*, 227.

[58] Rudolf Schützeichel und Birgit Meineke, eds., *Die älteste Überlieferung von Willirams Kommentar des Hohen Liedes: Edition, Übersetzung, Glossar* (Göttingen: Vandenhoek and Ruprecht, 2001), which supplements *Willirams deutsche Paraphrase des Hohen Liedes*, ed. Joseph Seemüller (Strasbourg: Trübner, 1878), and *The Expositio in Cantica Canticorum of Williram*, ed. Erminnie H. Bartelmez (Philadelphia: American Philosophical Society, 1967).

[59] F. Ohly, *Hohelied-Studien* (Wiesbaden: Steiner, 1958), 101f.

[60] See Erich Petzet and Otto Glauning, Deutsche Schrifttafeln des IX bis XVI Jahrhunderts (Munich and Leipzig: Kuhn, 1910–30), plate XV; Haubrichs, *Anfänge*, Abb. 12. There is an illustration in Brian Murdoch, "Williram of Ebersberg," in Hasty and Hardin, *German Writers*, 146–49.

[61] Braune XXIV.

[62] See *PL* 117, 295.

[63] Reproduced in Eggers, *Deutsche Sprachgeschichte*, II, 216, with discussion, 44–46.

[64] Eggers, *Deutsche Sprachgeschichte*, II, 45.

[65] Eggers, *Deutsche Sprachgeschichte*, II, 47–51.

[66] Waldtraut Ingeborg Sauer-Geppert, *Wörterbuch zum St. Trudperter Hohen Lied: Ein Beitrag zur Sprache der mittelalterlichen Mystik* (Berlin, New York: de Gruyter, 1972).

[67] Schützeichel, *Althochdeutsches Wörterbuch*, 220.

[68] *Biographisch-bibliographisches Kirchenlexikon*, VI, 1339–40; Bostock, *Handbook*, 300–301; Murdoch, *Old High German Literature*, 121.

[69] Braune, XXVI.

[70] Braune, XXII.

[71] The linguistic changes from Old to Middle High German are clear when one knows what to look for. There appear to be full vowels in unstressed syllables, but in fact, apart from the use of -*i*- to indicate umlaut of the vowel of the previous syllable (e.g., *guoti* "goodness"), the writer uses them haphazardly, as if he is unsure how to spell the word in an etymologically justifiable way. Thus we have *hungiro*, third person present singular subjunctive, with the vowel of a second class weak verb even though it belongs to the first class (forms of first-class verbs such as *lôstôst* "you have redeemed" probably contributed to the confusion); in the form *gilâzzast* (present second-person singular subjunctive), we would expect the vowel -*i*- or later -*e*-; in the past participle *erslagon*, an -*a*- or an -*e*- would be expected. Similarly, the old conjunction *ioh* "and" seems to have merged with *ouh* "also" (otherwise *unta* "and").

[72] P. Dinzelbacher, *Sachwörterbuch der Mediävistik* (Stuttgart: Kröner, 1992), with further literature.

[73] Parallel texts in Wilhelm, along with a commentary and critical edition of the Latin texts. See Nikolaus Henkel, *Studien zum Physiologus in Mittelalter* (Tübingen: Niemeyer, 1976).

[74] Ehrismann, *Geschichte,* II/i, 224–30; MSD LXXXII; St. XXVII.

[75] Klaus Grubmüller, "Latein und Deutsch im 15. Jahrhundert. Zur literar-historischen Physiognomie der 'Epoche,'" in *Deutsche Literatur des Spätmittelalters* (Greifswald: Ernst-Moritz-Arndt-Universität Greifswald, 1986), 35–49.

[76] Birgit Stolt, *Die Sprachmischung in Luthers Tischreden* (Stockholm: Almqvist and Wiksell, 1964).

[77] Eggers, *Sprachgeschichte* II, 183–211.

[78] *Middle High German Translation of the Summa theologica by Thomas Aquinas,* ed. Bayard Quincy Morgan and Friedrich W. Strothmann (Stanford and London: Stanford UP, 1950, repr. New York: AMS Press, 1967).

[79] Gall Morel, ed., *Offenbarungen der Schwester Mechthild von Magdeburg oder Das fließende Licht der Gottheit: Aus der einzigen Handschrift des Stiftes Einsiedeln* ([1869] repr. Darmstadt: WBG, 1963).

[80] Franz Pfeiffer, *Deutsche Mystiker des 14. Jahrhunderts* (Leipzig: Göschen, 1845) I, 309–405.

[81] F. Vetter, ed., *Die Predigten Taulers: aus der Engelberger und der Freiburger Handschrift sowie aus Schmidts Abschriften der ehemaligen Straßburger Handschriften* ([1910] repr. Berlin, Zurich, Dublin: Weidmann, 1968); extracts in Josef Quint, ed., *Textbuch zur Mystik des deutschen Mittelalters,* 3rd ed. (Tübingen: Niemeyer, 1978).

[82] Josef Quint, *Deutsche Predigten und Traktate* (Munich: Hanser, 1955).

[83] Reiner Hildebrandt, *Summarium Heinrici* (Berlin: de Gruyter, 1974) I, xxxvi–xliii.

[84] See Oskar Reichmann and Klaus Peter Wegera, *Frühneuhochdeutsches Lesebuch* (Tübingen: Niemeyer, 1988) for a review of the field with special reference to Early Modern German.

[85] Sonderegger, *Althochdeutsche Sprache und Literatur,* 33–36.

Bibliography

Primary Literature

Note that some works containing editions of Old High German glosses, for example, may be found under secondary literature. References to websites are not included here, and have in the endnotes also been kept to a minimum, given the uncertainty of longer-term availability in some cases. The bibliography, while necessarily extensive, is select, and titles are listed under one category only.

German Anthologies

Barber, Charles Clyde. *An Old High German Reader*. Oxford: Blackwell, 1964.

Braune, Wilhelm. *Althochdeutsches Lesebuch*. Ed. Ernst Ebbinghaus. Tübingen: Niemeyer, 16th. ed. 1979 [cited], 17th ed. 1991 = Braune.

Fischer, Hanns. *Schrifttafeln zum althochdeutschen Lesebuch*. Tübingen: Niemeyer, 1966.

Gentry, Francis C., and James K. Walter. *German Epic Poetry*. New York: Continuum, 1995 (English translations).

Gernentz, Hans Joachim. *Kleinere deutsche Gedichte des 11. und 12. Jahrhunderts: Nach der Ausgabe von Albert Waag herausgegeben*. Leipzig: Bibliographisches Institut, 1970; 3rd ed. 1977.

Holzmann, Verena. *"Ich beswer dich wurm vnd wyrmin . . .": Formen und Typen altdeutscher Zaubersprüche und Segen*. Bern: Lang, 2001.

Mettke, Heinz. *Altdeutsche Texte*. Leipzig: VEB Bibliographisches Institut, 1970.

———. *Älteste deutsche Dichtung und Prosa*. Leipzig: Reclam, 1976.

Maurer, Friedrich. *Die religiösen Dichtungen des 11. und 12. Jahrhunderts*. Tübingen: Niemeyer, 1964–70.

Miller, Carol Lynn. "The Old High German and Old Saxon Charms." Diss., Washington University, St. Louis, MO, 1963.

Müllenhoff, Karl Victor, and Wilhelm Scherer. *Deutsche Poesie und Prosa aus dem VIII–XII Jahrhundert*. Berlin: Weidmann, 1864; 2nd ed. 1873, 3rd ed. by Elias v. Steinmeyer 1892, reprint 1964 = MSD.

Petzet, Erich, and Otto Glauning. *Deutsche Schrifttafeln des IX bis XVI Jahrhunderts.* Munich and Leipzig: Kuhn, 1910–30.

Schlosser, Horst Dieter. *Althochdeutsche Literatur.* Frankfurt am Main: Fischer, 1970; revised ed. Berlin: Schmidt, 1998 = Schlosser.

Steinmeyer, Elias von. *Die kleineren althochdeutschen Sprachdenkmäler.* Berlin and Zurich: Weidmann, 1916, reprint. as 2nd ed. 1963 and 1971 = St.

Wilhelm, Friedrich. *Denkmäler deutscher Prosa des 11. und 12. Jahrhunderts.* Munich: Hueber, 1916, reprint 1960 = Wilhelm.

Wipf, Karl A. *Althochdeutsche poetische Texte.* Stuttgart: Reclam, 1992 = Wipf.

Latin Anthologies

Boretius, A. *Capitularia regum Francorum* I. Hanover: MGH, 1883.

Dümmler, Ernst. *Poetae Latini aevi Carolini.* Berlin: MGH, 1881.

Dutton, Paul Edward. *Carolingian Civilisation.* Peterborough, ON: Broadview, 1993 (English translations).

Godman, Peter, ed. and translator into English. *Poetry of the Carolingian Renaissance.* London: Duckworth; Norman, OK: U of Oklahoma P, 1985.

Haug, W., and B. K. Vollmann. *Frühe deutsche Literatur und lateinische Literatur in Deutschland 800–1150.* Frankfurt am Main: Deutscher Klassiker Verlag, 1991.

King, P. D. *Charlemagne: Translated Sources.* Kendal: King, 1987.

Kusch, Horst. *Einführung in das lateinische Mittelalter.* Berlin: VEB Verlag der Wissenschaften, 1957 (with modern German translations).

Langosch, Karl. *Lyrische Anthologie des lateinischen Mittelalters.* Darmstadt: WBG, 1968.

Raby, F. J. E. *The Oxford Book of Medieval Latin Verse.* Oxford: Clarendon, 1959.

Strecker, Karl. *Nachträge zu den Poetae Latini I.* Weimar: Böhlau, 1951, reprint Munich: MGH, 1978.

Waddell, Helen, ed. and translator into English. *Medieval Latin Lyrics.* London: Constable, 1929, 4th ed. 1933 and Harmondsworth: Penguin, 1952.

Other Anthologies

Gassner, John. *Medieval and Tudor Drama.* New York: Bantam, 1963; London: Applause, 1987.

Önnerfors, Alf. *Antike Zaubersprüche.* Stuttgart: Reclam, 1991.

Stokes, Whitley, and John Strachan. *Thesaurus Palaeohibernicus* [1901–3]. Dublin: Dublin Institute for Advanced Studies, reprint 1975.

German Works

Annolied (between 1077 and 1081)

Das Annolied. Ed. and translated (into German) by Eberhard Nellmann. Stuttgart: Reclam, 1975. Graeme Dunphy. Opitz's Anno. Glasgow: Scottish Papers in Germanic Studies, 2003.

Cologne Inscription (9th Century)

Bergmann, Rolf. "Zu der althochdeutschen Inschrift aus Köln." Rheinische Vierteljahresblätter 30 (1965): 66–69.

Bible, Early German Translations

Fragmenta Theotisca. Ed. Stephanus [Istvan] Endlicher and H. Hoffmann von Fallersleben. Vienna: Beck, 1834, 2nd ed. 1841.

Exodus, Altdeutsche (ca. 1120–30)

Die altdeutsche Exodus. Ed. Edgar Papp. Munich: Fink, 1968.

Genesis, Altdeutsche (ca. 1060–70)

Die altdeutsche Genesis. Ed. Viktor Dollmayr. Halle: Niemeyer, 1932. Die frühmittelhochdeutsche Wiener Genesis. Ed. Kathryn Smits. Berlin: Schmidt, 1972.

Genesis, Old Saxon (9th century)

Doane, A. N. The Saxon Genesis. Madison: U Wisconsin P, 1991.

Glosses (from 8th century)

Die althochdeutschen Glossen. Ed. Elias Steinmeyer and Eduard Sievers. Berlin: Weidmann, 1879–1922. Eckhard Meineke. "Unedierte Glossen zu Bibelkommentaren des Walahfrid Strabo in Handschriften französischer Bibliotheken." In Addenda und Corrigenda (II) zur althochdeutschen Glossensammlung, ed. Rudolf Schützeichel. Göttingen: Vandenhoeck and Ruprecht, 1985, 57–64. Lothar Voetz. Die St. Pauler Lukasglossen: Untersuchungen, Edition, Faksimile: Studien zu den Anfängen althochdeutscher Textglossierung. Göttingen: Vandenhoeck and Ruprecht, 1985. Lothar Voetz. "Neuedition der althochdeutschen Glossen des Codex Sangallensis 70." In Althochdeutsch, ed. Rolf Bergmann, Heinrich Tiefenbach, and Lothar Voetz. Heidelberg: Winter, 1987, I, 467–99.

Heliand (ca. 850)

Heliand und Genesis. Ed. Otto Behaghel, 11th ed. by Burkhard Taeger, Tübingen: Niemeyer, 1996. English trans.: The Heliand: The Saxon Gospel. Trans. Ronald G. Murphy. New York and Oxford: OUP, 1992.

Hildebrandlied (early 9th century)

Baesecke, Georg. *Das Hildebrandlied.* Halle: Niemeyer, 1945. *Das Hildebrandlied.* Ed. Hartmut Broszinski. 2nd ed., Kassel: Stauda, 1985.

Isidor (late 8th century)

Der althochdeutsche Isidor. Ed. Hans Eggers. Tübingen: Niemeyer, 1964.

Kaiserchronik (ca. 1147)

Die Kaiserchronik eines Regensburger Geistlichen. Ed. Edward Schröder. Hanover: Hahn/MGH, 1892.

Mechthild of Magdeburg (ca. 1207–ca. 1282)

Offenbarungen der Schwester Mechthild von Magdeburg oder Das fließende Licht der Gottheit: Aus der einzigen Handschrift des Stiftes Einsiedeln. Ed. Gall Morel. 1869. Darmstadt: WBG, reprint 1963.

Monsee Fragments (late 8th century)

The Monsee Fragments. Ed. George A. Hench. Strassburg: Trübner, 1890.

Murbach Hymns (early 9th century)

Die Murbacher Hymnen. Ed. Eduard Sievers. Halle: Waisenhaus, 1874. Reprint with introduction by Evelyn Scherabon Firchow. New York: Johnson, 1972.

St. Gallen Verse (ca. 900)

Müllenhoff, Karl. "Ein Vers aus Sangallen." *ZfdA* 18 (1875): 261–62.

Notker Labeo (Teutonicus) (ca. 950–1022)

Notkers des Deutschen Werke. Ed. E. H. Sehrt and Taylor Starck. Halle/Saale: Niemeyer, 1933–35; continued as new ed. by James C. King and Petrus W. Tax. Tübingen: Niemeyer, 1972ff.

Otfrid of Weissenburg (ca. 800–ca. 875)

Otfrids Evangelienbuch. Ed. Oskar Erdmann [1882], 7th ed. by Ludwig Wolff, Tübingen: Niemeyer, 1973. Partial German translation by Gisela Vollmann-Profe. *Otfrid von Weißenburg: Evangelienbuch.* Stuttgart, Reclam, 1987. Karin Pivernetz. *Otfrid von Weißenburg: Das Evangelienbuch in der Überlieferung der Freisinger Handschrift (Bayerische Staatsbibliothek München, cgm.14).* Vol. 1: *Edition;* vol. 2: *Untersuchungen.* Göppingen: Kümmerle, 2000 = GAG 671/I; 671/II.

Paris Conversation Book (10th century)

Wolfgang Haubrichs and Max Pfister. *In Francia fui.* Stuttgart: Steiner, 1989.

Summarium Heinrici (early 11th century)

Summarium Heinrici. Ed. Reiner Hildebrandt. Berlin: de Gruyter, 1982 = Quellen und Forschungen zur Sprach- und Kulturgeschichte der germanischen Völker, NF 61, 78.

Tatian: Gospel Harmony (ca. 830)

Sievers, Eduard. *Tatian: Lateinisch und altdeutsch mit ausführlichem Glossar.* Paderborn: Schöningh, 1884, reprint 1966. Masser, Achim. *Die lateinisch-althochdeutsche Tatianbilingue des Cod. Sang. 56.* Göttingen: Vandenhoeck and Ruprecht, 1991.

Tauler, Johannes (ca. 1300–ca. 1361)

Die Predigten Taulers: Aus der Engelberger und der Freiburger Handschrift sowie aus Schmidts Abschriften der ehemaligen Straßburger Handschriften. Ed. F. Vetter [1910]. Berlin, Zurich, Dublin: Weidmann, reprint 1968.

Thomas Aquinas (ca. 1225–1274)

Middle High German Translation of the Summa Theologica by Thomas Aquina. Ed. Bayard Quincy Morgan and Friedrich W. Strothmann. Stanford and London: Stanford UP, 1950; reprint New York: AMS Press, 1967.

Williram of Ebersberg (ca. 1020–1085)

Willirams deutsche Paraphrase des Hohen Liedes. Ed. Joseph Seemüller. Strasbourg: Trübner, 1878. *The Expositio in Cantica Canticorum of Williram.* Ed. Erminnie H. Bartelmez. Philadelphia: American Philosophical Society, 1967. *Die älteste Überlieferung von Willirams Kommentar des Hohen Liedes: Edition, Übersetzung, Glossar,* ed. Rudolf Schützeichel and Birgit Meineke. Göttingen: Vandenhoek and Ruprecht, 2001 = Studien zum Althochdeutschen 39.

Windberg Psalter (13th century)

Kirchert, Klaus. *Der Windberger Psalter.* Munich: Artemis, 1979.

Latin Works

Alcuin (ca. 732–804)

Commentaria in S. Johannis. PL 100, 735–1008. *Ars grammatica,* PL 101, 849–902.

Annals, Royal Frankish (from 791–)

Annales regni francorum inde ab a. 741 usque a 829, qui dicuntur Annales Laurissenses maiores et Einhardi. Ed. Fredrick Kurze. Hanover: Hahn/MGH, 1893.

Annals of Fulda (from 838–)

Annales Fuldenses. Ed. Fredrick Kurze. Hanover: Hahn/MGH, 1891. *The Annals of Fulda.* Ed. and translated by Timothy Reuter. Manchester: Manchester UP, 1992.

Astronomus: see Thegan

Avianus (late 4th century)

Aviani fabulae. Ed. R. Ellis. Oxford: Clarendon, 1887. Ed. A. Guaglianone. Turin: Paravia, 1958.

Baebius Italicus (1st century A.D.)

Kennedy, George A., ed. *Publius Baebius Italicus, The Latin Iliad: Introduction, Text, Translation, and Notes.* Fort Collins, CO: G. A. Kennedy, 1998.

Bede (ca. 672–735)

Bedae Venerabilis Anglo-Saxonis presbyteri opera omnia. PL 90–95. *Ecclesiastical History of the English People,* ed. Bertram Colgrave and R. A. B. Mynors. Oxford: Clarendon, 1969; repr. 1991.

Bible (Vulgate)

Roger Gryson, ed. *Biblia Sacra iuxta Vulgatem Versionem.* Stuttgart: Deutsche Bibelgesellschaft, 1994.

Cambridge Songs (ca. 1050)

Die Cambridger Lieder (Carmina Cantabrigensia). Ed. Karl Strecker. Berlin: Weidmann/MGH, 1926, 2nd ed. 1955. Karl Breul. *The Cambridge Songs.* Cambridge: CUP, 1915 [with facsimile]. *Carmina Cantabrigensia.* Ed. Walther Bulst. Heidelberg: Winter, 1950. *The Cambridge Songs (Carmina Cantabrigiensia).* Ed. and translated by Jan M. Ziolkowski. New York and London: Garland, 1994 and Tempe, AZ: Medieval & Renaissance Texts & Studies, 1998.

Cassidorus (ca. 468–562)

De institutione divinarum litterarum. PL 70. Ed. R. A. B. Mynors. Oxford: Clarendon, 1937.

Dhuoda (ca. 803–after 843)

Dhuoda. *Handbook for Her Warrior Son, Liber Manualis.* Ed. and translated by Marcelle Thiébaux. Cambridge and New York: CUP, 1998.

Ecbasis cuiusdam captivi (ca. 1045)

Ecbasis cuiusdam captivi. Ed. and translated by Edwin H. Zeydel. Chapel Hill,: U of North Carolina P, 1963.

Einhard (ca. 770–840)

Einhardi Vita Karoli Magni. Ed. G. H. Pertz, G. Waitz, 6th ed. by Oswald Holder-Egger. Hanover and Leipzig: Hahn/MHG, 1911; repr. 1947. *Einhard's Life of Charlemagne.* Ed. H. W. Garrod and R. B. Mowat. Oxford: Clarendon, 1915. Paul Edward Dutton. *Charlemagne's Courtier.* Peterborough, ON: Broadview, 1998 [English translation].

Eupolemius (late 11th century)

Eupolemius. *Das Bibelgedicht.* Ed. Karl Manitius. Leipzig: Böhlau/MGH, 1973.

Hermann the Lame, Her(i)mannus Contractus, Hermann of Reichenau (1013–54)

De astrolabio. PL 143, 389–408. *De mensura astrolabii. PL* 143, 481–490.

Hincmar of Reims (ca. 806–882)

De divortio Lotharii. PL 125, 659–680.

Homer: see Baebius

Honorius Augustodunensis (d. ca. 1152)

Valerie I. J. Flint. "Honorius Augustodunensis: Imago Mundi." *Archives d'histoire doctrinale et littéraire du Moyen Âge* 57 (1983): 7–153.

Hrabanus Maurus (ca. 776–856)

Opera. PL 107–12. *De Laudibus sanctae Crucis. PL* 107, 133–294. *De institutione clericorum. PL* 107, 295–420. *Commentariorum in Matthaeum. PL* 107, 727–1156. *De Universo (De naturis rerum). PL* 111, 9–614. *Hymnus de charitate. PL* 112, 1666–68.

Hrotswitha of Gandersheim (ca. 935–ca. 1000)

Hrotsvithae Opera. Ed. Karl Strecker. Leipzig: Teubner, 1906.

Isidore of Seville (ca. 560–636)

Etymologiae. PL 82, 73–728. Ed. W. M. Lindsay. Oxford: Clarendon, 1911.

John Sco(t)tus (Eriugena) (ca. 810–877 or 886)

Periphyseon (De divisione naturae). Ed. J. P. Sheldon Williams and Ludwig Bieler. Dublin: Institute for Advanced Studies, 1968–81. *De praedestinatione.* Ed. Goulven Madec. Turnhout: Brepols, 1978 = Corpus Christianorum cont. med.

Martianus Capella (5th century)

De nuptiis Philologiae et Mercurii. Ed. James Willis. Leipzig: Teubner, 1983.

Notker Balbulus, Notker the Stammerer (ca. 840–912)

Notker der Dichter und seine geistige Welt. Ed. Wolfram von den Steinen. Bern: Franke, 1948. Gesta Karoli Magni Imperatoris. Ed. Hans F. Haefele. Hanover: Hahn/MGH, 1959. Martyrologium. PL 131, 1029–1164.

Ratpert of St. Gallen (d. ca. 884)

Osterwalder, Peter. Das althochdeutsche Galluslied Ratperts und seine lateinischen Übersetzungen durch Ekkehart IV. Berlin and New York: de Gruyter, 1982.

Ruodlieb (ca. 1050–75)

The Ruodlieb. Ed. and translated by G. W. Grocock. Warminster: Aris and Phillips, 1985. Translated by Gordon B. Ford. Leiden: Brill, 1965. Ed. Gordon B. Ford. Leiden: Brill, 1966. Ed. and translated by Edwin H. Zeydel. New York: AMS Press, 1959. See also Waltharius.

Tatian (2nd century A.D.)

E. Schwartz. Tatiani Oratio ad Graecos: Texte und Untersuchungen. Leipzig: Hinrichs, 1888.

Thegan(us) (writing ca. 850)

Thegan: Die Taten Kaiser Ludwigs; Astronomus: Das Leben Kaiser Ludwigs. Ed. and translated into German by Ernst Tremp. Hanover: Hahn/MGH, 1995.

Venantius Fortunatus (ca. 530–609)

Personal and Political Poems. Ed. Judith George. Liverpool: Liverpool UP, 1995.

Walahfrid Strabo (ca. 808–849)

Walahfrid Strabo's Visio Wettini. Ed. and translated by David A. Traill. Frankfurt: Peter Lang, 1974. De imagine Tetrici. PL 113, 1089B–1092C. Michael W. Herren. "The De imagine Tetrici." Journal of Medieval Latin 1 (1991): 118–39.

Waltharius (9th or 10th century?)

Nachträge zu den Poetae Latini I. Ed. Karl Strecker. Weimar: Böhlau, 1951, reprint Munich: MGH, 1978. Karl Strecker. Waltharius, with German translation by Peter Vossen. Berlin: Weidmann, 1947. Gregor Vogt-Spira. Waltharius: Lateinisch/Deutsch. Stuttgart: Reclam, 1994. Marion Dexter Learned. The Saga of Walther of Aquitaine [1892]. Westport, CT: Greenwood, reprint 1970. Karl Langosch. Waltharius, Ruodlieb, Märchenepen: Lateinische Epik des Mittelalters mit deutschen Versen. 2nd ed. Berlin: Rütten and Loening, 1956. Dennis M. Kratz. Waltharius and Ruodlieb. New York: Garland, 1984, 1–71 (with English translation). Brian Murdoch. Walthari. Glasgow: Scottish Papers in Germanic Studies, 1989 (English translation).

Other Works

Stere hit well (late 15th century)

Hodgett, G. A. J. *Stere hit well: Medieval Recipes and Remedies from Samuel Pepys's Library.* London: Cornmarket, 1972.

William Langland (ca. 1332–ca. 1400)

Piers Plowman: A Complete Edition of the B-Text. Ed. A. V. C. Schmidt. London: Dent, 1987.

Liber de diversis medicinis (English, 15th century)

The Liber de diversis medicinis in the Thornton Manuscript (MS Lincoln Cathedral A.5.2.). Ed. Margaret Sinclair Ogden. London: OUP, 1938 = Early English Text Society/OS 207.

Secondary Literature

General and Historical Studies

Airlie, Stuart. "After Empire — Recent Work on the Emergence of Post-Carolingian Kingdoms." *Early Medieval Europe* 2 (1993): 153–61.

Bäuml, Franz H. "Medieval Literacy and Illiteracy." In *Germanic Studies in Honor of Otto Springer,* ed. Stephen J. Kaplowitt. Pittsburgh, PA: K and S Enterprises, 1978. 41–54.

Biographisch-bibliographisches Kirchenlexikon. Ed. Friedrich Wilhelm Bautz. Herzberg: Bautz, 1970–98.

Bischoff, Bernhard. "Wendepunkte in der Geschichte der lateinischen Exegese im Frühmittelalter." *Sacris Erudiri* 6 (1954): 189–279.

Bodmann, Gertrud. *Jahreszahlen und Weltalter: Zeit- und Raumvorstellung im Mittelalter.* Frankfurt and New York: Campus, 1992.

Bolgar, R. R. *The Classical Heritage and Its Beneficiaries.* Cambridge: CUP, 1963.

———. *Classical Influences on European Culture AD 500–1500.* Cambridge: CUP, 1971.

Borst, Arno. *Computus: Zeit und Zahl in der Geschichte Europas.* Berlin: Wagenbach, 1990.

———. *Die karolingische Kalenderreform.* Hanover: Hahn, 1998.

Boudriot, Wilhelm. *Die altgermanische Religion in der amtlichen kirchlichen Literatur des Abendlandes vom 5. bis 11. Jahrhundert.* 1928; reprint Darmstadt: WBG, 1964.

Bowra, C. M. *Heroic Poetry*. London: Macmillan, 1952.

Braunfels, Werner (vol. 1), and Bernhard Bischoff (vol. 2), ed. *Karl der Große: Lebenswerk und Nachleben*. Düsseldorf: Schwann, 1965.

Bullough, Donald. *The Age of Charlemagne*. London: Ferndale, 1980.

―――. *Carolingian Renewal: Sources and Heritage*. Manchester: Manchester UP, 1991.

Cantor, Norman. "The Crisis of Western Monasticism." *American Historical Review* 66 (1960): 47–67.

Clark, J. M. *The Abbey of St. Gall*. Cambridge: CUP, 1926.

Contreni, John J. "The Pursuit of Knowledge in Carolingian Europe." In *The Gentle Voices of Teachers*, ed. Richard E. Sullivan. Columbus: Ohio State UP, 1995, 106–41.

Curtius, Ernst Robert. *Europäische Literatur und lateinisches Mittelalter*. Bern: Francke, 1948; 11th ed. Tübingen and Basle, 1993. Trans. Willard R. Trask, *European Literature and the Latin Middle Ages*. London: RKP, 1953.

De Vries, Jan. *Heroic Song and Heroic Legend*. Trans. B. J. Timmer. London: OUP, 1963.

Dinzelbacher, P. *Sachwörterbuch der Mediävistik*. Stuttgart: Kröner, 1992.

Dronke, Peter. *Medieval Latin and the Rise of European Love-Lyric*. Oxford: Clarendon, 1966, 2nd ed. 1968.

―――. *The Medieval Lyric*. Cambridge: Brewer, 1968; 3rd ed. 1996.

―――. *Poetic Individuality in the Middle Ages: New Departures in Poetry, 1000–1150*. Oxford: Clarendon, 1970.

―――. *The Medieval Poet and His World*. Rome: Edizioni di Storia e Letteratura, 1984.

Duckett, Eleanor Shipley. *Carolingian Portraits*. Ann Arbor: U of Michigan P, 1962.

Fichtenau, Heinrich. *The Carolingian Empire*. Trans. Peter Munz. Oxford: Blackwell, 1968.

Godman, Peter. *Poets and Emperors: Frankish Politics and Carolingian Poetry*. Oxford: Clarendon, 1987.

Goez, Werner. *Translatio imperii: Ein Beitrag zur Geschichte des Geschichtsdenkens und der politischen Theorien im Mittelalter und in der frühen Neuzeit*. Tübingen: Mohr, 1958.

Green, D. H. *Medieval Listening and Reading*. Cambridge: CUP, 1994.

―――. *Language and History in the Early Germanic World*. Cambridge: CUP, 1998.

Grotefend, Hermann. *Taschenbuch der Zeitrechnung.* Hanover: Hahn 1898; 13th ed. 1991.

Grundmann, Herbert. *Geschichtsschreibung im Mittelalter.* Göttingen: Vandenhoeck and Ruprecht, 1965.

Haeusler, Martin. *Das Ende der Geschichte in der mittelalterlichen Weltchronistik.* Cologne and Vienna: Böhlau, 1980 = Beihefte zum Archiv für Kulturgeschichte, 13.

Hardison, O. B. *Christian Rite and Christian Drama in the Middle Ages.* Baltimore: Johns Hopkins UP, 1965.

Hay, Denys. *Annalists and Historians: Western Historiography from the Eighth to the Eighteenth Century.* London: Methuen, 1977.

Heer, Friedrich. *The Holy Roman Empire.* New York: Praeger, 1968.

Hildebrandt, M. M. *The External School in Carolingian Society.* Leiden: Brill, 1992.

Jackson, W. H. T. *The Hero and the King.* New York: Columbia UP, 1982.

Kaegi, Werner. *Chronica Mundi: Grundformen der Geschichtsschreibung seit dem Mittelalter.* Einsiedeln: Johannes, 1954.

Kieckhefer, Richard. *Magic in the Middle Ages.* Cambridge: CUP, 1989.

King, K. C. "The Earliest German Monasteries." [1961]. In K. C. King, *Selected Essays on Medieval German Literature,* ed. John L. Flood and A. T. Hatto. London: Institute of Germanic Studies, 1975. 98–124.

Knefelkamp, Ulrich, ed. *Weltbild und Realität: Einführung in die Mittelalterliche Geschichtsschreibung.* Pfaffenweiler: Centaurus, 1992.

Laistner, M. L. W. *Thought and Letters in Western Europe, AD 500–900.* 2nd ed. London: Methuen, 1957.

Lasko, Peter. *The Kingdom of the Franks: North-West Europe Before Charlemagne.* London: Thames and Hudson, 1971.

Lexikon des Mittelalters. Zurich: Artemis, 1976–99.

Lhotsky, Alphons. *Quellenkunde zur mittelalterlichen Geschichte Österreichs.* Graz: Böhlau, 1963.

McKitterick, Rosamond. *The Frankish Church and the Carolingian Reforms.* Cambridge: CUP, 1977.

———. *The Frankish Kingdoms under the Carolingians 751–987.* London and New York: Longman, 1983.

———. *The Carolingians and the Written Word.* Cambridge: CUP, 1989.

———, ed. *The Uses of Literacy in Early Medieval Europe.* Cambridge: CUP, 1992.

————, ed. *Carolingian Culture: Emulation and Innovation*. Cambridge: CUP, 1993.

Matthew, D. J. A. "Reflections on the Medieval Roman Empire." *History 77* (1992): 363–90.

Murdoch, Brian. *The Germanic Hero*. London: Hambledon, 1996.

Nelson, J. L., ed. *The Frankish World, 750–900*. London: Hambledon, 1996.

Prinz, Friedrich. "Monastische Zentren im Frankenreich." *Studi Medievali*, Ser. 3/19 (1978): 571–90.

Reallexikon für Antike und Christentum. Ed. Ernst Dassmann. Stuttgart: Hiersemann, 1988–93.

Reuter, Timothy. *Germany in the Early Middle Ages: 800–1056*. London: Longman, 1991.

Schaefer, Ursula, ed. *Artes im Mittelalter*. Berlin: Akademie, 1999.

Schmale, Franz-Josef. *Funktion und Formen mittelalterlicher Geschichtsschreibung: Eine Einführung*. Darmstadt: WBG, 1985.

Seidlmayer, Michael. *Currents of Medieval Thought*. Trans. D. Barker. Oxford: Blackwell, 1960.

Wagner, David L., ed. *The Seven Liberal Arts in the Middle Ages*. Bloomington: Indiana UP, 1983.

Wallace-Hadrill, J. M. *The Barbarian West, 400–1000*. 3rd ed. London: Hutchinson, 1967.

Wallach, Liutpold. *Alcuin and Charlemagne: Studies in Carolingian History and Literature*. Ithaca, NY: Cornell UP, 1959.

Wattenbach, Wilhelm. *Deutschlands Geschichtesquellen im Mittelalter*, new ed. Robert Holzmann et al. Berlin: Ebering, 1938–90.

General Studies of German Language and Literature

Baesecke, Georg. *Der deutsche Abrogans und die Herkunft des deutschen Schrifttums*. Halle: Niemeyer, 1930.

————. "Die deutschen Worte der germanischen Gesetze." *PBB* 59 (1935): 1–101.

————. "Die karlische Renaissance und das deutsche Schrifttum." *DVjs* 23 (1949): 143–216.

Benecke, G. F., W. Müller, and F. Zarncke. *Mittelhochdeutsches Handwörterbuch*. Leipzig: Hirzel, 1854–61.

Bergmann, Rolf, Heinrich Tiefenbach, and Lothar Voetz, eds. *Althochdeutsch*. Heidelberg: Winter, 1987.

Bergmann, Rolf. *Rückläufiges morphologisches Wörterbuch des Althochdeutschen.* Tübingen: Niemeyer, 1991.

Bertau, Karl. *Deutsche Literatur im europäischen Mittelalter.* Munich: Beck, 1972–73.

Werner Betz. "Das gegenwärtige Bild des Althochdeutschen." *Der Deutschunterricht* 5/vi (1953): 94–108.

————. *Lateinisch und Deutsch: Die Lehnbildungen der althochdeutschen Benediktinerregel.* 2nd ed. Bonn: Bouvier, 1965.

————. "Karl der Große und die lingua theodisca." In *Karl der Große: Lebenswerk und Nachleben*, vol. 2., ed. Werner Braunfels and Bernhard Bischoff. Düsseldorf: Schwann, 1965. 300–306.

Bostock, J. Knight. *A Handbook on Old High German Literature.* 1954; 2nd ed. by Kenneth C. King and David Robert McLintock. Oxford: Clarendon, 1976.

Braune, Wilhelm. *Althochdeutsche Grammatik.* Tübingen: Niemeyer, 13th ed. by Hans Eggers, 1975, 14th ed. 1987.

De Boor, Helmut. *Die deutsche Literatur von Karl dem Großen bis zum Beginn der höfischen Dichtung (1770–1170).* Munich: Beck, 1949, 5th ed. 1962, 8th ed. 1971.

Diebold, Markus. *Das Sagelied.* Bern and Frankfurt am Main: Lang, 1974.

Cyril Edwards. "German Vernacular Literature: A Survey." In *Carolingian Culture: Emulation and Innovation*, ed. Rosamond McKitterick. Cambridge: CUP, 1993. 141–70.

————. *The Beginnings of German Literature: Comparative and Interdisciplinary Approaches to Old High German.* Rochester, NY: Camden House, 2002.

Eggers, Hans. *Deutsche Sprachgeschichte.* Reinbek bei Hamburg: Rowohlt, 1963–77.

Ehrismann, Gustav. *Geschichte der deutschen Literatur bis zum Ausgang des Mittelalters.* Munich: Beck, 1932–34, repr. as 2nd ed. 1954–55; see esp. I, *Die althochdeutsche Literatur*, 1932/54.

Eis, Gerhard. *Altdeutsche Handschriften.* Munich: Beck, 1949.

Fiebig, Annegret, and Hans-Jochen Schiewer, eds. *Deutsche Literatur und Sprache von 1050–1200: Festschrift für Ursula Hennig.* Berlin: Akademie Verlag, 1995.

Flood, John L., and David N. Yeandle, eds. *mit regulu bithuungan.* Göppingen: Kümmerle, 1989 = GAG 500.

Geith, Karl-Ernst. *Carolus Magnus.* Bern and Munich: Francke, 1977.

Gentry, Francis C. *Bibliographie zur frühmittelhochdeutschen geistlichen Dichtung.* Berlin: Schmidt, 1992.

————, ed. *A Companion to Middle High German Literature*. Leiden: Brill, 2002.

Georgi, Annette. *Das lateinische und deutsche Preisgedicht des Mittelalters in der Nachfolge des genus demonstrativum*. Berlin: Erich Schmidt, 1969 = Philologische Studien und Quellen, 48.

Graff, Eberhard G. *Althochdeutscher Sprachschatz oder Wörterbuch der althochdeutschen Sprache*. Berlin: Nikolai, 1834–42; repr. Hildesheim, 1963; with alphabetical index (as Vol. VII) by H. F. Massmann, 1846.

Grimm, Jacob, *Deutsche Mythologie*. 3rd ed. Göttingen: Dietersche Buchhandlung, 1854.

Grimm, Jacob. *Deutsche Rechtsaltertümer*. 4th ed. by Andreas Heusler and Rudolf Hübner. 1899; reprint Darmstadt: WBG, 1989.

Groseclose, J. Sidney, and Brian O. Murdoch. *Die althochdeutschen poetischen Denkmäler*. Stuttgart: Metzler, 1976.

Grotans, Anna A. "Utraque lingua: Latein- und Deutschunterricht in Notkers St. Gallen?" In *Theodisca: Beiträge zur althochdetuschen und altniederdeutschen Sprache und Literatur in der Kultur des frühen Mittelalters*, ed. Wolfgang Haubrichs et al. Berlin, New York: de Gruyter, 2000. 267–71.

Harms, Wolfgang. *Der Kampf mit dem Freund oder Verwandten in der deutschen Literatur bis um 1300*. Munich: Eidos, 1963.

Hasty, Will, and James Hardin, eds. *German Writers and Works of the Early Middle Ages: 800–1170*. New York: Gale, 1995.

Haubrichs, Wolfgang. *Die Anfänge: Versuche volkssprachiger Schriftlichkeit im frühen Mittelalter (ca. 700–1050/60)*. Frankfurt am Main: Athenäum; Tübingen: Niemeyer, 1988 = Heinzle. Geschichte der deutschen Literatur 1/i.

Haubrichs, Wolfgang, et al., eds. *Theodisca: Beiträge zur althochdeutschen und altniederdeutschen Sprache und Literatur in der Kultur des frühen Mittelalters*. Berlin, New York: de Gruyter, 2000.

Haug, Walter. *Literaturtheorie im deutschen Mittelalter — von den Anfängen bis zum Ende des 13. Jahrhunderts*. Cologne: Böhlau, 1975.

Haug, Walter, and Benedikt Konrad Vollmann. *Frühe deutsche Literatur und lateinische Literatur in Deutschland 800–1150*. Frankfurt am Main: Deutscher Klassiker Verlag, 1991.

Heinzle, Joachim. *Geschichte der deutschen Literatur von den Anfängen bis zum Beginn der Neuzeit*. Königsstein/Ts. et al.: Athenäum, 1986ff.

Hoffmann, Werner. *Altdeutsche Metrik*. Stuttgart: Metzler, 1967.

Johnson, L. P., H.-H. Steinhoff, and R. A. Wisbey, eds. *Studien zur frühmittelhochdeutschen Literatur*. Berlin: Schmidt, 1974.

Karg-Gasterstädt, E., T. Frings et al. *Althochdeutsches Wörterbuch auf Grund der von Elias von Steinmeyer hinterlassenen Sammlungen.* Berlin: Akademie-Verlag, 1952ff.

Kartschoke, Dieter. *Altdeutsche Bibeldichtung.* Stuttgart: Metzler, 1975.

———. *Geschichte der deutschen Literatur im frühen Mittelalter*, 1. Munich: dtv, 1990, 3rd ed. 2000.

Keller, R. E. *The German Language.* London: Faber, 1978.

Köbler, Gerhard. *Wörterbuch des althochdeutschen Wortschatzes.* Paderborn: Schöningh, 1993.

Koegel, Rudolf. *Geschichte der deutschen Litteratur bis zum Ausgange des Mittelalters. Erster Band: Bis zur Mitte des elften Jahrhunderts. Erster Teil: Die stabreimende Dichtung und die Gothische Prosa.* Strasbourg: Trübner, 1894; *Zweiter Teil: Die endreimende Dichtung und die Prosa der althochdeutschen Zeit.* Strasbourg: Trübner, 1897.

Kolb, Herbert. "Himmlisches und irdisches Gericht in karolingischer Theologie." *Frühmittelalterliche Studien* 5 (1971): 284–308.

Krahe, Hans, and Wolfgang Meid. *Germanische Sprachwissenschaft I: Einleitung und Lautlehre.* 7th ed. Berlin: de Gruyter, 1969.

Kuhn, Hugo. *Dichtung und Welt im Mittelalter.* Stuttgart: Metzler, 1959; 2nd ed. 1969.

Lexer, Matthias. *Mittelhochdeutsches Handwörterbuch.* 1872; reprint Stuttgart: Hirzel, 1992.

Lloyd, Albert, Rosemarie Lühr, and Otto Springer. *Etymologisches Wörterbuch des Althochdeutschen.* Göttingen and Zurich: Vandenhoeck and Ruprecht, 1988ff.

Matzel, Klaus. "Karl der Große und die deutsche Sprache." *Rheinische Vierteljahrsblätter* 34 (1970): 172–89.

Maurer, Friedrich. "Salische Geistlichendichtung." *Der Deutschunterricht* 5/ii (1953): 5–10.

Maurer, Friedrich. "Langzeilenstrophen und fortlaufende Reimpaare." In Maurer, *Dichtung und Sprache des Mittelalters: Gesammelte Aufsätze.* Bern and Munich: Francke, 1967, 2nd ed. 1971. 195–213.

Meineke, Eckhard, and Judith Schwerdt. *Einführung in das Althochdeutsche.* Paderborn: Schöningh, 2001.

Meissburger, Gerhard. *Grundlagen zum Verständnis der deutschen Mönchsdichtung im 11. und 12. Jahrhundert.* Munich: Fink, 1970.

Murdoch, Brian. *Old High German Literature.* Boston: Twayne, 1983.

———. "The Carolingian Period and the Early Middle Ages." In *Cambridge History of German Literature*, ed. Helen Watanabe-O'Kelly. Cambridge: CUP, 1997, 1–39.

Nusser, Peter. *Deutsche Literatur im Mittelalter: Lebensformen, Wertvorstellungen und literarische Entwicklungen.* Stuttgart: Kröner, 1992.

Ochsenbein, Peter. "Lehren und Lernen im Mittelalterlichen Galluskloster." In *Cultura Sangallensis: Gesammelte Aufsätze, Peter Ochsenbein: Zu seinem 75. Geburtstag,* ed. Ernst Tremp. St. Gallen: Verlag am Klosterhof, 2000. 111–15.

Ohly, Friedrich. *Vom geistigen Sinn des Wortes im Mittelalter.* Darmstadt: WBG, 1966.

Polenz, Peter von. "Karlische Renaissance, karlische Bildungsreformen und die Anfänge der deutschen Literatur." *Mitteilungen des Marburger Universitätsbunds* (1959): 27–39.

Rupp, Heinz. "Über das Verhältnis von deutscher und lateinischer Literatur im 9–12. Jahrhundert." *Germanisch-Romanische Monatsschrift* 39 (1958): 19–34.

———. *Deutsche religiöse Dichtungen des 11. und 12. Jahrhunderts.* Freiburg/ Br.: Herder, 1958; 2nd ed., Bern and Munich: Francke, 1971.

———. *Forschung zur althochdeutschen Literatur 1945–1962.* Stuttgart: Metzler, 1965.

Schlosser, Horst Dieter. *Die literarischen Anfänge der deutschen Sprache.* Berlin: Schmidt, 1977.

Schreyer-Mühlpfordt, Brigitta. "Sprachliche Einigungstendenzen im deutschen Schrifttum des Frühmittelalters." *Wissenschaftliche Annalen* 5 (1956): 295– 304

Schröbler, Ingeborg. "Fulda und die althochdeutsche Literatur." *Literaturwissenschaftliches Jahrbuch der Görres-Gesellschaft* 1 (1960): 1–26.

Schröder, Werner. *Grenzen und Möglichkeiten einer althochdeutschen Literaturgeschichte.* Leipzig: Sächsische Akademie, 1959 = Berichte 105/ii.

Schützeichel, Rudolf. *Althochdeutsches Wörterbuch.* 5th ed. Tübingen: Niemeyer, 1969, 1995.

———. *Textgebundenheit: Kleinere Schriften zur Mittelalterlichen deutschen Literatur.* Tübingen: Niemeyer, 1981.

———. "Grenzen des Althochdeutschen." *PBB/T* 95 (1973 = Sonderheft/ *Festschrift für Ingeborg Schröbler*): 23–38.

Soetemann, C. *Deutsche geistliche Dichtung des 11. und 12. Jahrhunderts.* Stuttgart: Metzler, 1963, 2nd ed. 1971.

Stefan Sonderegger. "Frühe Erscheinungsformen dichterischer Sprache im Althochdeutschen." In *Festschrift Max Wehrli,* ed. S. Sonderegger et al. Zurich and Freiburg/Br.: Atlantis, 1969, 53–81.

———. "Reflexe gesprochener Sprache in der althochdeutschen Literatur." *Frühmittelalterliche Studien* 5 (1971): 176–92.

———. *Althochdeutsch in St. Gallen.* St. Gallen: Ostschweiz, 1970.

———. *Das Althochdeutsche von St. Gallen.* Berlin: de Gruyter, 1970.

———. *Althochdeutsche Sprache und Literatur.* Berlin: de Gruyter, 1974.

Starck, Taylor, and J. C. Wells. *Althochdeutsches Glossenwörterbuch.* Heidelberg: Winter, 1990.

Udwin, Victor Morris. *Between Two Armies: The Place of the Duel in Epic Culture.* Leiden: Brill, 1999.

Vollmann-Profe, Gisela. *Wiederbeginn volkssprachlicher Schriftlichkeit im hohen Mittelalter (1050/60–1160/70).* Königstein/Taunus: Athenäum, 1986 = Heinzle, *Geschichte der deutschen Literatur* I/ii.

Wagner, Kurt. "Hochsprache und Mundart in althochdeutscher Zeit." *Der Deutschunterricht* 8/ii (1956): 14–23.

Wegstein, Werner. "Die sprachgeographische Gliederung des Deutschen in historischer Sicht." In *Sprachgeschichte*, ed. Werner Besch, Oskar Reichmann, and Stefan Sonderegger. Berlin and New York: de Gruyter, 1985, 1/ii. 1751–66.

Wehrli, Max. *Geschichte der deutschen Literatur vom frühen Mittelalter bis zum Ende des 16. Jahrhunderts.* Stuttgart: Reclam, 1980.

German Authors and Works

Charms

Allard, Jean-Paul. "Du second charme de Mersebourg au viatique de Weingarten." *Etudes Européenes* 14 (1985): 33–59 (with a "Note additionelle" by Jean Haudry).

Bacon, Isaac. "Versuch einer Klassifizierung altdeutscher Zaubersprüche und Segen." *MLN* 67 (1952): 224–32.

Ebermann, O. *Blut und Wundsegen.* Berlin: Mayer and Müller, 1903.

Eis, Gerhard. *Altdeutsche Zaubersprüche.* Berlin: de Gruyter, 1964.

Fuller, Susan D. "Pagan Charms in Tenth-Century Saxony? The Function of the Merseburg Charms." *Monatshefte* 72 (1980): 162–70 (with a rejoinder by Heather Stuart and F. Walla in *Germanic Notes* 14 [1983]: 35–37).

Geier, Manfred. "Die magische Kraft der Poesie." *DVjs* 56 (1982): 359–85.

Genzmer, Felix. "Die Götter des zweiten Merseburger Zauberspruchs." *Arkiv för Nordisk Filologi* 93 (1948): 55–72.

Hampp, Irmgard. "Vom Wesen des Zaubers im Zauberspruch." *Der Deutschunterricht* 13/1 (1961): 58–76.

———. *Beschwörung, Segen, Gebet.* Stuttgart: Silberburg, 1961.

Ködderitzsch, Rolf. "Der 2. Merseburger Spruch und seine Parallele." *Zeitschrift für celtische Philologie* 33 (1974): 45–57.

Masser, Achim. "Zum zweiten Merseburger Zauberspruch." *PBB*/T (1972): 19–25.

Moser, Hugo. "Vom *Weingartner Reisesegen* zu Walthers Ausfahrtssegen. Gereimte Gebetssegen des frühen und hohen Mittelalters." *PBB*/H 82 (1961 = Sonderheft/ *Festschrift fur Elisabeth Karg-Gasterstädt*), 69–89.

Murdoch, Brian. "*Peri hieres nousou*. Approaches to the Old High German Medical Charms." In *mit regulu bithuungan*, ed. John L. Flood and David N. Yeandle. Göppingen: Kümmerle, 1989. 142–60.

———. "But Did They Work? Interpreting the Old High German Merseburg Charms in their Medieval Context." *Neuphilologische Mitteilungen* 89 (1988): 358–69.

———. "*Drohtin, uuerthe so!* Funktionsweisen der altdeutschen Zaubersprüche." *Literaturwissenschaftliches Jahrbuch der Görres-Gesellschaft* 32 (1991): 11–37.

Rosenfeld, Hellmut. "Phol ende Wuodan Vuorun zi holza." *PBB*/T 95 (1973): 1–12.

Schirokauer, Arno. "Form und Formel einiger altdeutschen Zaubersprüche." *ZfdPh* 73 (1954): 353–64.

Early Middle High German Works

Henkel, Nikolaus. *Studien zum Physiologus in Mittelalter*. Tübingen: Niemeyer, 1976.

Ohly, Friedrich. *Sage und Legende in der Kaiserchronik*. Münster, 1940; reprint Darmstadt: WBG, 1968.

———. *Hohelied-Studien*. Wiesbaden: Steiner, 1958.

Sauer-Geppert, Waldtraut Ingeborg. *Wörterbuch zum St. Trudperter Hohen Lied: Ein Beitrag zur Sprache der Mittelalterlichen Mystik*. Berlin, New York: de Gruyter, 1972.

Schützeichel, Rudolf. *Das Alemannische Memento Mori: Das Gedicht und der geistig-historische Hintergrund*. Tübingen: Niemeyer, 1962.

Voorwinden, N. Th. J. *Merigarto: Eine philologisch-historische Monographie*. Leiden: Leiden UP, 1973.

Glosses

Bergmann, Rolf. *Verzeichnis der althochdeutschen und altsächsichen Glossenhandschriften: Mit Bibliographie der Glosseneditionen, der Handschriftenbeschreibungen und der Dialektbestimmungen*. Berlin: de Gruyter, 1973 = Arbeiten zur Frühmittelalterforschung, 6.

Blum, Sybille. *Wortschatz und Übersetzungsleistung in den althochdeutschen Canonesglossen: Untersuchungen zur Hs. Frankfurt am Main Ms. Barth. 64.* Berlin: Akademie-Verlag, 1986 = Sitzungsberichte der Sächsischen Akademie der Wissenschaften zu Leipzig. Phil.-hist. Klasse 126, 7.

Frank, Irmgard. *Die althochdeutschen Glossen der Handschrift Leipzig Rep. II. 6.* Berlin and New York: de Gruyter, 1974.

———. *Aus Glossenhandschriften des 8. bis 14. Jahrhunderts: Quellen zur Geschichte einer Überlieferungsart.* Heidelberg: Winter, 1984.

Gadow, Henning von. *Die deutschen Aratorglossen der Handschrift Trier 1464.* Munich: Fink, 1974.

Hellgardt, Ernst. "Die lateinischen und althochdeutschen Vergilglossen des clm 18059. Plädoyer für eine neue Art der Glossenlektüre." In *Stand und Aufgaben der deutschen Dialektlexikographie: II. Brüder-Grimm-Symposion zur historischen Wortforschung: Beiträge zu der Marburger Tagung vom Oktober 1992,* ed. Ernst Bremer and Reiner Hildebrandt. Berlin, New York: de Gruyter, 1996. 73–88.

Mayer, Hartwig. *Die althochdeutschen Griffelglossen der Hs. Salzburg, St. Peter a VII 2.* Göttingen: Vandenhoeck and Ruprecht, 1994.

Meineke, Eckhard. *Saint-Mihiel Bibliothèque Municipale Ms. 25: Studien zu den althochdeutschen Glossen.* Göttingen: Vandenhoeck and Ruprecht, 1983.

Schröter, E. *Walahfrids deutsche Glossierung zu den biblischen Büchern Genesis bis Regum II und der althochdeutsche Tatian.* Halle: Niemeyer, 1926.

Siewert, Klaus. *Die althochdeutsche Horazglossierung.* Göttingen: Vandenhoeck and Ruprecht, 1986.

———. *Glossenfunde: Volkssprachliches zu lateinischen Autoren der Antike und des Mittelalters.* Göttingen: Vandenhoeck and Ruprecht, 1989.

Splett, Jochen. *Abrogans-Studien.* Wiesbaden: Steiner, 1976.

Hildebrandlied

Gutenbrunner, Siegfried. *Von Hildebrand und Hadubrand: Lied-Sage-Mythos.* Heidelberg: Winter, 1976.

Hatto, A. T. "On the Excellence of the Hildebrandslied." *Modern Language Review* 68 (1973): 820–38.

Hoffmann, Werner. "Das Hildebrandslied und die indo-germanische Vater-Sohn-Kampf-Dichtung." *PBB/T* 92 (1970): 26–42.

Kolk, H. van der. *Das Hildebrandslied: Eine forschungsgeschichtliche Darstellung.* Amsterdam: Scheltema and Holkema, 1967.

Lühr, Rosemarie. *Studien zur Sprache des Hildebrandsliedes.* Frankfurt am Main and Bern: Lang, 1982.

McDonald, William C. "Too Softly a Gift of Treasure: a Re-Reading of the Old High German Hildebrandslied." *Euphorion* 78 (1984): 1–16.

Maurer, Friedrich. "Hildebrandslied und *Ludwigslied.*" *Der Deutschunterricht* 9/ii (1957): 5–15.

Molinari, Maria Vittoria, and Ute Schwab, eds. *Ildebrando: Quattro saggi e i testi.* Alessandria: Edizioni dell'Orso, 2001.

Norman, Frederick. *Three Essays on the Hildebrandslied.* Ed. A. T. Hatto. London: Institute of German Studies 1973.

Renoir, Alain. "The Armor of the Hildebrandslied." *Neuphilologische Mitteilungen* 78 (1977): 389–95.

Schröder, Werner. "Hildebrands tragischer Blindheit und der Schluß des Hildebrandsliedes." *DVjs* 37 (1963): 481–97.

Schwab, Ute. *Arbeo laoso.* Bern: Francke, 1972.

Wagner, Norbert. "Cheiseringu getan." *ZfdA* 104 (1975): 179–88.

Wisniewski, Roswitha. "Hadubrands Rache." *ABäG* 9 (1975): 1–12.

Isidore-Translation

Ostberg, Kurt. *The Old High German Isidor in its Relationship to the Manuscripts (Eighth to Twelfth Century) of Isidorus, De fide Catholica.* Göppingen: Kümmerle, 1979 = GAG 203.

Wedel, Alfred R. "The Old High German Isidor." In *German Writers and Works of the Early Middle Ages: 800–1170,* ed. Will Hasty and James Hardin. New York: Gale, 1991. 248–51.

Ludwigslied

Beck, Heinrich. "Zur literaturgeschichtliche Stellung des ahd. *Ludwigsliedes.*" *ZfdA* 103 (1974): 37–51.

Berg, Elisabeth. "Das *Ludwigslied* und die Schlacht bei Saucourt." *Rheinische Vierteljahresblätter* 29 (1964): 175–99.

Fouracre, Paul. "The Context of the Old High German *Ludwigslied.*" *Medium Aevum* 54 (1985): 87–103.

Harvey, Ruth. "The Provenance of the Old High German *Ludwigslied.*" *Medium Aevum* 14 (1945): 1–20.

Homann, Holger. "Das *Ludwigslied* — Dichtung im Dienste der Politik." In *Traditions and Transitions: Studies in Honor of Harold Jantz,* ed. Lieselotte E. Kurth et al. Munich: Delp, 1972, 17–28.

Kemper, Raimund. "Das *Ludwigslied* im Kontext zeitgenössischer Rechtsvorgänge." *DVjs* 56 (1982): 161–73.

Händl, Claudia. *Ludwigslied: Canto di Ludovico.* Alessandria: Edizioni dell'Orso, 1990.

Lefranq, Paul. *Rithmus teutonicus ou Ludwigslied?* Paris: Droz, 1945.

Murdoch, Brian. "Saucourt and the *Ludwigslied.*" *Revue belge de philologie et d'histoire* 55 (1977): 841–67.

Naumann, Hans. *Das Ludwigslied und die verwandten lateinischen Gedichte.* Halle: Klinz, 1932.

Schwarz, Werner. "The *Ludwigslied* — a Ninth-Century Poem." *Modern Language Review* 42 (1947): 467–73.

Urmoneit, Erika. *Der Wortschatz des Ludwigsliedes.* Munich: Fink, 1973.

Minor Old High German Poems and Prose

Dittrich, Marie-Luise. "*De Heinrico.*" *ZfdA* 84 (1952/53): 274–308.

Haubrichs, Wolfgang. *Georgslied und Georgslegende im frühen Mittelalter: Text und Rekonstruktion.* Konigstein/Ts: Scriptor, 1979.

Heffner, R-M. S. "The Third Basel Recipe." *Journal of English and Germanic Philology* 46 (1947): 248–53.

Ludwig, Otto. "Der althochdeutsche und der biblische Psalm 138. Ein Vergleich." *Euphorion* 56 (1962): 402–9.

Rauch, Irmengard. "Basler Rezept I." In *Festschrift für Herbert Kolb,* ed. Klaus Matzel and Hans-Gert Roloff. Bern: Lang, 1989. 523–27.

Sanders, Willy. "*Imperator ore iucundo saxonizans.* Die altsächsischen Begrüßungsworte des Kaisers Otto in *De Heinrico.*" *ZfdA* 98 (1969): 13–28.

Scherer, Wilhelm. "*Memento Mori.*" *ZfdA* 24 (1880): 426–50.

Schwab, Ute. "Das althochdeutsche Lied *Hirsch und Hinde* in seiner lateinischen Umgebung." In *Latein und Volkssprache im deutschen Mittelalter 1100–1500,* ed. Nikolaus Henkel and Nigel F. Palmer. Tübingen: Niemeyer, 1992. 74–122.

Willems, Fritz. "Psalm 138 und althochdeutscher Stil." *DVjs* 29 (1955): 429–46.

Muspilli

Bergmann, Rolf. "Zum Problem der Sprache des *Muspilli.*" *Frühmittelalterliche Studien* 5 (1971): 304–16.

Finger, Heinz. *Untersuchungen zum 'Muspilli.'* Göppingen: Kümmerle, 1977 = GAG 44.

Kolb, Herbert. "*Vora demo muspille.*" *ZfdPh* 83 (1964): 2–33.

———. "Himmlisches und irdisches Gericht in karolingischer Theologie und althochdeutscher Dichtung." *Frühmittelalterliche Studien* (1971): 284–303.

Mohr, Wolfgang, and Walther Haug. *Zweimal 'Muspilli.'* Tübingen: Niemeyer, 1977.

Schmidt-Wiegand, Ruth. "*Muspilli.*" In *Handwörterbuch zur deutschen Rechtsgeschichte*, ed. Adalbert Erler et al. Berlin: Erich Schmidt, 1971–98. Vol. 3, 795–98.

Notker Labeo

Eilers, Helge. *Die Syntax Notkers des Deutschen in seinen Übersetzungen: Boethius, Martianus Capella und Psalmen*. Berlin, New York: de Gruyter 2003 = Studia Linguistica Germanica 66.

Firchow, Evelyn Scherabon. *Notker der Deutsche von St. Gallen (950–1022): Ausführliche Bibliographie*. Göttingen: Vandenhoeck and Ruprecht, 2000 (reviewed by John M. Jeep, *ABäG* 55 [2001]: 239–47).

Hellgardt, Ernst. "Notkers des Deutschen Brief an Bischof Hugo von Sitten." In *Befund und Deutung: Zum Verhältnis von Empirie und Interpretation in Sprach- und Literaturwissenschaft*, ed. Klaus Grubmüller et al. Tübingen: Niemeyer, 1979.

Schröbler, Ingeborg. "Zum Brief Notkers des Deutschen an den Bischof Hugo von Sitten." *ZfdA* 82 (1948–50): 32–46.

Otfrid von Weissenburg

Archibald, Linda. "The Seamless Robe and Related Imagery in Otfrid von Weissenburg's *Evangelienbuch*." In *mit regulu bithuungan*, ed. John L. Flood and David N. Yeandle. Göppingen: Kümmerle, 1989. 123–32.

———. *Cur scriptor theotisce dictaverit*. Diss., Stirling University, 1988.

Belkin, Johanna, and Jürgen Meier. *Bibliographie zu Otfrid von Weißenburg*. Berlin: Schmidt, 1975.

Ernst, Ulrich. *Der Liber Evangeliorum Otfrids von Weissenburg: Literarästhetik und Verstechnik im Lichte der Tradition*. Cologne and Vienna: Böhlau, 1975 = Kölner germanistische Studien 11.

Hartmann, Reinildis. *Allegorisches Wörterbuch zu Otfrieds von Weissenburg Evangeliendichtung*. Munich: Fink, 1975 = Münstersche Mittelalterschriften 26.

Hellgardt, Ernst. *Die exegetischen Quellen von Otfrids Evangelienbuch*. Tübingen: Niemeyer, 1981.

Kleiber, Wolfgang. *Otfrid von Weissenburg: Untersuchungen zur handschriftlichen Überlieferung und Studien zum Aufbau des Evangelienbuches*. Munich: Francke, 1971 = Bibliotheca Germanica 14.

———, ed. *Otfrid von Weißenburg*. Darmstadt: WBG, 1978.

McKenzie, Donald A. *Otfrid von Weissenburg: Narrator or Commentator? A Comparative Study*. Stanford and London: Stanford UP, 1946.

Patzlaff, Rainer. *Otfrid von Weissenburg und die mittelalterliche versus-Tradition: Untersuchungen zur formgeschichtlichen Stellung der Otfridstrophe*. Tübingen: Niemeyer, 1975.

Schützeichel, Rudolf. *Codex Pal. Lat. 52: Studien zur Heidelberger Otfridhand-schrift, zum Kicila-Vers und zum Georgslied.* Göttingen: Vandenhoeck and Ruprecht, 1982 = Abh. Der Akad. der Wissenschaften in Göttingen. Phil.-hist. Kl.; 3/130.

Vollmann-Profe, Gisela. *Kommentar zu Otfrids Evangelienbuch I.* Bonn: Habelt, 1976.

Tatian-Translation

Gutmacher, E. "Der Wortschatz des althochdeutschen Tatian." *PBB* 39 (1914): 1–83, 229–89, 571–77.

Henß, Walter. "Zur Quellenfrage im *Heliand* und althochdeutschen *Tatian.*" In *Der Heliand,* ed. Jürgen Eichhoff and Irmengard Rauch. Darmstadt: WBG, 1973. 191–99.

Wessobrunn Prayer

Edwards, Cyril, and Jennie Kiff-Hooper. "Ego Bonefacius scripsi? More Oblique Approaches to the Wessobrunn Prayer." In *mit regulu bithuungan,* ed. John L. Flood and David N. Yeandle. Göppingen: Kümmerle, 1989. 94–122.

Ganz, Peter F. "Die Zeilenaufteilung im *Wessobrunner Gebet.*" *PBB/T* 95 (1973 = Sonderheft/*Festschrift fur Ingeborg Schröbler*): 39–51.

Gottzmann, Carola L. "Das *Wessobrunner Gebet.* Ein Zeugnis des Kulturumbruchs vom heidnischen Germanentum zum Christentum." In *Althochdeutsch* ed. Rolf Bergmann, Heinrich Tiefenbach, and Lothar Voetz. Heidelberg: Winter, 1987. Vol. 1, 637–54.

Schwab, Ute. *Die Sternrune im Wessobrunner Gebet.* Amsterdam: Rodopi 1973.

Seiffert, Leslie. "The Metrical Form and Composition of the *Wessobrunner Gebet.*" *Medium Ævum* 31 (1962): 1–13.

Waldman, Glenys A. *The Wessobrunn Prayer Manuscript Clm 22053: A Transliteration, Translation and Study of Parallels.* Diss., U. Pennsylvania, 1975; Ann Arbor, MI; University Microfilms, 1988.

Williram of Ebersberg

Schupp, Volker. *Studien zu Williram von Ebersberg.* Bern and Munich: Francke, 1978.

Studies of Latin Language, Authors and Works

Allott, Stephen. *Alcuin of York — His Life and Letters.* York: William Sessions, 1974.

Archibald, Linda. "Notker Balbulus." In *German Writers and Works of the Early Middle Ages: 800–1170,* ed. Will Hasty and James Hardin. New York: Gale, 1991. 92–95.

Brincken, Anna-Dorothee von den. *Studien zur lateinischen Weltchronistik bis in das Zeitalter Ottos von Freising.* Düsseldorf: Triltsch, 1957.

Carabine, Deirdre. *John Scotus Eriugena.* Oxford and New York: OUP, 2000.

Ernst, Ursula. "Walther — ein christlicher Held?" *Mittellateinisches Jahrbuch* 21 (1986): 79–83.

Flint, Valerie I. J. "The Place and Purpose of the Works of Honorius Augustodunensis." *Revue Bénédictine* 87 (1977): 97–127.

Kottje, Raymund, and Harald Zimmermann. *Hrabanus Maurus: Lehrer, Abt und Bischof.* Wiesbaden: Steiner, 1982.

Langosch, Karl. *Profile des lateinischen Mittelalters.* Darmstadt: WBG, 1965.

———. *Waltharius: Die Dichtung und die Forschung.* Darmstadt: WBG, 1973.

———. *Mittellatein und Europa: Führung in die Hauptliteratur des Mittelalters.* Darmstadt: WBG, 1990.

Manitius, Max. *Geschichte der lateinischen Literatur des Mittelalters.* Munich: Beck, 1911–31, reprint 1964–65.

Murdoch, Brian. "Hrabanus Maurus," "Lupus of Ferrières," "Walahfrid Strabo," and "Williram of Ebersberg." In *German Writers and Works of the Early Middle Ages: 800–1170,* ed. Will Hasty and James Hardin. New York: Gale, 1995. 74–78, 88–91, 143–45 and 146–49.

Ondracek, Claudia. "Die lateinischen Weltchroniken bis in das 12. Jahrhundert." In *Weltbild und Realität: Einführung in die mittelalterliche Geschichtsschreibung,* ed. Ulrich Knefelkamp. Pfaffenweiler: Centaurus, 1992, 1–14.

Parkes, Ford B. "Irony in *Waltharius.*" *MLN* 89 (1974): 459–65.

Ploss, Emil. *Waltharius und Walthersage.* Hildesheim: Olms, 1969.

Raby, Frederic J. *A History of Christian-Latin Poetry from the Beginnings to the Close of the Middle Ages.* Oxford: Clarendon, 1927, 2nd ed. 1953.

———. *A History of Secular Latin Poetry in the Middle Ages.* Oxford: Clarendon, 1934, 2nd ed. 1957.

Stach, W. "Geralds *Waltharius.*" *Historische Zeitschrift* 168 (1943): 57–81.

Szövérffy, J. *Die Annalen der lateinischen Hymnendichtung.* Berlin: Schmidt, 1964–65.

Wehrli, Max. "*Waltharius.* Gattungsgeschichtliche Betrachtungen." *Mittellateinisches Jahrbuch* 2 (1965): 63–73.

Wright, Roger. *Late Latin and Early Romance in Spain and Carolingian France.* Liverpool: Francis Cairns, 1982.

———. *Latin and the Romance Languages in the Early Middle Ages.* University Park, PA: Pennsylvania State UP, 1996.

Ziolkowski, Jan. "Eupolemius." *Journal of Medieval Latin* 1 (1991): 1–45.

Zwierlein, Otto. "Das *Waltharius*-Epos und seine lateinischen Vorbilder." *Antike und Abendland* 16 (1970): 153–84.

Contributors

LINDA ARCHIBALD is Professor of German and Head of Modern Languages at Liverpool John Moore's University, and has written on a number of aspects of writers and works in the Old High German period, both Latin and German, particularly on Otfrid.

GRAEME DUNPHY studied German at Stirling University, Scotland, then Hebrew and Old Testament in St. Andrews. He wrote his Stirling doctoral thesis on Jans Enikel's *Weltchronik*. Since 1993 he has been lecturer in EFL and in German literature at the University of Regensburg. Recent publications include an edition of the *Annolied* commentary by Martin Opitz and an anthology of thirteenth-century verse chronicles.

BRIAN MURDOCH is Professor of German at Stirling University, Scotland, and has held Visiting Fellowships at Oxford and Cambridge, where he has delivered the Waynflete, Hulsean, and Speaker's Lectures. His main specialization is early medieval comparative literature, especially biblical and apocryphal writings; recent books include *Cornish Literature, The Germanic Hero, Adam's Grace,* and *The Medieval Popular Bible.*

STEPHEN PENN is a Lecturer in English Studies at Stirling University. He has a doctorate from York. He has written articles on Chaucer, John Wyclif, and diverse topics relating to late medieval literary culture. He is currently working on a collection of translations of selected Latin texts by Wyclif.

CHRISTOPHER J. WELLS is University Lecturer in Germanic Philology and Medieval German Literature at the University of Oxford, and Senior Modern Languages Fellow of St. Edmund Hall. His special interest is the history of the German language, and he is currently working on its postwar developments.

JONATHAN WEST is Senior Lecturer in German at the University of Newcastle upon Tyne, and a specialist in Germanic languages and philology. He is the author of papers on Gothic and Old High German, and books and articles on early New High German and modern German grammar.

Index